D1084340

Germany in Central America

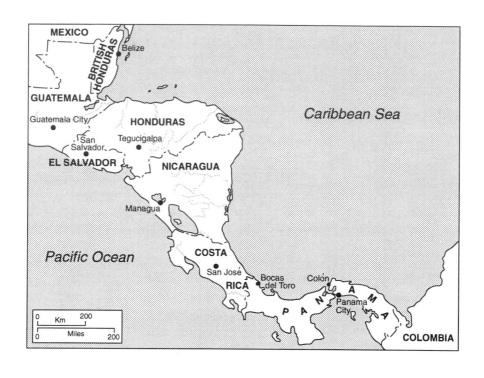

Germany in Central America

■

Competitive Imperialism, 1821–1929

THOMAS SCHOONOVER

The University of Alabama Press
Tuscaloosa and London

The maps on pages ii and xiv reprinted from Lester Langley and Thomas Schoonover,
Banana Men, copyright © 1995 by The University Press of Kentucky,
by permission of the publishers.

Library of Congress Cataloging-in-Publication Data

Schoonover, Thomas David, 1936–
Germany in Central America : competitive imperialism, 1821–1929 /
Thomas Schoonover.
p. cm.
ISBN 0-8173-0886-5 (cloth : alk. paper)
1. Central America—Foreign relations—Germany. 2. Germany—
Foreign relations—Central America. 3. Central America—Economic
conditions. 4. Germany—Economic conditions. I. Title.
F1436.8.G3S3 1998
327.430728—dc21   97-15111
                                                                      CIP

British Library Cataloguing-in-Publication Data available

To Ebba Wesener Schoonover
and Paco Schoonover

Contents

■

Preface

∎

After research on the interaction of ideology, the political economy, and social change in U.S.-Mexican relations during the 1860s, the study of ideology and change related to the liberal revolutions of Central America seemed a logical second project. From fifteen years' work in the archives and libraries of Central America, Europe, and the United States, I had ample material for three book-length manuscripts on the 1823 to 1929 period. In addition to this book, I completed a second volume (in 1993), which focuses on French relations with Central America. The third will treat U.S. relations with Central America. I decided not to add a study of British relations with the isthmus because so much work has already been done on the subject. I created a fourth book, *The United States in Central America, 1860–1911: Episodes in Social Imperialism and Imperial Rivalry in the World System* (Durham, NC: Duke University Press, 1991), from the 2,800-page manuscript on U.S.–Central American relations. An invitation to join Lester Langley on an uncompleted project led to a fifth book, *The Banana Men: American Mercenaries and Entrepreneurs in Central America, 1880–1930* (Lexington: University Press of Kentucky, 1995). The results of this excursion into international history should challenge scholars, teachers, and policymakers to broaden their view of relations with the world.

My interest in relations between the United States and Central America was an outgrowth of my fascination with the relationship of liberalism to imperialism and the New World reaction to French intervention in Mexico; Maximilian and Napoleon III intended to acquire influence in the isthmian area in conjunction with their Mexican empire. I began the pursuit of imperialism on the isthmus twenty-five years ago, while still deciphering U.S.-Mexican-European relations. In the intervening years I have acquired debts on a scale commensurate with the world system theory. Three people—Lee Woodward and Walt LaFeber, both dear friends and professional colleagues, and Ebba Schoonover, my wife—are well aware of my debt to them, for I have asked them for help many times over the years. Lee guided a National Endowment for the Humanities (NEH) Summer Seminar that I attended, supported my grant requests, responded to my research and conceptual problems, and encouraged me to continue a near never-ending task. Walt has read my manuscripts over the years, always supplying valuable critique and never ceasing to encourage me, even when I felt like postponing the project for a century or two (one gets a different perspective on time when one reads Fernand Braudel!). Ebba has helped me with research and has provided editorial and secretarial assistance since the beginning. Her own professional career as an instructor of languages has lately reduced the time she can give me, but it has not ended her support.

Many colleagues have read some part of this book in earlier versions. All have stimulated my thinking and helped me improve my work. Hoping I have not forgotten anyone, I gratefully thank James Dormon, David Pletcher, Steve Webre, Glen Jeansonne, Thomas Leonard, Amos Simpson, Vaughn Baker Simpson, Robert Kirkpatrick, Friedrich Katz, Carole Fink, Robert Berdahl, Knud Krakau, Hans-Jürgen Schroeder, and Reinhard Liehr. Additionally, James Dormon has done much more than critique parts of my manuscript. He has shared friendship, professional insights, and encouragement for the past two and a half decades. Gloria Fiero's friendship has sustained me in the mutual quest to understand mankind. Ann Grogg helped me think through problems in search of a better-organized and more explicit presentation of my research. Student aides EkJuana Fruge, Mayra Rodríguez, Victoria Woods, and Paula Lacombe helped with the word processing through several revisions. The translations of documents and secondary texts (from German, Spanish, and French) are my responsibility. I have listed the primary sources and opted for a bibliographic essay that omits many items cited once or twice.

My research, which was supported by a number of foundations, was rooted in my conviction that international history must be multicultural and multilingual to have lasting value. That will not surprise those who become acquainted with the cosmopolitan perspective I try to develop in my scholarship. Without the support of the National Endowment for the Humanities (NEH), the German Academic Exchange Service (DAAD), the Fritz Thyssen Foundation (in Germany), the American Philosophical Society, the Southern Regional Education Board, Tulane University's Mellon Travel Grants, and the American Historical Association's Albert Beveridge Fund, the research for this manuscript would have been inconceivable.

During a summer as visiting professor at Cornell University and a year as a Fulbright Senior Lecturer at the University of Bielefeld, I encountered colleagues, departments, and universities that supported scholarship in a most impressive manner. I am grateful for those experiences. About 1980, the French magazine *L'information* discovered that European historians considered the history department at Bielefeld one of the five best in Europe. In 1991, the *Chronicle of Higher Education* placed Cornell's history department at the top of those in the United States. I concur with both evaluations.

Germany in Central America

Introduction

∎

Since the sixteenth century, when the European maritime nations first realized that only a narrow strip of land separated the Atlantic and Pacific oceans at the Panama isthmus, Middle America (the Panama and Tehuantepec isthmuses and those states forming the Central American Federation—Guatemala, El Salvador, Honduras, Nicaragua, and Costa Rica) has engaged the imagination and energy of entrepreneurs, government officials, and military leaders. For many observers, a bridge between the vast Pacific and Atlantic Oceans represented the real wealth of the New World rather than the deceptively attractive glitter of many El Dorados. The Central American Federation (1823 to 1843) recognized that Great Britain, France, and the newly emerging powers—Germany and the United States—had interest in the isthmus as the key to a Pacific trade that promised enormous wealth. The economics and geography of Central America produced early competition for transit rights and trade opportunities among Holland, Britain, and the United States, and France and Germany quickly entered the fray. A strong German presence in Central America began in the 1870s. This book analyzes the relationship between Germany and the Central American societies within the framework of the rivalry of metropole and aggressive semi-peripheral powers on the isthmus in the nineteenth and twentieth centuries. The imperial rivalry occurred within a world integrating ever-larger shares of the globe's land, labor, capital, and distribution into a world economy. The nature of imperialism included more than accumulation and expansion; it was also competitive.

Scholars of German history have seldom pursued the *histoire événementielle* (the history of events, or narrative history) or the *histoire totale* (historical analysis of structure and change) of German–Central American relations. My efforts to understand the impact of ideology, industrialization, and an expansive *Weltanschauung* (a world view that is concrete and abstract) on U.S.–Central American relations were constantly handicapped by the intrusion of foreign powers into U.S.-isthmian relations. The few works on German, French, Mexican, Spanish, Italian, Dutch, or Belgian interests in isthmian affairs offered little help. The study of Central America's relations with the world was limited to involvements with Britain and the United States. Central America had attracted the attention of many metropole states (those states that controlled the factors of domestic production—land, labor, and capital—and distribution but that also possessed the power and technology to control the factors of production and distribution in the peripheral and semi-peripheral areas) or semi-peripheral countries (those that controlled some factors of production but not all) as the vital point for expanding into the Pacific basin. By the third quarter of the nineteenth century, both Germany and the United States had undergone wars of unification and were adapting to bastardized liberal socioeconomic orders (often called organized or corporate capitalism) and industrial transformation. World trade became a chief tool (and hope) for avoiding stagnation and collapse.

Some German states—especially those Prussia led, first in the Customs Union and later the German empire—wanted national unity, status in Europe (or the world), and pride in their accomplishments. To achieve these goals they encouraged industrialization and expansion and sought to bolster their security with formal and informal commercial and military ties to places around the globe. The Pacific basin seemed to offer more opportunities than most other spots on earth. The unified German empire sought access to that region and colonies there. Germany's share in the expanding trade with the Pacific side of the New World, Oceania, and Asia in the nineteenth and early twentieth centuries is not easy to establish. The U.S. share was appreciable and statistically more visible. The development of Pacific coast trade and transit from 1849 to 1854 (Cornelius Vanderbilt's Accessory Transit Company in Nicaragua, the Panama Railroad, and the Pacific Mail Steamship Company) played a role in the rapid expansion of U.S. trade with Asia in the mid-nineteenth century. Comparing data from the mid-1840s versus the pre–World War I years indicates that U.S. trade with the Pacific basin increased 966 percent, which is noticeably larger than the 520 percent increase for total U.S. trade during this period. I could locate only scattered comparable data for German trade that occurred after unification. From the 1870s to the 1920s, German exports to Chile grew 411 percent, and German imports from Chile grew 891 percent. From the 1890s to the 1920s, German trade with Peru grew 460 percent. In the first three decades of the twentieth century, German trade with both Ecuador and Bolivia increased about 95 percent. German entrepreneurs and politicians, who repeatedly expressed interest in a share of the Pacific trade, launched campaigns beginning in the 1850s to establish naval stations in Asia or on the Pacific islands. The Middle American isthmus was the battlefield for much of the struggle among expansive industrial powers to dominate interoceanic transit.[1]

Many diplomatic historians focus so sharply on domestic politics that they almost ignore the international aspects of foreign relations. Other historians look so intensely on international political, strategic, and national-interest matters that they slight the domestic role in shaping foreign relations and the impact of foreign affairs on domestic society. Appropriately, those who ignore the international aspects consider their subject to be the history of foreign policy or diplomacy. Yet even bilateral relations are not simply the affairs of two states. They encompass a variety of transnational elements that impact more than two nations.

My research design followed the broad, multi-state dimension of international affairs. The research encompassed public, business, organizational, and individual records from twelve countries; it was organized according to a world system approach and in recognition that social imperialism and dependency theory are useful tools for analyzing the international history of Central America in the nineteenth and twentieth centuries. For this study, social imperialism (defined here as metropole policies that ameliorated domestic problems such as labor dissatisfaction, undesired social behavior, social disorder, and unemployment by transferring them abroad) sheds light on the impulses operating within Germany. Social imperialism is a policy that aimed, in the words of Thomas McCormick, "to export the social problem" and "to export the unemployment" in an attempt to resolve internal social problems. Dependency theory (which focuses on matters of political sovereignty and economic and social autonomy) illuminates the consequences of German intrusions in the peripheral states (those states that did not effectively control the factors of production) on the isthmus.[2]

Economies are dynamic and changing. Since ancient times, some producers and middlemen recognized the profit to be made in long-distance trade. New products generated new markets and new markets, new products. Rising expectations of future material prosperity became the motor for economic growth. Some metropole entrepreneurs contemplated a distribution system over the Middle American isthmus that would encompass the whole world. (The Suez region, of course, offered a similar hope.) World system theory (the French historian Fernand Braudel and the American sociologist Immanuel Wallerstein are two of its best-known proponents) describes the relationships of the metropole (core), semi-periphery, and periphery within the world economy. A semi-peripheral state functioned both as exploited and exploiter in the world economy. Metropole and semi-peripheral states exploited the periphery.[3]

In the mid-nineteenth century, Germany (then Prussia and the states north of Austria) was a semi-peripheral society. It exercised only limited control over land, labor, capital, and distribution and was therefore dependent to some degree on other states. By the late nineteenth century, a unified German empire had transformed itself into a metropole state, in large part by using social imperialist policies to exploit the transit, market, and investment opportunities in various parts of eastern and southeastern Europe, Africa, Asia, South America, and the Central American–Caribbean region. This process cast some peripheral areas (Guatemala, parts of eastern and southeastern Europe, and colonies in Africa and Asia) into dependent relationships with Germany.

Metropole policymakers commonly discussed the impact of their foreign relations on the domestic economy, but they rarely examined the consequences of their policies on the host states in the periphery and semi-periphery. The industrial powers hawked liberal capitalism in the world system to overcome domestic weaknesses. A whole host of problems—persistent high unemployment, maldistribution of goods and services, deteriorating national prestige and patriotism, the uncertainty of preserving class privileges, the desire for more rapid accumulations of wealth, the unreliability of progress under laissez-faire, the restricted national markets, and a lack of productive investment opportunities—suggested to the industrial powers the need to expand their spheres of activity.[4]

By the late nineteenth century, leaders in Germany (and other metropoles) needed agencies to implement their policies of social imperialism and simultaneously to mediate the internal discord arising from bitter competition during the crises of industrial capitalism. The business leaders used political institutions to establish corporate (or organized) capitalism. They institutionalized cartel, oligopolistic, or holding company arrangements that joined government and business leaders into cooperative situations. Germany implemented social imperialism abroad in a variety of forms, but common instruments were multinational corporations (for example, Siemens and its subsidiary Empresa Eléctrica de Guatemala), nonbusiness transnational organizations (International Congress of Americanists), governmental or quasi-governmental agencies (Deutsches Auslandsamt [German Foreign Institute]), and private social and cultural bodies—German schools, clubs, and religious organizations.[5]

When German interests approached an area of the world economy as key as the Central American isthmus, they encountered other nations' businesspeople whose corrupted laissez-faire ideology—evident in free trade rhetoric covering government-supported multinational business ventures—generated intense competition. This competition was buttressed with strategic, political, social, and cultural language to reinforce the home countries' determination to assure maximum access to the wealth and security they expected from the transit linking the Atlantic and Pacific half-worlds.

The primary consequence for the periphery was dependency. *Dependencia* theorists point out that metropole development required the underdevelopment of the periphery. If the periphery developed, it would retain more of the value produced from its land, labor, and capital, and the reduced transfer of value would not serve the well-being of the metropole. Metropole states commonly sought to manipulate the sovereignty of peripheral states as a means to tilt the local factors of production in their favor. Dependency theory focuses on sovereignty and the international ties of the metropole-periphery relationship.[6]

By the late nineteenth century, much of the world had become colonies or protectorates of metropole states or had fallen under the influence of multinational corporations. Metropole firms often controlled the production and distribution systems that drove the political economies on the periphery. Large transnational firms dominated the shipping, transoceanic telegraph cables, maritime services, and marketing operations that serviced the Central American isthmus. Metropole states dominated the political, judicial, social, cultural, labor, and professional organizations of the periphery through other international organizations, which developed the capacity to interact with the gigantic firms on the level of the world economy.[7]

The metropole states and the multinational corporations commonly established informal political and economic alliances with compradors—both local individuals and groups. These compradors facilitated the entrance of foreign entrepreneurial and political or social influence, and they managed the domestic order so as to create attractive business opportunities and to avoid undesired political interference in foreign enterprises. Domestic peasant, worker, artisan, religious, cultural, and other excluded or marginal groups protested and resisted. Compradors stifled the discontent generated by the loss of sovereignty, infringement of cultural values, loss of land ownership, and the protests of exploited workers. But political repression generated violent resistance, and the ensuing spectacle alienated metropole supporters of the civilizing mission, the white man's burden, and human rights.[8]

German relations with Central America from 1823 to 1929 divide into four periods for analytical purposes. For much of the first period, 1823 to the 1850s, Prussian officials perceived of Central America as linked to the internal Grossdeutschland-Kleindeutschland (a union of all German states versus a union of selected German states) struggle with Austria over which power would dominate Germany's future. Only a Prussia capable of competing with Britain and the United States for isthmian transit rights would have a chance to attract the Hansa cities into the Zollverein [Customs Union] and to implement a kleindeutsch solution. During the second period, the 1860s to the 1880s, Germany unified (as Kleindeutschland) and expanded overseas to mitigate difficulties in its industrialized political economy. By the 1880s, Germans were well established in Guatemala, Costa Rica, and Nicaragua, and important shipping firms—Kosmos (Hamburg) and Roland (Bremen)—operated on the west coast of Latin America.[9]

In the third period, the 1890s to 1918, competition over peripheral areas increased as the great powers sought to resolve internal problems through free trade experiments, colonial and informal expansion, and war. A roll call of the large German firms active in Central America in the late nineteenth century—Siemens, Krupp, Deutsche Bank, Überseebank, Kosmos, Hamburg-Amerika-Packetfahrt-Aktien Gesellschaft (HAPAG)—underscored the rising stake of the German political economy in that region. The increased German role in Central America sharpened the rivalry between Germany and the United States. The inability of German and U.S. metropole leaders to resolve the domestic difficulties allowed them to blame foreign rivals for ineffective domestic policies until violence tore through the problems.

The fourth period, 1918 to 1929, delineated the recovery and renewal of competition as if little had been learned from the earlier struggles for material success. New entrepreneurial elements—such as Allgemeine Elektrizitäts Gesellschaft (AEG), public works engineer Walter Sprung in Costa Rica, and the construction firm Wayss-Freitag in El Salvador and Costa Rica—restored the profitability of German firms in Central America so quickly that they aroused the jealousy and suspicion of U.S., British, and French officials. The Central American governments gladly facilitated German reentry as a countervailing force to the U.S. hegemonic position.

The leaders on the isthmus were often attracted to the vision of material growth that liberalism and metropole promoters conjured up. Pressured by the competition of the metropole powers, the small Central American states tried to play them off against each other and to create some breathing space for themselves. In the early nineteenth century when Britain was aggressive, they periodically sought U.S. aid. Later, when the United States and Germany played the leading roles, these Central American states called on France, Austria, Italy, Mexico, and even Britain. Seduced by the wealth and power of the industrializing states, the Central American societies replaced subsistence with a plantation cash crop system.[10] Only after being incorporated into the world economy did leaders of the isthmian countries discover the severe limitations its system placed on their sovereignty and self-government.

Central America's relationship to the colonial and imperial powers of the North Atlantic had been weak throughout the Spanish colonial era and the first half-century of independence. Until the 1850s, the region had been marginal in the political economy of Spain; it exported some cacao, tobacco, gold, silver, hides and skins, indigo, cochineal, and hard woods, but the total value of these products was modest even by the standards of Spanish trade with the New World. The gold and hardwoods were frequently removed by illegal British operations on the Atlantic coast of the isthmus—an area that Spain never controlled well during 300 years of colonial rule. Central America in the era of the federation had few products to offer the world market, and the metropole states had not yet begun determined competition for the transit.

In the 1840s, however, the expanding metropole economies began competing more earnestly for land, economic opportunities, and political authority. Some of the foreign penetration was welcome, some was not. One early sign of increased importance in the world economy occurred with the development of coffee in Costa Rica around 1840. By 1850 Costa Rican coffee was a major export crop. A second sign of foreign interest in the isthmus involved various transit concessions that reflected the attraction of Pacific trade. Between 1820 and 1854, Mexico, Central America, and New Granada negotiated about a dozen unfulfilled contracts. The first interoceanic projects completed—the Panama Railroad (1854) and the Accessory Transit in Nicaragua (1849)—did not satisfy the transit needs of the metropole economies; they merely whetted their appetite. Appeals for a canal, a railroad, or an all-weather carriage road multiplied in the next half-century. The French initiated a canal project in 1879, and U.S.-British interests undertook transisthmian railroad projects in 1869 and 1871 at Honduras and Costa Rica. German entrepreneurs operated steamship lines and built several railroads in Guatemala, and German officials scouted for a naval station in the Caribbean–Central American region to protect their growing presence. All metropoles suspected that the intensified activity in the region might impair their national well-being and security. Despite their free trade rhetoric, U.S. officials and businesspeople did not welcome German competition in the area.[11]

In the 1880s, foreign entrepreneurs developed new export-oriented coffee, banana, and mineral activities requiring considerable capital for production, processing, or distribution; these products formed the heart of Central American export activity until after World War II. In the 1880s, the Costa Rican railroad had fostered banana operations that grew until United Fruit, an early multinational firm in Central America, was formed in 1899 from about twenty existing fruit and steamship companies. French, German, and British companies attempted to compete in the banana business, but with little success. Other export products—cotton, meat, hides, live cattle, and sugar—proved transitory and secondary in producing exchange or attracting foreign capital.[12]

Economic growth commonly produces instability, not stability, because growth alters the production and distribution of wealth, power, security, and status within a society. It challenges the status quo. In mid-nineteenth-century Germany, the aristocrats and large landowners faced a quandary common to many governing elites. The traditional elite employed authoritarian devices to strengthen its legitimacy and authority. Many urban entrepreneurs and some rural landowners wished to unleash the forces of an unfettered market system to reap greater rewards of wealth, power, and prestige. But the free market required a modest-sized, mobile, educated, flexible labor group and a large unskilled workforce. These laborers demanded greater political and social liberty as a price for their participation in the liberal economic order. The reluctant extension of political and social liberty to the laboring class and the concession of release from remnant serflike control for rural laborers challenged the monarchical, aristocratic, large landowning classes, and even urban entrepreneurs. Many in the elite, desirous of power and profits, struggled to preserve their class's authority while freeing the laboring class as much as possible. The path of economic transformation was neither easy nor smooth.[13]

German leaders recognized that informal or formal ties to the cheap labor of overseas peripheral societies could compensate for some of the costs and burdens of conceding material and social privileges to a domestic laboring force. The division of labor that industrialization fostered produced a domestic labor elite that, although divided, could marshal opposition to any perceived infringements of its position, and a foreign labor force that was commonly divided and only meekly challenged the domestic elite's wealth, power, and prestige. German historian Hans-Ulrich Wehler has contended that "German imperialism is to be seen primarily as the result of endogenous socio-economic and political forces, and not as a reaction to exogenous pressures, nor as a means of defending traditional foreign interests." He identified the loci of expansion: an industrial state seeking well-being and security through a philosophy that defined progress as material and expansive (growth), and the leadership in a nonindustrialized state that saw "borrowing" of development as the key to its social, economic and political progress.[14] Thus, the metropole leaders and the compradors both expected major benefits from the development (or "progress") of the periphery. More important, metropole entrepreneurs would distribute the gains of economic activity. And the Central American societies possessed limited resource bases, smaller and less-educated populations, and less capital, communications, and technological development than metropole states. Yet, they were made to bear some of the burden of metropole unemployment and social disorder in addition to their own.

The leadership in these peripheral societies interpreted the theoretical treatises of Adam Smith, John Stuart Mill, and Auguste Comte as descriptive of their best chance for progress. They believed that the external link was vital in achieving the material benefits that would shape their new society. In the nineteenth century, the new society would be what the metropole state wished—laissez-faire capitalism—for while the metropoles themselves were developing state-regulated corporate institutions, they championed the unrestrained and potentially more profitable free market system abroad. The metropole states, in fact, exported a system truer to their past than either their present or the future for which they were striving.[15]

1

■

Foundations of German Interest in Central America, 1820–1848

The alliance of European powers that defeated Napoleon twice dissolved in the post-1815 years. In a series of congresses, conferences, and confidential negotiations, the great and near-great powers of Europe, Great Britain, Austria-Hungary, Russia, Prussia, Spain, and Savoy each hoped to facilitate a (favorable) balance of power. The Napoleonic era left a mark on unification in Germany and on the isthmus. The German-speaking population stirred slowly toward national awakening. Student and professorial organizations grew in strength in the 1810s and 1820s and sponsored regional and national assemblies that reinforced nationalism. The July 1830 revolution in France stimulated German nationalists. Other clubs and organizations sponsored regional meetings, culminating in large national gatherings at the Deutsches Sängerfest [festival of German singing clubs] (1845) and the Gelehrtencongress [academic congress] (1846). The Central American provinces organized a central federation in 1824 that, however, survived less than two decades. Despite the shared language, culture, and historical experiences of the European creole and peninsular elites, the federation split into five separate states.

The Napoleonic era had a profound effect on the geographic and cultural area of Germany, which consisted of about seventy autonomous political units that varied in size from tiny city-states to large states like Bavaria, Prussia, and Austria. The political and ethnic geography was complicated. Austria (a Catholic state) was the German-speaking cultural and political center of the Hapsburg empire, a conglomerate of ethnic groups—Poles, Czechs, Slovaks, Slovenes, Magyars, Romanians, Serbs, and others—in which the Austrian Germans were a small minority. Napoleon drastically reduced the number and redrew the boundaries of the German states, and the wars suggested to some German leaders that if unification produced prosperity, they might escape powerful British and

Dutch economic influences. In the post-Napoleonic era, the German Confederation [Deutsche Bund], consisting of thirty-nine tenuously organized states, sought a place in the reconstructed European state system.[1]

Prussia, the largest German state north of the Hapsburg empire, had
a Lutheran aristocracy and populace. Both it and Austria sought preeminence among the Germanic states. Austrian influence and alliances were
pervasive in the overwhelmingly Catholic south of Germany. While both
states had strong monarchical traditions, the Prussian government built
its power base in a confederation of North German states [Nord Deutscher Bund] and in the Customs Union [Zollverein] that encouraged free
trade and other liberal economic practices. The Prussian government labored to unify the German political economy. It exercised a major role in
negotiating the Customs Union, in encouraging state participation in
transportation, communications, and industrial development, and in foreign commerce. Plans for a south German customs union and a middle
German customs union produced no viable alternatives to the Prussian-
led Customs Union.[2] The movement toward political and economic unity
lasted until the 1870s, and uniform cultural norms survived several decades more.

The Hansa cities—Hamburg, Bremen, and Lübeck—and some other
German states sought to expand overseas trade as a means of combating
the economic crisis that followed the Napoleonic wars. Individual states
pursued different objectives. Many parts of Germany were adapting to
the industrial and technological progress of late-eighteenth-century
Europe, especially the capacity of armies in the Napoleonic era to consume industrial and technological production in massive quantities.
Prussia's aristocratic and industrial elites wished to use this wave of industrialization to buttress the political system and to accumulate personal wealth and power. The Prussian government and entrepreneurs in
Germany built transportation, production, distribution, and financial institutions that would hasten industrialization. The Prussian nation
moved along a course that hinted at conflict between Junker aristocratic
landowners and bourgeois liberal groups, both searching to direct that
nation's internal and external development. The Hansa cities and Hanover appeared ready to adapt to the liberal trade movement and to enter
the commercial and industrial transformation of the world system.[3]

Prussia, however, intended to manipulate the commerce and maritime activity to gain advantage inside Germany. Some Prussian leaders believed that their government's role in Central American isthmian
affairs could be used advantageously in the internal Grossdeutschland-

Kleindeutschland struggle with Austria to dominate Germany's future. After the Napoleonic era, Austria wished to unite a splintered body of German states to its north into one large Germanic federation [Grossdeutschland], under its dominance. Bavaria and Württemberg, two large Catholic states just north of Austria, generally accepted Austria's leadership. Prussia intended to avoid a Grossdeutschland by building a Kleindeutschland (meaning all German princes and populations except Austria and independent Switzerland) under its tutelage. Most German states subordinated their policy to Prussia or Austria.[4]

The idea of a customs union to expand the German market for industrial goods took preliminary form in the early nineteenth century. Many Germans considered a customs union essential to unify the German domestic economy and to tie it to the world economy. By 1828 Prussia had organized a small customs union. Around 1830 Prussian leaders adopted free trade and removed tariffs in order to accommodate domestic producers entering international competition. Prussia sought the maximum material and political benefits from its role in the Customs Union. Historian Hubert Kiesewetter argued that the "Customs Union of 1834 had at least overcome the politically unproductive particularism of the individual states. In some states . . . it came to an industrial growth phase between 1835 and 1848 and to rapid growth after 1850." German exports of half-finished and finished products increased noticeably after 1835 and thus industrial producers needed to import more raw materials.[5]

German and Prussian leaders expected the development of economic and political power to give the German "nation" a proper place in European affairs. Economic growth and political unity were the goals, but it was difficult for German leaders to capture nationalism in an area where several magnets (Prussia, Austria, Bavaria, and the Holy Roman Empire) competed for political loyalties. For historian Hagen Schulze, "the history of the German national movement is simultaneously the history of social and political opposition to the dominant forces of the time—first against Napoleon's order and then against the German Bund." Moreover, the internal German political borders were also trade barriers, hence the relationship between nationalism and the customs union movement reflected the link between the political and economic development of Germany. Kiesewetter concluded that "the German Union did not give the impression, . . . in comparison with England, France, or the United States, that in less than a hundred years it could become the most powerful national economy in Europe."[6]

The Central (and Latin) American societies have been linked to the

European state system since the sixteenth century, either in formal colonial relationships or through protection and informal economic and cultural ties. Of course, the chief trading partner for Central America was Great Britain. Statistical data on commercial, migration, investment, and maritime interaction of the German and Central American states for the period from 1820 to 1848 are sparse. The data for Guatemala—the capital of the Central American Federation and its largest, wealthiest, and most developed state—probably incorporated most of Central America's international trade until the federation dissolved around 1840. The German states sold directly about 2 percent of Guatemala's imports in these years (Table 1). Germany was the source of 3 percent of Guatemala's direct imports (items going directly between two nations) in the years from 1839 to 1847. (In the eighteenth and nineteenth centuries, Great Britian often served as intermediary for an indirect trade between Germany and Central America—that is, German goods were sold to British merchants for resale in Guatemala, just as German merchants purchased Central American products in London.) German vessels supplied 6 percent of the tonnage and 8 percent of the ships that serviced the foreign trade of Corinto, Nicaragua, from 1836 to 1839. For the early decades of the nineteenth century, the sparse data on German residents in Central America suggests a moderate to large number of colonists or businessmen in Guatemala (425 in 1844) (Table 9).[7]

Latin America, which experienced periods of prosperity and decline in the first half of the nineteenth century, remained an area of economic potential and unpredictable development. Generally, Central America's economy was depressed like that in much of Latin America. After 1823 the Central American societies slowly broke out of the colonial export production cycles. They continued to produce the same items as those traded during the colonial period—cochineal (*grana*) in Guatemala; indigo (*añil*) in El Salvador; minerals, cattle, hides, and hardwoods in Honduras; and cattle and hides in Nicaragua. Isthmian liberals and foreign entrepreneurs urged the development of export products from agriculture and mining. Costa Rica first altered the colonial export production cycle. Its farmers experimented with coffee trees in the early nineteenth century and began to export coffee in the late 1830s. Only coffee-producing Costa Rica and Guatemala experienced reasonably good days in the fourth and fifth decades of the nineteenth century.[8]

In the nineteenth century, Germans entered a Central America where the individual states were physically isolated from each other. The major cities, agricultural areas, and populated regions were poorly interconnected. The movement of people and goods was difficult except by water. The social and political leadership was divided. The conservatives, called *serviles* in Central America, wished to preserve traditional sources of authority—the Creoles, the church, and the landowning classes. In their view, political, economic, and social life required few major adjustments. The liberals wanted to open Central America's political economy to the educated and advantaged persons of European stock. They wished to reshape isthmian society according to ideas borrowed from U.S. and French revolutionary experience and from European liberal thinkers. Neither the liberals nor the conservatives could govern effectively through the Central American Federation, however. The modest political success of the liberals in the 1820s and 1830s was eroded through inexperience, a miscalculation of the power of tradition (especially among the Indian peasants), the failure of many reforms, and the reaction to foreign intrusions into isthmian society. Although Old World states had drawn some New World areas loosely into the world economy through trade in their chief ports, indigenous cultures were only gradually transformed.[9]

During the era of Latin American independence from 1810 to 1830, the Germanic states and other European nations threatened to help restore Spanish power in the New World colonies, a step that would challenge the British predominance in Latin America and undermine further U.S. territorial ambitions. In the early 1820s, the Spanish government confronted domestic unrest, the danger of war with Portugal, and defeat everywhere in Spanish America. With Spain governing its colonies ineffectively, President James Monroe and the U.S. Congress gained political influence in the New World by recognizing the Latin American republics. In the years from 1821 to 1823, European congresses at Troppau and Verona authorized the use of armed force to bolster Spain's legitimate authority in the face of widespread revolution in Latin America. These agreements collapsed when England refused to participate unless the United States was invited. In 1823 Monroe announced a policy to prevent European interference in Latin America, even while several Latin American states sought European recognition. Responding to the Latin American initiatives, the Hansa cities and Hanover proposed to enter into official relationships. Prussia and Austria adopted a guarded stance because they feared that the Latin American liberal movement threatened the legitimacy principle (the idea that governing authority was rooted in a religiously ordained hereditary aristocracy and in no way tied to popular will), and they portended European upheavals related to the recognition of "revolutionary" governments. The Monroe Doctrine kept the supporters of the Old World and legitimacy from accepting U.S. participation because that doctrine required European nonintervention as a precondition.[10]

England's recognition of several Latin American states in late 1824 prompted a strong protest from Prussia, which exposed its forked-tongue policy. Prussia's distinction between "diplomacy" and "private initiative" permitted it to recognize Spain's de jure rights in Latin America, while Prussian merchants entered de facto arrangements with Spanish American revolutionaries. If Prussia wished to lead the drive for German unification, it could not allow the Hansa cities to establish economic and political ties to Latin America that left Prussia behind. England's advantageous position (supported by diplomatic and economic institutions) was reducing the opportunities of German businesspeople, who had to operate without the political support of their government. French merchants benefited from general inspectors for trade questions sent to Latin America. German merchants sought trade in Latin America to ease the marketing problems associated with the troublesome domestic economic crisis of 1825 and 1826. Under pressure of petitions from the Rhine and Silesia, Prussia negotiated a commerce treaty with Mexico in 1827 but failed in other negotiations because it feared alienating Austria and Russia, which supported legitimacy. Uncertain of its support within the German states and unwilling to precipitate a crisis with Austria, Prussian policy evolved toward independent activity on the isthmus.[11]

The aspirations of the Hansa cities and other commercial interests directed special attention to Germany's role on the isthmus. Although the Napoleonic wars had encouraged various forms of industrial growth in Germany, especially in textiles, iron and steel, and chemicals, the lack of isthmian consumers for quality linens and iron works and the inaccessibility of the west coast Central American harbors meant that only a modest trade developed. Germans had traded largely indirectly with Latin America until Hansa merchants slowly built direct connections in the 1820s.[12]

In the 1820s German trading interests entered Central and South America seriously. In 1821 the Rheinish-West India Company was formed in Elberfeld, with the support of the Prussian government, to trade German wares in the Caribbean area. In the late 1820s the Prussian chancellor urged the king to encourage trade with South America. In 1830 the German Union Parliament [Deutsche Bundes-Versammlung] decided that commerce had an essential influence on the well-being of a state because of its link to industry. It praised German trading companies that handled domestic craft products and thus preserved intermediary profits for German merchants. The Union Parliament expected German industry to compete with European industry if it received support from the state governments.[13]

Prussia, paralyzed between trade and legitimacy, allowed Hanseatic consular agents—the most effective German agents in Latin America—to represent its commercial interests. Still, its inability to attract the Hansa cities into the Customs Union hindered that body's growth. While the free trade policy of Hamburg and Bremen reduced the economic impact of their reluctance to join the Customs Union, Prussia exercised little influence on the policies guiding the Hansa cities as long as they remained outside the economic and political system Prussia was constructing. Without Germany's chief ports, the Customs Union could not develop optimum overseas connections.[14] Moreover, a Prussia dependent on Hansa agents in Latin America and Hansa free trade did not cut the figure of a strong leader in a Kleindeutschland.

In the 1830s the Hansa cities negotiated trade and navigation pacts to protect their merchants, while the Prussian government waffled between its concern for its reputation among conservative European governments and its wish to develop markets for its new Rhineland provinces. Clearly expecting the Customs Union to provide political and economic benefits, the Prussian government regularly granted subsidies (bribes) to German states that were hesitant about joining or unsatisfied once they had joined. The total of Prussia's direct payments to members of the Customs Union often amounted to more than the combined revenue Prussia collected from these states. The member states, however, profited from the central location of the Customs Union within Europe and the accelerated development of a railroad system and river traffic in Germany. For decades, the Prussian government underwrote the extension of the Customs Union. By 1842, twenty-eight of the thirty-nine members of the German Union belonged to the Customs Union. Prussian leaders hoped to couple the growing need for markets with their desire to lead within the German Confederation. They recognized that a capacity to compete diplomatically with Britain and the United States in international commercial matters might draw the Hansa cities into the Customs Union.[15]

Foreign appeals for concessions peppered the Central American Federation. Commonly these requests aimed at developing communications to facilitate exploitation of the area. Successful projects—U.S. and European steamship lines, the Panama railroad, a variety of roads and ports—and a multitude of failed schemes for interoceanic canals, railroads, the clearing of rivers, and port and road construction dot the chronology after the 1820s. Although the majority of such schemes had U.S. or European roots, Central American elites occasionally appointed agents to solicit metropole technology, capital, and entrepreneurial skills for favored projects. The competition often assumed a dangerous character when an interoceanic scheme appeared a realistic possibility. Some foreign diplomats and promoters perceived business opportunities in the disintegration of the federation into five sovereign states that occurred between 1837 and 1843.[16]

During the turmoil from the 1820s to the 1840s, Britain's historic position in the Caribbean and its ties to Belize and the Mosquito region of Honduras and Nicaragua predominated in Central America. The Dutch and Belgians vied with the British on the isthmus, not so much for political authority as for access to economic opportunity and transit rights. In the 1840s the United States, which was experiencing rapid population growth and a rising individualism that encouraged resistance to the domestic social and the international order, challenged British authority in Middle America. The British resisted for a while and then retreated before the aggressive Yankees.[17]

The sudden spurt of British and U.S. activity on the isthmus in the 1840s, focusing on the canal routes, attracted German interest. The Prussian government moved toward a role that would safeguard Germany's permanent interest in such a vital area. It refused to adhere to the Hansa cities' treaties with Guatemala and Costa Rica, however, because such a course would mark it as subordinate to the Hansa states. Since Prussia intended to magnify its political capital in Germany by obtaining access to Central America's valuable transit routes for German industry, commerce, and shipping, it could not accept even the appearance of an inferior, dependent role.[18]

The Prussian government suspected that it could not win the support of the Hansa cities and the industrializing states of Germany for a kleindeutsch resolution to a splintered Germany unless it could offer them access to world trade routes. The rising productivity of Prussia and other German states and the demands of Latin American governments for formal recognition eventually compelled Prussia to reconsider its nonrecognition policy. More extensive direct trade with Latin America needed shipping ties and friendly tariffs. While Prussian minister Albrecht Alvensleben-Erxleben wanted Prussian ships to face customs conditions similar to other nations in the Caribbean area, some Prussian spokesmen expected shippers from the Hansa cities and the North German states to bear the burden required to overcome the disadvantages placed on German vessels in Latin American trade. Prussian trade was handicapped without consular or diplomatic representation. In the early 1840s, Carl Friedrich Rudolph Klee, the Hansa and Hanoverian consul general in Central America, pointed out to the Prussian government that the disappointing trade data did not measure the considerable indirect German trade conducted through British or French intermediaries. Lamentably, he observed, indirect trade left the sales of German products at the mercy of foreigners. If Prussia intended to expand German trade in Central America, Klee advised establishing a consul general.[19]

In 1845 Prussia named Klee consul general in Central America. He faced his first major challenge as a Prussian agent on June 9, 1845, when a Guatemalan decree moved the main east coast customs office to Izabal. This new location produced costly delays in processing customs papers, increased the likelihood of damage to goods, and favored foreign countries that traded in lower-quality products. The decree greatly disadvantaged German trade in high-quality products—such as iron, steelwares, and middle- and high-grade textiles—which had been increasing in the mid-1840s. The lack of reciprocity in commercial exchange also disturbed Klee. Guatemalan goods could enter German ports under consignment and pass inland without delay, while German goods had to remain in the port until inspected. Klee claimed that this decree undermined efforts to increase Germany's share of the Central American market more gravely than did the British or French traders who dealt in lower-quality goods.[20]

With the introduction of labor-saving machinery during the early stages of industrialization, the German political economy could not gainfully employ all of its artisans, rural day laborers, and urban unskilled workers. It supplied the world with numerous emigrants, beginning in the second quarter of the nineteenth century. The development of passenger service to export people displaced or unemployed by the economic transformation occupied an important role in the growth of trade in the Hansa cities by making imported products a valuable return cargo. In the 1840s Germany exported on average 469,000 people annually, in the 1860s it exported 833,000 annually, and in the 1880s it exported 1,342,000 annually. These emigrants also represented a significant outward flow of capital. They carried out 200 million talers (1 taler was worth slightly less than a silver dollar, circa 1820s) between 1832 and 1852 and about 20 to 30 million talers per year in the 1860s. This emigration was stronger in the economic conjunctures than in the crises, perhaps because the ongoing crises displaced the workers and made them ripe to depart as soon as economic conditions facilitated departures.[21]

Many German leaders reacted with mixed feelings to large-scale emigration. Central America was attractive (as was the U.S. Midwest, where 90 percent of migrating Germans settled at this time) because its virgin lands needed labor and promised wealth. In the 1830s, a Belgian colonization project at Santo Tomás in Guatemala attracted many German immigrants. In 1845 Central American colonization associations organized in Berlin and Königsberg. The Prussian government recognized that colonization on the frontiers of the New World offered economic and diplomatic opportunities but also involved risks, including possible difficulties with the United States and Great Britain.[22]

German entrepreneurs and speculators sought to profit from colonization schemes in Central America. One particular colonization scheme from 1844 to 1846 raised special problems for Prussian officials. Prince Carl of Prussia, the brother of King Frederick William IV, and Prince Otto Victor von Schönburg-Waldenburg became active partners in a company that contracted to settle a large area in the Mosquito king's realm. The British government confidentially warned the Prussian government that it disapproved of this pact and would oppose any effort by Prince Carl and Prince Otto Victor to obtain sovereign rights there. The Prussian government followed the scheme's development with great interest because it involved the reputation and honor of the Prussian royal family and entailed a possible confrontation with Britain. In late 1846 this company sent 110 German settlers to the Mosquito Coast where they founded Carlstadt in honor of Prince Carl. A second expedition stranded its colonists in the Danish Virgin Islands because it lacked funds. Aided by Louis Beschor's Bluefields merchant firm, many of these stranded Germans opted to go to the United States, but some continued on to Central America. The Carlstadt colony broke apart in 1852, undone by quiet British unfriendliness. In addition to Prince Carl's project, over half of the 850 settlers present in the Belgian Santo Tomás colony in 1846 were German. In the late 1840s and early 1850s, over 1,000 Germans migrated to Middle America.[23] The Prussian government supported projects to export surplus labor, but it did not want these projects to undermine its prestige nor to produce confrontations with a major power.

Despite the revolution of 1848 and the subsequent constitutional crisis, Prussia intended to preserve a significant German role in future Central American affairs. The economic costs of the Customs Union and its success in uniting jealous, self-conscious, independent states under Prussian leadership indicated Prussia's determined political and economic objectives. By the early 1840s the Customs Union, the building of railroads, and state encouragement of and investment in economic activity had produced considerable capital accumulation and a modest rise in the standard of living within the Customs Union states. In the mid-1840s general European economic stagnation, an increasing German population, the dislocation of the crafts and agrarian sectors, and faltering efforts at political modernization in Germany collectively helped to produce the sociopolitical crisis of 1848. In early 1848 Prussia encouraged the formation of chambers of commerce with powers to oversee and advise the bureaucracy serving commerce in order to coordinate business activity.[24] After the revolution of 1848, Prussia wished to regain some of the prestige it had lost in its awkward response to the Frankfurt Parliament and in the unhappy settlement of the Hessian and Schleswig-Holstein problems that Austria and Russia had maneuvered Prussia into accepting. A successful role in colonization, interoceanic transit, and commercial matters might recoup some lost prestige, induce the Hansa cities to join the Customs Union, and create markets for Prussia and other German states.

A clash of British and American plans to control the Middle American transit routes between 1848 and 1850 was, at heart, a great power contest to secure future access to the world economy. If the German states intended to use the world economic system to foster their internal growth, they needed to preserve access to transit between the Atlantic and Pacific. Many Germans recognized that power, prestige, economic growth, and internal order and stability would be linked in some fashion to the fate of Central America.

2

■

Prussia and Commerce
with the Pacific Basin, 1848–1851

The revolutions of 1848, especially the Frankfurt Parliament, profoundly affected Prussia and Austria. German liberals were discredited for their indecisive conduct in 1848–1849. The Frankfurt Parliament swayed between a gross- and kleindeutsch resolution to stabilize the German political order. Since the Parliament liberals formed no consensus on what was German, they could not draft a constitution. The military and monarchical forces in Berlin and Vienna regained authority. Prussian authorities wished to quell the liberal nationalism of Frankfurt, yet they asserted nationalist leadership in diplomacy and commerce by protecting all German interests on the isthmus.

From 1846 to 1850 affairs on the isthmus heated up, as Britain and the United States negotiated, acted preemptively, and shifted military forces around to gain advantage of isthmian transit. Transit would play a central role in connecting the Atlantic area with the whole Pacific basin, from the Yukon down to Chile, across to Australia and the Indian Ocean, up through southeast Asia and China to Japan and Alaska, and to all the islands within this great circle. The string of events elevating the tension between the United States and Britain began with the U.S.-Colombia Bidlack treaty (1846), which gave the United States special advantage on the isthmus. Then followed a series of events in succession: the treaty of Guadelupe-Hidalgo ended the Mexican War and recognized special U.S. rights at the Tehuantepec isthmus; the British extended their authority along the Atlantic side of the Central American isthmus from Honduras to the Panamanian province of Colombia in agreement with the puppet Mosquito king; and the British expanded their political authority in Belize and on the Bay Islands. Finally, U.S.-British agreement via the Clayton-Bulwer treaty in 1850 calmed matters.

During the time the Anglo-American contest was running its course,

Prussia was not a preeminent power. It had had glory in the past, and its leaders looked to the future with stars in their eyes, contemplating the energy of a unified Germany. The Prussian government wished to avoid a contest over the fate of the Middle American isthmus in the late 1840s and 1850s. Its attention was drawn to the isthmus because it did not want to be excluded from the transit and because the Central American states sought the aid of Prussia's German rival, Austria. Prussia had few options but to pursue influence on the isthmus in view of German economic growth, its own social transformation, and its political competition with Austria. It could best exit from the ranks of secondary powers by unifying the industrial, agricultural, and commercial heart of Germany in Kleindeutschland. To this end, Prussia needed to assure German entrepreneurs access to the Pacific basin under its auspices and to prevent Austria from becoming a dispenser of trade access to Central America and the Pacific.[1]

Various forces shoved Prussia toward Central America. One push came from Austrian competition for leadership of a unified Germany, while another came from various expansive powers that sought to maximize their rights to transit over the isthmus. Germany's internal communications revolution blossomed in the 1840s and 1850s, mostly in canals, steamships, and railroads, but the value of these improvements was related to world communications routes as well as internal pressure to export products and people. Railroad investment rose from 800 million talers in 1851 to 6,800 million talers in 1875. Industrialization shifted wealth from rural, aristocratic groups to urban entrepreneurs and financiers. The remnants of the feudal agrarian order ended about midcentury in most German states. Industrialization and the adoption of capital-intensive agriculture dislocated rural and artisan labor and left many unemployed. Surplus labor, a by-product of the technological revolution, was exported through emigration.[2]

In the 1840s and 1850s, German leaders presumed that closer ties with Central America would alleviate some domestic ailments and facilitate security and prosperity for Germany. Aspects of Germany's domestic economic development in the mid-nineteenth century were linked to Prussia's isthmian politics. Early industrial modernization led to surpluses of some products and, in some sectors, yielded appreciable accumulation of capital that could not be profitably reinvested in the same product lines. Some of the more successful industrial areas increased exports to new markets. A few German entrepreneurs ventured capital above their firms' needs in unfamiliar domestic or foreign outlets or in

search of industrial raw material imports. Thus industrialists and financiers participated in the commercial expansion. Central America became
one area of particular attractiveness, not merely for its direct economic
role but also because of its political and strategic potential for Prussia's
future.[3]

An analysis of German competition with metropole or semi-peripheral
states would benefit from a detailed, empirical study of Germany's colonization and its investment in shipping, trading, extractive, and plantation enterprises. Total German trade grew from 1.1 billion marks in 1850
to 6.5 billion marks in 1875. Per capita trade increased from 31 marks in
1820 to 156 marks in 1872. Initially, German traders and shippers aimed
at the United States and South America; after the 1840s they also targeted
Asia, Australia, and Africa.[4]

Unfortunately, little data was available on German trade and shipping
connections with Central America before the mid-nineteenth century. In
the late 1840s, the Hansa cities expanded trade with the region. About 1.6
percent of total Bremen exports went to Central America; however, this
percentage declined steadily throughout the nineteenth century. Also
during the late 1840s, Central American products constituted only 0.3
percent of Bremen importation, but this percentage rose over the next
decades (Table 4). During the period 1848 to 1851, the Germanic states
furnished 2 percent of Guatemala's imports (Table 1). The empirical data
buttresses an argument that from 1848 to 1858, Prussian trade policy in
Central America aided projects to assure access to the vital communication routes of the world market. Both trade and colonization advanced
the Prussian goal of developing influence in this crucial region.[5]

German historiography associates German imperialism with the per-
sonality and era of Bismarck. Yet Prussia exhibited a social imperialist
policy toward Central America before Bismarck's rise to power. Just as
the Prussian government had intervened to regulate the domestic economy in the 1830s and 1840s when it judged the contemporary tendencies
dangerous to its (and Germany's) well-being and security, so would it intervene in foreign affairs—for example, assuring German access to world
trade routes—when it judged the actions necessary to secure Germany's
well-being and security. Such broad concerns were discussed in the
Frankfurt Parliament, in the Prussian government, and among a wider
German community around 1850.[6]

Since the consular service was viewed as an integral element of the
national economy, the Frankfurt Parliament asserted authority over German international representation. It studied the need to reform the con-

sular service with regard to both the expansion of commercial interests and the broader concerns of German nationalism. Consul candidates and veteran consuls should study languages, statistics, history, and maritime, international, and commercial law in the foreign ministry and in chambers of commerce. Many observers argued that, to serve their industrial, agricultural, and commercial enterprises well in international trade, the German states needed more consulates.[7]

The parameters defining German links to the world economy influenced the course of German nationalism. The new consular service should be national and professional. One study argued that only with consulates operating under a common flag could "Germany's trade power become as great and respected as was suited to a mighty nation." It suggested that a national consular service could be implemented without slighting the federal states by permitting the consuls to correspond directly with a specific state whenever a matter was of interest only to that state. Several reports to Parliament underscored that the competition among the consular agents of German states produced ridicule, endangered German subjects by reducing the credibility of their consuls, and decreased German prestige. "One important argument against retention of consuls from the individual states," one report claimed, was the "necessity for Germany to appear as a compact powerful state in the eyes of foreigners."[8]

Another major step toward building a dynamic consular service involved replacing the merchant consuls with civil servant consuls. Salaried, full-time consuls would distribute regular reports to every German state and would develop better relations with the host country (which would not consider them merchant adventurers) and with their compatriots (who would not see them as commercial competitors). Furthermore, the professionalized consular service would employ only German citizens. The fragmented consular services had handled German interests carelessly, a legislative study reported, because responsibility rested with a divided nation, an ineffective commercial system, and inadequate sea power. These flaws were correctable, particularly when one considered the potential value of German trade and the modest sum needed to staff a consular service adequately.[9]

The Prussian government studied the internal pressures. The revolution of 1848, emigration activities, the tension related to the Anglo-American crisis in Central America, and information from diplomats, colonization and missionary groups, and merchant interests outlined Prussia's role in Central America (and in world trade) and shaped a policy that could best fulfill its vision of Germany's objectives. In particular, Prussian Privy Counselor Franz Hugo Hesse detailed a plan for expanding German interests while alleviating internal disorder. In September 1850 Hesse's memorandum to the king's government interchanged Prussia and Germany freely as it analyzed the significance of potential British-American control of Middle American transit rights on Germany's future in world commerce. Reviewing the historical, strategic, economic, and political factors that sustained great power competition on the isthmus, Hesse proposed a plan for assuring German interests in Middle America.[10]

Hesse judged much of the political and diplomatic activity on the isthmus—for example, the flood of new diplomatic and consular appointments to Central America in the 1840s—closely linked to transit. Britain, the United States, France, Sardinia, and Belgium maintained diplomatic agents, while Hanover and the Hansa cities relied on consul generals in Central America. Most of these states had formal trade and navigation treaties with at least one Central American state. Hesse assigned special significance to British relations with the Mosquito state, which lay astride the Nicaraguan transit route, and to Belgium's colony at Santo Tomás, which was, more than coincidentally, a major harbor area capable of conversion into a superb naval station. Santo Tomás and certain other points represented valuable strategic locations, if Hesse's assessment of the importance of future trade over this isthmus to Australia, China, and the Pacific islands was correct.[11]

The Clayton-Bulwer treaty (which assured a shared access to any interoceanic canal) revealed that the great trading nations had refocused attention on the link between the Atlantic and Pacific Oceans. First the British, then, in Hesse's view, "the United States recognized very well that the nation which ruled the transit route connecting the oceans must also win the trade with the west coast of America, with the East Indies, Australia, and the east coast of Asia, in other words, the world." He described how the United States used the Mexican War to conquer the best harbor on the northwest coast of America, parlayed its involvement in Yucatán to achieve control of the Tehuantepec route, and finally, moved to dominate the Nicaraguan route. British consul general Frederick Chatfield, however, used Britain's position in Belize and the Bay Islands, its relations with the Mosquito Indians, and the seizure of Tigre Island in Fonseca Bay on the Pacific side to stymie U.S. designs. The Clayton-Bulwer treaty resolved this stalemate. Hesse understood that these two giant trading nations were contesting for "Middle America because it was destined to give rise to a transformation of world trade of monumental importance."[12]

Britain and the United States normally determined the significance of foreign trading areas, Hesse observed, while the German states quietly accepted a subordinate position. Germany should be prepared, in his view, to take advantage of internal Central American changes. For example, independence had encouraged a liberal ideology that favored trade. And European trade, mostly in manufactured goods, had grown to 4 million piasters (about $800,000) by the late 1840s and was paid for with indigo, cochineal, and coffee. While some German manufactures from the Ruhr went directly to Central America, other German goods arrived indirectly through Britain, France, and the United States. Often, Hesse lamented, German entrepreneurs entered areas too late to participate appropriately in trade activity. Although the transit potential of the isthmus had been acknowledged since the beginning of Spanish rule, the route had not been developed because it was considered unprofitable, unfeasible, or capital was lacking.[13]

In the late 1840s and early 1850s, Klee, Minister Friedrich von Rönne in Washington, and Minister Christian Karl von Bunsen in England directed Prussian attention to the British-U.S. struggle regarding transit and influence in Middle America. The British retreated politically in the 1850s yet retained their transit rights in the Clayton-Bulwer treaty. German officials studied the Anglo-Saxon crisis over transit because German commercial interests were attracted to trade opportunities on the west coast of the New World, in the Pacific, and in east Asia. In the summer of 1850, the *Nassauische Allgemeine* declared Costa Rica a promising goal for German migrants because "we must look beyond [America], if we want to participate in world trade and if we wish, despite the unfavorable political relations, to create the proper opportunity for the German people and to demonstrate the way in which the emigrants can harvest the fruits of their courage and industry." In addition, German colonization societies and several missionary groups peppered the population with propaganda tracts. The evaluations of the Prussian agents, while contradictory at times, warned that the U.S. government sought a protectorate arrangement that threatened to limit European opportunities on the isthmus and beyond, into the Pacific.[14]

The 1840s and early 1850s were marked with German colonization activity and sprinkled with thoughts that a properly guided colonization program might help extend Germandom to parts of the world essential for the homeland's well-being. The Prussian government accepted

Hesse's contention that colonization, trade, and the acquisition of political influence would nullify the negative effects of the Clayton-Bulwer pact on Prussian interests and would contribute toward a satisfactory resolution of the internal German economic and social turmoil. German colonization was closely related to Prussian concern about the importance of Central America.[15]

Foreseeing no interference from either Britain or the United States, Hesse assumed that 1850 was an ideal time to plant German colonists quietly. Various colonization societies aimed to settle Germans in Central America. About 1851, the Hamburg Society for the Transportation of Emigrants to Central America, the Hamburg Society for German Trade Colonies in Central America, and similar bodies in Leipzig, Cologne, and elsewhere formed to promote trade and colonization in Central America. These groups supplemented the German participation in the Belgian project at Santo Tomás, which ultimately received about 800 German colonists. In addition to the Germans who entered under Belgian auspices, from 1843 until 1854 the various colonization societies sent between 1,000 and 2,000 Germans to the isthmus. The United States, temporarily wrapped up in its internal development, did not interfere with the colonization because Germany did not appear to be a dangerous trade competitor.[16]

Hesse and other German observers were disturbed because many German emigrants lost contact with the fatherland. Each lost son or daughter contributed labor and services to a new country that might well be competing with the fatherland. Each year, Hesse lamented, some 80,000 to 90,000 Germans emigrated, carrying with them liquid assets of about 15 to 20 million taler. He applauded the Prussian law that proposed to protect and guide emigrants of the Customs Union. He sought to coordinate emigrating Germans in order to preserve their ties with the fatherland. He hoped to guide them to locations like Central America, where they might preserve their culture and serve German national interests.[17]

These German settlers were important because everything pointed to Central America's key role in the next transformation of world trade. North German trading and shipping firms and the industry of the Customs Union, Hesse insisted, should not observe this development inattentively. He perceived the German relationship to Central America within a social imperialism framework. "German business activity and production are in the midst of irresistible growth," he boasted, "yet if this growth is to become a blessing and not a curse, Germany needs new markets which could still be found in the Middle American states if it immediately applies the right means." Earlier, one of Germany's foremost economic thinkers, Friedrich List, projected that Middle America was a new rich market for manufactures and a goal for colonization.[18]

Germans expected the colonies in tropical lands to help locate the raw materials to expand production and markets to absorb the increased domestic production. Germany would use informal colonies to increase direct imports of tropical products and to emancipate itself from foreign controlled markets. Social and political conditions on the periphery had to be made acceptable for German colonists and businesses. The Prussian government sought British support to persuade Guatemala to legislate in favor of mixed marriages with Protestants. This step was considered essential to attract German settlers. Hesse lamented that the radical element among Germany's emigrants strengthened the democratic direction of the New World. Since most emigrants had no predetermined geographic goal, he proposed guiding them to healthy locations suitable to Prussian policy goals and where Prussian influence might establish an informal protectorate. Central America, he observed, had natural and political advantages that would permit "a talented and energetic Prussian agent to found a new overseas Prussia" in an area vital to German transit and trade objectives. It was one of the few areas where German emigrants could preserve their nationality and strengthen Germany's reputation.[19]

Supporters of an existing colonization scheme in Mexico opposed Hesse's proposal. The Prussian minister to the United States, Baron Friedrich von Gerolt, feared that a second project in the Middle American area would diffuse Germans into small bands. Moreover, he considered the experience of the colony in Mexico discouraging. In Hesse's judgment, the Mexican colonization venture, which merely placed independently emigrating Germans together, was not comparable to his proposal. The Central American project rested on several significant political assumptions: first, colonization represented the enterprising spirit of the German people; second, the migrants needed steering; third, Germans generally approved the project; and finally, liberals, who unceasingly expended their energy in fruitless fields of reform, would participate. He believed that the Berlin Colonization Society's plans for settlement in Nicaragua offered a promising prospect to establish long-term influence on the isthmus and to generate the experience needed to make the Mexican project realistic. The Mexican colonization project was not an alternative to his Central American project, which was needed, in any event, because "the Prussian government must secure transit through the Middle American isthmus for its colonists and its goods." He expected the Nicaraguan canal to become the focal point for a transformed world trade.[20]

Without burdening the state treasury, Hesse intended quietly to manage the capital and labor of the numerous German emigrants who normally became the booty of foreign nations. Success, he observed, required "Prussia to turn its full attention to the states of Middle America in the interest of German trade and in harmony with the suggestions manifested in the draft Customs Union bill to protect German emigration and colonization." He insisted that a salaried, full-time consul general accredited to the Mosquito kingdom, New Granada, and the five Central American republics should replace Klee, who could remain as consul for Guatemala. The new official would prevent California's rapid development from unduly influencing these isthmian states. Hesse also recommended moving the consulate general to Granada, Nicaragua—a central site, closer to the vital transit routes. Since the Nicaraguan government urgently desired a Prussian agent, the move might foster important advantages for German trade and settlements in Nicaragua. Moreover, the appointment of a consul general would respond to the legislative resolutions to expand Germany's consular and trade representation. "Only if we quickly respond to these resolutions will Prussia still manage to gain the influence which it needs for itself and for Germany," he warned, because "relationships are in the midst of very rapid development. If Prussia hesitates, then other powers will win the influence in Central America which Germany's hesitation has previously disdainfully lost everywhere."[21]

In October 1850 the Berlin Colonization Society for Central America complained to the king that Prussia had neglected world trade and focused on internal German affairs. It suggested that Middle American transit meant that "an unlimited field of activity had opened to world competition." It reinforced Hesse's arguments relative to the immense potential of the canal route, the sharp British-American competition, and Germany's loss of population and wealth through uncontrolled emigration. Then it arrived at a similar conclusion—Prussia needed to secure access to Central American transit. The king should "direct attention to an essentially Prussian colonization of Middle America on both sides of the ship canal since this would initiate the desired influence of Prussia on world trade." Moreover, it alleged that English, U.S., and French agents intended to use German immigrants to win control in Central America. The Berlin society hoped that the king would aid its project, just as Belgian King Leopold had protected Santo Tomás. It argued that Prussian influence could still capture Middle America if a government-controlled emigration policy was adopted quickly.[22]

Initially, the Prussian cabinet reacted favorably to suggestions about Central America's importance for Germany's future. Minister of Foreign Affairs Otto von Manteuffel recommended Hesse's memorandum to Finance Minister Arnold von Rabe and Commerce Minister August von der Heydt. Manteuffel proposed creating a consulate general, and Hesse and the Berlin Colonization Society lobbied in support. Von der Heydt, convinced that an isthmian transit route would become important for Europan participation in Atlantic-Pacific trade, agreed that Prussian objectives required more attention than an unsalaried businessman-consul like Klee could command. Since Britain and the United States had already acted to obtain advantage in Middle America, he urged Prussia to set its plans in operation quietly and quickly.[23]

In March 1851 Manteuffel, Rabe, and von der Heydt informed the king that, recognizing the importance of the isthmian route to trade with the west coast of America, the Pacific islands, and Asia, Britain had sought to seduce Middle America into a dependent relationship through political and economic penetration and through its protectorate over the Mosquito nation. British success had awakened U.S. opposition, until the Clayton-Bulwer treaty eased a tense situation. Meanwhile, France, Belgium, and Sardinia sought to extend their trade in Middle America. The ministers did not believe that Prussia could ignore these developments any longer.[24]

In early 1851 the Prussian government, viewing German trade with the Pacific basin as vital for domestic well-being and for unification, recommended Hesse to head a special mission to acquire trade and colonization opportunities and to protect German transit interests. The king appointed him and covered his salary of 8,400 marks (about $2,000) for 1851 from the extraordinary legation budget. Rabe, displaying an agrarian aristocratic perspective, objected to a salary increase merely because Hesse was undertaking a mission to advance trade. He also objected to the appointment of a secretary for Hesse at a salary of 1,500 marks (about $360). Despite such misgivings, the king ordered Hesse's salary incorporated into the foreign ministry budget for 1852. After the mission had been approved, Hesse followed von der Heydt's proposal to visit those areas in Germany that traded directly with Middle America before departing.[25]

Just as Hesse was about to depart, the Ministry of Commerce, Crafts, and Public Works proposed revising his instructions to obtain agree-

ments with the maximum personal, property, and religious advantages
for German settlers. Manteuffel agreed and listed other treaty advantages
worth striving for—such as freedom from tariffs for certain goods the
settlers might use and freedom from the domestic military duty of the
Middle American states, or, if emigrants must perform military duty, at
least service in a separate unit with German officers. He pointed out that
a majority of the emigrants came from Prussia and the Customs Union.
Thus, early in the industrial transformation, the surplus population
came more from the industrializing rather than the agrarian states of
Germany. Since the Central American states often preferred German immigrants, Prussia used its Customs Union association to obtain the best
terms for German immigrants. Prussian politicians preferred settlements
that would preserve the culture through churches, schools, clubs, and societies, supply most of the technical skills and labor force for establishing the colony, and draft their own community governmental document. Prussian officials presumed that their agent would persuade the
local government to protect the German settlements without promising
material support from Prussia, yet he would nurture the inclination of
these lands toward Germany.[26]

Hesse took the first step toward solidifying the Germandom of the
colonists before he departed for Central America. In April and May 1851,
he contacted the central organization of Germany's Protestant churches,
the Evangelical Church of the Union [Evangelische Kirche der Union, or
EKU], to solicit bibles, song books, and spiritual assistance for the emigrating Germans. Hesse and the EKU leadership agreed to cooperate to
preserve the culture and the Protestant religion among the emigrants.
Hesse, with his wife and six sons accompanying him, recognized the
value of a regular religious service to attract migrating German families.
Since the Central American states only subsidized the Catholic religion,
any other religion had to generate its own funds. While the EKU eagerly
offered song books and bibles, Hesse hoped that it could fund a minister and, later, a teacher with a religious orientation. He volunteered to report to the EKU on the situation of the Protestant Germans in the various
countries, for if the colonization projects succeeded, the need for Protestant church ties would be strong.[27]

The competitive nature of the industrialized countries prompted poli-
ticizing Central American internal disputes. Germans became increasingly involved in these disputes. During the winter and spring of 1850
and 1851, when fighting broke out between El Salvador and Honduras
on one side and Guatemala on the other, Klee and U.S. consul Stephen

Weems guided the belligerents to a conference that ended the struggle. In early 1851, in the midst of the cooperative mediation, Henry Savage, who replaced Weems, complained that Weems had trusted Klee, who was "subservient to political ends in opposition to the policy of the United States government." U.S. officials on the isthmus shared Savage's suspicion of German activity in Guatemala.[28]

The increased involvement of great powers in the isthmian routes prompted the small Central American states to test the other major European powers to find protectors, trading partners, or a counterforce to British and U.S. pressure. Austria received solicitations for protection from Nicaragua and Costa Rica, which feared for their independence during the Anglo-American contest to control isthmian transit. Austria cautiously awaited word about French and Russian intentions before acting on a joint guarantee of Middle American transit. Soon after the Clayton-Bulwer treaty was signed, Guatemala and Honduras also contacted Austrian officials about recognition. While Austria lacked a large navy or a sizable world trade, it hoped its trade would expand. Its trade minister anticipated that trade expansion would require an interest in the Panama canal project (in addition to the Suez Canal) and support for the treaty guaranteeing neutrality of an isthmian canal. However, he contended that Austria should concern itself more with the guarantee of neutrality of a New World canal than with its construction. The Austrian bureaucracy was sensitive to the reality of New World power. Although the Nicaraguan minister to London and Paris had initiated the negotiations, the documents were classified top secret and filed in the U.S. section. The Austrian government was interested in relations with all of Latin America and in isthmian transit, but it wanted no political entanglements to follow recognition or trade arrangements.[29]

Prussia drifted into the competition over the isthmus transit routes between 1848 and 1851. It sought to regain lost prestige, to draw strength from its isthmian policy to undercut Austrian aspirations in Germany, and to fortify German nationalism while subordinating it to the Prussian monarchy. Prussia, acting to capture support for German unification, became an early defender of German interests on the isthmus. A key factor in understanding Prussia's position was the nature of the competitive forces acting upon it. It competed with Austria for leadership of a unified Germany and with the imperial powers seeking to maximize their rights to transit over the isthmus. If Prussia ignored the isthmian competition, it would probably lose ground in the competition for dominance in Germany, just as a weak response might reduce its likelihood of creating a world role for a Prussian-led Germany. German migration was calculated as labor, capital, and a security force in the New World distribution system. The role of Germans in Middle America increased following the arrival of Hesse's mission in late 1851. After Prussian leaders recognized the relationship of Prussian-German growth and development in Central America with Prussia's role in world trade, German leaders never again perceived German interests as dissociated from Middle America for an extended period.

3

■

Franz Hugo Hesse's Mission to Central America, 1851–1858

During the decade of the Hesse mission, German interests were permanently established in Middle America. Mid-nineteenth century Prussian policy and activity revealed much about the worldwide nature of imperialism and about the integration of industrializing centers with peripheral agrarian and raw material producing areas. The epoch of industrialization and national unification fundamentally changed the social, economic, and political thought and institutions of German society. Productivity expanded, although pockmarked with periods of stagnation and high unemployment. Industrialization included the building of a communications system (especially railroads), the development of a factory system, internal migration from agrarian areas to urban centers, and substantial emigration. Naturally, any ruling class would view an era of social transformation with misgivings, particularly when interspersed with periods of stagnation.[1]

The Customs Union entered a crisis in the 1850s. Other mid-sized German states wanted Austria included, but Prussia was opposed. An attempt to form a competing customs union failed: Austria had little to offer and many German states were closely intertwined with the Customs Union. Most German states accepted the idea of Hapsburg political leadership in principle (attracted by the grandeur of the Holy Roman Empire), but Prussia's economic policy had undermined the implementation of this idea.[2]

The dynamic growth in Germany shifted wealth from certain areas or groups to other areas and groups (in this case from rural, aristocratic, large landowners to an urban entrepreneurial and financial bourgeoisie). Wealth creation became increasingly financial and industrial. German banks founded and financed industrial enterprises on the model of the French financial institution, the Crédit Mobilier. The adoption of a unified national currency, the paper mark, aided economic growth and nationalism. The mark replaced the taler in the north and the gulden in the south in the mid-nineteenth century. By 1870, 30 percent of the exchange medium was paper. The economy of the German states grew steadily from the 1820s until the world economic depression of 1857–1859, which coincided with the political crises of the Prussian budget, army, and constitution.[3]

In this period of change and increasing nationalism, Prussia sought prestige and status. During the Crimean War, it sought an intermediary role, but the great powers considered it so weak that they leaned toward France as an intermediary with the Ottoman Empire. Within Germany, however, the prestige of France was eroding. Public opinion in favor of a German state grew so strong after 1848 that by 1859 no mid-sized German state dared to seek an alliance with a non-German power. Even the attempt to rebuild a Rhine federation behind French protection entailed too great a risk.[4] The fruit of unification was ripe.

When evaluating the trade of any foreign country with Central America, it is necessary to recall that Central Americans represented roughly 0.3 percent of the world population from 1823 to 1930. This fact should temper the expectations of people who study trade, maritime activity, or investment in the isthmian states. Since metropole and semi-peripheral political economies tended to concentrate their exchange and investment among themselves, any instance where Central America achieved a share equal to or larger than 0.3 percent of a metropole's economic activity should be interpreted as a significant connection.

Nineteenth-century commercial data requires careful analysis because indirect trade, smuggling, bribery of customs officials, and imprecise bookkeeping affected the figures. While the precision in recordkeeping may have been the same for all trading partners, cultural value systems may have affected the propensity of nationals to smuggle or bribe, and the state of a nation's merchant marine could have influenced the amount of its indirect trade. Apparently, the level of trade was as responsible as poor recordkeeping for the incomplete data.

The figures for German trade with Central America (Tables 1 to 6) are misleading because they do not take into account the considerable indirect trade of German merchants using British, Dutch, Belgian, and French ports to reach Belize, Greytown, and the Bay Islands. Hamburg and Bremen reported sporadically on trade with Central America in the 1840s. Regular recording of trade with that region began in 1850 in Bremen and in 1853 in Hamburg. Hamburg and Bremen sources indicate that Guatemala received 4 percent of its imports from Germany in the 1850s and suggest that 11 percent of Costa Rican imports came from Germany (Table 1). Two percent of Guatemalan exports and 6 percent of Costa Rican exports went directly to German ports. German direct trade grew markedly after the mid-1850s, when, according to rather full data series for Guatemala and Costa Rica, a persistent upward trend began. German vessels constituted 5 percent of the foreign tonnage serving Guatemalan and Salvadoran ports and 2 percent of the numbers and tonnage registered in Costa Rican ports.[5]

There were several severe crises in Central America in the 1850s. The Central American Federation had dissolved because of deep differences between liberal and conservative factions. The political, economic, and social tension was amplified with crises in cochineal and indigo, two chief products of Central America that were losing market share, first to alternative production areas and then to synthetic dyes. Dissatisfied artisans and landowners of mid-sized estates who wished to produce coffee instead of dyes both objected to unresponsive state policies. The liberals in Nicaragua saw their authority eroding before conservative forces and opted to invite foreign mercenaries to bolster their forces, even as conservative leaders contemplated the same step.

During the period from 1823 to the 1850s the major objectives of isthmian liberals and foreign metropole promoters and entrepreneurs were the development of products for world trade, the improvement of roads, harbors, and rivers, and the construction of an interoceanic canal to serve world commerce. The continental powers, Belgian consul Martial Cloquet maintained, all wanted the opportunity to enter the isthmian economies, and the metropole entrepreneurs competed for developmental projects.[6]

Privy Counselor Hesse's mission was considered a useful step in aid of Prussian policies responding to the socioeconomic problems of an industrializing society. After some study of Central American commerce, Hesse reported that Silesian trade had been forced out of the Middle American market and only Elberfeld and Krefeld silk goods and Solingen and Remscheid iron manufactures continued to represent Prussian industry. French and British firms often handled even these products because there were few German commercial houses. After a year in Central America, he made suggestions to develop market opportunities for dry goods, paper and paper products, umbrellas, porcelains, glass goods, furniture, musical instruments, metal products, eau-de-cologne, flour, mustard, all forms and colors of textiles, shawls, towels, and fine wool blankets. German silks and half-silks enjoyed high demand, but the credit arrangements often made sales difficult. Although Silesian linens would encounter little demand as long as the native Indians remained the chief customers, Hesse speculated that the influx of foreign settlers might create a market for them.[7]

Hesse studied German production and learned quickly about Central American needs. The key to increasing German trade, Hesse insisted, was to raise the number of firms trading in Central America. He boasted that German houses had initiated businesses in Costa Rica, Panama, El Salvador, and Guatemala. For example, before 1850 Hamburg was receiving orchids from Central America. Hesse heartily endorsed the orchid trade because the only cost was the very low daily wage of Indians to harvest the flowers that grew wild. Trade expansion, however, suffered from improper conduct. Many manufacturers undermined trade when they attempted to market their own products abroad, often through ill-advised practices or dishonest conduct. The disreputable conduct prompted Leipzig's big exporters to turn from trade in Middle America. Hesse also criticized a lack of "esprit de corps" among German manufacturers.[8]

German businesspeople and political analysts in the third quarter of the nineteenth century frequently espoused the social imperialist outlook that Germany must export either people or products. In 1851 Hesse expected Klee's return trip to Germany to help the merchants in Cologne, who sought to establish profitable commercial contacts. The Prussian and Customs Union entrepreneurs expected a direct steamship line soon after appreciable trade developed with Middle America. While Bremen and Bremerhaven shipping firms referred to "the market" for immigrants and to the emigrants as "this modern freight goods," Hesse hoped that any group wishing to send immigrants to Central America would first consult him.[9]

On his way to Central America, Hesse made long stopovers in London and New York, where he gathered valuable information on commercial affairs and personalities in Central America. In London he had fruitful meetings with key British and Central American personalities. From Foreign Minister John Henry Temple, Third Viscount Palmerston, he heard accolades for the British consul general in Central America, Frederick Chatfield. The consul general for Guatemala and Costa Rica, Edward Wallerstein, applauded the growing German interest in Central America. Felipe Molina, minister for Guatemala and Costa Rica, and the Marquis José de Marcoleta, minister for Nicaragua, indicated that their countries would welcome Hesse. Hesse characterized Marcoleta as a talkative Spaniard and a monarchist who had little knowledge of Nicaragua. In New York, he was warned that Palmerston promoted turmoil on the isthmus to strengthen Britain's dominant position. Still, Hesse reserved judgment about British policy in Central America.[10]

Soon after arriving in Central America, Hesse analyzed the personalities of the three-man Guatemalan cabinet. He considered Manuel Pavón, minister of the interior, public instruction, and religious affairs, jealous of anyone else's influence. J. Mariano Rodríguez, minister of foreign affairs, was Chatfield's good friend and a clever lawyer whose "skin color reminded us that his ancestors had come into contact with the Indian population." Both Pavón and Rodríguez were reactionaries; Rodríguez was openly monarchist. José Najera, minister of the army and finance, was a creole of limited ability possessing unmixed blood and strong Catholic leanings. Hesse reported that collectively the cabinet sought to keep the country free of democratic ideology and that many of the Guatemalan elite were attracted to the House of Orleans, Louis Napoleon, and the French.[11]

French consul Leonce Angrand considered Prussian consul Klee and Pavón (rather than Rodríguez) "Chatfield's creatures." Angrand claimed that Hesse had been greeted in Guatemala with a personal insult and insults to the Prussian flag because Chatfield wanted no agent who was not subservient. Hesse prepared to depart for Nicaragua because Guatemala evaded his remonstrance, but Cloquet and Klee persuaded him that his complaint would receive satisfaction. Angrand, however, doubted that Hesse would receive satisfaction after his ill-considered decision to remain.[12]

Hesse remarked during his reception by Guatemalan president Rafael Carrera that Germany had decided to pursue commerce and navigation treaties more actively in that part of the world. Guatemala welcomed his announcement even though it had just informed Austria and Sweden-Norway that it held no desire to conclude such treaties. He boasted that Guatemala recognized the difference between the commercial significance of treaties with Austria or Sweden-Norway and one with Prussia. Since most of the German residents in Guatemala came from Customs Union states, he was not surprised when the Guatemalan government indicated a willingness to negotiate a commercial pact. It proposed that Hesse should send a signed and ratified document to Prussia for perfection. Hesse interpreted this proposal as an indication of the great importance Guatemala assigned to the treaty.[13]

Hesse marshaled reasons for approving the treaty in its actual form. First, the burdensome communications of the isthmus could make a return to Guatemala City difficult. Second, the rapidly developing German trade with Guatemala suggested the desirability of such a pact. For example, the prevailing treaty status would determine in part how the goods on one Prussian and two Hamburg merchant vessels, which were expected soon at Istapa, would be handled in customs. Among the unusual treaty provisions Hesse defended were stipulations granting extraterritorial powers to Prussian consular agents to supervise estates and to intervene in disputes between Prussian nationals. Prussia would seem weak if its consular agents did not obtain rights similar to those exercised by other consuls in Central America. Besides, if the German settlers assumed that the consul could not protect their rights and property, he would lose influence and his countrymen might become his opponents. To accelerate approval of the pact and to strengthen relations between the two countries, Hesse proposed granting a Prussian order to Carrera, Mariano Rodríguez, and three other Guatemalan politicians. Ultimately, he believed that the cabinet would recommend that the legislature ratify the treaty.[14]

After his initial euphoria, however, Hesse became perturbed at the chicanery of Guatemala. It inexplicably hesitated to ratify a commerce treaty and immigration convention before he departed. He suspected that Guatemala hesitated to ratify the draft treaty because Jesuit-Catholic influence opposed article 5, which granted religious tolerance to German Protestants. Chargé Angrand recognized the poor prospects for Hesse's commercial treaty because the Catholic Church was determined to oppose it. Angrand judged that a powerful and widespread fear of rising Protestantism had "imposed its will on the councils of government," despite Hesse's demand for the treaty's ratification. Later, it was rumored that Hesse faced recall because he had abandoned the claims of German businesses in order to obtain ratification.[15]

Prussian desires for broader commercial access to Central America underlay relations with all isthmian societies. Hesse expected the Panama railroad and the Pacific Mail steamer service between Panama and Istapa to eliminate the chief difficulty in expanding German trade ties: the long Cape Horn ship route. A proper response to some existing situations promised ample reward. The many annual trade fairs and products of El Salvador made that country attractive to Customs Union commerce and industry. He considered the Salvadoran government inclined toward a commercial treaty. He urged the Prussian government to ratify the draft commercial treaty with El Salvador before California became the established trading center for the isthmian states. Although revolutionary activity would limit the attractiveness of the Central American countries as trading partners, the treaty should produce advantageous developments for Prussian trade and influence in Central America.[16]

In mid-1853 the Prussian council decided to ratify Hesse's treaties with Guatemala and El Salvador. Ministers von der Heydt and Ernst von Bodelschwing agreed that if only Prussia were involved, they would recommend immediate ratification. However, both were concerned because some provisions permitting Guatemalan or Salvadoran consuls in Prussia would not be in harmony with German laws. They recognized that the treaty gave Prussian consuls financial and commercial advantages their Guatemalan counterparts would probably never use. Yet, other foreign consuls might claim equal privileges under the most-favored-nation clause. Justice Minister Louis Simons contemplated whether foreign consular officials should be given attributes that Prussian law reserved for courts. He leaned toward an affirmative reply because international agreements often required states to modify their domestic order.[17]

Hesse's instructions connected foreign relations with Customs Union politics. He was ordered to seek, consistent with Prussia's ambitions in Germany, opportunities in Central America that might entice states to join or remain in the Customs Union and treaties that contained provisions of interest to Customs Union members. He was to evaluate the advisability of Prussia or the Customs Union adhering to the Clayton-Bulwer treaty.[18]

In early 1854, Hamburg Sindicatus C. L. Merck notified the Hansa agent in the United States, Rudolph Schleiden, that Nicaragua and El Salvador desired commercial treaties. Schleiden, who negotiated for Lübeck and Bremen as well as Hamburg, proposed that Nicaragua accept the Guatemala-Hansa treaty of 1847 as a model. He suggested modifications to include broader religious toleration, a stipulation that any port opened to a third party would accept Hansa vessels, a most-favored-nation clause, an exemption from tonnage fees for Hansa ships carrying at least twenty immigrants, and some revision of consular rights.[19]

Schleiden tried to persuade Marcoleta that the Hansa demands, particularly the exemption of vessels carrying at least twenty immigrants from tonnage duties, would increase Nicaraguan commercial activity. The Hansa cities proposed a general law to encourage migration so it would not be an exclusive privilege. They had to deny reciprocity to Nicaragua on this article, he argued, because their territory was among the most densely populated regions in the world. Hansa officials claimed that the vessels would use this exemption to load Nicaraguan products as return cargo. Responding to Nicaraguan concerns about too many nations taking advantage of such a general law without stimulating trade, the Hansa cities were prepared to incorporate a qualifying provision rather than insist on a general law.[20]

Hesse was eager to use treaties of commerce and navigation to nudge some German states, particularly the Hansa cities, into the Customs Union. The Prussian-Salvadoran treaty, for example, conceded benefits to any state that entered the Customs Union. While some Bavarian officials were convinced that Prussia intended the treaty to strengthen the Customs Union, others were uncertain that the Customs Union partners would approve it. The Prussian government wished all Customs Union states would approve the Prussian-Salvadoran treaty, but it was prepared to accept a negative response, even though a rejection might affect future trade relations with El Salvador. The response was mixed. Most Customs Union states agreed to the commercial treaties, provided the pacts could be amended. Hesse speculated that the economic value of the Prussian-Guatemalan treaty and the prospect of similar agreements with the other Middle American states persuaded some German states to renew the Customs Union.[21]

Von der Heydt suspected that in mid-1855 Hanover rejected participation in the Prussian-Salvadoran treaty because it did not wish Prussia to appear as the leader of the Customs Union. However, he expected the Hanoverian government would face strong domestic pressure to reverse its decision because the Salvadoran treaty offered advantages to Customs Union shipping interests equal to those won by Britain, France, and Belgium in their navigation treaties. Still, he counseled caution in approving any of Hesse's commerce treaties. Later, he opposed the trade and navigation treaties with New Granada, Honduras, Nicaragua, and El Salvador when he learned that German merchants would obtain access to these areas through free trade principles. He cited the problem with Hanover to justify taking no action at that time.[22]

By the 1850s the need for regular and speedy communications with trading areas such as Central America was generally recognized in Germany. One Prussian official argued that regular steamship lines would produce better organized export-import business, lower prices, and more satisfied customers, and would help medium-sized and small manufacturers sell their products with smaller profit margins. Von der Heydt expected that regular steamship connections would expand German commercial opportunities along the west coast of South America.[23]

The numerous public meetings and clubs organized in the early 1850s to colonize Central America reflected Prussian and German interests in the isthmus. These meetings and clubs seconded the views of Hesse and Klee that Nicaragua and Costa Rica were best suited for German colonization and that Guatemala needed time before Germans should settle there. In 1851 the Berliner Verein zur Centralisation deutscher Auswanderung und Colonisation [Berlin Association for the Centralization of German Emigration and Colonization] created a committee devoted to Central America and held two public lectures exclusively on Central America, in addition to their other lectures at which speakers mentioned that region. In 1852 the Central-Verein für die deutsche Auswanderungs-und Colonisations-Angelegenheit [Central Association for German Emigration and Colonization Affairs] praised the excellent reports from Klee and Hesse that facilitated emigration to Central America. The annual report of the Hamburg Colonization Club listed only thirteen of some 100,000 emigrants as specifically headed for Central America, although large numbers were marked as bound for the Caribbean region or for some undetermined destination.[24]

Central Americans commonly favored German colonists. Hesse learned that foreigners were generally disliked and labeled *inglés* (English), except for the Germans, who were called *alemanes* (Germans). While *inglés* was a pejorative word, *alemanes* was not. Carrera's Guatemala sought German colonization, but Klee and Hesse recommended caution. The Guatemalan government hesitated to grant the German communities municipal charters that would permit the settlements to elect judges and control their own defense force. Without judicial and military control, Hesse doubted that a colony could be successful, despite the richness of the land. He considered the Guatemalan bureaucracy too willful and the brigand bands too aggressive.[25] The Germans needed significant privileges to establish a successful colony.

Although many schemes failed, Germans found their way to Central America. Baron Alexander von Bülow developed various projects to bring Germans there. He established several settlements in Costa Rica, where about 164 Germans were enumerated in the 1864 census (Table 9). Given that the purpose was to establish a permanent, agricultural settlement, yet the census most likely counted only adult males, one could estimate that 400 German men, women, and children were living in Costa Rica in

1864. The balance sheet on colonization reveals that during the 1840s and 1850s, about 2,000 colonists migrated. Some German emigrants obtained prominence in Central America because they inhabited an area where modest capital, personal links to a metropole economy, and the benefits of metropole education, cultural ties, and contacts facilitated success far beyond anything they could have expected at home. Not all German emigrants became wealthy and influential, however. The records describe drunks, scoundrels, and people of modest achievement.[26]

In mid-1852 Hesse learned that Alexander von Bülow had sent colonization agreements with the Costa Rican government and the Costa Rican Junta Itineraria [Transportation Board] to the Prussian king for approval. He avoided much comment on the projects, but he hoped to examine the location personally and report on the healthfulness of the area prior to a final decision. Bülow had arrived in Central America as a private citizen, Hesse complained, yet aboard a Prussian war vessel, thereby compromising Hesse's position.[27]

Very early, Hesse had trouble with Bülow. Hesse had traveled to Central America with Carl von Bülow, nephew of Alexander von Bülow. Carl had solicited funds from Hesse for passage and then had become insolent, reforming his manners only long enough to acquire a letter of credit from Hesse. Upon landing in Belize, Carl overdrew the letter of credit without informing Hesse. Alexander agreed at first to make good his nephew's debts, but then changed his mind. Instead, he questioned Hesse's financial role in colonization and mining activity in Guatemala. Hesse denied the allegations.[28]

About 1852 Bülow had settled a colony of Germans in the hill land near the central plateau in Costa Rica. Later, reports from Costa Rica indicated that Bülow's activity was detrimental to German interests. The Henry L. Kinney filibustering expedition on the Mosquito Coast established a tenuous link with Bülow, who hoped to build roads from Costa Rica's Atlantic coast area to San Juan del Norte, Nicaragua. The son of Lieutenant Colonel von Stupfnagel of Berlin, a member of the Ducal family of Lippe and a merchant in Costa Rica, complained to Hesse of the brutal group linked to Bülow. Hesse had not opposed Bülow's activity initially; nevertheless, Bülow had openly attacked him. With Bülow about to return to Berlin, Hesse wanted to be consulted prior to any decision with regard to the project.[29] Thus, with prestige and wealth at stake, two important Germans in Central America fought rather than cooperated.

Other colonization schemes seemed even less likely to succeed than the Bülow project. The Guatemalan government used contractual lapses to terminate the colonization agreement for Santo Tomás. Since Hesse had criticized German participation in the Santo Tomás colony, he wanted the revocation of the Belgian concession publicized in Germany. The impact on the Germans at Santo Tomás was mitigated when El Salvador agreed to accept any German colonists who wished to leave. French diplomat Angrand saw religion linked to commerce in the plan of some German promoters to convert Santo Tomás into a market for German products and a "foyer" of Protestant propaganda for Central America.[30]

In the mid-1850s, Carl Scherzer considered creating a huge German-speaking colonization company for Central America with a capital of about $10 million. The Austrian government spurned his project because it had land for expansion in Hungary and Transylvania. Scherzer memorialized the German Bundestag about "the advantages which the German nation, German industry, and German commerce would derive from colonizing Central America with Germans." He expected emigrants to preserve more of their language, culture, and ethnic identification in Central America than they would in the United States. He needed about 100,000 pounds sterling to found the company and to build several vessels to transport colonists. Scherzer, unable to attract German or Austrian capital, became enamored with former U.S. diplomat Ephraim George Squier's Honduras railroad and colonization project. But by December 1856, Squier still had not offered to employ Scherzer, so he joined a world scientific cruise with Archduke Ferdinand Maximilian. Despite the decision, he declared his heart remained in Central America and with the Honduras project.[31]

Tensions related to personal problems could produce misinformation. Thus, Hesse warned the Prussian government to discount negative reports from Klee, a resident since the 1830s and a participant in the English firm Klee, Skinner and Company, who had owned large dyestuff plantations in Guatemala and El Salvador. Klee liquidated his holdings in preparation for a quick departure for Europe because he had suffered considerable losses from the sharp price decline caused by competing cochineal from the British Empire. Hesse hinted that Klee had exaggerated reports of disturbances in Guatemala in order to justify his preparations to flee.[32]

Economic well-being in Germany and Central America were linked. Germans were participating in Guatemala's development, but that entailed risks as well as profit. In 1852, for the second straight year, Hesse reported that heavy rains had destroyed much of Guatemala's cochineal, which meant a reduced income and a shrunken demand for European manufactures. Since the merchants had not anticipated the damage to cochineal, the market was overrun with English and German goods. Customs Union goods were not immune from this overloaded market condition. Hence, Hesse was concerned about the large quantities of German goods German merchant C. H. Feldmann had ordered. Most were on consignment, and unless a miracle occurred, the consignors would absorb great losses, while Feldmann would retain his commission on any goods sold. Moreover, Feldmann, who had a flawed reputation among the local population, had obtained permission from the Guatemalan government for his family to emigrate, which suggested a precautionary move for possible flight if his business turned bad. When Hesse inquired about this dangerous speculation in consigned German products, Feldmann admitted to misreading the market. He refused, however, to explain the market conditions to his consignors or to supply them information about Guatemalan business conditions. He even stopped communicating with Hesse. Since Feldmann's activity created the impression that he was about to depart, Hesse notified the consignors for their protection. He recommended that German entrepreneurs interested in the Guatemalan market should turn to the British firm Klee, Skinner because Feldmann's conduct seemed injurious to German manufacturers, shippers, and merchants. Later, an agent representing the Hamburg consignors arrived to prevent Feldmann's funny business.[33]

Commercial conditions were different elsewhere in Central America. German goods were in demand in Costa Rica. Hesse hoped that mistaken views about the Guatemalan market and the Feldmann affair would not harm the Two Lippe firm in Costa Rica. The duke of Lippe complained about misinformation coming from Bremen merchant Edward Delius. Delius—reported to have failed twice in the United States before migrating to Central America—and his wife had requested Hesse's cooperation to force the Lippian firm out of Costa Rica. Hesse lent little credence to the complaints of the Deliuses. Delius's antagonism was traceable to his failed ventures in Central America. Hesse regretted that Germans often became bitter enemies when their plans went awry.[34]

Hesse reported on economic opportunity throughout Central America, but not always accurately. Since the Atlantic side of Central America was known to be unhealthy, he claimed that the chief ports in Central America were located on the Pacific side. Panama served as the terminal for goods coming from California and the Central American countries. Puntarenas, Costa Rica, exported coffee, commonly shipped around Cape Horn. San Juan del Sur, Realejo (Nicaragua), and Fonseca Bay—which contained both La Unión and Tiger Island and touched the Nicaraguan, Honduran, and Salvadoran coasts—were commercial centers. The Pacific Mail Steamship Company initiated regular mail service in the 1850s, which increased the value of the Pacific coast. Hesse enthusiastically recommended Fonseca Bay and observed that the chief firm on Tiger Island (Honduras) was a joint venture of the Sardinian consul Dardano and the Hamburg merchant Christian Möller. Although Central America's population and several active ports were on the Pacific coast, Belize, San Juan del Norte, and Greytown on the Atlantic side remained large commercial centers in the 1850s.[35]

While Germany's involvement in Central America was increasing and the United States was seeking a dominant position, other countries also pursued their interests. The key development was, in Hesse's view, the retreat of the British before the United States. He interpreted Consul General Chatfield's recall in 1852 as a sign that Britain would leave Middle America to the North Americans. Klee warned that the U.S. proposal to accept dyestuffs duty-free in California might eliminate German trade because U.S. entrepreneurs would try to direct other Central American products via San Francisco, New Orleans, and New York. German trade would survive, he argued, chiefly because U.S. trade agencies were inadequate to handle greatly increased volume and U.S. industry was not capable of delivering enough goods to pay for the whole of Central American production. Confronting a rising U.S. empire, the Guatemalan government was ready to conclude a trade and friendship agreement with Prussia, even against the wishes of Interior Minister Pavón, who opposed the introduction of German influence. The Guatemalan government, in Hesse's interpretation, welcomed the opportunity to escape British influence, while avoiding U.S. expansionism.[36]

The Central American states also responded to increased U.S. activity on the isthmus with projects for union or closer ties to other foreign countries. Nicaragua, Honduras, and El Salvador claimed that a federal republic of Central American states would be their "salvation," protecting them against a U.S. invasion; but the movement for the union stagnated. In early 1852 both Costa Rica and Guatemala solicited recognition from Austria. The Guatemalan government encouraged the Marquis de Lorenzana, Guatemalan minister to the Vatican, to pursue the possibility of relations with Austria. Costa Rica's president and foreign minister speculated that commercial opportunity and emigration to Costa Rica might interest Austria. In 1853 Austria decided to recognize Nicaragua, Guatemala, and Costa Rica but to avoid political engagements, to refuse a protectorate, and to deny the Central American states any guarantee. It even rejected commercial treaties at that time because the existing commercial contact did not justify them.[37]

Hesse understood the need to build an adequate consular service. He frequently reviewed the state of Prussian consular representation in Central America. In 1851 a manufacturer had recommended Thomas Alexander Maclean Portes as Prussian consul in Panama. Hesse agreed that a consul was urgently needed because the movement of goods and passengers for California and the haste to complete the Panama railroad enhanced Panama's transit value. However, Portes could neither write nor speak German. In addition, no one in London or New York cared to discuss Portes or his firm, Portes, Logan and Company. Hesse feared that Portes may have been one of the adventurers who had migrated to Middle America in the mid-nineteenth century. He recommended postponing any action until he could investigate further.[38]

In early 1852 Hesse saw a visiting card on which Portes claimed to be the Prussian consul in Panama. Still, Hesse learned that Portes was affiliated with an old, reputable firm and that a Mr. Hülsenbeck, an independently wealthy merchant and supposedly the Hanseatic consul in Panama, would most likely join Portes as an "associé." In this situation, Hesse preferred Hülsenbeck or some other German merchant in Panama as consul. Ultimately, Portes's nomination was rejected.[39]

Hesse considered Klee the German most knowledgeable about Central American matters. However, he disliked Klee's business association with the English merchant George Skinner because he suspected that their firm primarily advanced British interests. Furthermore, Klee occasionally served as Belgian and U.S. consular representative, and in late 1851 he applied to become Austrian consul general. Hesse excused Klee's applications to hold the Prussian and Austrian posts simultaneously because his long residence in Middle America left him naive about Central European politics. Yet, Klee had eagerly pursued the possibility of developing a fruit oil, mahogany, and dyestuff commerce with German entrepreneurs. Hesse contended that Klee, dedicated to royalism and conservatism, had earned a generous welcome during his visit to Germany in mid-1852. While Klee's role in commercial matters was suspect, Hesse considered him quite German in culture and sentiment.[40]

Before leaving, Klee had refused to help select a temporary replacement because he did not know the "capacity or thought lines" of the other Prussians. He had appointed an employee from Hamburg to represent him as Hanoverian and Hanseatic consul. Hesse acted as Prussian consul, but he intended to name Friedrich Springmühl, a purchasing agent for an Elberfeld firm, as provisional vice consul. With Klee in Europe, Hesse, who was preparing to leave Guatemala, needed a qualified Prussian to act as consular agent. Hesse had to reconsider his intention to name Springmühl because of many stories circulating about the firm employing him. Hesse considered naming Gustav Willemsen, manager of Feldmann and Company, as vice consul. Willemsen, from a well-to-do family, possessed the proper education and had served as a noncommissioned officer in the Landwehr [national guard], but he lacked mastery of the Spanish language. Finally, although Springmühl made himself independent, he was without capital, so Hesse appointed Willemsen as vice consul.[41]

Willemsen's appointment disturbed Klee, who threatened to resign if Willemsen's employer, C. H. Feldmann, who lacked honor and integrity, were named vice consul. When Hesse invited Willemsen, but not Feldmann, to festivities honoring the Prussian king's birthday, Feldmann dismissed Willemsen. Willemsen won a court judgment that ordered Feldmann to reemploy him. Though Feldmann complied, he hired Willemsen as a traveling agent; thus, Willemsen could no longer be vice consul because he no longer resided in Guatemala City. When Hesse returned to Germany briefly in early 1853, Feldmann was named chargé. The French minister reported that German residents complained because Feldmann abandoned their claims for Guatemalan approval of a trade treaty. The French diplomat suspected that the abandonment of the claims would haunt German businesses in the future.[42]

Although Guatemala was the key post, Hesse knew that other ports and countries needed consular representation. He encountered difficulty in his effort to appoint Prussian consular agents elsewhere. A consular agent in Guatemala City could serve the palmhouse village of Istapa on the Pacific coast. Although the most frequented Guatemalan port, Izabal near Santo Tomás on the Caribbean coast, had no German-speaking resident, Hesse hesitated to recommend any of the German, French, or Belgian residents of Santo Tomás. Still, the number of German residents in Santo Tomás and the volume of German goods moving through Izabal demanded a consular agent. Hesse presumed that William Baily—a partner in the highly respected forwarding firm Baily and Castille and a conservative, Protestant, educated man with a command of French, Spanish, and English—would accept the Prussian consular agency for Izabal and Santo Tomás. Since Hesse saw no prospect of a suitable German settling near Izabal, he asked for indulgence in his appointment of Baily as provisional Prussian agent. He contended that Baily's long relationship as middleman for German merchants would hinder any slighting of Prussian interests should a conflict arise with British interests.[43]

When Klee departed for Europe in 1852, Hesse entrusted him with the petition naming Baily as Prussian consular agent for Izabal and Santo Tomás. Once on the coast, Klee advised Baily to refuse the post. Baily, already the British consular agent, was considering an offer from the Hansa agency that Klee maintained would provide ample protection for Prussian interests. Hesse speculated that "Consul-General Klee does not wish a Prussian consul to be named for Izabal and Santo Tomas" because that step might undermine the British firm Klee, Skinner. German goods had not penetrated Central America, Hesse stated, largely due to the heavy influx of British goods through Klee, Skinner. If German commercial interests were to be well served, he felt compelled to name another candidate for the Izabal area as soon as possible.[44]

Upon Klee's death in 1853, Herman Gaedaekens, the Hansa vice consul, succeeded as Prussian consul. Hesse reported that Gaedaekens lacked energy, avoided contact with the Guatemalan bureaucracy, and was creating enemies for Prussian trade. In the competitive situation in Central America, even the process of selecting consular agents, Hesse lamented, tended to produce enemies of increased Prussian trade where previously friends had existed.[45]

The Prussian government repeatedly instructed Hesse to name a consul for San José, Costa Rica. The Berlin Society for Colonization in Central America advised Germans to emigrate to Costa Rica, an ordered and economically sound state eager to attract Germans. Germans in Costa Rica pursued the important coffee trade and the Berlin Society's settlement project. Hesse could not locate a qualified unsalaried consul from among the local Germans. Several residents refused an unsalaried consular post because it entailed some expense and usually made enemies among one's fellow Germans. The divergent goals of coffee production and trade versus settling colonies bitterly divided the German residents and made agreement on a consul unlikely. After Hanover and the Hansa cities named consuls to Costa Rica, Prussia came under extra pressure to name an agent. Hesse needed to meet the Germans in Costa Rica in order to name a consul wisely. He postponed a trip, however, until he received instructions for a commerce and navigation treaty he expected would bolster the situation for the new consul. He suspected that his nemesis,

Bülow, encouraged the Costa Rican government to receive him with reserve. Even without a treaty, the Berlin Society urged the immediate appointment of a Prussian consul from among the German settlers.[46]

Hesse continued to hesitate in regard to Costa Rica. In late 1856 Heinrich F. W. (Guillermo) Nanne applied to serve as Prussian consul in Costa Rica. He recognized that the importance of Central America resulted from the interest of great powers in the region's primary materials and trading prospects and from Central America's position between the Eastern and Western Hemispheres. He was convinced that the United States would derive the greatest advantage from the transit to the East Indies, China, and Australia. Still, Nanne insisted that the Prussian government needed representation in order to safeguard German interests.[47]

Regarding other consular posts, Hesse was disappointed that a capable businessman named Wassmann was not appointed for San Juan del Norte, where German interests needed the services of a consular agent. Since Hesse also had to withdraw his nominee for El Salvador, in late 1853 he was temporarily without consular assistance anywhere outside Guatemala. He found no suitable German on Tiger Island, but in mid-1854 he persuaded Doctor Carl Bernhard to accept the consular post in Nicaragua. Although Hesse's instructions prohibited naming non-Germans to consular agencies, he slowly recognized the necessity, if not the virtue, of naming local merchants to consular agencies, provided they possessed a minimal knowledge of English.[48] Since energetic Germans moved where opportunity appeared, these developmental years on the isthmus made finding stable, consular agents difficult.

U.S.-dominated San Juan del Norte and British Greytown (a few miles north of San Juan) experienced violent rivalry because of their location near the proposed transit route. In addition, San Juan possessed a traditional role in the commerce of Nicaragua and Costa Rica. Although Hesse considered San Juan one of the securest and best harbors in Central America, it was in fact heavily silted up, forcing most vessels to anchor offshore. He believed that Germany had a special interest in the rivalry because the Accessory Transit Company moved about 12,000 people annually through San Juan to California. The transients purchased supplies for the five-day trip across the isthmus, and the passenger and merchant vessels restocked ship provisions. German businesses—Wassmann and Company linked to Bremen and Wiedemann and Beschor linked to Hanau—served most of the flourishing provisions trade. German imports, mostly from Customs Union states, had increased considerably after Wassmann opened branch agencies in Greytown and Granada. Hesse noted that both Wassmann and Wiedemann had generously helped German refugees from the failed Mosquito and Costa Rican colonization schemes settle in Nicaragua. These colonies should contribute to increasing trade. Furthermore, both Greytown's doctor and its health official were German. The area could easily support another German doctor, he added, as well as a number of artisans, such as cabinet makers, carpenters, and blacksmiths. He conceded U.S. and British preponderance at San Juan and Greytown, however, because U.S. coins, measures, and weights were used. North Americans and the British were the most numerous residents, and English was the business language.[49]

North American activity in Nicaragua affected German businesses and residents. In August 1854 the faction called Democrats in Nicaragua, with aid from U.S. mercenaries led by William Walker, had defeated Conservative president Fruto Chamorro. Then, the Democrats had gone on a rampage destroying property, including that of Hesse's agent in Granada. Given the disrupted economic situation, Nicaraguans had increased the tariff significantly, which Hesse suspected would prompt the Customs Union states to cease exporting there. After a dispute between Nicaraguan officials and a U.S. diplomat, a U.S. naval vessel had destroyed Greytown. This violent action further deterred Customs Union commercial ventures. Hesse expected the local German merchants to file sizable claims against the United States, rather than against the Mosquito kingdom or Nicaragua. Although a Hamburg firm had started a mining colony in the gold region of Chontales, he claimed that Nicaragua was important to Prussia chiefly for its transit and commerce.[50]

German relations with Costa Rica became friendlier, in part due to tensions transferred from U.S. sectionalism. In 1856 Hamburg consul Juan Knohr reported that the Texas Know-Nothing party's antiforeigner activity was driving Germans from Texas to Costa Rica. Costa Rica welcomed them as a counterweight to growing U.S. influence in Nicaragua. Commercial conditions seemed ready to improve. A Bielefeld businessman and a Hamburg shipper contemplated a regular steamship service along the Caribbean coast of Central America. Then, Hesse warned that William Walker's filibustering was causing coffee losses that would diminish purchasing power and made it inadvisable to send large quantities of German goods to Costa Rica until the coffee business recovered. Costa Ricans hoped that German and European interests in speedier isthmian transit would undermine U.S. influence and work against Walker.[51]

Hesse constantly returned to the central theme of nineteenth-century imperial relations with Central America: transit and communication routes. In the early 1850s, he intended to hasten to Granada, Nicaragua, to be near the center of transit developments. The move did not occur, however, because Guatemala offered tradition and a fine climate, and Nicaragua's civil war found no end. He hoped Prussia would accept a more prominent role because Britain's refusal to challenge the United States on the isthmus and Walker's invasions underscored the danger of U.S. expansionism to Germany's future. All Europe, he believed, would pay for the British decision to withdraw. These developments shifted great advantages to U.S. navigation and trade in the Pacific basin. If U.S. expansion were halted and the British remained cautious, however, he foresaw a good opportunity to increase Prussian influence.[52]

In the mid-nineteenth century, canal routes competed with railroad lines to connect the Atlantic and Pacific Oceans. The completion of the Panama railway attracted more attention to that mode of transit. In the 1850s, the movement of people, goods, and mail across Guatemala was very difficult, requiring weeks by means of human carriers or pack animals for most of the distance. Occasionally, luxury goods made the difficult overland journey between Guatemala and the Caribbean coast at Belize. A railroad crossing Guatemala, Hesse calculated, would connect the two oceans in about seven hours. Later, when Squier's Honduras Interoceanic Railway actually began construction, Hesse decided that the cost—about $25 million—was excessive for the limited traffic it would attract. He assumed that passengers would continue to opt for Panama or Nicaragua.[53] The high cost of land travel gave advantage to routes like Panama and Nicaragua, which used more water and less land for transit.

By late 1853 Hesse had lost much of his original enthusiasm for Central America and departed for New Granada, never to return. Nevertheless, he reported on isthmian affairs for four more years. He made Bogotá, New Granada, his residence because that country offered coasts on the Pacific and the Caribbean with harbors superior to Central America, and it possessed the Panama route, the commercial potential of the Magdalena River region, and a larger population than the 2 million inhabitants of the five Central American states. Hesse insisted that German economic activity could expand in New Granada with less likelihood of a jealous U.S. or British reaction. While the United States strove to dominate Central America, it wanted merely to control the Panama route. Moreover, he claimed, the hatred of foreigners found in Central America did not exist in New Granada. Religious freedom did. In mid-1856 he declared that the disrupted communications—Walker had canceled the Accessory Transit Company's concession and the Panama Railroad faced problems with robbery and derailments—prevented him from supplying further reliable reports on Central America.[54]

During his formal reception in New Granada, Hesse recalled German links dating back to Alexander von Humboldt's reports on the local economy. Since the Magdalena River was opened to free trade, the Prussian view of New Granada had improved and Germans were attentive to business opportunities. Hesse expected more Germans to conduct business in New Granada, provided the government preserved order and security. During his last four years as minister on the isthmus, he labored to tie Prussia and the Customs Union states more closely to New Granada.[55]

When Hesse's work seemed to stagnate after 1856, some Prussians sought to revitalize rather than eliminate the mission. One legislator suggested that perhaps the public nature of the mission hindered its success. He proposed that more secretive officials might bolster the role of Prussia in that region while reviving the colonization project. Updated information and the required studies could come from simple traveling people without official character.[56]

When Hesse left New Granada in late 1858 to serve as Prussian minister to Persia, he considered his success in making the isthmus better known in Germany one of his central achievements. In 1859 British writer Anthony Trollope attested indirectly to the success of Hesse's mission. After a trip through the Caribbean–Central American region, he praised the German planters and merchants who were "wedded to the country" with a reputation for being the best builders, coffee planters, and professionals in the region.[57]

Central American development persuaded even more Germans to seek out that region. The balance sheet reveals that Hesse achieved considerable success during his eight years. He negotiated various treaties and signed several contracts related to trade and migration. About 2,000 colonists migrated to that region. German trade became more regular and direct, and German cultural activity built a strong foundation. In the late 1850s, however, a major recession and the sharpening constitutional crisis in Prussia over the army budget redirected the energies of the Prussian government inward. While official Prussian-German interests on the isthmus receded during the era of German unification, the role of Prussian-German citizens and firms never reached its low level of the pre-1850 years. The Hesse mission—a response to the social, political, and economic dynamic within Prussia and Germany—permanently established German interests in Middle America. Hesse's labor in transmitting information to Germany and his success in creating goodwill, treaties, and informal agreements in Central America was evident in later years, after German society had absorbed the products of his labor.

4

■

Bismarck and the Foundations
of the German Empire, 1858–1871

In the 1860s and 1870s, the Prussian government unified most German-speaking states into an empire. After decades of group activity sponsored by bodies ranging from political clubs to singing associations, a series of wars—against Denmark in 1864, Austria-Hungary in 1866, and France in 1870—led to the elevation of Prussia's king to German emperor. Central Europe's German speakers were united in a Kleindeutschland that excluded Austria, parts of Switzerland, and a few small enclaves of German speakers scattered throughout Central and Eastern Europe. The states of the North German Union grew rapidly in industrial and commercial activity during these two decades. German nationalists were exalted, and their numbers grew dramatically. The new empire, however, lacked overseas colonies. While some historians have underscored preliminary projects to establish colonies and naval support points, German entrepreneurs and officials did not overlook opportunities to build an informal empire as one response to social imperialistic politics.[1]

The economy of the German states grew steadily for several decades before the world depression of 1857–1859. Prussia's constitutional-military crisis of the late 1850s and early 1860s and German unification drew attention from the problems of industrialization and the need for expansion. Increasingly in the nineteenth and early twentieth centuries, Germany engaged in a struggle to maximize its role in the world economy. After Hesse's mission, the Prussian government subordinated its interests in Central America to pressing matters of security and well-being in and near the homeland. In the third quarter of the nineteenth century, German grains met sharp competition from the capital-intensive agricultural industry of the United States and the grain fields of Russia. A rising standard of living for many Germans generated a demand for new imported products. These developments increased the desire for enlargement of the national market (encouraged through an informal alliance between the traditional aristocracy and the new industrial and financial bourgeoisie) with tariff protection. A unified Germany improved access to a wider range of domestic resources, diversified opportunities for investment, and assured access to foreign markets and raw materials through the Hansa cities. Even plant expansion became more rational within the larger national economy.[2]

Prussian Chancellor Otto von Bismarck's resolution of the constitutional crisis and Prussian leadership in industrialization and unification entailed wars and internal tension that dislocated life in some agrarian areas and threatened the lifestyles of Bismarck's beloved Junker class as well as other conservatives and aristocrats. His resolution of the budget crisis was, in some ways, a victory for laissez-faire German entrepreneurs who wished to replace local markets with a national market and who looked abroad for new economic endeavors. The success of the Customs Union encouraged the idea of one large, protected market under a government willing to subsidize railroad and industrial expansion and to unify commercial and business law and custom. Still, many German nationalists opposed the government until Bismarck made peace with the leaders after 1866. Yet, even during these tumultuous years, the place of Central America in Germany's development was not forgotten.[3]

In the Caribbean–Central American area, Germans sought to use the local economies as a sponge to absorb the small but growing surpluses of German textiles, iron wares, capital, and population, and as a supplier of additional raw materials and new products to satisfy demands for an improved lifestyle. German entrepreneurs became more active in Central America during the U.S. Civil War. The Caribbean also presented opportunities in mining, plantation production, and land speculation. The number of German firms (perhaps fifty by 1870) and residents (perhaps 700 males) in Central America in the 1860s sketched a modest but growing presence (see Tables 9 and 10). German settlers continued to arrive, engaging successfully in agricultural, commercial, and financial affairs, and building clubs and schools.

German direct commerce with Central America, particularly Guatemala and Costa Rica, grew from 1840 to 1873. At their peak in this period, German products accounted for over 15 percent of Guatemala's and over 18 percent of Costa Rica's imports (Table 1). Germany's share of Guatemalan exports rose from 1 percent in 1860 to nearly 25 percent in the early 1870s (Table 2). Germans purchased around 7 percent of Costa Rican products in the mid- and late 1860s. Hamburg and Bremen commercial statistics reveal a rapid rise in trade with Central America from the late 1860s to the mid-1870s (Table 3). Hamburg's exports to Central America rose from only 79,500 current marks in 1853 to over 3 million current marks by 1873. Bremen's upward trend was not as dramatic as Hamburg's. Bremen exported goods worth over 100,000 gold marks to Central America in 1863, and over one-half million current marks in 1872. Bremen's imports from Central America exceeded 100,000 gold marks in 1861 and reached 3 million current marks in 1874. In the late 1860s and early 1870s, Bremen sent 0.5 percent of its exports to Central America and received 0.6 percent of its imports from the region in return (Table 4). German vessels made up 5 percent of foreign vessels in Guatemalan harbors in the early 1860s and 11 percent around 1870. Eleven percent of the vessels visiting Salvadoran harbors and about 6 percent of the vessels in Costa Rican ports in the 1860s were German.[4]

During the political turmoil and the early development of a communications system before 1871, the Central American societies continued to trade largely in the products of the Spanish colonial period. In the 1850s and 1860s, the production of cochineal and indigo in other parts of the world and the development of artificial dyes in Germany undermined the Guatemalan and Salvadoran political economies. The landowners in both societies found escape routes. They studied Costa Rica's coffee production and planted coffee trees. When the U.S. Civil War disrupted the exportation of southern cotton, all Central America expanded cotton production. El Salvador and Guatemala—in crisis because of the sagging market for cochineal and indigo—benefited in particular from the boom in world cotton prices.[5] Metropole markets and conditions had a major role in the success or failure of investment in cochineal, indigo, or cotton on the isthmus.

While merchants, producers, and exporters from the Hansa, Rhine, and Ruhr areas had long urged commercial advances, elements of the traditional ruling classes increasingly recognized that overseas commercial and capital expansion eased the troubles of an industrializing economy. A host of problems—the breakdown of guilds, migration to urban areas, chronic high unemployment, growing socialist or activist labor groups, and rising crime rates—lent themselves to amelioration through social imperialism. A successful policy of social imperialism needed the capacity to reach societies on the periphery. Trade ties over the isthmus to the west coast of the New World and the Pacific region would require a German naval presence. Colonization in Central America (and in places made more accessible through isthmian transit) would relieve some of the pressure of surplus German population, while building markets and increasing German cultural and political influence in an area of commercial and strategic importance. Prussian officials recognized the connection between the costs and regularity of mail and passenger service and economic expansion, so they recommended reducing mail rates in order to increase emigration and trade. Social imperialism generated support to pay for the army and other institutions of order (the formal and informal expansion allegedly would create jobs and increase the standard of living), while it also reduced the threat of liberalization in German politics by placating (or exporting) dissatisfied groups or individuals.[6]

German officials risked career, reputation, and life in these competitive yet isolated peripheral places. In 1860 the Prussian consul at Greytown, George Theodor Beschor, cited his poor financial situation to defend himself against charges of wrongfully seizing money entrusted to him during the U.S. bombardment of Greytown in 1854. Since anyone with a modest amount of money in Nicaragua's sad state could make a fortune, his defense rested in his inability to take advantage of the economic situation. Contrary to the common claim that poor countries offer few good opportunities for capital accumulation, he asserted that "although Nicaraguan exports are insignificant and play no role in the world markets, one can earn much money with money here[;] indeed capital can easily more than double itself annually. Given the poverty of the land, a foreigner being free from the contributions [taxes and fees] . . . could easily purchase the native products at unbelievably cheap prices." He innocently proclaimed that foreigners received advantages over natives in the competition for power and wealth in peripheral areas. Still, opportunities for Germans had decreased, he argued, because U.S. policy aimed to limit foreign participation in Central American transit.[7]

German journals suggested ways to preserve access for Europeans facing a growing U.S. presence on the isthmus. *Westermann's* observed that "the Panama Railroad had not served European trade as one had expected" because it was "a monopoly of the North Americans." Thus, the magazine welcomed British naval captain Bedford Pim's Nicaraguan railroad project. It offered European goods a shorter route to the Pacific and effective competition for the Panama route. U.S. activity was not the only restrictive one. French officials charged that the Prussians used their economic system to gain political influence.[8] The U.S. and North German governments competed first and foremost for influence on the isthmus, not principally to promote access.

Germans took special interest in Costa Rican trade and communications. In 1864 the Prussian consul in Costa Rica, Juan Knohr, reported that President Jesús Jiménez's administration had labored to realize the long-held wish of many Costa Rican mining and agricultural entrepreneurs for a transportation route to the Atlantic. He judged that the Costa Rican government had sufficient credit in Europe to borrow $1 million to finance the Atlantic coast road. One option led from the *mesa central* (central plateau) to Puerto Limón. A second popular option ran overland to the Sarapiquí River and then down that river to the Nicaraguan port of San Juan del Norte. A Berlin company had inspected the Puerto Limón route but chose not to pursue the project. By 1864, German trade with Costa Rica had increased significantly and U.S. minister Mirabeau B. Lamar considered German influence powerful there.[9]

By the late 1860s, the Prussian government was searching for naval stations in Asia, the Pacific, and the New World. Longtime German consul in Central America, Dr. Carl Bernhard, argued that contemporary European events—Prussian victories in the Danish and Austrian wars—made it necessary either for Prussia to obtain a naval station on the west coast of America to protect "the interests of German subjects" or for its ships to visit that coast at least once a year. Bremen entrepreneur Edward Delius urged a Prussian naval presence at the Chiriquí region on the border of Panama and Costa Rica. He had acquired from the defunct Berlin Colonization Society a valuable contract with Costa Rica for a prime canal site at the Chiriquí isthmus. His contract included large land grants that could serve as a home for German settlers. By locating this land wisely, he argued, Prussia could control the best harbors in the Chiriquí area. His contract did not conflict with the Monroe Doctrine, he stressed, because Costa Rica would retain sovereignty, while ownership would pass to Germany. In his view, a mail service, a well-situated naval station, and the best harbor in Central America would give Prussia a premier position near any interoceanic route. He offered the contract for whatever the Prussian government considered fair. He expected to accompany the expedition in order to negotiate an extension of the contract.[10] Although Prussia did not adopt Delius's proposal, his and Bernhard's suggestions were consistent with its goals.

In 1866 Chancellor Bismarck was attracted to a variation of Delius's proposal that involved U.S. frontier hero, politician, Civil War general, and speculator John C. Frémont, who had obtained a Costa Rican government contract to build a railroad from Puerto Limón to the Pacific coast. Since Frémont's speculative company lacked capital and administrative and engineering skills, he offered to sell his "rights" to the U.S.

government. When Washington showed no interest, he offered the Prussian government bonds in his company, employment for German surplus labor, and a naval station in Puerto Limón as compensation for capital participation. German engineer E. E. Verebelij, who had worked near Puerto Limón, claimed that the port was suited to function as a naval station and to handle Costa Rica's foreign trade and a considerable interoceanic trade besides.[11]

The search for trade and naval station sites lent the Prussian consular post in Costa Rica more importance. Knohr's resignation in 1867 unleashed a struggle among German interest groups intending to use the consulate to support or oppose the acquisition of Frémont's port and railroad concession. In addition, the Prussian commerce minister insisted on filling the post quickly. Acting on the advice of U.S. minister to Costa Rica Charles N. Riotte, the German minister in the United States recommended R. Friedrich Lahmann to replace Knohr.[12]

Despite other preoccupations, the Prussian government was interested in the Frémont proposal. It sent Captain Friedrich Wilhelm Franz Kinderling and the war vessel *Augusta* to conduct a naval survey along the Caribbean coast of Central America in early 1868. Kinderling made the difficult overland trip from Puerto Limón to San José, where he encountered strong resistance to the transfer of rights over Puerto Limón to the Prussian government. Costa Rican foreign minister Julio Volio wanted a private company to manage Prussian interests near Puerto Limón. Costa Rica wanted no treaty with Prussia on this matter, but it would consider a contract with private Prussian groups. Kinderling was so impressed with Puerto Limón that he recommended it wholeheartedly to the Prussian government.[13]

Historians have disagreed on the meaning of Kinderling's mission. Was it a personal venture or a sly Prussian scheme to penetrate the isthmus by presenting the world with a fait accompli? Historian Helmuth Polakowsky claimed that the mission represented Kinderling's overly ambitious personal initiative, which Bismarck disapproved of as soon as he learned of the affair through the inquiry of an unnamed foreign banker. Polakowsky also accepted Bismarck's disclaimer of any intention of acquiring a naval station. His interpretation has not gone unchallenged. Historian Tulio von Bülow has convincingly argued that Kinderling was Bismarck's confidential agent, floating a trial balloon. Bülow contended that when word of Kinderling's objectives in San José, Costa Rica, became public, the Prussian government immediately declared that the *Augusta* had entered Caribbean waters only for the protection of

North German Union commerce. It immediately withdrew the ship and reprimanded Kinderling as if he had acted on his own. Naturally, Bülow pointed out, Bismarck denied any covert, expansive plans, especially in response to undesired public inquiry.[14]

There is considerable evidence to support Bülow's interpretation. U.S. consul Arthur Morrell kept the state department well informed about Kinderling's visit to San José. His relationship to the Costa Rican government allowed him to obtain a copy of the captain's note to Lahmann of April 30, 1868, which revealed that the Prussian government expected this mission to lead to the acquisition of a base for its West Indies squadron. Morrell expected Lahmann to recommend the formation of a colonization and road construction company to Prussian officials. Morrell's access to the correspondence jeopardized Lahmann's position until Morrell certified that he had received copies of the relevant Prussian–Costa Rican correspondence from Volio.[15]

Costa Rican officials, still fearful that the U.S. government sought annexation, welcomed the prospect of German immigration. Lahmann supported some of Kinderling's contentions, but he urged caution in interpreting Costa Rican wishes. The Costa Rican government had been generous with land grants to immigrants, but its earlier generosity had distributed most good land. While immigrant craftsmen had previously done well in Costa Rica, by the late 1860s Lahmann claimed that the demand for handworkers was saturated. Additional handworkers would merely drive down the income levels. Moreover, the Costa Rican government was not consistently friendly to foreign entrepreneurs. He related the story of a German brewer who had negotiated the right to open a brewery. After he invested his capital and opened the brewery, the Costa Rican government started a brewery that was giving him considerable competition. Lahmann argued that Costa Ricans viewed foreigners as the labor force necessary for the development of their country—in other words, as machines to be exploited.[16]

Kinderling was instructed to evaluate the reliability of Lahmann and the possibility of advancing him to consul or consul general for the North German Union. He considered Lahmann subservient to his father-in-law, José Manuel Carazo, the former finance minister and director of the state bank, who disliked foreigners. Kinderling was displeased to learn that Lahmann had converted to Catholicism to marry Carazo's daughter. He declared that Lahmann was unfit to serve as the North German Union consul while under this man's influence. He considered Adolph Knohr, brother of Juan Knohr, best qualified to serve as North German consul.[17]

Bismarck's denial of any interest in the Frémont project in 1868 appears disingenuous. The most convincing evidence in support of Bülow's argument was not available to the historians of that period. The Prussian naval ministry archives contain Kinderling's confidential report to the Prussian Naval High Command. His report indicated that he was responding to specific instructions. Likewise, his promotions in 1871 and 1878 hint at service to, rather than hindrance of, Bismarck's objectives.[18]

Prussia's search for overseas naval stations supported the argument that Kinderling was instructed to inquire about a naval station at Puerto Limón. Bismarck's government had shown interest in a naval base in Asia before the 1868 incident. In fact, the affair in Costa Rica led to correspondence between the renowned German-American statesman Carl Schurz and Prussia's minister in the United States, Friedrich von Gerolt, on the subject of naval bases. Schurz pointed out that Germany should find U.S. friendship more valuable in the long run than a naval station in the Caribbean, although the North German Union and the United States might assist each other's quest for security and naval stations. He hinted that the U.S. government might agree to Germany acquiring some sort of naval facilities in the New World consistent with the Monroe Doctrine in return for access to naval facilities in Europe.[19] The U.S. government did not pursue Schurz's proposal, however.

Kinderling eventually disappears from the naval base story, but Bismarck maintained interest for years. In the early 1870s Gerolt added another dimension to the Prussian–Puerto Limón affair. He learned from Riotte that Dr. Streber, an associate of Frémont, was conspiring to replace Lahmann as North German Union consul. In response to Streber's query, Gerolt declared that the North German Union had no plan to acquire a naval station or a railway in Costa Rica or Central America. Still, Delius pursued Prussian officials. Under his urging in 1876, Frémont's New York Company again offered Puerto Limón to Germany. Bismarck's interest remained. He instructed the consul general in New York to investigate the standing of the chief members of the Frémont company with the intention of reopening negotiations for Puerto Limón. When the consul general assured him that Frémont's group consisted of small-time speculators, he dropped the matter.[20] Bismarck's interest in Puerto Limón as a Caribbean base for the German fleet endured because it was rooted in the dynamic growth of the German economy.

An expanding German consular representation on the isthmus signaled an increase of German activity in Middle America. Bernhard wanted his area extended to include New Granada so that he could effectively respond to the complaints of German colonists dispersed throughout Middle America. Hamburg Mayor Kirchenpauer cited the appreciable German shipping and trading interests in Nicaragua to justify the appointment of Paul Eisenstück as consular agent for Chinandega, Nicaragua. He recommended against the appointment of Georg N. K. Morris at Amapala, Honduras, however, alleging that Germany (meaning Hamburg?) had little commercial interest in that port. In contrast, Bernhard urged Morris's appointment because vessels of the North German Union visited Amapala frequently. The North German Union appointed three new consular officials for Nicaragua in 1869 and 1870 because it expected increased commercial and transit activity if the U.S.-Nicaraguan negotiations actually produced a canal project.[21]

Around 1870 the North German Union considered elevating Bernhard to consul general for El Salvador, Honduras, and Nicaragua. He lobbied for the consul generalship, citing his experience, the value of centralizing representation, and the need to protect Germany's interests. Many Germans in Central America supported his candidacy. When the North German Union finally established a consulate general, Guatemala and Costa Rica were not added to the area under Bernhard's supervision, most likely because consuls Friedrich Augener in Guatemala and Lahmann in Costa Rica had cultivated good relationships with officials in those countries. Bernhard hoped to establish various consuls and consular agencies to serve the greater presence of Germans and German enterprises in Middle America, but he denied the need for a diplomatic agent. He understood that initiating a diplomatic position would mean the arrival of an official from Germany and a reduction of his authority and status. According to Bernhard, who laid the basis to protect his own position, many foreign businesspeople argued that they best understood local customs, personalities, politics, and the needs of the foreign colony in Central America. Thus, they preferred one of their own as representative if a ministerial post were established.[22]

The consular appointments might strengthen German resistance to rising U.S. interests on the isthmus. Gerolt warned Prussia that the 1868 draft of the Nicaraguan-U.S. treaty would, in certain cases, permit the U.S. government to introduce troops for the protection of U.S. interests without Nicaraguan approval. He expected President Ulysses S. Grant to redirect some of the energy of the State Department to Central America and the Caribbean because of his special interest in that region. In fact,

Gerolt considered the expanding U.S. trade with China and Japan as a warning sign that the U.S. government would ultimately dominate isthmian interoceanic transit to protect a growing Asian trade.[23]

In 1870 Riotte reported that "many Germans have settled [in Nicaragua], particularly merchants. They import heavily from the fatherland and . . . German shipping in Nicaraguan ports is only second to Great Britain's." He protested to Washington because Nicaragua had granted the Central American and California Steamship Company, largely German-owned, advantages in flour importing that violated the most-favored-nation clause. Yet, various friends of the United States, mostly Germans, had tried to persuade the Nicaraguans to deal with the U.S. government regarding a canal.[24] It is not clear why the German residents looked to the U.S. government in this transit matter. Conceivably they preferred that this plum fall into the hands of a power that could not challenge German power in Europe—meaning the United States rather than Britain or France—or perhaps they assumed there would be greater security if U.S. power dominated Nicaraguan society.

Three German intellectuals commented on Germany's role in transit and colonization. In 1873 Karl von Seebach compared Panama and Nicaragua as canal sites. After considering technical problems and isthmian political stability, he noted that both Anglo-Saxon powers and several German states had a long tradition of involvement in Central American affairs. He recalled that earlier,

> the celebrated name of Alexander von Humboldt assured the German traveller of a friendly welcome . . . and the scientific proficiency of German doctors and the solid and unpretentious labors of Bremen and Hamburg merchants had won an extraordinary respect for Germany throughout Central America. Today, after our national rebirth, . . . with the ever expanding horizon of our nation, with the ever thicker net of external communication links, with the rising national standard of living, Germany also wishes to cooperate in the labor and share in the harvest.

Seebach argued that an isthmian canal project called for world cooperation in construction and open access after completion.[25]

Julius Fröbel, a German intellectual and education specialist, predicted excellent prospects for a well-conceived, properly supported colonization project. In the mid-1860s, some settlers, mostly German, remained at the old Belgian Santo Tomás colony. The Santo Tomás project, he argued, revealed that a settlement with only modest support, established at an unsuitable location and with ill-defined economic objectives, could survive on the rich productive soil of Central America. He contended that there were outstanding colonization sites away from the coastal areas for agriculturally oriented German emigrants. Carl Scherzer noted that many German immigrants had found the high plateau in Guatemala more suited to their agricultural inclinations than much of the land in the United States. For Scherzer and Fröbel, these areas offered settlers the opportunity to preserve their culture and to retain mutually beneficial ties with the fatherland.[26]

A social imperialist perspective often guided colonization advocates in Germany (and other dynamic industrial states) to consider their projects as only marginally related to the area being settled but important for their homeland. The German governments considered colonization a means to link its surplus population to some part of the globe that could be integrated into the domestic economy. The colonists, once in the peripheral territories, would consume home country manufactures, produce raw materials or exotic items to satisfy the industry or to enhance the living standard of consumers in the fatherland, generate enterprises that absorbed surplus capital, and build influence near communication routes. Colonization projects did not, however, receive uncritical approval. In 1870 Bismarck's government warned Silesian authorities that Costa Rican officials had contracted to introduce between 80 and 160 German families on a site that was fever-ridden and had little likelihood of success.[27] Sending Germans abroad to die was not social imperialism.

Admittedly, the 1860s were difficult years for German interests and officials on the isthmus when compared to the 1850s or the 1870s. This lower level of activity, however, did not reflect a decline of fundamental German interest in Central America or the Caribbean. German settlers continued to arrive, building clubs and schools as well as engaging in agricultural, commercial, and financial affairs. They were engaged in a wide variety of activity up and down the isthmus. Franz Rohrmoser, Franz Kurtze, and Guillermo Nanne labored as engineers in Costa Rica in the 1850s and 1860s, although Nanne moved to Guatemala to continue his career. J. Friedrich Lahmann and George and Louis Beschor were merchants in Costa Rica and Nicaragua. Alexander von Bülow headed an agricultural colonization project. Erwin Paul Dieseldorff and Franz Sarg were among the early large landowners in Guatemala. In addition to the private activity of some Germans, the Prussian government pursued a naval station at Puerto Limón or elsewhere in Central America. During the 1860s, U.S. and other foreign officials expressed concern over the expanding wealth and influence of the Germans. The pointed warnings of various U.S. officials that began in the 1860s and grew in subsequent years best measured the German presence in Central America and forewarned of the rapid expansion of the 1870s and 1880s.

Even during years in which German activity appears limited, Prussia undertook steps to increase its role in Central America. After 1860 German politicians, military leaders, and entrepreneurs increasingly assumed that expansion abroad would help resolve the mounting internal problems of the political economy. During industrialization, Germany experienced spasmodic economic cycles that raised a host of problems its leaders sought to alleviate abroad. When German interests approached such a key area of the world economic system as the Central American isthmus, they encountered the business interests of other nations. Competition with these businesses revealed a corrupted laissez-faire ideology relying on government diplomatic and military activity to shelter their property, schemes, and speculative ventures. This intense competition was clothed in strategic, social, and cultural language to reinforce the home countries' determination to assure access to interoceanic transit, land, or opportunities. These understandable German aspirations confronted similar agendas from the respective leaderships of the United States, Britain, and France.

5

■

Defining Germany's Role
in Central America, 1871–1885

Prussian success in guiding a kleindeutsch unification into an empire ruled by the Hohenzollern family was a marvel of insight, determination, and slyness. The peace signed at Versailles in the Hall of Mirrors in 1871 extracted a large gold indemnity from France. Historian Wolfgang Zank observed that the French decision to accelerate the reparations indemnity led to stock and real estate speculation. The boom delayed a downturn in the German economy, postponing its entry into the world economic crisis (*grosse Depression* [1871–1895]) in 1874. Partial, sporadic recovery soon followed. Bismarck guided the new German empire into alliances in central and eastern Europe to stymie any French aspiration for revenge. The young German empire needed to sustain economic growth and to increase its prestige.[1]

Prussia had unified the empire, but to maximize the value of unification, it needed domestic policies that would preserve order and foreign policies that would bind the Hansa merchant and shipping interests to the empire. A uniform tariff and increased security would support the economic growth of the newly created empire. The German economy had to be integrated more thoroughly into the world economy in order to fulfill the materialistic expectations of the bourgeoisie, the nobility, and elite elements of the working class. Security and well-being became increasingly identified with protectorates, naval and military stations, and agreements to assure access to the world economy. German officials and businesspeople assigned Central America significance as a transit area, market, and a source for the investment opportunities and products the new German lifestyle demanded.[2] German officials on the isthmus became more assertive and demanded treatment corresponding to their imperial ambitions and pretensions.

Despite the 1870s depression, the German political economy experienced rapid industrial expansion and capital accumulation during up-swings. These developments were consistent with policies establishing a national market (the means to distribute readily the national production) and governmental subsidies or laws to encourage mining, textile production, metal industries, and railroad building. Historian Wolfgang Hardt-wig contended that the chief elements of the German industrial economy were instituted between 1835 and 1875 and then remained relatively stable until World War I. The economic transformation of Germany led to the decay of the old order: one's social status and occupation were altered, child labor in factories and mines grew, and a wage pyramid fostered internal colonialism that marginalized part of the laboring class. These developments allowed the elite to accumulate the capital necessary to advance the economic transformation.[3]

Historians have long puzzled over the character and meaning of the 1871 to 1918 period in Germany. Historian Knut Borchardt characterized "Germany's rise between 1871 and the outbreak of World War I as without example," while historian Imanuel Geiss argued that "the first massive industrialization boost brought compensation for the political failure of the bourgeoisie in 1848–1849[;] the second boost after the new empire's economy faltered in the crash of 1873 and the subsequent depression, which briefly delayed industrial growth, made Germany the strongest industrial power on the continent, even surpassing England in the leading sectors (chemical industry, electric industry) during the next conjuncture which began in 1896." Historian Michael Stürmer outlined the social imperialism that accompanied this rapid growth: "Bismarck was prepared to use the lessons of history on the future. What he wanted was a truce in middle Europe and the redirection of all rivalry, all struggles, and all danger onto the periphery. Germany's role in world trade grew faster than the rest of Europe in this period."[4]

Some historians have recognized that prior to World War I, Germany turned to social imperialism to transfer tensions related to Central Europe abroad and to mitigate the conflict between the old elite and the powerful new industrial and financial interest groups and parties. The German Parliament moved toward interest representation rather than constitutional representation. Germany's social imperialism operated under the rubric *Weltpolitik* (world policy), a term describing steps to meet the needs of the industrial groups while simultaneously seeking the resolution of internal problems abroad.[5]

Historian Geoff Eley sought to carve out a special territory for the German empire. He emphasized that "the Kaiserreich should be viewed on the basis of its own conditions, not as the arena for the conflux of preindustrial continuity, and also not as mere preface to the later Weimar period and the thirties, forced between a trusted past and a known future, but in contrast, as an important foundation era with its own signature."[6] This is fine as long as it recognizes the continuity linking the past, present, and future.

German penetration of the isthmus in the 1870s and 1880s was evident in the record of migration and merchant activity. In 1884 a French evaluation suggested that only 100 Germans resided in Guatemala. Possibly this low figure only counted adult males or was biased through the difficulty of counting the German settlers, many of whom resided on coffee plantations in the northern highlands, rather than near the capital city (Table 9). In the 1870s, direct German purchases of Central American products increased noticeably. German merchants acquired over 20 percent of Guatemalan exports, 11 percent of Costa Rican exports, 10 percent of Salvadoran exports, and 7 percent of Nicaraguan exports. German products constituted 12 percent of Guatemalan importation, 8 percent of Costa Rican, 6 percent of Salvadoran, and 5 percent of Nicaraguan. The place of German shipping in Central American trade strengthened in the third quarter of the nineteenth century. German vessels furnished 15 percent of the foreign tonnage at Corinto, 7 percent at San Juan del Norte, Nicaragua, 7 percent in Salvadoran ports, 4 percent in Guatemalan harbors, and 2 percent in Costa Rican harbors.[7]

Economic stagnation in the metropoles increased competition between metropole states and enterprises to guide the material and ideological restructuring of the Middle American societies. After a generation of conservative governments, a liberal resurgence transformed Costa Rica and Guatemala in 1870 and 1871. In 1870 General Tomás Guardia began a dozen years of moderate liberal reforms in Costa Rica. In 1871 Miguel García Granados and Justo Rufino Barrios led the Guatemalan liberals (coffee planters, professionals, and others) who ousted conservative General Vicente Cerna. Barrios led a group of entrepreneurs and political activists who intended to expand Guatemala's economy (initially focusing on coffee production) and to tie it more effectively into the U.S. and European political economies. These ties were expected to enhance Guatemala's growth. For security, Guatemalan leaders sought to replace nearby conservative governments with friendly liberal regimes. By 1876 Barrios had helped liberal factions overturn conservative governments in El Salvador and Honduras that he suspected were aiding the defeated Guatemalan conservatives. Only Nicaragua resisted liberal reform, largely because liberalism had been discredited by its links to the filibusterer William Walker.[8]

An expanding world economy required institutions to handle the migration of labor and the movement of raw materials, capital, and manufactured products that reordered the factors of production. It also required intellectual developments to explain and justify the dislocations of lives and the distribution of accumulation. Ideas from one European (largely French) philosophical movement—positivism—inspired the isthmian leaders of reform in the 1870s. Positivism claimed to be a more realistic version of liberalism, an ideology widely discredited on the isthmus because of its ineffective reforms in the 1820s and 1830s and because it was Nicaraguan liberals who had called Walker to the isthmus in 1854. The positivists on the isthmus subordinated political liberty to material progress. They advocated development and economic accumulation as the first step toward producing order and practical, material progress, necessary for the educational and cultural progress upon which they would found democratic political reform. They rejected Marxism and socialism, viewing private development as superior to community. Positivism lent itself to elitism and authoritarian directions, hence it was acceptable to wealthy, landed, military, and religious people. The Central American leaders acted as if appearing to be like Europe was considered a sign of progress and development. Positivism was often combined with parts of Herbert Spencer's social Darwinism. Both positivists and social Darwinists thought that despite some sacrifice of political liberty, free market competition and natural selection would produce material success and ultimately facilitate social and political liberty.[9]

The Central American liberals championed material progress. They facilitated the private acquisition of land, created a wage-dependent labor force, freed domestic capital by undermining the *cofradías* (religiously inspired socioeconomic brotherhoods) and other church-controlled sources of capital, and encouraged the formation of banks (especially hypothecary or mortgage land banks). They also offered inducements to foreign settlers and financial and entrepreneurial interests to develop transportation, communications, extractive enterprises, and agro-export production.[10]

The Central American desire to induce foreign assistance for its material progress corresponded to growing interest in Germany to explore foreign areas for partial relief of domestic economic problems. The German elite responded to social unrest and the weak capacity of urban-industrial areas to employ the dislocated rural laborers with expansionist programs that circumvented, rather than confronted, the social ills. Nevertheless, these policies of social imperialism generated support among German laboring groups for formal and informal expansion. U.S. agents became apprehensive about the expanding influence of Germany's "excess capital" and its displaced semiskilled and unskilled workers and agricultural laborers who entered Central America, especially Guatemala and Costa Rica.[11]

In the late nineteenth century the German workforce became proletarian and Central American labor was subordinated to and incorporated into the world economy. Metropole entrepreneurs liked semiproletariat peripheral labor because these laborers could be paid less than subsistence wages while members of their household performed nonremunerated work that kept the household afloat—thereby sustaining the employed laborers' contribution to international trade and transferring part of the labor value of the whole family to the entrepreneur. The driving forces of expansion were core demand, not peripheral demand, and the search for raw materials to cheapen production and the cost of living in the metropole, not markets—except, and it is a significant exception, the development of the periphery required surplus core products to institute the infrastructural changes inherent in liberalism's progress. Railroads, for example, demanded the exportation of core materials and technology. As domestic profitmaking opportunities shrank, Germans looked to the low-cost labor (and other factors of production) in the periphery, but any significant German interest there increased the activity among the metropole competitors.[12]

The drive to link the German domestic order to the world system had positive and negative side effects. It greatly improved the standard of living and opportunities for some Germans. The search for access to areas considered vital led to protectorates, naval and military stations, and an imperial system. German expansion justified a large military establishment. Social imperialism permitted the new German empire to apply liberal, unrestricted expansionist views (of a social Darwinian nature) to external affairs, yet allowed for a slower internal reordering of power, status, and prestige.[13]

Historians of U.S.-German relations have often viewed the 1870s and early 1880s as years of comparatively good diplomatic relations because Germany had sympathized with the United States during the Civil War and the United States had sympathized with Prussia during its crisis with France. This friendliness deteriorated, according to some historians, with the economic rivalry of the 1880s. In fact, two decades earlier U.S.

diplomats, consuls, and businesspeople in Central America had repeatedly cautioned the State Department about a modest yet dynamic German expansion into an area of special U.S. interest. The U.S. agents recognized the potential undesirable political consequences from numerous German residents and investments on the isthmus.[14]

Most observers of German presence in Middle America underscored the increasing trade. In late 1872 veteran German consul Friedrich Augener proposed using the leverage from the increased trade and shipping to pry a favorable treaty from Guatemala. The need for a treaty had become urgent during the revolution in 1871, when the Guatemalan government had sought to conscript the citizens of all nations not possessing treaties with Guatemala. His vice consul had prevented the implementation of that decree against Germans. Instead, seventy-five males had registered at the German consulate to obtain a certificate of exemption from military service. In 1874 Augener expected his good relations with the Guatemalan foreign minister to produce an advantageous treaty on trade and the rights of German settlers. The German government appointed Werner von Bergen as chargé and consul general in 1876 to achieve trade conditions that would expand markets for industrial goods and capital. Bergen quickly negotiated a treaty covering trade, navigation, and consular representation.[15]

In the 1870s and 1880s, the role of Germans in all phases of Central American life, from business to the military to cultural activity, alerted U.S. officials to the possibility of German preeminence in that region. In 1872 German minister to the United States Kurt von Schlözer disclaimed any German desire to obtain a political foothold anywhere in Latin America. German entrepreneurs only sought commercial or investment opportunities, he assured the U.S. government, and the German government recognized a special U.S. influence derived from proximity. U.S. diplomats and consuls agreed that German investment and commerce formed the most formidable foreign competition for Americans in Guatemala. U.S. consul John Graham determined that German businesses used a liberal credit system to obtain trade that otherwise might have gone to U.S. merchants. Metropole or semi-peripheral powers competed, at times fiercely, to acquire advantageous conditions or exclusive rights.[16]

Central American governments acted when necessary to protect the class interests of their landowning or merchant elites, thereby conflicting with German (and other metropole) entrepreneurs. In 1874 Honduras decided to terminate duty-free entry at Amapala, where foreign merchants had opened warehousing and wholesale firms. The British government protested this action vigorously, citing its 1856 treaty with Honduras. Without a treaty, the German foreign ministry lacked a basis to object, but it wanted the decree withdrawn. The German government hoped to draw support from British protests.[17]

French diplomats were concerned about competition with German firms and entrepreneurs. Frenchman Gustave de Belot, Guatemala's chargé in France in 1872, requested the appointment of Juan (Johan) Grisar as Guatemalan consul general in Berlin. Grisar was a wealthy Prussian banker with headquarters in France and branches in Frankfurt, Hamburg, Koblenz, and Berlin. He sent a machine gun to Guatemala as a sign of his esteem and offered his services to arrange a loan, emigration project, the establishment of a bank, or arms acquisitions. His Franco-German firm did not receive a concession. In 1875 the French chargé claimed that French firms suffered because gigantic German stores with ample credit built excellent consumer acceptance despite the superior quality of French goods. He lamented that many products handled as French goods were actually German manufactures ordered from large French export houses, while German merchants traded extensively in German products. He regretted that these customs allowed German products to hold a position second only to Great Britain.[18]

There was constant tension in the minds of German businessmen-consuls between their duty to serve the empire and the prospect of personal wealth from business opportunities. Their conduct reflected this tension. In mid-1875, Bernhard, long an advocate of expanding consular services, liquidated his holdings in San Miguel, El Salvador, and resigned to accept employment from the Honduran government related to the interoceanic railway. He suddenly discovered that a consul was not needed because there were few Germans in the Fonseca Bay area or in Honduras, and Salvadoran-German trade was declining. Honduras's termination of Amapala's free port status may have been responsible for altering this situation.[19]

Germans remained interested in completion of an interoceanic transit route in the 1870s. They appeared less concerned with which route was chosen than whether they had access to it. In 1872 U.S. minister Riotte insisted that "many indications . . . show that if our people will not undertake [the Nicaraguan transit], then the English or Germans will." In mid-1876 Manuel María de Peralta, Costa Rica's most experienced diplomat, informed Secretary of State Hamilton Fish that the German empire sympathized with the desire of French engineer Ferdinand de Lesseps to build a canal somewhere on the isthmus. The emperor had publicly confirmed the importance of Germany's treaty with Costa Rica because of its geopolitical position. The recurring rumors of German projects to control some strategically valuable port or area in the Caribbean troubled Fish, but he generally rejected the rumors.[20]

In 1877 an episode involving brothers Paul and Christian Moritz Eisenstück, German merchants and sometime consular officials, and Nicaraguan official Francisco Leal unfolded into a major affair juxtaposing Nicaraguan sovereignty and German prestige. Many aspects of the new German empire's role in Nicaragua and the world were exposed when the marriage of Leal to the stepdaughter of Paul Eisenstück was transformed into a personal and cultural conflict that escalated into an international affair. The German government alleged that Leal so mistreated his wife that she returned to her parents and initiated divorce proceedings. Leal tried unsuccessfully to restore the situation to its previous state. German reports claim that Leal then harassed and threatened the Eisenstücks. An incident occurred in October 1877 in which Paul and Christian Eisenstück were the recipients of gunshots, physical detainment, and other alleged abuse. After delayed, indecisive judicial handling and the Nicaraguan government's lackadaisical intervention, the German government ordered Bergen to go to Nicaragua to expedite a resolution of the incident. Since the U.S. government initially supported Germany, U.S. minister George M. Williamson accompanied Bergen to Nicaragua. Viewing their reception as disrespectful and insulting, the metropole diplomats departed a few hours before their scheduled meeting and only two days after their arrival in Managua. In fact, the Nicaraguan government had only delayed the meeting one day because of a long-planned national celebration. The British and French naval commanders found the German claims exaggerated.[21]

Foreign Minister Bernhard Ernst von Bülow, Bismarck's closest and most trusted lieutenant at this time, considered this incident and similar events in Greece, Africa, and Spain insults to the empire. He decided to make the Eisenstück affair a test case to demonstrate Germany's capacity to respond to insults. Rejecting a diplomatic solution, the empire used an ultimatum and a display of force to defeat Nicaragua publicly. In early 1878 the German government gathered six war vessels off Nicaraguan coasts to sustain its ultimatum. The German commanders landed forces at Corinto to seize weapons that could be used against them if the Nicaraguan government chose to resist. The Nicaraguan government was compelled to pay a sizable indemnity and to salute the German flag. In the aftermath, the German government expressed its appreciation to the U.S. government for support during the crisis. It even awarded the Royal Order of the Prussian Crown to those Guatemalans who undertook a special mission in 1878 to persuade Nicaragua to accept the ultimatum. German officials believed that this display of force strengthened the economic position of Germans in Central America. However, the Eisenstück affair embittered German-Nicaraguan relations. Nevertheless, the naval action produced a domestic bonus. After this success, even Hansa officials and organizations supported the diversion of funds to naval construction programs. The German government had demonstrated its ability to marshal diplomatic and military force to protect its expansion activities in peripheral areas from attack or insult. When an incident erupted in Colombia in 1879, the German government made near identical demands and enforced the same ceremonial activity.[22]

Before the Eisenstück affair ended, Williamson had altered his attitude toward German interests in Central America. He noted that U.S. trade with Guatemala had risen steadily from 1864 until 1874, but then U.S. merchants lost interest just as French and German merchants became energetic. German merchants apparently profited more from this trade than merchants from other countries because they managed the chief commercial establishments and traded in goods from all countries. He concluded: "The Germans and not the British are our real competition for the trade of the whole of Spanish America."[23]

U.S. minister Cornelius Logan, a pronounced Anglophobe when he arrived in Central America, also came to recognize that German competition, not British, represented the chief economic and political challenge to the United States. Bergen's outspoken nature dispelled any lingering doubts in Logan's mind regarding which nation most seriously challenged U.S. objectives in Central America. A variety of facts attested to the depth of Germany's penetration. A large majority of merchants and most of the sailing vessels on the west coast were German. German-born naturalized Americans often headed American firms, a situation Logan thought contributed to the success of foreign imports, the low volume of U.S. imports, and bias against U.S. citizens. By 1880 he categorized the German presence in the Central American–Caribbean area, both economically and strategically, as threatening. He concluded that "the nation which is now more directly and openly aspiring to supremacy in Central America is that of Germany." The size of the German investment and the increasing number of settlers and firms by the 1890s supported the evaluations of Williamson, Logan, and others. The fear of German competition reflected respect for the diligence and hard work of German shippers, merchants, diplomats, and entrepreneurs.[24]

In conjunction with a drive to extract more commercial information for German businesspeople, Foreign Minister Bülow reminded Bergen that "your chief task is to advance German trade interests." Bülow expected extensive reports about each Central American country, its products, transportation routes, commercial institutions, and trade. He believed that budding economies frequently offered valuable concessions to early comers, if they arrived well before much competition was attracted to the opportunities. Bergen had prepared an extensive foreign trade report even before Bülow solicited such information. The foreign ministry praised his initial report, which embodied a magnitude of information scarcely equaled by a consular representative. Nevertheless, Bergen began a further, more detailed report based on information gathered from all German merchants in Central America.[25]

When the *Preussisches Handelsarchiv* labeled German merchants in Central America ineffective, described German steamer service between the homeland and Central America as inadequate and reported that new trade regulations along the Mississippi Valley might have a detrimental impact on trade with the Caribbean area, Bülow expected Bergen to respond to these criticisms. Bergen called the author of the article ignorant of the situation in Central America. He cited Williamson's published observation that local merchants gladly imported German industrial products, when feasible. Bergen considered the charge of inadequate steamship connections between Germany and Middle America ill-informed. The Hamburg-Amerika-Packetfahrt-Aktien Gesellschaft (HAPAG), the Hamburg–West Indies Mail Steamship, and their connecting lines offered some of the best steamer service available without government subvention. He strove to preserve existing communications. He wanted to expand the protection of personal and property rights because only when foreigners were physically secure and had legal recourse to collect debts would German merchants expand their activity in Central America. When these conditions were realized, he presumed that these countries would experience advancement and progress.[26]

When Bergen's final report appeared in the *Preussisches Handelsarchiv,* the German government directed the attention of chambers of commerce and business associations to the opportunities in Central America. It insisted that lack of information was no longer an excuse for insufficient exportation to Central America. The trade minister indicated that "he would be prepared to examine thoroughly any well-founded proposals relative to the possibility and purposefulness of intervention on the part of the government."[27]

Bergen continued his abrasive support of German economic expansion in the early 1880s. In 1880 he vigorously defended German merchant Edward Lehnhoff against Guatemalan charges of tariff fraud, even though he had not investigated the facts. In response, Guatemalan foreign minister Lorenzo Montúfar informed Germany that Guatemala's only problem with Germany was "the hostility of its representative, his irritating character, and the magnitude of pleasure he gets from offending." He explained that "instead of fomenting the friendship between the two countries, [Bergen] weakened it; instead of augmenting the mutual sympathy, he diminished it because he censured the president, the cabinet, those supporting government policy, the laws, and even those passing them." Montúfar preferred the recall of Bergen to the embarrassment of giving him his passport. Bergen held his ground and sought Logan's support. Logan refused after his investigation suggested that Lehnhoff was guilty. Logan suspected that Bergen's antagonistic behavior had prompted the Guatemalan government, supported by other Central American governments, to request his recall. In August 1880 the German government instructed Bergen to move to another Central American republic, at which point he asked the Guatemalan president for a letter attesting to the harmony between them. Instead, the minister received his passport. When the president, wishing to show friendship toward imperial Germany, said that he had not wished to give Bergen his passport, the German minister made it appear that the president had asked to meet him in order to make explanations. Montúfar demanded a note that properly described the events and reluctantly informed the German chancellor of the matter. Bergen sought to expand Germany's official role into areas where Germans were successful. His arrogance created friction and at times burdened German-Guatemalan relations.[28]

There was broad agreement that German servicing of trade in Central America was superior to U.S. commercial services. There was no agreement, however, on which nation's industry offered products better suited for that market. H. H. Leavitt, U.S. consul in Managua, confirmed that German manufactures competed well with U.S. goods. He found that lower-quality German goods were often modeled on American products and occasionally even copied the trademarks. Yet, German businesses claimed that U.S. firms used unfair means to undermine German success. In 1880 when French canal entrepreneur Ferdinand de Lesseps purchased the Panama Railroad, he discovered freight agreements favoring the Pacific Mail Steamship Company. He apparently freed any German maritime enterprise that wanted to initiate a Panama–to–San Francisco line from this monopolistic opposition. In August 1881 a group of German merchants complained that the Pacific Mail discriminated against them in the San Francisco–to–Panama commerce by capriciously refusing to load properly packaged and freight-ready goods. They called for a competitive steamship line on the Pacific coast. Hamburg officials calculated that such a line could be profitable without government subventions if it could count on the business of German export and import firms. In the early 1880s the Kosmos line (Hamburg) introduced regular steamer service during the coffee season; the Roland line (Bremen) joined Kosmos in the coffee trade less than ten years later.[29]

Kosmos negotiators obtained an attractive contract from Guatemala that drew the attention of Pacific Mail's superintendent John Dow. In 1883 he protested that Kosmos received a $9,000 subvention for three visits to Guatemalan ports while Pacific Mail received only $2,000 monthly for its several stops in Guatemalan harbors. Moreover, Guatemala was behind in these modest subvention payments. He complained because Kosmos vessels only loaded coffee for Europe while Pacific Mail steamers carried passengers, mail, and freight going north or south. In early 1884 President Barrios apparently agreed not to offer Kosmos better terms than Pacific Mail (which Dow maintained violated their contract) if it agreed not to raise its rates. Dow agreed. Afterward, both German and Guatemalan coffee producers and merchants continued to complain about Pacific Mail's inadequate service.[30]

German businesses viewed Central America as a client for products and capital, a supplier of primary commodities, and an intermediary to reach valuable areas of the world economy. In late 1885 the Guatemalan government, despite its arrangement with Dow and expecting to encourage trade with Germany, agreed to a $1,000 subvention for each Kosmos ship stopping in a Guatemalan harbor. Since Pacific Mail remained hostile to German competition, Guatemala insisted on excluding the subvention clause from the draft treaty. El Salvador and Nicaragua also contracted to subsidize regular Kosmos service. The Central American countries, however, wanted news of their participation distributed confidentially to the proper circles in Hansa cities. In fact, Kosmos and other German shipping interests contemplated trade on the whole west coast of the New World and out across the Pacific.[31]

The competition to win Central America's Pacific coast freight and passenger service was not restricted to Germany and the United States. French naval officers regretted that French commerce had been outstripped along the Central American coast where "German commerce had the lead." In one officer's view, Germans exercised the preeminent role among the foreign elements everywhere in Central America, except in Nicaragua where French interests occupied a good position. French diplomat Emile LeBrun found the chief elements of power in Guatemala still in U.S. hands, despite the ascending German role in shipping and coffee.[32]

The presence of Siemens, Krupp, Deutsche Bank, Überseebank, HAPAG, Kosmos, and many smaller enterprises in Central America in the late nineteenth century underscored the stake of the German political economy in that region. The success of the German entrepreneurs, however, produced jealousy and confrontations with North Americans. In the early 1880s Bergen repeatedly accused the United States of imperial ambitions. At a dinner to celebrate the opening of the Guatemala Central Railway, built by U.S. concessionaires, he asked Salvadoran foreign minister Salvador Gallegos how long he believed El Salvador could retain its freedom and autonomy. When Gallegos asked for an explanation, Bergen warned that this railroad would bring a flood of Yankee immigrants to submerge the Central American states. The Central American states, he suggested, could best protect themselves by forming an alliance with some other power. The affair vanished when Secretary of State William Evarts accepted an explanation from Germany. Diplomatic contacts in Middle America participated in the intensifying U.S.-German rivalry worldwide.[33]

In 1881 Logan assumed that the U.S. government would need money, arms, munitions, and war vessels to shape Central American political affairs to serve its interests. Despite his call for determined U.S. political and military activity, he expressed surprise when German, French, and British officials distrusted the USS *Lackawanna*'s search for a coaling station site near Amapala, Honduras. "The only real danger of foreign influence or acquisition," Logan warned, "lies in the commercial competition of the great exporting nations"—Britain, France, and Germany—which "fully understand the necessity of markets for their own products." Both France and Germany needed possessions on the Pacific side of Central America to advance their commerce, he noted, but the danger to U.S. transit and security interests lay in intrigue and treaties, not conquest.[34]

The busiest diplomat coordinating European opposition to U.S. objectives in Central America, Logan observed, was Bergen: "His zeal in opposing the United States was remarkable. He constantly called private conferences of the European representatives, at which he revealed some new plan of our Government against the interests of their respective countries." When the French, British, and Germans acted in unison, Logan assigned Bergen the leader's role.[35]

German leaders recognized that U.S. leaders manipulated Central (or Latin) American policy for domestic political purposes. In addition to matters of trade and prestige, Bergen feared that the Guatemalan-Mexican dispute over their common border might create a situation that would favor U.S. over German interests. Guatemala, confronting a powerful Mexico, raised the options of submitting to a protectorate or annexation by the United States as a means to warn Mexico to act more circumspectly. Bergen hoped that the European diplomats in Washington might persuade the U.S. government to reject a protectorate, thus preserving Middle America's independence in the interest of world trade. The German minister in Mexico hoped that the border dispute might induce Central American cooperation to resist U.S. expansion.[36] German officials understood that any metropole might pry an advantage out of trouble between isthmian states.

Logan doubted that Germany, France, and Great Britain would willingly allow the best routes to their large commercial interests in Central America to fall under sole U.S. control. In 1884 German diplomats learned that Secretary of State Frederick Frelinghuysen sought congressional approval for a $250,000 secret fund to survey a Nicaraguan route and, perhaps, as a down payment to acquire the Maritime Canal Company of Nicaragua, a private U.S. firm. Although Frelinghuysen lobbied the House Foreign Affairs Committee, the money was denied. Daniel Ammen, a partner in the Maritime Canal Company, complained bitterly to German minister Casimir von Leyden that Frelinghuysen's conduct had defeated the appropriation and weakened public sympathy for the company. Ammen proposed a German-British capital venture under a joint government guarantee of at least 3 percent interest. German officials, however, intended to secure access to transit for German expansion into the Pacific, while avoiding involvement in U.S. projects.[37]

German leaders, disturbed at the continual loss of population, talent, and capital through emigration, sought to guide the migration to serve imperial interests. The extension of German influence into this peripheral region and the surge of entrepreneurs, promoters, and conveyors of culture, technology, and values increased the number of Protestants residing in Middle America. In 1879 the royal-chartered Evangelical Society for Protestant Germans in North America wished to drop "North" from its name so it could work with the Protestant Germans throughout the New World.[38]

Colonization and investment played major roles in Germany's more prominent position on the isthmus in the late nineteenth century. Speculators, publicists, dreamers, and even the Central American governments created imaginary stories of wealth to attract investment and settlers. German vice consul E. Kraft challenged the exaggerated story of the wealth of the east coast of Honduras. He noted that "the trade of this land is very low, great poverty rules the land, and the exports are very meager." He found a great gap between the real Honduras and the country described in Honduran newspapers.[39]

While German emigration and entrepreneurial activity influenced Honduran society, it had a larger, more lasting impact on Guatemalan society. German entrepreneurs largely developed the Alta Verapáz region of Guatemala, beginning in the 1870s. Historian Guillermo Náñez Falcón has noted that the Guatemalan government encouraged German colonists, who "remained a tightly knit, unassimilated foreign group" that maintained close cultural, social, and economic ties within the colony and with the fatherland. He concluded that "the closeness of the Germans meant that coffee production, the leading industry in the department which they developed and controlled, remained in the hands of an unintegrated foreign group, and profits yielded by Guatemalan coffee, rather than benefiting native-born citizens, Indians and ladinos, enriched a foreign group living in Guatemala." The records of the German Club at Cobán, Guatemala, one of the oldest German clubs in Central America, indicate that almost 500 Germans signed the club records between 1888 and 1937, but, except for several women who had occupations (teacher, nurse, and so forth), they were exclusively adult males. They also recorded eighty-nine marriages—most involving German women, although Spanish-surnamed women made up a large minority—and 162 births. Because this record shows only those who registered in the Cobán region and includes few German women, it suggests that at least 1,000 Germans resided in this part of Guatemala between 1888 and 1937. The political and social power this colonization achieved undermined U.S. efforts to increase North American commercial, investment, and security interests in Guatemala.[40]

In the 1870s and 1880s, Guatemala's Immigration Society encouraged projects to bring in North Americans, Irish, Germans, Spanish, and Italians to work the land. German settlers came so eagerly that Guatemalan officials had to deny that they had conceived a policy to undermine U.S. influence. Some Guatemalans objected to all foreign colonization, arguing that the country's population was adequate for the modest quantity of good land available. Others objected because the colonists interacted principally with the Guatemalan elite, who undermined the alleged civilizing mission of the colonists. Germans quickly countered any steps taken in Guatemala that they interpreted as unfriendly to immigration.[41]

German colonization proposals responded to the transformation of the German political economy. In 1883 U.S. minister to Germany Aaron A. Sargent observed the continued enthusiasm in Germany for colonization in Latin America among "influential statesmen, university professors, colonization societies, and a large part of the press." Opposition and the difficulties of realization hindered the fruition of colonial projects. Proponents commonly argued that colonization should facilitate the exchange of German finished goods for products of other climates and should identify agricultural land for displaced German farmers. Sargent argued that Germany was not a prime candidate for building a colonial empire because its geography and political economy, its modest naval force, and its neighbors, which forced it to maintain expensive military preparations, undermined its capacity to meet the financial burden of a colonizing nation.[42]

The *Kölnische Zeitung* claimed that Germany profited from a rising export trade in Central American products. While Guatemalan, Nicaraguan, and Salvadoran trade had stagnated during the early 1880s, German exchange with these countries trended upward. The newspaper insisted that Germany benefited more from trade with Central America than other metropole competitors. The *British Trade Journal* confirmed that while British goods remained in first place, German trade had grown most rapidly in the early 1880s. Specifically, German cotton and woolen textiles were displacing British, U.S., and French products.[43] Several factors defined the commercial penetration of Central America. First, the British commanded the traditional trade routes and financial agencies, and second, the rising commercial activity in the whole world in the late nineteenth century reflected the expansion of a half-dozen European states and the United States.

In the mid-1880s the Hamburg Chamber of Commerce and the Hamburg Senate agreed that U.S. attempts to secure new treaties with Mexico, Spain (covering Cuba and Puerto Rico), and the Central American states seriously challenged Germany's trade position. The Hamburg Chamber wanted the imperial government to arrange satisfactory treaties with the countries touched by the U.S. campaign. The Hamburg Senate feared, for example, that U.S. tariff manipulations might place German exports of iron products at a disadvantage. It wanted German industrial goods to receive the same customs treatment in Central America and the Caribbean that U.S. goods received.[44]

Although the archives of the Friedrich Krupp firm are incomplete for the late nineteenth century, they show that the iron works entered the Central American arms market in the mid-1870s. In the late 1870s, El Salvador and Guatemala purchased Krupp cannons. The extant bills from the 1870s and 1880s report Guatemalan purchases for $2,156, 10,169 marks, and 4,297.8, 32,600, 21,245, and 43,190 francs, which indicate the regularity and the increasing size of the orders. The German government refused to send an active artillery officer to function as Guatemala's artillery instructor. Conscious of U.S. sensitivities, Germany refused to link itself to Krupp arms sales.[45]

In addition to arms, Krupp agents were interested in bidding for the delivery of rails because "all these little republics have railroad fever." The prospects for sales to railroad companies prompted a Krupp agent to recommend German engineer and longtime resident of Central America Guillermo Nanne as unofficial Krupp agent for railroad materials. Krupp followed each development and pursued most opportunities.[46]

In the 1870s, Minister Williamson succeeded in removing U.S. consul Henry Houben, a good man but a German citizen who had declared his intention to become an American citizen. Williamson suspected that Houben was inclined "in favor of the large German interests in Guatemala." German business, Williamson insisted, was "conducted by men of enterprise and sagacity, whose influence cannot readily be resisted by a man who is only theoretically an American and who represents American interests only by the slender tenure of a commission." He was particularly concerned because the Germans were the paramount foreign interest in Guatemala.[47]

German scholars often view the 1880s as a key period for German expansionism. They refer to the founding of the German Foreign Institute in 1880, the dynamic German trading companies, and the establishment of several German colonial societies to buttress their position.[48] In fact, by the 1880s, German expansionism was a third of a century old in Central America. German officials in the 1870s and 1880s outlined new means to expand Germany's commercial and colonial activity and to protect Germans who participated in that expansion. Bergen underscored the abrasiveness when he confronted the Nicaraguan government over the Eisenstück incident, blindly protected Lehnhoff, and publicly warned El Salvador of U.S. ambition. The German government expected incidents like the Eisenstück affair to occur repeatedly as the consequence of German penetration of Africa, Asia, and Latin America. In the Eisenstück affair, the government tested a policy of impatient demands, ultimatums, and naval force that would guide the future defense of imperial subjects, honor, and dignity on the periphery.

The German government recognized that access to transit routes was essential to any nation with expectations of expansion. The vital role of communications was also evident in the aggressive conduct of German shipping lines, which sought to participate in Central American commerce. Germany upgraded its representation in Central America in the 1870s and 1880s, concurrent with its trade and investment expansion. German entrepreneurs engaged in the infrastructure projects—railroads, steamship lines, and urban utilities. To the extent that competition among the metropole powers could be reduced to a contest for local services, a comprador group best arranged for the political, social, and cultural filtering of metropole values. Social imperialism guided German relations with Central America in the 1870s and 1880s. Revived German migration to the isthmus, new paths of investment, and arms marketing responded to continual high unemployment, exhausted domestic opportunities for risk capital, and stagnation in arms-related industries. The German economy expected Middle America or transit through the isthmus to offer some relief for persistent problems of surplus labor, capital, and production.

6

■

Aggressive Participation in the New World, 1885–1898

Unified Germany was a great power in the center of Europe. With several great powers and a dozen ethnic minorities, most politically organized, near its borders, Wilhelmine Germany pursued vigorous economic growth to cover the material costs of security and to establish a living standard worthy of a great people. The domestic economy could not generate sufficient resources or capital to expand and diversify production, so it looked abroad to facilitate economic well-being and accumulation.[1] Central America was one place that offered attractive opportunities.

Any aspiring metropole state had to interest itself in the Central American isthmus or risk being eliminated from the immense accumulation of wealth latent in the demography and geography of the Pacific basin. The U.S. government, however, considered both the Caribbean–Central American region and the Pacific basin areas of special interest. Leaders of Germany also viewed participation in the world economy essential for prestige, well-being, and security. By 1889 U.S.-German competition in Samoa, the Caribbean–Central American region, and other places stimulated the German government to study the possibility of war between the two powers. In the event of war, German Admiral Guido Karcher expected the fighting to focus in the Caribbean area, so he compared the naval strengths of the two countries in the Caribbean and Central American area. He concluded that the German navy could successfully curtail U.S. power in and preserve German access to the Caribbean.[2]

In the late nineteenth century, German trade, investment, emigration, and navigation activity increased appreciably without causing visible friction with the isthmian governments. German settlers and businesses used private and governmental policy to shape their fate in Middle America. Germany, like other metropole governments, provided social overhead capital abroad in the form of diplomatic and consular services, naval forces to protect people and property and to maintain order and respect, and special commissions, experts, subsidies, and tariff and tax advantages—all services that aided overseas firms. Such activity can be obscured abroad and, because the host society's workforce had greatly reduced standards of living and lower expectations, usually required smaller sums. The arrogance involved in performing these services and the consequent denigration of local authorities often generated difficulties. German nationalism (political manifestations of culture) eroded the favorable Central American perception of Germans and stimulated native nationalism in response. German activity in Central America also attracted attention in the United States. While the German government generally sought to appease U.S. public opinion, occasionally it appeared indifferent. The U.S.-German relations in Middle America reinforced the suspicions and tensions of their broader rivalry.[3] The German and U.S. governments frequently cooperated on matters of access, then clashed over the fruits of access—influence, strategic matters, and the distribution of the wealth.

By the 1880s the German political economy challenged the British Empire. German trade swelled as did the accumulation of capital. The concentration of capital (a characteristic of laissez-faire in practice) accompanied the growth of production and distribution enterprises, the building of maritime and commercial institutions, the acquisition of colonies, and the establishment of businesses abroad. In 1887 Germany legalized cartels, which became the principal economic units at home and abroad. German overseas firms engaged in mineral extraction, agricultural production, infrastructure projects, and distribution. German entrepreneurs scurried to invest in public utilities—water, lighting, power, urban transit, and roads—in order to market the technological products of firms like Siemens and Allgemeine-Elektrizitäts-Gesellschaft (AEG). German workers and labor organizations accepted expansionism because they thought it would assure their jobs. They became part of the metropole worker aristocracy.[4] The metropole societies observed the rapid expansion of German activity with the apprehension due a powerful competitor.

Historian Wolfgang Mommsen described how organized capitalism fostered imperialism in the 1880s when "first, the principle of the free market was subordinated to the principle of state control, second, the principle of free trade was totally undermined, and third, it was no longer thinkable to limit state activity in the economy and society to the most minimum role and to hold the guidance as small as possible." Moreover, the touted sense of cultural mission was tainted. Historian Karl Hammer pointed out that "especially the educational objectives could be perceived by the natives over time as 'imperialistic,' since the instructional model derived from European models. On the other hand, the missions mostly assumed a neutral position in the political and social conflicts of the colonial powers with the natives, by which course they 'fell between two stools' and could be considered enemies by both parties of the conflict."[5] The German empire mixed free trade rhetoric with a conservative political system; it was less open than the U.S. or British empires and less inclined toward mission, but when it followed the "white man's burden," it was more patriarchal in form.

By the 1890s, Germany's stake in the Central American economies was impressive. Central American products rose from 0.3 percent of the total German importation in the late 1880s to between 0.8 and 1.0 percent in the mid-1890s (Table 5). Costa Rica exported from 7 to 10 percent of its products to Germany in the late 1880s and 1890s. Germans purchased 7 percent of Nicaraguan exports in the mid-1880s. However, Central America did not become a significant market for German exports in the 1880s or 1890s. Central America's share of German exports rose from less than 0.1 percent to 0.2 percent from 1880 through 1897 (Table 6). German products, however, achieved a sizable share of some Central American markets; they supplied 18 percent of Costa Rican imports, 15 percent of Guatemalan imports, and 5 percent of Nicaraguan imports. In 1886 the German consul in Panama judged that the export trade on the west coast of the New World was in German hands and the import trade was in British hands.[6]

In 1898 foreign office economic specialist Friedrich C. von Erckert detailed German investment in Central America (Tables 7 and 8). He calculated that Germans in Guatemala owned 50 main merchant houses with 18 branches and 64 million marks of rural and 600,000 marks of urban real estate, which represented a total of 2,725 square kilometers and included 17.7 million coffee trees and 14.3 square kilometers of sugar plantings. He found little German capital in railroads and none in banking or mining. He estimated German working capital in Guatemala at 183.5 million marks. Berlin officials estimated the gross profit of German firms in Nicaragua during 1898 at 1.8 million marks on an investment of 14 million marks.[7] The information on settlers and firms suggests that Costa Rica, El Salvador, and Honduras also benefited from sizable German investment (Tables 9 and 10).

Foreign interests took advantage of new liberal laws to establish enclaves in the Central American societies. Enclaves are inhabited regions of development in which foreign authority and custom supplant domestic law and custom. In the 1880s three single-product enclaves were established—bananas in Costa Rica, mining in Honduras, and coffee in Guatemala. The banana and mining enclaves—located in areas near the Caribbean coast of Costa Rica and Honduras where Central American authority had traditionally been weak—were characterized by extensive foreign control. The German coffee planters and merchants in Guatemala possessed less effective governance because their community was located near the older settled areas in the highlands on the Pacific coast. A second area of German coffee in Alta Verapáz had more autonomy. In addition, a fourth enclave of mixed commercial, agricultural, and mining activity on Nicaragua's Caribbean coast had served since the seventeenth century as an adjunct "colony" to British (and later U.S.) commerce and extractive industries (cattle, hides, hardwoods, minerals, and foodstuffs).[8]

Enclave exploitation required the transformation of much of isthmian society. The compradors were expected to facilitate the access of foreign entrepreneurs to the land and labor. Most notably, a reformed tax structure burdened the Indians with cash tax obligations (rather than in-kind services), which compelled them to abandon subsistence farming. Conscript labor practices took others away from subsistence living. Further, legal changes separated many Indians from communal lands. The liberal laws converted the Indians into a mobile, seasonal, wage-earning labor force, one more amenable to employment in enclave projects.[9] The forced wage labor system and altered landownership produced tension between the compradors and the peasant communities.

When the peasant societies resisted the new labor role assigned them, the comprador leaders of the Central American governments used rural police forces and a professionalized military, which metropole experts organized and trained, to enforce compliance. These new agencies of authority, with increased loyalty to a central government rather than to a caudillo (military leader of Spanish or mestizo roots) or cacique (political and military leader of Indian areas), enforced tax collection—which accelerated the trend toward wage labor—and facilitated the privatization of *ejido* (communal land). The armed forces periodically restricted peasant attempts to occupy unused land. Peasants who settled on vacant lands became less dependent on wage labor and hence endangered enclave production units, which were geared to a world cash crop system. Still, the military often drove the peasants from the land only when producers needed labor.[10] Foreign entrepreneurs profited from a system that allowed laborers to feed themselves when not employed—yet made them available when needed—and shielded the foreigner's image because enforcement of the unpopular laws was left to domestic forces.

The conduct of the professionalized forces of law and order occasionally haunted the metropole powers. These armed forces could intrude on international affairs also. Guatemala's war to unify Central America in 1885 attracted the attention of Mexico, the United States, and the major European powers. Guatemalan president Barrios's proclamation of Central American union, Mexican president Porfirio Díaz warned, threatened the independence of New World nations because it increased the risk of foreign interference. German officials recognized that disturbances between the isthmian states might create opportunities for a metropole power to embellish its influence. Naturally, they intended to outmaneuver U.S. agents in the competition for influence. The German minister in Mexico hoped to nullify any need to call on the United States by appealing to Mexico "to play the role of protector" in Guatemala. Although Guatemalan officials claimed that union attracted universal support, Bergen found widespread opposition.[11]

Bergen regretted that Guatemala's ill-considered project jeopardized the concept of union, disturbed Mexico, and attracted U.S. interference. He favored union, but not by force, so he quietly labored to defeat Barrios's project. His position produced some misunderstanding. The Nicaraguan foreign minister accused him of supporting Barrios's scheme. Bergen affirmed support for the idea of union, just as did the Nicaraguan foreign minister and president, but he denied assigning a specific time or method to his remarks. After the Mexicans threatened intervention, he suggested a union of Honduras, El Salvador, and Guatemala to bolster peace in Central America. He considered stability and order in northern Central America "urgently important in the interest of German trade." He advised Guatemala's president to invite Nicaragua and Costa Rica to join this partial union project and to reject a proffered Mexican alliance.[12]

The tension on the Guatemalan-Mexican border heated up as a result of French engineer Ferdinand de Lesseps's plans to build a canal at Panama. This decision sparked U.S. officials to reopen negotiations for a Nicaraguan canal; however, Barrios intended to obtain a large share of the expected revenue stream from a canal in Nicaragua, and his only claim would come through Guatemalan leadership of a Central American union with shared revenues. Guatemala's scheme upset Nicaragua, Costa Rica, and Mexico. Nicaragua and Costa Rica had intended to share the revenue of a Nicaraguan canal. Mexico distrusted what Guatemala's attitude toward Chiapas and Soconusco would be once the Guatemalan treasury was full. Germany feared that Barrios's disorder would bring more U.S. intervention into isthmian affairs.[13]

The German government worked during the crisis to obtain U.S. approval and to limit the U.S. role. It welcomed cooperation to protect German trade and to undermine Mexican penetration into Central America. Bismarck appreciated Bergen's ability to protect German trade and to work with Hall, "the representative of the chief power on the American continents."[14] But cooperation became less common as time passed. U.S., Mexican, and German economic and security objectives diverged at many points.

U.S.-German competition in Central America increased in the late nineteenth century. While U.S. vessels remained major carriers in Middle America, Hamburg's Kosmos line and Bremen's Roland line compelled the Pacific Mail to consider improving its service. When U.S. vessels obtained a few commercial advantages, Secretary of State Thomas Bayard explained to the German government that the geographical proximity of the United States gave it special rights in the New World that German enterprises would not receive.[15] U.S. officials insisted that proximity merited special privilege in Latin America, although they rejected that argument in Asia and Europe because it clashed with the "Open Door" policy statement.

About 1890 when the German minister in Santo Domingo persisted in "his unfriendly action," which consisted of a protest of special privileges to U.S. trade, the State Department marked the whole Central American–Caribbean region as an area of special privilege. The U.S. minister in Germany explained that special arrangements were made with "adjacent American Republics" on "the basis of the mutual convenience and close geographical proximity [to the United States]" but that similar terms for Europeans, without corresponding concessions, would bankrupt these small states.[16] The U.S. government molded the proximity argument to control access to any interoceanic transit.

Governance in Guatemala was important because the German stake in that country was high. Bergen reported privately to Friedrich von Holstein, the "grey eminence" of the foreign ministry, about political changes in Guatemala. After Barrios's death in 1885, Bergen praised the new government as one of the best during his ten years in Guatemala. He claimed that he and the U.S. minister had jointly recommended Fernando Cruz as foreign minister to President Manuel Lisandro Barillas. In Bergen's judgment, Barillas, who had worked as a furniture maker in a

German firm and as a police official under Barrios, lacked knowledge of the external world or the instincts for conducting foreign relations. He had meager intellectual ability and inadequate education. Despite Barillas's reputation as an honorable man, Bergen expected him to dip into the state treasury. Ultimately, corruption would force the good, inexperienced corps of ministers to leave government service. On several occasions, Bergen's informants enabled him to warn the Guatemalan government about preparations for revolt.[17] His ability to gather information served his compatriots by preserving order and stability.

In 1887 the German government adopted the strategy of negotiating a commercial pact first with Guatemala to serve as a model for discussions with the other Central American states. Bergen recognized that the German-Guatemalan treaty of 1876 was in conflict with Guatemala's constitution of 1887. He negotiated a new treaty with Guatemala in 1887 that was compatible with German ambitions. It preserved and expanded commercial ties and increased protection of German nationals and their investments. He received immediate praise from his home government, but Guatemalan suspicion of the role of Germans in their country grew steadily in the succeeding decades. After the Guatemalan treaty was signed, Honduras quickly ratified a modified version of it. In 1887 the Salvadoran legislature approved a revised version of an earlier treaty with Germany.[18] Completing treaties with three of the five Central American states in the late 1880s reflected respect for Germany's political economy and a desire to use Germany as a counterweight to U.S. presence in Middle America.

More German residents, larger investments, and sharper competition led the German government to revise its representation in Central America (see Tables 8 and 9). German interests in Guatemala were evident in the swelling wealth and status of German individuals and firms and the German domestic economy's surging surpluses of production and capital. The German government wanted to protect existing interests, expand business ties to Central America, and promote interoceanic transit. Bergen's low formal rank embarrassed Germany by conceding many foreign officials precedence at ceremonial functions. The German government acknowledged that promotion was reasonable given the German stake in Guatemala's economy, but it did not wish to embarrass Central American governments that did not maintain permanent representation in Berlin. A solution was worked out. In June 1888 Bergen was promoted to minister resident, but his new rank was only valid in those states maintaining a similarly ranked official in Germany. Guatemala lacked permanent representation in Berlin, but German officials preferred to wait until the Guatemalan budget allowed a permanent resident minister rather than accept a temporary official.[19]

The French chargé interpreted the elevation of Bergen to minister resident as a further sign of German ambition to achieve a preponderant position in Central America. The promotion confirmed German progress in commerce, capital investment, and shipping. The chargé suggested that the French government should name a minister to halt further erosion of its competitive situation. The success of Germans in Guatemala, he argued, encouraged German entrepreneurs and migrants to move to other parts of the isthmus. Already in the mid-1880s, German emigrants were participating prominently in agriculture and commerce throughout Central America.[20]

In U.S. consul James Hosmer's view, Bergen merited promotion because of his "ability, integrity and judicious handling of questions and his very ample success in advancing German interests." In part due to Bergen's skill, many important positions in the Guatemalan government and society were filled with Germans. The director of Guatemala's national teachers' institute and the directress of its national female college were Germans. From 1885 until mid-1888, German consul Francis C. Sarg managed President Barillas's private business, while another German served as Barillas's majordomo and succeeded Sarg in the management of Barillas's private holdings. The government engineer was a German-American. Germans owned the leading mercantile houses and many of the most profitable coffee plantations. "Indeed, I am compelled to assert," Hosmer reported, "that the Teutonic element of the foreign population of Guatemala is a financial and commercial octopus which threatens to grasp in its tentacles and to devour everything containing possible entrepreneurial and developmental value throughout this Republic." He wanted State Department policy to assure that "in the competitive race, our countrymen shall have a fair opportunity to secure at least an equal share in the rich pecuniary enterprises and positions which are now so generally controlled by their German opponents." Hosmer was alarmed. Bergen's promotion acknowledged that the Germans were creating a competitive edge that would be difficult to overcome.[21]

The United States was not Germany's only competition in Central America. Kosmos officials informed the Hamburg government in mid-1887 that a Spaniard, the Marquis de Campo, was initiating a steamship line to various ports in Central America. The Campo line would pay no port fees in Guatemala and receive a 5 percent tariff reduction on the freight of its regular service. Bergen complained that such a concession might drive German vessels and goods from Guatemala. Kosmos officials wanted the German government to join other diplomats who were protesting the concession to Campo.[22]

Unfortunately, no German-Guatemalan treaty covered economic relations. The 1847 Guatemalan-Hansa treaty, which guaranteed mutual tariff equality, had lapsed. The Hamburg Chamber of Commerce admitted partial responsibility because it had opposed a treaty in the mid-1870s. By 1887 it had changed its view. Hamburg's imports from Central America had increased 500 percent over the 1875 figures, while its exports to that region had also increased significantly. At the urging of Kosmos and the Hamburg Chamber, the German government informed the Central American governments that it expected Kosmos to receive a rebate similar to Campo's. The Guatemalan president decreed a similar tariff reduction on the freight goods of all steamship companies making regular, direct trips to Guatemalan ports.[23]

The Campo line also negotiated a 5 percent reduction with the Costa Rican government. Costa Rica's foreign minister informed Bergen that if Hamburg ships met the same conditions as Campo's line, they would probably receive the same tariff reduction. By early 1888 Bergen assumed that Campo would withdraw his vessels from Guatemalan and Costa Rican service because complaints from British, U.S., and German officials and shipping firms like Pacific Mail prompted the removal of Campo's tariff advantages. Several weeks later, the Campo line entered receivership.[24]

Deteriorating French communications service undermined the sale of French products. This was especially inappropriate because de Lesseps was constructing a canal at Panama. French diplomat Emile LeBrun regretted that French steamer lines were not profiting from the opportunities in Central America that German and U.S. companies found so attractive. French agents monitored the rise of U.S. and German economic activity and the decline of France's exports of cotton textiles and manufactures of iron and steel. In 1886 L. Debos complained that "in recent years German commerce [which] has expanded extraordinarily in Costa Rica" was replacing French products. French chargé Paul Louis Reynaud reported that "Germany placed everything in the works to extend its influence in Central America." The French cabinet contemplated the establishment of direct steamer connections to improve the competitiveness of French industrial production and to reduce German influence.[25] However, when de Lesseps's canal project floundered in the late 1880s, French shipping firms shied away from the isthmian trade.

Shipping and mail service were essential for German firms planning to enter Central American markets. In 1891 the German consul at Santa Ana, El Salvador, reported that "American industry energetically pursues its goal to drive European competition from the field in this as in the other Spanish American republics." Communications were central to the competition. However, he reported, HAPAG freight was delivered slower than goods from the Royal Mail Steamship Company or the Compagnie Générale Transatlantique. Bergen argued that a parcel post convention might encourage direct, rapid ties between Costa Rica and Germany. Many Germans were unhappy when Pacific Mail renewed its contract with the Guatemalan government because it served the German coffee barons so poorly. Their campaign to undermine the contract with a barrage of rumors failed, however.[26]

The German government sought more than a maritime edge in its drive to increase its economic role on the isthmus. Bergen clarified for the Nicaraguan government that German trade policy in Latin America rested on the most-favored-nation concept, which placed German industry in a position to compete equitably with all. He added that creating a climate attractive to businesses was also important. Nicaraguan officials did not do so. They often postponed decisions, forcing German businesspeople to seek a slow diplomatic settlement of disputes. The German government preferred to arbitrate all reclamations that resulted from not having a trade or consular treaty.[27]

The isthmian states also recognized opportunities to use metropole economic power and aspirations to help them accomplish their goals. This process was easier in conception than implementation because, unlike the peripheral states, the metropoles could not be coerced to adopt a specific course. The peripheral state had to persuade them that the economic and political risks were worth the potential reward. In 1888 former Nicaraguan president Adán Cárdenas traveled to England, Italy, and Germany as minister extraordinary, ostensibly searching for trade treaties. Bergen recalled that Cárdenas, during his presidency, had displayed friendliness toward Germany. Bismarck was prepared to welcome him in Berlin. The Nicaraguan government wanted more than trade, however. It was displeased because the U.S. government had not responded to de Lesseps's project at Panama with steps to build an alternative canal in Nicaragua. Since U.S. policymakers projected a depressed economic future for Nicaragua, Cárdenas scouted British and German capital for a Nicaraguan canal project.[28]

Competition on the isthmus involved interplay among metropole and peripheral states over transit, political influence, investment and commercial opportunities, and colonization. Bergen, eager to win the support of Central American political forces, occasionally overstepped the boundaries of proper conduct in defense of German interests. In early 1888 the Salvadoran government honored him with a banquet at which he spoke flatteringly of President Francisco Menéndez and his supporters and disrespectfully of the opposition. Bergen praised the dominant Salvadoran political forces in the hope of weakening the efforts of U.S. shipping, merchant, and railroad interests. The opposition interpreted these remarks as interference in Salvadoran politics. When the German colony held a dance in Bergen's honor, the opposition announced that Salvadorans who attended would be honoring an enemy of the nation. Bismarck admonished Bergen for failure to observe the European standard of noninterference in internal affairs. In early 1888 French chargé Reynaud observed, "there is no doubt in my mind that German interests labored energetically to seize a preponderance in El Salvador, as much political as commercial." Reynaud thought that Bergen's willingness to speak out on issues important to Central Americans—his support of the idea of union—earned him praise and influence.[29] But his outspoken activity also raised opposition outcries.

German officials considered union a device for stymieing U.S. influence. Existing European economic interests resisted the new U.S. entrepreneurial activity. Some Americans expected to use political capital to open economic opportunities. In the U.S. elections of 1888, Central American affairs became intertwined with domestic politics in a manner that affected German interests. The German minister in the United States argued that the Democrats intended to use Panamericanism as the cornerstone of a policy designed to reduce foreign influence and to increase the U.S. role in Latin America. Guatemala resisted the Democratic strategy. Bergen believed that the Guatemalan government would submit to U.S. pressure only if he could not mediate an end to the perceived Mexican threat. "In order to oppose permanently the U.S. threat to all European trade interests in Central America," he found it "necessary to improve in every possible way the atmosphere among the five free states and to prepare them for union." He reported that "friendlier Guatemalan-Mexican relations would benefit German isthmian interests. A rapprochement would prevent the U.S. government from using discord between the two countries to win a dominating influence in Central America. Such an influence would damage the extensive German material interests." Both Guatemalan and Mexican officials praised Bergen's mediation during the tension in the late 1880s.[30]

Guatemalan foreign minister Enrique Martínez Sobral recognized that war would injure economic activity along the Guatemalan-Mexican border, where Germans owned about 4 million marks worth of choice land and dominated trade. Beginning in the 1890s Germans invested heavily in plantation corporations; two Hamburg plantation corporations operated in Guatemala (the Hamburg Company of Guatemalan Plantations and the Hanseatic Plantation Company), and Frankfurt investors were developing a large plantation corporation worth about 5 million marks. "There was probably no land outside of Europe," Bergen surmised, "in which such large interests had developed a relationship to the national resources as was the case in Guatemala." But war between Mexico and Guatemala would threaten these interests.[31] German diplomats were engaged, alone or with U.S. diplomats, to mediate tension between Mexico and Guatemala.

By 1890 foreign observers acknowledged German success in acquiring a premier position in Guatemala's political economy. "The ever increasing influence of the German element in [Guatemala]," the U.S. consul reported, "has culminated in the purchase of many of the principal coffee plantations by Hamburg firms. Now that our commercial and financial interests are beginning to pay attention to the wealth of these countries, these points may be of use to show how firmly the roots of European interests are being planted." French diplomat Reynaud conceded that the tireless work habits of German officials and entrepreneurs contributed to their success. Unless French capitalists entered the competition, he expected the Germans to build sufficient influence to nullify any French role. German merchants dominated the wholesale trade and flooded Guatemala with German products. Germans increasingly dominated Guatemala's coffee production and commerce.[32]

In mid-1890 a mobilization of Guatemalan armed forces in response to internal problems endangered Germany's trading situation. Since investment suffered during periods of disorder, German businesspeople complained of the prospective injury to their businesses. In search of order, 100 German, Austrian, and Swiss residents offered to perform military service for Barillas's administration. The Hamburg government, however, claimed that German property had only suffered the indirect injury that occurred when businesses reacted to innuendo. Hamburg officials in Guatemala agreed that a rumored U.S. intervention posed a greater challenge to German interests than an uprising. Continuous disorder unsettled investments and business.[33]

The nature of the world economy made it difficult to separate national from international economic characteristics. In the world economy, nationalism, the terms of exchange, and the procedures of accumulation and exploitation favored legal distinctions that allowed some wealth to lose value while other wealth did not. The world economic crisis from 1873 to 1898—which disrupted the silver-gold ratio, international exchange rates, and monetary systems around the world and which was often harmful to foreign businesses in the short term—facilitated the extraction of value from peripheral societies in the long term. Between the 1870s and 1910, each Central American society devalued its money and introduced paper currency. In 1891 Guatemala arrested those who refused to accept the compulsory exchange rates between paper and silver. This compulsory exchange rate fixed the value of foreign currencies. Foreigners vigorously protested the laws requiring the acceptance of paper currency. The commercial community wanted the government to issue the paper as debt, recall it within three months, and pay 12 percent interest. Consul Sarg cautioned that if the merchants were required to accept the paper as currency rather than as certificates of debt, they would be ruined within a few months. Bergen warned the Guatemalan government that he was personally responsible to the emperor for the property of every German, but his protest was weakened because no German naval vessel had entered a Guatemalan port since the mid-1880s.[34] In time, and with some help from German officials, entrepreneurs learned to manipulate the multiple currencies to enhance profits.

Business organization and infrastructure acquired importance as the volume of goods entering and exiting the isthmus increased and as the capital placements grew. By the early 1890s the frequent German victories that occurred in commercial competition with the United States appeared threatened. German firms needed to modernize their sales organization. One consul noted that only 3 percent of El Salvador's drug imports came from German firms, while U.S., British, and French drug firms regularly used traveling agents. He argued that German iron and machine industries would only increase their exports to Central America when German engineers directed projects and influenced the ordering of materials. Since only U.S. engineers resided in El Salvador, they naturally selected U.S. machinery and equipment when called on to do construction work.[35] Technological transfer implied economic benefits for a metropole because its agents and technological experts would order tools and materials from the homeland.

Alfred Krupp's business transferred advanced technological products early. The Krupp firm became a leader in the sale of metal products and arms. In the 1880s and 1890s its sales of weapons and munitions met serious challenges from French, British, and U.S. producers. In the early 1890s ballistics and field tests conducted in Central America demonstrated the superiority of French Bange cannon over Krupp weapons. Still, Krupp continually modernized its organization in an effort to promote sales. From 1893 to 1905 it used one agent for all of Central America. Beginning in 1905 it named one agent for each country. Then, in 1911 it reorganized again with a general agent for Central America and separate agents in each country. The Guatemalans requested three German officers to instruct in its military academy, Escuela Politécnica. Politécnica students would determine future weapons purchases. The metropole leaders realized that sales of weapons interacted with the training and organization of isthmian forces to promote influence.[36]

While German-Guatemalan relations were generally warm in the 1890s, the German insistence on a most-favored-nation status was a thorn. German diplomats were pleased when José María Reina Barrios assumed the Guatemalan presidency in 1892. Bergen had friendly relations with Reina Barrios, who had served German interests well when he headed the foreign affairs committee of the Guatemalan Congress. Erckert described Reina Barrios as a man who "has constantly shown cooperativeness towards our interests," because he wanted good relations with Germany. Yet the relations were strained. German officials claimed advantages through the most-favored-nation clause of the U.S.-Guatemalan trade treaty of 1893. Guatemalan officials sought U.S. support to rebuff the German claim. Guatemalan diplomat Lazo Arriaga, upset with German persistence about the most-favored-nation clause, considered abrogating the German-Guatemalan treaty. He doubted that Germany could act decisively against Guatemala because the United States was preoccupied with the Monroe Doctrine.[37]

Costa Rican officials were uncertain about the protection of the Monroe Doctrine, so they responded cautiously toward German projects for colonization and investment in commerce. In 1893 and 1894 the Deutsche kostarikanische Land-Gesellschaft [German–Costa Rican Land Association] advertised cheap land and an annual profit rate of 58 percent within three years for German immigrants who would pursue wine culture. The Costa Rican consul general in Berlin also received inquiries about banana lands and railroad projects within the company's concession. He suspected fraud because the project rested on exaggeration, miscalculations, and false data. In 1895 Costa Rica's foreign minister advised prudence in granting concessions after the German government used force to collect an international debt in Venezuela.[38] Exuberant promises might bring reclamations while the Monroe Doctrine was an uncertain shield.

The Hamburg Senate circulated commercial information among chambers of commerce, industrial associations, and other interested organizations to sharpen the competitiveness of German merchants. Several reports encouraged German industries and exporters to compete in Costa Rica. However, some German officials complained that the low quality of reordered merchandise damaged the reputation of German products. The reputation of a metropole's technology often rested on a few areas of production. For example, the German consul to Costa Rica suspected that if German industry could not demonstrate its ability to supply coffee cleaning and sugar preparation machinery at the Chicago World's Fair in 1893, its sale of machinery in Costa Rica would suffer. The following year, English traders claimed that the poor quality and shoddy packaging of German goods allowed the traders the opportunity to make inroads into German markets.[39] Metropoles competed in quality as well as price and service.

Maintaining quality representation was important to any plan to expand Germany's role on the isthmus. In the late nineteenth century, the German government judged that only its links to Guatemala and Costa Rica merited diplomatic agents. Consuls sufficed in the other Central American states. In 1891 when the German government ordered Consul Gustavo Lembke, an importer of chemicals, drugs, and manufactures, to move back to León, Nicaragua, after a year in Managua, he argued that Managua was the center of German warehouse and import-export interests and the surrounding area was home to eight German firms, fifteen resident families, and various German-owned coffee plantations. If the consulate must be returned to León, he asked to remain as vice consul in Managua.[40] For nonprofessional consuls, business and family rather than duty dictated the location of their service.

The German merchants in Guatemala concluded that an honorary consul—presumably a merchant with knowledge of the language, people, and country—might serve German interests better than a professional consul. The professional consuls and diplomats spoke English and French, which could not replace Spanish in Central America. Moreover, the German government often transferred a professional consul after he had finally accumulated the necessary language and experience. Local experience was valuable, the merchants argued, in evaluating situations and communicating with foreign officials. Moreover, the professional diplomat often received status and honors, while the honorary consul got the increasing burden of paperwork. The merchants proposed to reduce the workload and to grant honorary consuls proper recognition as an inducement for merchants to accept the appointments. Bergen and other professional diplomats disagreed. They argued that because competition in the political and commercial areas had sharpened, the consular service had to function at an elevated niveau. The honorary consuls were not competent to fulfill the more demanding duties. Bergen believed that the merchants' desire for an agent to respond to narrow local interests conflicted with the German government's need for agents to advance imperial objectives.[41]

In 1895 the Hamburg government received serious complaints from "reliable merchants" against German minister Otto Rudolph Peyer in Guatemala. The disgruntled Germans contended that Peyer seemed indifferent to the interests of his compatriots and unable to make himself the centerpiece of the German colony. They argued that he had not established a good relationship with the government or used his influence on behalf of the German community. Germans withdrew from him socially, they continued, and his successor would have difficulty regaining respect for the German government.[42]

French chargé Challet in Guatemala, jealous of German diplomatic and commercial successes, regretted that his government refused to act to assure French interests a competitive opportunity. He described how the German colony helped persuade the Guatemalan government to replace the army's French military uniform with a German one. German settlers and commercial houses contributed to the home country's well-being, he noted, because they "imported German products in exchange for coffee and sugar grown on German fincas" via two German transatlantic shipping companies. Thus, German businesses drew large profits from abroad while French capital remained stagnant at home. He was impressed with the patriotism and cultural awareness of the German colony. French consul in Costa Rica Emile Joré noted that the business success of the German residents augmented their influence. He envied the German government's ability to extract profit from its nationals in that rich country. When the French government urged its diplomats to organize chambers of commerce in order to achieve commercial success, Challet pointed out that German, U.S., and British merchants in Guatemala were doing well without chambers of commerce.[43]

German capitalists and banks sought stability for their investments in Guatemala. In 1896 Bergen asked the Guatemalan government to renounce its right to terminate the 1887 treaty for five years because various German enterprises were leery of investing in projects that could not be completed in the time left. Some 50 million pesos of German investment under this treaty could be terminated in two years. For example, the London branch of the Deutsche Bank helped finance the Northern Railroad.[44] German investors needed a favorable investment climate until they had turned a profit.

Hamburg commercial spokesmen encouraged activity in Central America—at times, however, without good information. A leading commercial periodical, the *Hamburgische Börsenhalle*, recognizing the swelling economic and political activity in Central America, recommended steps to assure German entrepreneurs the chance to develop Honduras, a country the Yankee colossus had not swallowed. In fact, one of the largest U.S. investments on the isthmus was the New York Honduras Rosario Mining Company. Wharf, logging, shipping, and banana interests supplemented U.S. mining interests in Honduras. The chairman of the Union of Hamburg Shippers responded to rumors that the German government intended to close its South American naval station with statistical evidence of the significance of Latin America for German exports, imports, and shipping. Ships from the South American station visited Central America. German ties with these regions, in his view, demanded extension, not reduction.[45]

German migrants were attracted to Central America, especially Guatemala. The fatherland commonly supported their efforts to avoid taxes, even if native merchants faced such fiscal duties. German colonists often carried some capital with them or discovered ties to capital in the homeland as they acquired position abroad. State Department employee Alvey A. Adee analyzed the imperial aspect of a dispute between Germany and the United States over Samoa with remarkable insight and candor and in a manner applicable to metropole-periphery relationships. He recognized that "when foreign capital established its foothold in the islands, commercial profits were diverted from the small native channels of production and barter to the larger organized foreign enterprises. . . . This disparity of resources and profits grows more marked each year against the native producer, and he becomes less and less able to pay taxes on nominal possessions from which he is prevented from deriving adequate profits." Competition among foreign entrepreneurs in Samoa reduced the income of local producers and merchants, Adee recognized, while it increased the taxes on their property and the cost of building infrastructure to facilitate access to the peripheral economy.[46] A comprador group approved the projects and consequently increased the tax burden. In short, real income tended downward while taxes shot up. Adee's analysis of metropole-periphery relations on Samoa applied aptly to Central America, where taxes increased on many native classes and businesses, but foreign interests benefited from tax relief, so they increasingly controlled the land, labor, and capital.

For decades German officials and entrepreneurs had perceived economic opportunity in colonization, coffee, commerce, or communications projects in Nicaragua. The government generally welcomed such projects because they increased Nicaragua's value as a site for interoceanic transit. By 1896 the German government discovered that Nicaraguan-German trade had grown without a treaty. It estimated that Germany purchased 60 percent of Nicaragua's chief export item (coffee) and 40 percent of all Nicaraguan exports, and supplied 20 percent of its imports. German shipping played an important role in Nicaraguan trade. After President José Santos Zelaya's government had terminated all treaties, he quickly signed one with Germany, using the Guatemalan-German treaty as a model. German officials suspected that Zelaya wanted this treaty in order "to parry some uncomfortable demands of the United States." The German colony in Nicaragua expected this treaty to protect its growing interests.[47]

Bergen's willingness to negotiate a commercial treaty had earned Germany the appreciation of the Nicaraguan people, who viewed Germany as the best alternative to the ambitious English and North Americans. New commercial and treaty arrangements altered Nicaraguan conduct toward metropole businesses. U.S. minister Lewis Baker complained that Nicaraguan officials at Bluefields were "insolently unfriendly towards Americans. . . . the citizens of both England and Germany were treated with more consideration." He made no effort to investigate the cause of that attitude. Despite the assassination of four German citizens in Nicaragua during a brief period, Baker still contended that Germans are "regarded by the more enlightened native citizens [in Central America] as the most desirable immigrants who come to these shores for permanent settlement."[48]

German businesspeople became important participants in the economic revival under Zelaya. The Nicaraguan government sought to interest German capitalists in Nicaraguan communications. A German firm obtained a railroad concession, but the government insisted that the locomotives, railway cars, and rails had to come from the United States, because German products were not suited for the construction methods used in Latin America. German entrepreneurs fared better in the consumer markets. British manufacturers encountered tougher competition in Nicaragua from German textiles, manufactured metals, clothing, beer, candles, and a variety of other items than from U.S. and French products. Later, an agent peddling infrastructure concessions for Nicaragua solicited German businesses to compete with British and American businesses.[49]

The appointment of a U.S. Interoceanic Canal Commission (chaired by Admiral John G. Walker) in 1898 revived the interest of German leaders in isthmian transit and world trade. An isthmian canal had special strategic meaning for the United States, Great Britain, and Germany. The Central American canal, a German agent noted, offered the possibility of a chain of naval and cable stations from the homeland, over St. Thomas in the Virgin Islands, the Galápagos, and Samoa, to Kiaochou, China. German naval attaché Gustav Adolf von Götzen interpreted the increase in the U.S. merchant marine and navy and the development of the Pacific coast states as signs of the strategic impact of a canal route. Germany also needed to protect its increased investment and numerous residents on the isthmus. In light of half-civilized bureaucrats and revolutionary changes in the New World, he assumed that German dignity and its commercial and strategic objectives needed a secure naval station in the West Indies. The empire did not have to dominate Middle America, he noted, but a strong point near any canal would allow it to expand trade with the Central American countries and the Pacific coast areas of the New World.[50]

Zelaya built a subservient political union, the Greater Republic of Central America—Nicaragua, Honduras, and El Salvador—to sustain him against Guatemalan encroachment and to bolster his plans to develop a Nicaraguan canal route. As formed in the late 1890s, the Greater Republic preserved the presidents of the member states in power and made foreign representation ineffective because great power diplomats would not adapt to the movement of the capital annually among the three member states. Bergen considered, but rejected, a protest against the itinerant capital. Since Guatemala was the center of German interests, he proposed that the German diplomat should continue to reside in Guatemala and make periodic visits to the current capital of the Greater Republic. He recommended recognition of the Greater Republic in order to protect German citizens and their property. In addition, he suspected that the United States and the other European powers would leave Germany isolated if it protested.[51]

In late 1897 foreign ministry official Wolfram von Rotenhan claimed that Germany held the premier economic position in Guatemala. When disturbances occurred there, German officials presumed that Reina Barrios, honored in 1896 with Germany's Order of the Red-Eagle (first class), would protect Germans and their interests. Fifty-seven firms and merchants supported Hamburg's petition for the dispatch of a naval vessel, after a thirteen-year absence, to protect Germany's trade. They were wary that reliance on British, U.S., or French naval vessels might injure German prestige. In response, the government recommended Central America for the next available cruiser.[52]

The predominance of German coffee planters and merchants encouraged German manufacturers and financial institutions to enter Guatemala. Coffee planter G. A. Dieseldorff was the agent for a group of Guatemalan Germans who planned to build short line railroads to assure the prompt delivery of German coffee to the nearest port. After several rejections, a Hamburg group agreed to raise at least 1 million marks for his venture. German entrepreneurs built several small railroads. In 1895, however, the Guatemalan government, hoping to avoid U.S. capital, solicited German or French capital to finish the nation's chief transportation artery, the Puerto Barrios railroad. In the midst of a worldwide depression, it found none. Guatemalan conduct toward existing investments endangered the flow of additional capital. In 1899 German minister Konstantin von Voights-Rhetz alleged that Guatemalan court proceedings against Nottebohn and Company, Wyld Brothers, and J. F. Romero in which Commerz-Disconto Bank and H. Meyer of Hamburg were interested parties undermined the confidence of European bankers and might damage Guatemala's credit in foreign countries. While numerous railroad schemes failed, German interests did participate in various small railroad projects to tie the coffee-producing areas to nearby ports. Some German capital supported the successful railroad projects as well as coffee production and commercial businesses in Guatemala. But, in general, capital was repatriated to Germany.[53]

When civil disturbances erupted in 1897, the financially strapped Reina Barrios received an offer from a "German syndicate which had long waited a favorable opportunity to purchase the Northern Railroad," the heart of the Guatemalan transportation system. His death in 1898 endangered the Northern Railroad because the president had sustained the project inadequately with national initiative and capital. The new government, Erckert reported, intended to finish the project either by mortgaging the finished sections to foreign capitalists or by selling the constructed sections to foreign interests. This railroad would open large areas to exploitation and would connect Guatemala directly to the eastern and southern United States and Europe. Resident Germans would benefit greatly because about 40 million marks of goods that moved annually between Guatemala and Germany on the Kosmos or Kirsten shipping lines around the Magellan straits or on HAPAG after transit over the Panama Railroad would find cheaper direct routes. Scarcely anywhere outside the fatherland, Erckert reported enthusiastically, "would a German railroad find a rear area where so many German interests exist in so small a space, where a larger part of the land belongs to Germans, another part is mortgaged to Germans, where two-thirds of the exports go to Germany and almost one-fourth of the imports come from Germany. One can also allude to the earnings offered to our industry from the deliveries for the railway." Given the enormous German investment in Guatemala, he preferred German capital to complete the railroad project.[54]

French officials marveled at German success in Guatemala. Challet, who considered German migration "the best modern system of colonization," described how it infiltrated the Guatemalan economy effortlessly with encouragement from an able diplomatic corps and competent businesspeople. It drained the wealth of the area for the benefit of the metropole. He cited an extreme case of German extraction of wealth from Guatemala: around 1890 Bergen had purchased a property for 100,000 marks, which he sold for 4 million marks in 1897. The French commercial attaché reported in 1897 that about 500 Germans who owned the major coffee plantations had made "a veritable German farm out of Guatemala." He added that at best a third of the 23 million marks gross profit German entrepreneurs earned each year remained in Guatemala, largely to cover the costs of exploitation. The rest was repatriated to Germany.[55] Germans dominated Guatemala's economy, but the profits were used to modernize the German economy.

The world economic crisis of 1873 to 1898 profoundly affected the Central American political economies. The crisis manifested disorders in the periphery that endangered metropole investment and commerce. When a revolt occurred in Guatemala in late 1898, the German minister requested that a war vessel visit Ocos, where a German-owned railroad serviced German coffee plantations. Likewise, the tension between Costa Rica and Nicaragua in 1898, related to the sharing of any canal fees, made the Germans in Costa Rica fear a war. When potential immigrants inquired about opportunities in Guatemala, the German minister cautioned them that recurring disturbances made considerable capital reserves essential to develop a stable enterprise.[56]

In the 1880s and 1890s German settlers, merchants, and entrepreneurs accumulated wealth and power in Central America, while developing extensive cultural institutions. These accomplishments owed much to the Prussian policies of the 1850s and to German economic growth in the nineteenth century. German interests in Central America were also shaped by the fierce competitive nature of liberal, industrial states. Germany and the other metropole states attempted to cooperate in "civilizing" societies on the periphery to international law and norms of conduct. The cooperation, however, dissipated when the sharpening domestic "overproduction" crisis (in fact, a maldistribution phenomenon) underscored the importance of exploiting these peripheral societies in order to alleviate domestic pressure. The metropole states discovered the limits of cooperative activity when they perceived imbalances in the utility of mutually acquired access.

The Dieseldorff family and friends and five Indian ball boys on the finca, Santa Margarita, Cobán, drying patio (for coffee) being used as a tennis court, ca. 1902. Johanna Gressler Dieseldorff, second from right (standing); Erwin Paul Dieseldorff, fourth from right (standing).

The Dieseldorffs' Christmas at San Margarita in Cobán with a tree and music, 1902.

The marketplace of the village Morazán with the *cabildo* (town hall) in the background, ca. 1903.

Erwin Dieseldorff (far right in back) and Johanna (seated in front of him) on the veranda of Mr. Gwatkins [G. Watkins?] (middle of front row) at his home in Gualán, ca. 1903.

Rockstroh, Maret, Ascoli, and Thomsen in the *Siedehaus* (cooking house) at the sugar works on the sugar plantation, Ceniza, ca. 1903.

Cane fields on the sugar plantation, Ceniza, ca. 1903.

Candelabra, clock, and other decorative pieces on a sideboard in the Dieseldorffs' living room in Cobán, ca. 1903.

Johanna, dressed in Cobanera, preparing masa for tortillas on metate with Indian servant, 1903.

Administrator and Indian laborer on the Dieseldorff finca, "las Amazones," an experiment with rubber trees in the lower Polochic Valley, ca. 1903.

Bareheaded Col. Guy R. Molony, soldier of fortune in the Honduran forces of Manuel Bonilla, and captured Krupp artillery, ca. 1910.

7

∎

Aggressive Penetration
and National Honor, 1898–1906

In 1898, after several decades in which U.S. authorities commonly used firm language or ship movements to enhance their desired policy in the Caribbean, the U.S. government underscored its willingness and intention to use force to define and extend its control in the Caribbean. It went to war with Spain to secure access to the Caribbean basin and the isthmian route to the Pacific basin (which encompassed close to half the world's population), and to expel a feeble European power whose inability to control its colony—Cuba—might allow that colony to become prey to a European metropole. German conduct in the Philippines, Cuba, and Samoa unsettled public figures and officials in the United States. The growing numbers of Germans in Mexico, Haiti, Venezuela, Costa Rica, Nicaragua, and Guatemala had disturbed some observers for decades. The German empire became strong in Europe because of economic and military growth and Bismarck's impressive alliance system. The economic and political power of Germans in Guatemala and elsewhere on the isthmus disturbed those countries competing for trade, prestige, and security.

Germany established protectorates in Africa in 1884, Samoa in 1889, and China (in Kiaochau province) in 1897. Bismarck appeared a reluctant participant. His focus was on Europe and informal empire seemed cheaper and less obtrusive. Still, for many German entrepreneurs, the combination of formal and informal empire offered an opportunity for a mixed exploitation of land, labor, and capital, all in the form of raw materials, a local workforce or a place for surplus German population, and investment ventures. Securing suitable communications was a reason for many German actions, from Manila Bay, Samoa, and Kiaochau to the Caribbean.

By the end of the nineteenth century, the German political economy strained to continue rapid internal growth and to secure its material gains against erosion from competition in the world economy. The population of Germany rose from 36 million in 1856 to 56 million in 1900. Germany (like any core state pursuing a hegemonic role) sought a share of the wealth and power from the world system, or, if possible, a competitive edge in its quest for preeminence. Believing that the nation's well-being and security were interlaced with its formal and informal colonies and the world economy, Germany's leaders pushed for markets, investment opportunities, raw materials, and naval support points around the world. To realize its aspirations, the German government opted for a naval building program that challenged the security and well-being of other metropoles. The German-British naval competition was one manifestation of this contest.[1]

Just as German leaders differed about how best to respond to British preeminence, they disagreed about the best response to the Monroe Doctrine and U.S. hegemony in the New World. German officials and business interests understood the importance of ties with Latin America, and particularly Middle America, in securing the nation's welfare. Few presumed that German entrepreneurs could withdraw from Latin America's economy and still deliver a high standard of living at home. The stakes—in effect, a comfortable future for the German nation—were simply too high to risk withdrawing. The mixture of free enterprise rhetoric, individualism, and organized capitalism hampered Germany's ability to control its nationals in Middle America. Their expansionist activities challenged U.S. geopolitical interests on the isthmus.[2]

Successful expansion abroad alerted other metropole societies that a German challenge merited serious attention. Historian Helmut Böhme, describing Germany's rise to world economic power before 1914, argued that "Germany fell ever deeper into a dependence on the world market, and the mightier the production volume of its economy became and the more the German entrepreneurs had to measure themselves with the competition in the world market, the more obvious became the limits of the German economy's resources. The search for assured raw material sources for its industry was judged the central problem of national development." German investment in Central America before 1914 centered in Guatemala; estimates of the total amount ranged from 185 to 300 million marks ($45 to $73 million [$1 equaled about 4.15 marks]) (Table 7). Nicaragua, Costa Rica, and El Salvador also received significant German investment. Around 1905, Germans had invested perhaps 50 million marks ($12 million) in Nicaragua, 35 million marks ($8 million) in Costa Rica, and 30 million marks ($7 million) in El Salvador.[3]

Some of the German long-term investment resulted from failed loans and followed a pattern that disturbed Guatemalan officials. During hard times, Hamburg and Bremen merchant firms often had to accept land in payment for debt, thus they acquired numerous coffee plantations. Gradually an animosity developed that found expression in antiforeignism. The Guatemalan government impeded foreign acquisition of new coffee plantations.[4] Guatemala's elite did not relish loss of control over the production of the nation's chief crop for the world market.

Much of the data on foreign residence in Central America comes from the German military—which gave physicals and placed conscript-age overseas Germans on its rolls—and hence often reflects only adult males. Estimates for the years 1898 to 1917 indicate between 900 and 1,400 German males (1,500 to 3,000 settlers) in Guatemala (Table 9). The estimate of 120 (male) Germans residing in Costa Rica in 1904 seems low. In 1906 a French consular official estimated that 350 German males resided in Costa Rica. The number of German settlers in Nicaragua grew steadily, reaching about 400 in 1905. In 1906 about 150 German males resided in Honduras. The data on German firms in Central America support estimates of the number of German residents (Table 10).[5]

From 1898 until 1906, Central American products declined to 0.5 percent of German imports, and Central America absorbed 0.1 percent of German exports (Tables 5 and 6). German merchants acquired 14 percent of Salvadoran exports and 5 percent of Costa Rican exports. German products captured 14 percent of El Salvador's import trade and 13 percent of Costa Rica's. German vessels supplied 20 percent of the foreign vessels operating in Salvadoran ports in 1901 and 1902.

In the late nineteenth century, most industrial states stepped up the transfer of technology and business organization to the isthmus. Central American communications and infrastructure developed and enclave production expanded, especially along the Atlantic coast. Foreign capitalists eagerly submitted projects involving railroads, street lighting, streetcar lines, electric power, and sewage, telephone, and water systems. German entrepreneurs played a major role in the building of Central American infrastructure. Germany, like other metropoles, used technology to expand the market base for its industrial order and to extract value for the homeland, not as a means to transfer the industrial revolution to Central America.[6]

The Central American economies suffered major disruption as they were incorporated more closely into the world economy in the late nineteenth and early twentieth centuries. Since all accumulators competed for limited surplus value, Central American anti-imperialist and comprador factions arose, expecting a greater share for themselves. Some factions sought to exploit the divisions and rivalries among the core states. A seldom-mentioned socioeconomic disruption followed the devaluations, as the Central American governments had to replace the shared, unifying silver peso with divisive, national paper currencies. The French chargé commented on German entrepreneurs during the financial crisis in Guatemala: "In effect, the German capitalists have profited from the depreciation of the silver currency in the country to acquire at bargain prices (in gold terms) important real estate properties. . . . the Germans have engaged about 250,000,000 marks in Guatemala." He marveled that German entrepreneurs had even extracted profit from the currency depreciation.[7]

By the 1890s German colonists, merchants, entrepreneurs, and financiers were engaged extensively in the Central American political economies. The imperial government and business leaders pondered how best to extend their position. German officials urged the development of communications to enhance the dominant position of German entrepreneurs in Guatemala. A German-financed Northern Railroad offered a quicker connection between the fatherland and its emigrant entrepreneurs and would enhance the value of German coffee plantations, coffee processing works, banking, shipping, and merchant activity.[8]

Many German and other foreign businesses recognized the need to facilitate Guatemala's north coast development and to open communications to the Caribbean. Around 1900 President Estrada Cabrera refocused attention on the capacity of the Northern Railroad to aid general development in Guatemala. Estrada Cabrera initiated a search for capital to complete the project. Arguing that foreign entrepreneurs would benefit immensely, his government was determined to persuade foreign investors to construct the railway and to start a bank. The combined railroad and bank project was estimated to require $6 million capital (25 million marks), but it promised ample rewards. Several French groups studied the project, and a U.S. consortium, which included Collis P. Huntington, made an attractive offer; but the Guatemalan government apparently preferred a German-led group. German officials and residents preferred German capitalists to complete the Northern Railroad because otherwise their hard won earnings might fall victim to a U.S. monopoly of transportation. Minor Cooper Keith and United Fruit won the concession to complete the railroad, however. They obtained a considerable loan from Deutsche Bank. Foreign capital dried up when Estrada Cabrera's reelection in 1906 produced protest, persecution of his opponents, and an invasion by forces acting on behalf of former president Barillas. Deutsche Bank refused further funds, but Keith tapped all the sources he could and brought in William van Horne, a railroad entrepreneur in Cuba, to see the project to completion in 1908.[9]

While loans from metropole capitalists generated influence, metropole diplomats were often unenthusiastic about ill-conceived or corrupt loan projects. The status of the debt of the isthmian states was intimately tied to matters of communications, commerce, investment, and general stability and order. Minister Voights-Rhetz persuaded Guatemala's president to postpone a moratorium on debt repayment until foreign interests were heard from. In his view, Guatemala needed a large loan under foreign control to bring order to its disarrayed finances. Although the German chancellery advised extreme prudence regarding a loan of $2 million secured by customs revenue, and although Estrada Cabrera rejected the first offer, German financiers remained interested in a loan. Legation secretary Baron Hans von Eyb suspected that much of any loan would disappear into private pockets without significantly altering the state debt. Nevertheless, in 1900 he cautioned that if a joint U.S.-German syndicate could not raise the capital for the loan in Hamburg, someone would seek funds in the United States.[10]

Metropoles competed sharply for loans because they carried some leverage related to the borrowing nation's debt and tariff policies. One German consul complained that the practice of linking the Central American tariff revenue to debt retirement unduly burdened trade and allowed speculators to make large, effortless profits. Financiers in the metropoles needed to tie tariff revenue to debt repayment in order to make Central American bonds attractive. Then, as the debt grew, the tariff rose and restricted trade, which ultimately shrank the income of the peripheral state. The reduced income undermined the state's capacity to repay its debt, so it borrowed just to service the debt until its credit was exhausted.[11] Finally, a severe financial crisis followed, sometimes with foreign intervention to protect the bondholders.

Guatemalans and Germans frequently clashed over the incompatibility of the home country's sovereign right to manage its domestic currency and the lender's right to fair debt repayment. In 1899 when the government repeated its 1894 act of withholding bond interest, the British and

German governments ordered vessels to both coasts of Guatemala. In late 1901, Britain, Germany, France, Belgium, and Italy jointly demanded that Guatemala make payment on the English debt from the postal convention and begin repayment of a 1.6 million pound sterling ($8 million) external debt. Guatemalan authorities turned to the U.S. government for assistance. Since no New World power was asked to participate, U.S. minister W. Geoffrey Hunter convinced Guatemala's president that the United States would intervene on his behalf, thus injuring European bondholders. Assistant Secretary of State Alvey A. Adee labeled Hunter's dispatch describing joint European demands for debt servicing "important correspondence, in view of our traditional jealousy of any concerted action of European powers to coerce an American state into payment of its debts." After the German government asked the U.S. government to join in requesting Guatemala to arrange debt repayment, the State Department decided merely to observe developments.[12]

In early 1902 the European powers proposed a joint loan to facilitate Guatemala's repayment of the English debt. Hamburg agents assigned Guatemala's dilatory behavior to the belief that the U.S. government would not join in the loan. The Hamburg Chamber of Commerce reported little interest in lending; most merchants suspected that the loan would only succeed if the U.S. government participated.[13]

U.S. chargé McNally worried that the pressure to settle the debt threatened the stability of the Guatemalan currency and the public image of the foreigners. The currency devaluation could create uncertainty for all investors, bondholders, and trading partners. "The German Minister seems to be the spokesman for the other Diplomats," he observed, "and his daily visits to the President are not relished by that Gentleman." British and German war vessels and an ultimatum achieved a settlement, but it generated antiforeign sentiments even against Americans, because they also brought claims before Guatemala. An earthquake salvaged the reputation of the Germans. The German colony was praised for its service following the disaster, which occurred in the midst of the debt settlement crisis.[14]

In early 1904 the Guatemalan president decreed a loan to stabilize the exchange rate between the national currency and foreign currencies. German creditors protested that the decree encouraged Guatemalan debtors to refuse to repay hard currency debts because the courts would compel the foreign creditor to accept repayment from a defaulted debtor at the discounted exchange rate. Thus foreign creditors had to tolerate a period of nonpayment or accept court-ordered repayment at less than one-sixth the silver value of the debt. German merchants and investors faced heavy losses unless their government resisted this manipulation of currency exchange. They expected the French, British, and U.S. governments to protest. The chief German investors conceded that Guatemala should manage its own currency but rejected its authority to decree a value for foreign currencies.[15] Unfortunately, the value of a currency was subject to foreign and domestic activities.

In addition to tension in regard to debt and currency exchange problems, the metropoles pursued conflicting objectives with regard to interoceanic transit. Some German agents, sensing that the U.S. government might use the Panama canal to support its dominance in Middle America, proposed that European capitalists should resume the project of Ferdinand de Lesseps. "If the European states could not raise the capital necessary for the construction of the Panama canal," one German agent warned in 1900, "then the United States has the opportunity through further clever maneuvers with the Nicaragua canal to exhaust the New [Panama Canal] Company" and obtain even more advantageous conditions that "might further restrict the role of other foreign powers on the isthmus." A German diplomat in France speculated that Germany, by leading a project so important for world commerce, would receive benefits both strategic and commercial and would bolster its own prestige.[16] Germany could capture advantages in both isthmian transit and an improved image.

U.S. policy undercut even these unlikely dreams of German diplomats. The British surrendered their right to share in the military protection of transit in the [John] Hay-[Julian] Pauncefote agreement of 1901, after U.S. officials made clear their intention to acquire the French canal concession at Panama. Tension developed between German and U.S. objectives because the isthmus's role in world trade and communications lent it a major part of any effort to exert military and economic primacy or hegemony. The goals were, of course, not the raw materials, trade, and investment options on the isthmus, although they were a bonus, but the trade lines over that isthmus to the labor and raw materials of the west coast of the New World, the Pacific, and Asia.

German entrepreneurs recognized the competitive value of the isthmus in the world market. Albert Ballin, director of HAPAG, claimed that a Panama canal would be a powerful weapon in U.S. hands. Professor Koch from Darmstadt, a Ballin associate, reflected on the "unhealthy consequences [which sole U.S. control over the canal] would have for German trade and navigation and even for its position in East Asia." The scandals enveloping the Universal Interoceanic Canal Company negated any possibility of raising funds in France, so Ballin tested German financial circles. He was convinced that "success [in raising funds in Germany] was unthinkable without effective support from the Imperial government." He trusted Foreign Minister Bernhard von Bülow to recognize the need to safeguard German interests.[17]

Koch emphasized the value of an internationally supervised canal. He expected the French firm to sell its rights at Panama to the U.S. government, which would then control both canal routes. If German officials acted quickly and resolutely, they might prevent the Panama canal from falling under U.S. control. Ballin's and Koch's concern about U.S. control of the Panama canal was echoed by Secretary of the Navy Admiral Alfred von Tirpitz. He claimed that the fighting navy and merchant marine shared interests in a shortened route from Europe to the Pacific Ocean "because our growing foreign interests will constantly compel us to increase our occupation of foreign stations." Without assured access to the canal, he warned, German economic interests would be endangered.[18]

Tirpitz believed that the imperial government had to recognize "the possibility of military entanglements in the Central American–Caribbean region . . . given the present and future significance of our varied economic relations to Latin America and the Pacific." "During military entanglements with states within the North American sphere of interest," he assumed that "Germany would face a closed canal." Participation in control of an isthmian canal, he noted, would enhance Germany's value as an ally and add to its prestige. Yet, "Germany's strategic position in the eastern areas of the Pacific Ocean, including the west coast of the Americas, would be very tangibly weakened by a transfer of the future isthmian canal to sole North American control," he warned, because "extensive areas [would] be removed from the effective operations-area of our fleet." One escape from Tirpitz's dilemma came from a German diplomat in Washington who suggested that German and U.S. capital might cooperate in the canal project.[19] However, neither government demonstrated any interest in a joint project at this time.

Some German leaders hoped to avoid direct confrontation with the U.S. government by undercutting an exclusive U.S. canal. The British and German ministers in Washington indicated that their governments would offer "all the encouragement of whatever nature necessary to facilitate the continuation of the [French New] Panama [Canal] Company as a private company," assuming that no agreement occurred between Colombia and the United States. In early 1901 Minister to the United States Theodor von

Holleben presumed that a canal could be built through the cooperation of France, Germany, and Britain. However, the Hay-Pauncefote agreement marked a British withdrawal from the shared canal rights arranged in the Clayton-Bulwer treaty and the surrender of an isthmian canal to U.S. control. Since the agreement persuaded Holleben that German capital would not participate in the canal, he supported the bloated demands of the Panama Canal Company because the longest postponement of construction served Germany best.[20]

German naval planners assumed that the United States was most vulnerable in the Caribbean and isthmian region. Tirpitz observed that the Panama canal shortened the distance from German North Sea ports to the west coast of America, which translated into reduced consumption of fuel and supplies and less operational time—important factors in any war plan based on quick mobilization and a rapid attack. Valuable U.S. naval possessions in the Caribbean—Puerto Rico and Guantánamo Bay in Cuba—protected the canal, but German naval officials planned to seize these poorly fortified bases if necessary. Naval attaché Herbert von Rebeur-Paschwitz warned that Germany "could not be disinterested [in events in the western Caribbean] without neglecting its very extensive interests there. And . . . Germany's difficulties increase with every step the North Americans take to strengthen their power position there." Since acquiring a naval station in peacetime was doubtful, the German navy planned, immediately upon outbreak of war with the United States, to seize a position that would allow its forces to attack U.S. trade centers.[21]

In conjunction with isthmian transit, Germans were concerned about steamer service, cable links, and naval stations. The Kosmos and Roland lines did well on the west coast, despite Pacific Mail's use of its privileged position with the Panama Railroad to raise its freight rates. Kosmos even extended its service to San Francisco to create more competition for Pacific Mail. When Kosmos steamers encountered health regulation problems in Guatemala, Minister Eugen von Seefried auf Buttenheim advised the Guatemalan government to encourage competition with Pacific Mail if it hoped to avoid monopoly freight rates for its trade. The Panama Railroad was expected to encounter stiff competition from either the Guatemalan Northern Railway or the Tehuantepec route, which served German interests in northwestern Guatemala better.[22]

A wide variety of German interests participated in the public discussion about world communications and transportation facilities. The All German Union [Alldeutscher Verband] understood the value of communications in the world economy. It assumed that "the United States would hardly be in a position to raise objection," if private German interests purchased communications facilities in the Virgin Islands. It envisioned a cable over the isthmus to Samoa and East Asia. Less ambitious plans merely sought a coaling station. In late 1898 Voights-Rhetz suggested the Cocos Islands, a Costa Rican possession, as a coaling station in the Pacific. After study, the German naval ministry rejected the Cocos as unsuitable, but the lure of the islands persisted. In mid-1901 a German civil engineer alleged that Costa Rica wished to sell the Cocos.[23] The U.S. government would scarcely have allowed Costa Rica to sell the Cocos in light of the Lodge Corollary to the Monroe Doctrine.

German officials and merchants wished for a support point for naval and commercial affairs. The Galápagos Islands, an Ecuadoran island group in the Pacific, were frequently the object of rumors because they possessed strategic value as the Pacific islands closest to an isthmian canal. A German diplomat in Ecuador proposed purchasing them to obtain "the first rank for [Germany's] power position in the Pacific Ocean" and to "prevent another world power from acquiring these islands." Holleben knew that "the Americans [and British] have also cast an eye on this island group." He was disheartened because it was now too late for his "youth's dream"—"the acquisition of the Galápagos Islands for Germany," but "it could not hurt our interests if England should break the Monroe Doctrine, through the acquisition of South American islands." He questioned whether the Galápagos was a wise option to complete Germany's chain of coaling and naval stations around the world because the United States and every South American state on the west coast would protest a foreign acquisition of the Galápagos.[24]

Despite the warning, the foreign ministry asked Holleben to ascertain the U.S. government's reaction to German acquisition of the Galápagos. The acquisition would be viewed as a violation of the Monroe Doctrine, he responded, but "the establishment of coaling stations is naturally another matter. [The U.S. government] could hardly raise objections to an agreement with Denmark [for a coaling station in the Virgin Islands] or Ecuador [in the Galápagos], even if the agreement touched an uncomfortable spot." The German minister in Mexico was incensed that the Monroe Doctrine forbade any "European nation to acquire even a handful of American soil, yet raised not the smallest scruple for America to acquire what it wished from this territory." Both Germany and the United States hoped to block the other's acquisition of the Galápagos.[25]

The German embassy in Washington was not certain that the U.S. government would allow foreign acquisition of key naval or coaling sites lying across the entrances to the Panama canal. It saw no sign that the United States intended to restrict the Monroe Doctrine umbrella to the Caribbean region. "While President [Theodore] Roosevelt apparently goes very far in his friendly sentiments towards Germany," Holleben received "the decided impression that these sentiments would end at once if Germany revealed a lust for land in the Americas." Even if the United States might ultimately accept "German sovereignty over a naval station," he warned that "this would probably only occur after America made its own demands in Europe or Asia which Germany might have doubts about granting."[26] The U.S. government would demand at least a quid pro quo for any concessions to Germany related to interoceanic transit.

German military interests in Middle America went beyond naval matters. The Friedrich Krupp firm supplied some Central American armies and was not adverse to sharing this information with the German government. Between 1875 and 1903 the Guatemalan government purchased at least thirty-eight new Krupp cannons. Alfred Krupp supplied the German government with detailed information about contracts with Nicaragua and Guatemala for munitions, weapons, and powder. In the early twentieth century, however, Guatemala contracted for a French military mission that quickly made inroads into Krupp's near monopoly of artillery and small arms sales.[27]

German leaders hoped to expand a wide variety of market and business ties on the isthmus. When the government solicited input while structuring tariff policy, various interest groups focused almost exclusively on their narrow, immediate needs. Berlin's oldest merchant organization expected social imperialist goals. It recommended that tariff policy promote the total interests of "Germany's political economy in its relations with the exterior. The commercial policy should contribute to increase as much as possible the productivity of German labor, to stabilize the economic life, to place economic goods in the greatest possible quantity and quality at the disposal of the German consumer, and to soften the struggle for survival of the poor and needy classes." The private sector activity of merchants, industrialists, and workers had the primary role in developing foreign trade relations. It argued that the "protecting and supporting activity of the state only enters into consideration in a secondary place. If the workers who produce an export article are not industrious and talented, and the entrepreneurs are not intelligent, energetic and far-sighted, then foreign trade cannot grow, even if the state makes the greatest effort to advance it." The merchants believed that "artificial obstacles to foreign trade or to the international division of labor can only be damaging."[28]

Consistent with its liberal perspective, the Berlin merchant organization wanted foreign economic policy coordinated with domestic economic policy. Misunderstanding the "close relationship existing between importation and exportation," according to the merchants, "often leads to a one-sided value judgment of exportation . . . it must be stressed anew that importing and exporting are of equal importance. Foreign trade rests on the exchange between two nations of products which each society can best produce." But it did not pursue its premises consistently. In a crisis it expected Germany to avoid foodstuff strangulation through a centralized state policy to assure the food supply: "If the German people wanted insurance with regard to wartime dangers, it would be better to pay the risk premium in the form of increased naval expenses rather than in higher prices of imported foodstuff and raw materials." The first solution was centralized planning; the second was a free market. In fact, this merchant association conceded that "a serious disturbance of our foreign trade relations would . . . have ominous consequences for almost the whole population," thus conceding that pursuit of social imperialism in the world economy was so essential for prosperity that state action was mandatory.[29]

Both Guatemala and El Salvador appeared slated for closer commercial ties with Germany. In 1900 Guatemala's consul in Bremen, Guillermo Kuksiek, observed that Bremen's trade with Guatemala more than doubled that year because the Guatemalan economy was in recovery and needed to restock the products of Bremen. El Salvador sent former president Rafael Zaldívar to Germany in late 1902 to conclude a trade pact similar to the Franco-Salvadoran treaty. Germany's need to expand its markets became a central topic. When El Salvador hesitated to make concessions similar to those granted France, the German government threatened to bar Salvadoran exports unless German goods could enter El Salvador more freely.[30]

Commerce was only one aspect of German economic expansion. German firms utilized investment and managing skills in Central America. In 1900 a Siemens subsidiary, Empresa Eléctrica de Guatemala, which had invested about 3.4 million marks ($825,000)—3 million marks from the Siemens firm and family and the Deutsche Bank and 400,000 marks from Hamburg interests—in the lighting and electrical business during the 1890s, asked Estrada Cabrera to renegotiate its concession. It sought to double the life of the concession and to obtain the right to convert into a German corporation. In exchange, it offered to pay the outstanding Guatemalan debt related to the electrical works and to purchase the president's thirteen shares of Empresa stock at about twelve times the market price. Estrada Cabrera's profit would have been appreciable, but he expected more. He broke off negotiations, attempted to appropriate 5,500 pesos worth of lighting equipment the company had lent him, and ordered Empresa to move light posts even though its concession freed it from such tasks. Chargé Eyb intervened energetically—in the form of an ultimatum that threatened to sever relations—to protect the firm's property.[31]

Soon after his intervention on behalf of Empresa, Eyb was assaulted in the streets of Guatemala City. Siemens officials, believing the word of some resident Germans, told the German foreign office that the Guatemalan government acted publicly correct toward Eyb, while hiring thugs to assault him in the night because of his humanitarian labors—he had monitored and criticized its detention system—not because of his defense of Siemens's interests. Still, Siemens director Tonio Bodiker requested the fullest support for Eyb's conduct, including the use of force if necessary.[32]

Most likely, Eyb was attacked because he successfully defended German interests and because German material success produced jealousy. U.S. minister James McNally saw a relationship between the attack on Eyb and Germany's imperialistic relationship with Guatemala. "The Germans," he noted, "have the trade of this country in every branch[;] they get the Government loans, and are in reality the financiers of the Guatemala Government." German businesses, in his view, were "taking unfair advantage of the financial misfortunes of this Government [because they were] unrelenting, aggressive, and exacting to the point of exasperation." Their persistent demands, in his opinion, created a widespread "enmity towards the Germans." McNally and the French chargé concurred that Eyb's ultimatum had strained ties.[33]

Siemens agent and general manager of Empresa Eléctrica, Ernst Greve, suspected that Guatemalan officials had a false sense of security following the assault. Other diplomatic agents had little to fear, he reported to the Siemens home office, because "none of them had dared previously to oppose the local government and its scandalous intrigues with the same energy and perseverance as Eyb." After the assault, Eyb's insecurity limited his ability to protect Germans who were subjected to administrative and bureaucratic harassment. German planters could not obtain the necessary labor force; other Germans found judicial matters postponed or decided unfavorably; and still others were ordered to fulfill extracontractual tasks. According to Bodiker, the government directed its hatred of foreigners chiefly at Germans because the situation temporarily denied them diplomatic protection. German businesspeople expected meaning-ful improvement only if the United States or Germany controlled Guate-mala, but the isthmian states and the remaining metropoles would op-pose such a move.[34]

In addition to economic and judicial problems, German residents faced a psychological burden because any disturbance threatened their per-sonal safety. Since Guatemalans respected armed foreigners, Bodiker be-lieved that a visit from a warship would persuade the government to act to avoid the landing of German forces. He assumed that the assault on Eyb would not have occurred if the cruiser *Geier* had not left the coast. In mid-1901, under pressure from the German government, the Guatemalan government began repaying its debt to Empresa. The Guatemalan presi-dent, however, denied Empresa the right to become a foreign corporation as long as a Guatemalan owned one share. Claiming it no longer laid value on becoming a German corporation, Empresa thanked the foreign ministry for its support.[35] This clash was only one of Guatemala's prob-lems with foreign powers at the turn of the century.

Greve noted that the U.S. minister often hindered German activity. He heartily approved the decision to combine the consulate with the legation in the person of Seefried. Greve praised Seefried's support of Empresa and his effort to repair an existing split in the German community. See-fried, Greve, and others agreed that U.S. and German trade interests in Central America overlapped too frequently to allow much free play.[36]

Entrepreneurs from metropoles commonly extended economic and so-cial benefits to domestic comprador leaders who advocated the interests of foreign firms. At times, the compradors requested favors for their serv-ices. In 1903 the Guatemalan government offered uncleared land to each of twelve foreign communities to construct a pavilion for the annual fall Minerva festival—a popular celebration with music, dancing, and free drinks. All twelve graciously declined. The government then selected ten economic groups (most likely grouped by industry) and the Ameri-cans and Germans, the most populous and wealthy colonies, to construct pavilions. The American director of the Central Railroad, Daniel B. Hodgsdon, and Greve declined to supervise the fund raising. The Ger-man colony had already made significant contributions to the festival, but Greve excused it from further contribution with the argument that a preferred position might wound the sensibilities of the New World states. Although Greve expected the railroad and Empresa to experience difficulty, he successfully solicited electric rate increases of 50–100 percent.[37] Greve rejected additional material support for the Minerva celebration, yet he expanded the accumulation of his Siemens affiliate.

Empresa won a material and moral victory in the Minerva affair, but it irritated a government already antagonistic to foreigners. While reporting to the home office on the affair, Greve explained how he had deceived the government about price and profit in a clever manner that would facilitate deception in the future. He fixed the accounting to show a small loss for the past year in order to wring price increases from the Guatemalan government. He could have shown an even greater loss, but then he would have been hard-pressed to control the appearance of high profits in future reports. His method allowed him to hide future profits by manipulating the exchange rates through early transfer of funds to the amortization account or by booking profits under the account for earthquake damage. Werner von Siemens held it "completely practical and desirable that [Greve] retain good relations with the [U.S.-owned] Central Railroad Company . . . since two so powerful opponents can better oppose even the Guatemalan government than one alone." He hoped that the failure to interest the foreign community in the Minerva festival might persuade the government to avoid such irritations in the future.[38]

Later, Greve was piqued by a Guatemalan decree of December 12, 1903, which regulated future price increases. He considered this unwise step a response to his requests for the president to repay his long-standing debt of $6,000 to Empresa. Greve used the completion of a section of railroad as an opportunity to describe privately the president's service as "chiefly limiting his [bribery] demands to what the enterprise could afford to give him." Siemens had confidence in Greve's ability to defend Empresa against Guatemalan chicanery. By 1908 Greve was promoted to a place on the four-man board that directed Siemens's overseas operations.[39]

Even without deceptive bookkeeping, the Siemens operations in Guatemala were immensely profitable. Ownership remained solidly in German hands. In 1910 the Siemens firm and family owned 65 percent of the Empresa Eléctrica, another 29 percent was in the hands of German-surnamed stockholders, and only 6 percent belonged to Spanish-surnamed stockholders. After subtracting large sums for contingency expenditures, Empresa's management calculated the gross profit at 40 percent of the revenue in 1910. Much of the profit was repatriated to Germany.[40]

Peripheral wealth ends up in core countries, according to political economist Arghiri Emmanuel, because of "unequal exchange." The exchange is often implemented through the use of creative accounting, bookkeeping, price transferring, and financial institutions in the core, as profits are organized and manipulated from the core (just as the Siemens director did in Guatemala in 1905). Core managers determined the policies of bookkeeping and transfers. Management and exchange mechanisms were needed for long-distance trade. Core management of peripheral activity assured that high wages remain at the core while wages for similar work in the periphery remain low. For example, agricultural or railroad workers were paid much less in Central America for similar work performed in a metropole setting.[41]

As German commercial and investment activity diversified, complicated problems arose for German entrepreneurs. A fall in coffee prices around 1900 produced a crisis in Costa Rica that endangered German capital. Some German diplomats hoped to improve trade relations with Costa Rica and to protect German products there from goods bearing false trademarks. The Costa Rican government preferred a law to protect German trademarks rather than a treaty. A German firm was irritated because Costa Rica required more information than Germany prior to allowing firms to do business. It objected vehemently that the decree mentioned "foreign companies" (sociedades extranjeras) rather than "limited liability companies" (sociedades anónimos). For many years, however, no major problems disturbed relations between the Costa Rican government and German residents.[42]

Some lesser problems nagged German–Costa Rican relations, however. For example, the Costa Rican Petroleum and Coal Company represented a speculative, perhaps dishonest, scheme organized in the United States, which involved the reputation of Germany. In September 1901 the San Francisco *Evening Post* reported that W. E. von Johannsen, the Costa Rican consul in San Francisco, helped form an American-German syndicate that had received unspecified concessions from Costa Rica and would issue 5 million shares in the Costa Rican Petroleum and Coal Company. Presuming that the shares would be offered in Germany also, the German consul in San Francisco warned his government about any activity in which Johannsen was engaged. Johannsen was incensed when he learned of this confidential message. Since prominent Costa Ricans had suggested that there should be coal and oil in Costa Rica, he argued that Costa Rican national honor required the chastisement of the German consul. The consul had possessed shrewd insight, however, because claims and counterclaims arising from this company—it produced no oil, gas, or coal—plagued Costa Rican, U.S., and German officials for decades.[43]

A German foreign ministry official discovered unexpected business opportunities for Germans when he traveled through Nicaragua in 1900 to survey the transit route. The trip revealed that though there was limited German activity on the Atlantic coast, extensive and profitable German merchant and coffee interests had developed on the Pacific side since the 1880s. Germany's role appeared ready to increase after a German firm acquired the Atlas steamship company, which operated in the Caribbean region, from United Fruit. If German entrepreneurs built the railroad connecting the interior to Nicaragua's Caribbean coast, the German stake would increase further.[44]

German consul Hans Ernst Schlieben traveled into the interior of Nicaragua in mid-1903 to visit the Germans there and to learn more about the extensive concession granted a U.S. group headed by James Deitrick of Pittsburgh. Deitrick's group oversaw an area for mineral exploitation equal in size to Saxony. In Schlieben's judgment, "this concession . . . can teach us how the Americans manage to achieve commercial advantage in these countries and which conditions German entrepreneurs can demand of Spanish American governments in similar cases." A new technology—the introduction of trucks to replace ox-carts for transporting coffee—intrigued him. "The Americans have carved out a sphere of interest," he observed, "when German, especially Hamburg, circles have looked distrustingly towards Central America because of losses in the coffee business. The American sphere grows in the richest region of Nicaragua where it will force out all other undertakings in a few years. Unfortunately, the [Deitrick] concession encompasses several mines which German engineers in Jinotega were in the process of denouncing." Schlieben discerned a mixed blessing in U.S. penetration. German coffee barons would suffer because "the American miners pay five or six times the wages prevailing on the German coffee plantations," which will strip away the planters' laborers. However, since Germans dominated the merchant activity, he expected the native workers, employed full-time in mines instead of part-time on coffee plantations, to purchase more German exports.[45]

While Deitrick's project overwhelmed Schlieben, other Germans advocated copying U.S. organization and tariff policy to boost exports. A German promoter, impressed that the private Philadelphia Commercial Museum—a center for commercial, statistical, and cultural information that established ties with all the Latin American countries and Europe—had achieved success in promoting trade in Latin America, persuaded his government to found a similar agency: the Central Bureau [Centralstelle]. There was at least one major difference: The Central Bureau was closely linked to its government, while the Philadelphia Museum only lobbied the U.S. government. U.S. tariffs could also serve as a model. In 1903 for mer minister of the interior Georg von Rheinbaben proposed measures to assure German industry of market opportunities behind tariff walls. Germany could protect its domestic market, he advised, just as the United States had protected its industry earlier, without avoiding friendly competition elsewhere around the world. He rejected criticism of cartels, effortlessly shifting focus from the home market to the world market as decisive for the survival of German values. Earlier many observers had warned that English manufactures would wipe out German industry, he recalled, but Germany used rapid technological and scientific advances to surpass Britain in most industrial areas. He believed that German enterprise and technology would meet the U.S. challenge in a similar fashion.[46]

Germany's advanced technology created opportunities for German manufacturers in Middle America, but German technology did not always overcome practical considerations. For example, one German manager who purchased industrial machines confidentially compared German and U.S. electrotechnical products. The U.S. producers were more customer-oriented than their German counterparts. They changed models less frequently and hence spare parts were available for a longer time. Although the German electrotechnical industry had a reputation for high quality, he cautioned that American marketing techniques created serious competition.[47]

As leaders of the U.S. political economy became determined to build and control an isthmian canal, they became increasingly sensitive to German expansion in the Caribbean. Some German agents speculated that the U.S. government might hinder further Central American conflict in order to encourage U.S. capitalists. Voights-Rhetz judged that the new U.S. policy would attempt to assure peace and order and to restrict foreign influence in the region. German officials reassured North Americans that "the rumors about German plans of conquest in Central or South America are lies and distortions of our opponents." Diplomat Botho von Eulenberg considered a successful trade campaign the only German challenge confronting the United States in South America. The difficulties between the United States and Germany, the embassy contended, were economic not political.[48]

U.S. officials suspected any German activity near canal sites. In early 1903 Secretary of State John Hay ordered discrete investigation of the allegation that the German government had offered $40 million for the Panama Canal Company interests and had proposed to purchase Colombia's shares. This rumor raised Colombia's hope to avoid an unwelcome agreement with the United States. Germany's large commercial stake in interoceanic transit and the public pronouncements of entrepreneurs like Ballin and naval officers like Tirpitz nurtured such rumors. Minister Werner Grünau rejoiced that "Germany is on everyone's tongue," but he denied knowledge of any forthcoming intervention on behalf of Colombia. The U.S. government distrusted the Germans in regard to Panamanian independence. German diplomat Hilmar Bussche surmised that the U.S. conduct in Panama served "Germany's position with regard to the South American republics because their eyes are now open to what they can expect from the great sister republic." Yet he assured Hay that Germans wanted the United States to build the canal. He avoided the State Department, however, and remained silent on Panama.[49]

The German government's reaction to the Panama "revolution" of November 1903 was shaped with U.S. wishes in mind. Since a landing of Colombian troops "would render U.S. efforts to keep the isthmus open to world commerce more difficult," Hay wanted proper instructions issued to German vessels that were "about to convey Colombian forces to Panama." The German minister counseled the Colombian president that his government would probably not intercede with the U.S. government. Once the U.S. government made its sympathy for the Panamanian revolutionaries clear, the emperor favored quick recognition of the Panamanian government.[50]

German leaders generally did not see a U.S. canal as a major burden for German commerce, but it presented disadvantages to the military. A canal gave the United States a two-ocean navy without the cost. In 1905 a foreign ministry official concluded that "the canal is chiefly an American establishment which principally serves naval strategic purposes." It will not "change the face of the commercial world," he argued, because "German shipping and trade with their . . . superior cleverness and energy will draw an advantage out of the canal," although U.S. goods would become more competitive in Asia. Writer Georg Wegener, however, believed that a competitive German steamship line in the Pacific would be adventuristic after the United States obtained a canal. Foreign ministry official Gustav Michahelles expected that "German interests would greatly benefit if German shipping firms would exploit the constantly increasing traffic better and not miss the advantage which can be extracted at the Panama isthmus."[51] The resolution of the political and strategic issues regarding a Panamanian canal increased the value of efficient steamer service along Central America's west coast.

The German navy occasionally was called on to monitor German residents, shipping services, and investments in Central America. German coffee exporters and merchants on the west coast of Guatemala were disgusted with the poor service of the Pacific Mail and its subsidiary, Agencia Marítima Nacional. Captain Paul Behneke, commander of the *Falke*, expected Kosmos and HAPAG to expand into the Pacific. In response to the many complaints, the Guatemalan government authorized three U.S. citizens to form a lighter company, the Express of Central America, to service the west coast ports. Later, attempts to combine the Express with the Agencia suggested a North American plan to monopolize Guatemala's west coast trade. Several German firms—Schlubach and Company, Nottebohm and Company, Koch, Hagmann and Company—proposed to purchase control "of the Agencia Marítima Nacional and the San José Wharf Company in order to influence the administration of these companies for German merchants and plantation owners."[52] The quality of the isthmian ports and the services and improvements in the ports both shaped and reflected metropole involvement in trading activity.

The German government, like other metropole governments, used its navy to undertake commercial intelligence gathering as well as traditional enforcement and protection tasks. In mid-1905 Behneke visited Middle America to analyze Germany's options to protect its influence. Costa Rican officials received him warmly and spoke well of the German colony. Behneke noted that "Bishop [Johann] Storck won praise regarding the respect and influence of Germandom and the German educational system." An interoceanic railroad in Costa Rica would offer competition to the Panama railroad, he believed, but it would reduce German trade with Costa Rica because it would open direct service to the U.S. east coast. Germany's share of Costa Rica's trade had fallen from one-fourth to one-eighth, while U.S. merchants held over half. Behneke expected that "with the increase in American influence the demand for American goods will also rise. Even German businesses are compelled to import American goods." Foreign ministry officials, nevertheless, believed that the small Costa Rican market offered good opportunities for German industrial products. Wegener noted that Costa Rica's per capita trade with Germany was "the strongest among the five Republics, and the total value of German capital invested in Costa Rica, except for Guatemala . . . was the absolute largest." Behneke reported that Germans were the most respected foreign businesspeople in Costa Rica, yet they had lost ground to the North Americans. German activities formed considerable cultural presence, including four clubs—the German Club, the Welfare Club, the Fleet Association, and a Polo Club. There was no German school in Costa Rica, although advanced plans existed to found one.[53]

Behneke learned that Nicaraguan president Zelaya was particularly friendly to Germans. Declining coffee prices and transportation routes that led only to the west coast had burdened Nicaragua's economy. The country's political factions had exploited the finances of the national railroad system so thoroughly, however, that it had become a liability. When efforts to sell the only completed section to Americans failed, the Nicaraguan government leased it to German engineer Julius Weist. A confidential German study reported that "if Weist should overcome the obstacles which oppose a growing development of the rail business, then his project would produce an essential strengthening of Germandom in Nicaragua." Weist also contracted to build the San Miguelito–Monkey Point railroad, which would connect the interior to the Caribbean coast and permit direct steamship ties with Germany. Germans could benefit from this project in various ways. Weist preferred German construction materials whenever they could meet the price and qualities of U.S. goods. Some Germans planned banana plantations along the projected railway. The Germans in Nicaragua supported two naval associations and one German club.[54]

Germany's role in Nicaragua seemed strong. Zelaya endured, Vice Consul Friedrich August Heye pointed out, because "his weapon" was his army. A Bavarian captain directed the cadet school on a German model with German aid and support. "Germany had in any case no grounds to be unsatisfied with the continuation of Zelaya's rule," Heye observed, since Zelaya had been "generally friendly toward German interests, and . . . a strong government like his offered the best guarantee against U.S. intervention." German penetration of Nicaragua grew in relation to Zelaya's disenchantment with U.S. canal policy, which threatened Nicaragua with a dark economic future. Rather than surrender to the U.S. decision to drop a Nicaraguan canal and build at Panama, Zelaya searched in Germany, France, Great Britain, and Japan for investors to replace U.S. capitalists. Zelaya and his associates sensed that the prospects of attracting German capital for a canal correlated in some fashion with the number and size of German enterprises that would benefit from the canal, thus they encouraged German investment.[55]

Behneke was unable to obtain much information about El Salvador and Honduras. German officers were warmly received in El Salvador, where three German-trained Chilean officers instructed El Salvador's army and where Germans, mostly Jewish merchants from Alsace-Lorraine, had sizable investments. Behneke noted that though Germans commanded great respect in El Salvador, there were few German residents and no clubs. He declined to report on German interests in Honduras because his visit was too brief.[56]

Behneke received a friendly welcome from the large German community in Guatemala. Cultural activity was extensive and varied. He recommended that the imperial government help the German school in Guatemala, which had about 115 students, find badly needed teachers. The Germans supported a German Club, a School Club, a Welfare Club, a Riding Club, and a Naval Association, which grew out of his visit. "There is," he boasted, "no foreign land in whose economy Germany is, relatively, so strongly engaged and in whose development, therefore, Germany is so interested, as Guatemala. Unfortunately, that does not often enough reach the public[;] the U.S. influence dominates here also."[57]

Behneke described German economic impact on Nicaraguan and Guatemalan societies in great detail. Although nineteen German merchant firms operated in Nicaragua, trade flowed strongly to the United States. Still, he estimated that the German investment of 24 million marks—12 million in trade and 6 million each in land and credit—was slightly larger than the U.S. placement. The next year, a German consular agent surprisingly estimated the German investment at 250 million marks in contrast to 60 million for the United States and 66 million for the British. It is unlikely that German capital doubled the combined U.S. and British investment. However, already in 1899, a U.S. consul had estimated the German placement in Nicaragua at $10.47 million (44 million marks), or double the U.S. investment. If the figure for 1899 is credible, Behneke's estimate must be low and the German consular figure of 1906 high.[58]

Behneke estimated that German investment in Guatemala had reached about 300 million marks ($73 million): 150 million in land (Germans owned 60 percent of the coffee plantations); 110 million in credit; 30 million in trade; and 10 million in a railroad, the Empresa Eléctrica, and other small enterprises. German capital was several times larger than the total of all other foreign investment.[59]

Behneke found that either a modest economic penetration or sparse information hampered his evaluation of German investment in Panama, El Salvador, and Costa Rica. He estimated 55 Germans had invested about one-half million marks in Panama. German investments in El Salvador totaled about 30 million marks. In Costa Rica, 176 Germans had invested 15 million marks in nine large businesses, about 7 million marks in land, and 3 million in credit.[60]

By the early twentieth century, Germans were engaged primarily in business, but colonization projects still surfaced occasionally. German officials evaluated such schemes in regard to national policy. When Dr. José Leonard sought a contract to bring 150 German or European immigrants per year for nine years to Honduras, the Bavarian government cited the unfriendly climate to advise against participation. Heye warned that a booklet prepared to attract settlers and capital to the banana regions of Costa Rica contained much that was false or misleading. For example, much of the land described in the brochure was in dispute between Panama and Costa Rica, while United Fruit dominated most of the rest. Moreover, the colonization site was not served by a railway. A successful banana operation, he warned, needed a fully independent banana-purchasing company, a railway, and land beyond United Fruit control. Despite obstacles, he indicated that "if a well-capitalized [German] company established itself in this area, linked to a large German shipping firm, it would have a good prospect to control the banana business in Germany and its neighboring areas. Otherwise . . . United Fruit might also conquer this valuable market area and thereby establish a sort of world monopoly" of bananas.[61]

The increased contact with Central American societies promoted interest in German scientific, educational, and cultural development. In 1901 German officials reported that 300 German residents enjoyed great respect and contributed significantly to Costa Rican social and cultural affairs. For example, a German doctor directed the largest mental institution in San José, which employed German staff and equipment. Education was also seen as a way to advance cultural interaction and possibly to make money. The Frankfurt Chamber of Industry and Commerce proposed translating German medical texts to capture the "health market" in Latin America. In 1900 Eyb discussed the founding of a Colegio Alemán in Guatemala City with the Guatemalan government. Later, when the German government endowed a school in Guatemala City under the direction of German professors, McNally thought that this school had "some political significance, but as of yet nothing of that sort appears, at least on the surface."[62] The influence of foreign schools went beyond language instruction. The schools acquainted the children of the native elite with the metropole culture, thus building a friendly comprador group.

Priests of German nationality played an important role in Costa Rica's Catholic church from the 1870s to the 1920s. Bishop August Gaspar Thiel, a German who served until his death in 1901, was succeeded by Johann Storck, a German Paulist. Among other things, these bishops attracted additional German priests to Costa Rica. French consul Emile Joré complained that the German bishops and priests persuaded some Costa Rican youth to study in Germany who might otherwise have gone to France. Thiel and Storck served German interests in Costa Rica for about fifty years.[63]

In addition to clashes in Samoa, the Philippines, China, the Congo, and conflicts over pork sales, the United States and Germany competed for access to the canal, naval stations, investment, commerce, and political influences in Middle America. German and British investments in Central America were greater than U.S. investment prior to World War I (Table 8). The United States also trailed the major European metropole powers in the number of settlers and firms before World War I. The nature of imperial competition and the peculiar U.S. sense of insecurity—the United States acted as if it posed no threat to any power when it increased its own investment and markets but was threatened when other powers did so—prompted the U.S. government to improve its economic and strategic position in Central America in those areas where it considered German interests the most aggressive and threatening.

German society turned outward in response to internal problems. It sought foreign outlets for surplus capital and for German technology—particularly electrical and military industries—to allow them to develop. The German navy gathered information on Central American political economies and societies and reported on the competition for investment, trade, and transit. While German elites wanted no unnecessary confrontation in Central America, they planned to attack the United States in the vulnerable Caribbean–Central American region if hostilities broke out. German elites also concerned themselves with preserving German-dom because they recognized the value of a large, successful, influential, and loyal German colony on the isthmus.

8

■

Apogee of German Power in Central America, 1906–1914

Germany needed to sustain its economic growth to satisfy the demands of its capitalists, workers, and those various patriotic groups that considered security and well-being a byproduct of the nation's material growth. Historian Wolfgang Mommsen recognized that "German banks were more likely cautious when confronted with imperialistic enterprises whether of a formal or an informal character," such as the Ottoman Railroad, but that it would be erroneous to believe that "German high finance had not participated in other financial imperialistic enterprises of greater style." He found that "the [German] state [was], under the command of imperialistic capitalism, that direct or indirect tool of the bourgeoisie class, which served two objectives . . . the suppression of the working class to the utility of the capitalists and . . . the protection, even in special cases the forceful expansion, of the economic interests of domestic capitalists to the disadvantage of rival capitalists beyond the national boundaries." Conflict arose over the implementation that would best convert the expansion into security and well-being.[1]

The numerous German firms and investors in Middle American economic life increased Germany's role, but they also produced jealousy, suspicion, and confrontations with the United States. Germany's expansion into Middle America disrupted U.S.-German relations at a time when Germany's naval building program was souring relations with England. The Mexican revolt of 1910 against Porfirio Díaz unleashed a decade of civil strife, some occurring on Guatemala's northern border. U.S. officials found the ties between Mexico and Germany, especially in the Mexican military, unsavory. This relationship reinforced U.S. distrust of German motives in the New World.[2]

Franco-German relations remained strained after the war of 1870; nevertheless, historian Raymond Poidevin has claimed that German and

French interests did not compete in Middle America. While Germans sought commercial, industrial, and investment opportunities, he noted, the French invested in government railroad bonds. In his view, Germans developed commercial and cultural ties through numerous colonists who conducted business, while France's few colonists commonly pursued personal, religious, or cultural goals. German colonists facilitated German commercial success, and the lack of French migrants made it difficult for France to hinder the spread of German influence. The French chargé in Guatemala conceded German preeminence in commerce, agricultural exploitation, and ownership of *fincas* (rural land holdings), and Guatemalan diplomat Emilio Gómez Carrillo argued that character, intelligence, honesty, and "extraordinary activity" made the Germans "admirable colonists."[3]

Poidevin recognized that metropole businesses and politicians often acknowledged a competitive framework yet cooperated to obtain common objectives, such as access or protection, for foreign firms and capital. German officials and businesspeople constantly weighed their need to compete and their need to cooperate with other metropoles. They expected to win a fair share of Central America's economy without antagonizing the United States, the predominant power on the isthmus.[4]

Historian Witt claimed that some politically and economically weak states, such as those in Central America, sought to accommodate their economy to that of Germany. They tried to manage the competition of industrial goods from other states in exchange for a privileged role as a raw material source for Germany. Witt argued that "these steps occurred either through massive direct German investment in the important leading sectors of the economy of the specific lands—as a rule in the infrastructure while simultaneously striving for long-term indebtedness to Germany, or through much cheaper, but not less effective, methods such as aid in the expansion and training of the military arms of these small countries and not the least through a muzzling policy of commercial treaties."[5]

The German physical presence on the isthmus had increased significantly by 1914. Around 1910 German investment was estimated at 35 million marks ($8.5 million) in Costa Rica and 42 million marks ($10 million) in Nicaragua. In 1914 German investment in Guatemala was about 300 million marks ($73 million) (Tables 7 and 8). Over 1,000 German males resided in Guatemala, with lesser but appreciable numbers present elsewhere in Central America. The growth of German firms supported estimates of increasing numbers of German residents (Tables 9 and 10).

German trade generally increased rapidly between the 1880s and World War I. The Central American share of that trade held steady, although imports from Germany fared better than the export of Central American products to Germany. Around 1913 the value of Central American products declined to 0.6 percent of German importation (Table 5). Central America absorbed only 0.1 percent of German exports (Table 6), but the German market and products were important for Central American trade. In 1913 Germany absorbed 53 percent, 20 percent, and 18 percent, respectively, of the value of coffee exported from Guatemala, Nicaragua, and El Salvador. Costa Rica and Honduras each sent about 4 percent of their exportation to Germany. German manufacturers captured 20 percent of the Guatemalan importation market, 15 percent of the Costa Rican market, 11 percent of the Salvadoran market, and 9 percent of the Honduran market. German vessels supplied 15 percent of the shipping tonnage serving Salvadoran foreign trade.[6]

Germany pursued objectives to enhance its commercial role. The German search for naval bases and advocacy of the open door in Middle America represented an unexpected challenge to the United States. Minister in the United States Hermann Speck von Sternburg observed that Secretary of State Elihu Root's chief area of interest was Latin America. The U.S. minister in Guatemala was disconcerted when Minister Seefried called for an "open door and fair play" everywhere. The U.S. open door policy—a fair field and no favor—which proclaimed equal access to trade and investment, excluded Latin America because the Monroe Doctrine asserted U.S. priority there. The Henry Cabot Lodge Corollary (1911) to the Monroe Doctrine, for example, rejected any foreign acquisitions that threatened U.S. security. However, German commercial interests needed secure harbors if they intended to participate in the Pacific coast's economic upswing. German diplomat Seelinger observed that "the Americans have followed essentially their own interests in deciding questions related to the canal . . . and they have proceeded with absolute ruthlessness." The United States, another German diplomat argued, hoped to use Panamericanism to achieve "America for the North Americans." Despite Latin American grumbling, he warned, in any serious conflict with a European power, the Latin Americans would cry out for the United States.[7]

European leaders acknowledged the aggressive expansionism of U.S. society at the turn of the century. Russian minister Count Serge Witte expressed his concern to German officials about a Monroe Doctrine that limited Europe but not America. He saw "a great political and economic danger in a United States which pushed itself forward and pursued its goals with raw force and unscrupulous brutality." The German emperor, who shared similar concerns, dreamed of building a European block—anchored in Russian and British support—to challenge the United States. The United States was not the only dynamic nation, however. While German leaders wanted European alliances to stymie U.S. expansion, Great Britain looked at U.S. power as an ally to curtail German expansion.[8]

A German diplomat in Rome speculated that a U.S.-German alliance was possible because U.S. imperialist impulses in the Pacific pitted it against two great sea powers: England and Japan. The naval ministry believed that U.S.-Japanese naval competition increased the need for a German naval presence in Middle American waters. While Germany's reputation demanded a ship in that area, the naval ministry found it impossible to assign a vessel permanently, thus an informal alliance might benefit German interest near the isthmus.[9]

German Ambassador in Washington Johann Heinrich Bernstorff cautioned that the United States and Germany, as expanding states, would find few areas for close cooperation. U.S. participation at the Algeciras conference on North African affairs in 1906 (an outgrowth of Franco-German competition for influence in Morocco) had produced no advantages for Germany. "Since at best German interests can expect only unpleasantness from the United States . . . in South America," he suggested that "only East Asia offers a field where we can work together." He expected efforts to reach an agreement on German-U.S. trade policy to remain the central problem.[10]

Several Central American states seemed eager to encourage European participation on the isthmus. President Cleto González Víquez was conscious of Costa Rica's dependence on the United States. Consul Heye believed that González Víquez, who favored closer ties with Europe and acknowleged Costa Rica's considerable debt to Germans, would encourage the projects of the German residents. The German merchants and planters expected steady economic progress under his administration. The Costa Rican government influenced railroad rates to benefit German interests. Seefried believed that his visit in 1906 had strengthened cooperation within the German colony and helped Costa Ricans form a more favorable opinion of Germany.[11]

Some Central Americans assumed that German-U.S. competition would facilitate the enlistment of German enterprise. In Honduras, Guatemala, and Nicaragua, Seefried encountered interest for a German bank in Central America. In 1906 a German branch bank was ready to open in

Guatemala when, in response to a new banking decree requiring that the manager and some directors of banks with a majority of Guatemalan stockholders be Guatemalan, the German investors canceled the project. In Costa Rica, Schwerin warned that although González Víquez publicly encouraged the formation of a German bank, United Fruit would strive to prevent any alternative source of economic power. Schwerin reported that a widespread fear of the United States, "less of a military intervention than of a business absorption, currently builds the only common ground among the Central American republics." He noted that German capital was desired with a naive openness as a counterweight to U.S. influence. Heye found opportunities for German concessionaires and capital, mentioning specifically a bank, "if unobtrusively formed and, if necessary, its German character were veiled."[12]

German investment, commercial, and communications interest in Nicaraguan projects rose markedly in the early twentieth century. Heye and Hamburg merchants differed vastly about Germany's role in Nicaragua's economy. Heye sharply criticized German economic activity in Nicaragua. For example, German planters chartered French vessels and sold their products in France because Kosmos levied excessive freight charges. German goods were absent from Bluefields because no German merchants resided there. In 1906 a commercial report evaluated extensive U.S. financial and security interests prior to recommending that German capital consider investing in Nicaraguan railroads. When the railroad to Monkey Point, a port on Nicaragua's Caribbean coast, was finally completed, Heye hoped that HAPAG would serve it and Bluefields. He considered banana plantations more profitable and less risky than the railway, but Germans would have to act quickly because Americans were buying up the best banana land. He found it "very regrettable that Germany leaves the exploitation of these lands entirely to the Americans" because Germany's trade and investment were greater than those of the United States.[13]

Heye stressed the need to replace ill-suited German customs with successful U.S. business practices, such as more catalogs in Spanish, more traveling salesmen, and less credit. Hamburg merchants and officials took strong exception to his misleading criticisms. Their sources indicated that Germans purchased most of Nicaragua's coffee, German exports to Nicaragua were not declining, and German manufactures held a major share of the Nicaraguan market. Moreover, they doubted the wisdom of particular U.S. businesses—electric lighting, an ice factory, and a steam cleaner. Furthermore, Hamburg sources insisted that German firms supplied Spanish language catalogs more consistently than any other country and extended credit to take markets away from U.S. products.[14] The Hamburg observations were well-taken.

Hamburg officials also expressed concern about German relations with Honduras. In late 1906 Honduras canceled the Honduran-German postal treaty of 1898, claiming lack of reciprocity. It also canceled the exequatur (a consul's official permission to serve) of Consul Theodore Köhncke at Amapala. The Hamburg Chamber of Commerce asked the German government to intervene on Köhncke's behalf. Without some form of protest, Hamburg officials feared that Germany might appear weak and ineffective, and its trade would suffer. They offered no course of action if Honduras resisted German demands, but they rejected the option of removing exequaturs from Honduran consuls because that step would merely increase the injury to German trade.[15]

In 1910 some German officials saw rosy prospects for German enterprises in Honduras if a loan were negotiated between the House of Morgan and Honduras. Rumors of revolt, however, halted the agreement. The Honduran president told the German minister in the presence of the U.S. minister that Honduras "would gladly welcome a constantly increasing German immigration." The German minister envisioned advantages in mining and agriculture from "a properly directed immigration of Germans under simultaneous investment of German capital." He welcomed the Honduran government's encouragement of a bank to support German businesses because there appeared only sufficient business for one bank and English interests might act first. German capitalists probably needed communications on the east coast to extract full benefit from a bank concession. Since German merchants wished to compete and the fear of unrest had resided, the German government named a commission to study a more effective commercial exchange with Honduras.[16]

Chinese merchants and local disturbances added to the challenge in Honduras. During a disturbance at Amapala in October 1910, a German naval officer suggested that either a German or an allied force should oversee the reestablishment of order. An American druggist, J. E. Foster, whose business was in Nacaome, Honduras, underscored the role of foreign merchants, particularly German and Chinese, who quietly controlled the mercantile interests of nearly all Latin America. He complained that German entrepreneurs often held and used U.S. consular agencies to advance German trade objectives. A prominent German merchant admitted that U.S. power frequently protected other metropole enterprises and he reluctantly hoisted the U.S. flag in time of trouble. He considered the formidable Chinese the future masters of isthmian commerce. He conceded that troubles in Honduras and sharp competition from European and Asiatic merchants who were protected by metropole warships were driving the native merchants out of business.[17]

The efforts of German entrepreneurs to enter Central American fruit and transportation businesses revealed how the metropoles clashed over the distribution of rewards after their cooperation had secured access to economic opportunities in the periphery. Entrepreneurs contemplating entrance into the banana industry had to consider the existing international and domestic transportation systems in the region. In 1908 an agricultural expert attached to the German consulate in Chicago recommended that given the rising demand for bananas in Germany, German capital should invest either in plantations or the importation of bananas to avoid dependence on United Fruit. He advised German entrepreneurs to develop a banana industry in the empire's African colonies or in areas like Nicaragua where suitable land was still available.[18]

The increased foreign penetration of the isthmus hastened the alienation and exploitation of the labor force, which had traditionally followed subsistence work rhythms. The liberal order molded the native workers to fit a wage-labor compensation system that facilitated the exploitation of land and natural resources for the world market. Isthmian labor leaders (especially those employed by foreign enterprises) struggled to organize unions and strengthen workers' capacity to bargain with embryo transnational firms for a fair wage and safe working conditions. An intriguing aspect of the formation of Central American labor movements was their dual antibourgeoisie (as a response to local conditions) and anti-imperialist (as a response to the world economy) characteristics—a contrast to early U.S. and European worker organizations, which focused on antibourgeoisie activity.[19] Isthmian workers recognized the fundamental international aspect of their exploitation.

Racism and assumptions of ethnocentric superiority reared their heads often and served to limit German–Central American relations. Schwerin recommended frequent visits from German warships "to tame the arrogant, absent-minded Latin-Indian race," to rekindle the patriotism of the settlers, and to conduct the military physical required of young German males. He expected such visits to bring "the power of the Empire once again before the eyes of the Central American republics."[20]

German diplomats and businesspeople, given the enormous German stake in Guatemala's economy, were gravely concerned about the possible repercussions of the assassination attempt (probably inspired by President Estrada Cabrera, to eliminate a potential challenger) on former Guatemalan president Manuel Lisandro Barillas in exile in Mexico. Mutual suspicions among the governments of Mexico, Guatemala, and the United States over the incident hindered the reduction of tension. While Germany might obtain short-term commercial gains from a conflict between Mexico and Guatemala, the German minister in Mexico believed that no one would accept responsibility for war damage to German investment in Guatemala. Foreign capitalists generally hoped for U.S. mediation because Mexico felt seriously aggrieved and did not fear war, but the capitalists also hoped to avoid an undesired U.S. puppet state in Guatemala.[21]

Guatemala became an area of considerable U.S.-German political and economic competition. In mid-1909 an analysis of Guatemala's internal and external communications—increasingly dominated by U.S. enterprises—pointed to potential danger spots for German interests. The U.S.-owned Guatemala Central Railroad absorbed the Oriental and Ocos railroads, which virtually ended internal competition, according to German diplomat Eckart von Bonin. He was apprehensive about leaving German businesses dependent on a transportation monopoly in the hands of a powerful competitor. The only exception was Schlubach, Dauch and Company's small Verapáz railroad, which moved the coffee of a few German planters to Livingston or Puerto Barrios. Elsewhere the Guatemala Central Railroad and the Northern Railroad had reached a rate agreement that could bankrupt the poorly maintained Pacific Mail. Then Guatemalan coffee might exit on the Atlantic, causing the Kosmos and Jebsen ship lines, which had maintained their investment, to suffer much more than the Pacific Mail.[22]

In 1913 a German diplomat saw an opportunity to secure the land communications necessary to market Guatemala's coffee. The London firm C. J. Hambro and Son acquired Minor Keith's stock in United Fruit and the International Railways of Central America. Reportedly, Hambro was building a syndicate to control the International Railways of Central America. The German consul general in Great Britain considered the sale of Keith's stock an opportunity to assure German banana and coffee exports through participation in the rail system.[23] He hoped the German government would notify German financial circles. The financial institutions made no large acquisitions of International Railroad shares.

Securing an ample share of the limited opportunity on the isthmus required ingenuity. In 1909 Adolph Stahl formed a syndicate of U.S. participants that negotiated a loan to Guatemala as a thinly veiled scheme to acquire mineral resources and mining concessions. The syndicate asked for land and mineral rights rather than customs revenue as security in case of default. Mining threatened coffee production. Bonin predicted that the higher wages and year-round employment of mining would undermine the labor needs of German coffee plantations. He protested that the U.S. economic conquest of Guatemala "should not occur at the expense of the 160 million marks of German money invested in agricultural land, nor . . . of the 30 million marks invested in German trading firms, nor at the cost of German credit which preserves the market here for German industry." Traveling through Guatemala, he observed, left the impression of traveling through a German colony. This syndicate threatened the accomplishments of the German entrepreneurs.[24]

Hard competition engulfed U.S. and German enterprises more frequently, as businesses from both nations strove to achieve success in a wide variety of ventures. About 1910 a bitter struggle developed between United Fruit and an HAPAG–Atlas shipline–Atlantic Fruit combination. In 1901 United Fruit had sold HAPAG its unprofitable Atlas line, which carried United Fruit bananas from the Caribbean to New York. United Fruit officials were so impressed when HAPAG restored the profitability of Atlas that they offered to repurchase the company. HAPAG rejected the offer. United Fruit then discontinued the use of Atlas vessels in an attempt to erode Atlas's profitability. Atlas, losing this freight, agreed to ship Atlantic Fruit bananas. If Atlantic Fruit "fell under United Fruit control," Seelinger warned, United Fruit would "make it very difficult, if not eternally impossible, for Germany to penetrate that business."[25]

United Fruit controlled the Costa Rican railroad that hauled bananas from the interior, influenced the courts, and exercised power so ruthlessly throughout Middle America and the Caribbean that it enjoyed little sympathy. Its struggle with Atlas and Atlantic Fruit became ugly. Since passenger service revenue was important for Atlas, newer United Fruit ships cooled the passengers' cabins with electric fans and air from the refrigerated fruit rooms. United Fruit delayed the departure of Atlas banana vessels (chartered by Atlantic Fruit) by claiming that the perishable fruit was stolen from its plantations. Atlantic Fruit counterattacked with a suit in the U.S. courts alleging that United Fruit violated antitrust laws.[26]

In 1910 United Fruit spread damaging rumors in Colombia that Atlantic Fruit—which was linked to Atlas and the banana operation of the Hamburg-Colombian Banana Company, Albingia—lacked capital, had inadequate facilities for landing banana boats, and had failed to attract a foreign purchaser. Editorially, the Colombian newspaper *Nuevo tiempo* refuted the charges. The maligning of these German capitalists, the editors concluded, would make attracting other capitalists more difficult. The German minister in Colombia considered the profitability of Albingia a gauge for future investment in the banana trade.[27]

HAPAG was also under attack. It owned Atlas and had participated in founding Albingia. Additional investment in Atlantic Fruit and in banana plantations would probably establish a profitable banana business. Seelinger charged, however, that the Warburg financial firm of New York—with German origins—had withheld capital from Atlantic Fruit in its confrontation with United Fruit. Max Warburg insisted that his firm had joined a European loan syndicate but that because Atlantic Fruit could not meet the conditions, the offer was withdrawn. Seelinger feared that German capital and shipping interests were on the verge of defeat because of woefully inadequate planning. By the fall of 1912, HAPAG was distributing bananas in Holland, Belgium, and the Rhine region to test consumer appeal. Yet Germany only imported 6 percent of Colombia's banana exports. United Fruit competed in Europe for a while, then closed its operation. The intense contest between United Fruit and Atlantic Fruit involved venture and merchant capital and reflected the expectation that bananas would be consumed in sufficient quantities in the United States and Europe.[28]

In mid-1912 the German foreign ministry learned that the railroad carrying bananas and other products to the port of Santa Marta, Colombia, was for sale. A German businessman wanted a Germano-Franco-English syndicate to acquire the railroad. A European syndicate, he stressed, could undercut any charge of violation of the Monroe Doctrine while creating advantages for HAPAG, German banana and mining enterprises, and Germany's export trade. Seelinger presumed that the isthmian states would welcome German capital and entrepreneurs, given their apprehension of U.S. domination.[29]

Failure could occur from competition in the marketplace, but it also existed in other forms, such as criminal activity. When economic depression threatened merchants in Central America with catastrophic losses, some burned down their failing businesses to collect the full value in an insurance settlement. Insurers responded by raising rates or by terminating coverage in certain business sectors. In 1909 Bremen and Hamburg export firms faced major losses when wholesale and retail commerce almost ceased because the Guatemalan government, to prevent business arson, ordered the imprisonment of the owners of insured buildings destroyed by fire until they could prove their innocence. This law threatened foreign wholesalers because local entrepreneurs who wished to avoid the risk of imprisonment did not insure their businesses, yet foreign export firms would not sell to uninsured firms. The Hamburg and Bremen Chambers of Commerce requested the government to prevent the law's application against Germans or any foreigner because non-German merchants handled German products.[30]

French officials and businesses sought to compete more effectively against Germans on the isthmus. Replacing German bankers was not easy. The Deutsche Bank lent $2 million for building a railroad from Guatemala City to Zacapa, but Keith's International Railways of Central America took over the project, intending to pay off the German bank. U.S. capitalists and French officials declined to participate in Keith's loan, which was then floated in London. Beginning in 1908 the French investment firm Banque de Neuflize hoped to claim a niche for French investors despite the powerful position of Germans in Guatemala. The Neuflize agent found that important German-American financiers—the Adolph Stahl firm and the Schwartz brothers of San Francisco—worked regularly with German enterprises. Neuflize's most likely customers in Guatemala were German businesses—Maegl and Company; the Hanseatische Plantagen Gesellschaft [Hansa Plantation Company]; and E. Peper, as agent for various Hamburg firms. Elsewhere in Central America, the Neuflize agent did not discover a predominance for German business and banking.[31]

The French government lamented that German businesses displaced French firms in Latin America and expressed displeasure with the loss of France's material and cultural position. It appreciated the German government's careful reading of the psychology of the Latin American elite, which led Germany to send to Latin America wealthy, ostentatious chiefs of missions whose lifestyle generated influence. French agents needed to exploit elegance and seductive appearance. Yet when French diplomats, for example, extracted favorable terms in the Franco-Salvadoran trade treaty after difficult negotiations, the German government quickly obtained similar concessions. German commercial success was not unblemished. The mark was unstable, so most German businesses billed in dollars rather than marks. Still, French minister Augustin Julien Rigoreau observed, "the German colony in Guatemala was numerous and due to . . . the prosperity they had acquired, their members occupied a preponderant place among the foreigners who came to seek fortune in Guatemala."[32]

The German presence in Central America was strengthened through the successful dissemination of language and culture on the isthmus. Still, the ability and the loyalty of the isthmian Germans were unclear. Many German firms, which considered the natives unreliable, employed large numbers of Germans who would not have advanced far at home. Most Germans wished to preserve their heritage and did not want to become Guatemalans, but Bonin warned of disastrous consequences for the preservation of German influence if young Germans opted for U.S. citizenship because Germany lacked political influence in Guatemala.[33]

Imperial Germany supported the preservation of German culture among migrants to Latin America. The isthmian Germans wanted to build schools and hire teachers, but the imperial government could not fund all the requests it received. In 1912 the German foreign ministry noted that while Guatemala had one of about 700 German schools in Latin America, the Guatemalan school had three of about thirty German teachers in Latin America under contract with the German government (the others were paid from local funds). Latin America was a prime recipient when the Reichstag appropriated 1.5 million marks in 1914 to support schools outside Germany.[34]

Cultural matters intertwined with the political economy. The German-led Catholic church in Costa Rica became enmeshed in politics during the presidential election in 1909. After German businesspeople complained that twenty German priests were campaigning for Rafael Iglesias, Consul Wilhelm Münzenthaler advised Bishop Storck that the activity reflected on other Germans. Storck refused to modify his stance. He publicly endorsed Iglesias and excommunicated a priest who campaigned for another candidate. The bishop pursued policies he thought vital for preserving religious objectives, yet he remained committed to promoting German culture in Costa Rica.[35]

Although Germany occupied third place behind the United States and Britain among Costa Rica's trade partners, the large import firms were German. In addition, Captain Ernst Goette judged that the Germans played a larger social role than any other foreign colony. The German consul in San José warned that the presidential election in 1913 might produce economic disorder, a misfortune for German interests. He argued that the U.S. government welcomed disorder, which it manipulated to subordinate the Latin American governments. He pointed to Nicaragua, where the U.S. government had created disorder because President Zelaya had raised Nicaragua's culture, honor, and justice above the norm for Central America and had threatened to remove Nicaragua from U.S. subservience. The consul warned that a similar U.S. domination of Costa Rica would be a heavy blow to German exportation. While many Germans in Costa Rica "regretted that Germany did not lend [Nicaraguan] President José Madriz at least moral support," Goette disagreed because encouragement of Madriz "would have aroused as much distrust in the United States . . . and thus would have damaged our interests more than aided them."[36]

The Costa Rican government intended to use a German firm and capital to free itself from dependence upon United Fruit. It employed German engineer D. Walther Sprung to evaluate proposed projects on the north coast and the construction firm Julius Berger of Berlin to select a harbor site north of Puerto Limón. Private individuals close to the Costa Rican government approached HAPAG and the Deutsche Bank about investing in the project, but both firms indicated that they would only consider participation once the work was more advanced. The German consul recognized that "certain circles" in Costa Rica "hope for German financial help to counteract the groping influence of Americanism."[37]

Costa Ricans praised Germans, the German minister reported, and expressed a strong anti-American sentiment. President Jiménez was eager to attract Germans and to avoid U.S. immigrants. Schwerin endangered the culture bonding that underlay the sympathy for German residents when he called the marriage of young German males to local women a cancer in the German community. The praise for Germans as immigrants was derived in large part from their willingness to commingle with Central Americans.[38] German financial interests seldom ventured beyond the realm defined by German entrepreneurs on the isthmus.

German influence from intermarriage was well represented in the new Costa Rican cabinet of 1914. Although the minister of trade and finance had worked for United Fruit, German consul Wilhelm Erythropel did not consider him particularly responsive to U.S. influence because his brother-in-law was the German vice consul. The minister of public works had a German business partner and a German sister-in-law. The minister of war had a German brother-in-law. Erythropel observed that "most of the ministers have sympathy for Germans, from which sympathy we can hopefully win some advantage for our trade relations."[39]

The German consul general in New York interpreted the U.S. protectorate of Nicaragua as an effort to eliminate European trade from Central

America. Naturally, German agents devoted special attention to U.S. monopolistic tendencies, which were hostile toward German entrepreneurial spirit. An article in the *Commercial and Financial Chronicle,* a journal "J. P. Morgan and his friends influence," acknowledged German entrepreneurs as energetic and methodical in developing control of trade on the west coast of South America. When U.S. merchants finally awoke, the article warned, they would confront an established German presence. In early 1910 the New Orleans *Times Democrat* expected that J. P. Morgan's New York banking firm would bring Central American trade "under American control, and German trade, especially the coffee trade which had gravitated toward Hamburg, should be pushed out if possible."[40]

German firms pursued weapons sales on the isthmus. Nicaragua's military successes against Honduras and El Salvador in a brief war in 1907 impressed on Costa Rica its own inferiority to the Nicaraguan army. Costa Rica intended to purchase Remington weapons, but the Krupp agent captured the order. When the situation in Central America became less hostile, the order was canceled. Then, new perceived dangers prompted the Costa Rican government to plan to spend approximately 1 million marks to acquire weapons secretly in Europe. Since Krupp demanded cash, the government sought a 1 million mark loan from a German bank, but it had a poor credit rating because it had stopped payment on some loans. The president asked Congress to negotiate with Costa Rica's creditors, and he appealed to the German government for "assistance to get out of its current embarrassment" because Costa Rica had "given large orders to German firms." Costa Rica was good for 1 million marks, Münzenthaler insisted, because its customs income and alcohol tax were unencumbered.[41]

German industry pursued arms orders elsewhere on the isthmus. In 1911 agents for German arms producers lost a Honduran order for 30,000 carbines to the French arms industry. The German arms industry competed in Guatemala despite the powerful hold of the French military. Guatemala instructed its minister in Europe to visit the German Arms and Munitions Factory [Deutsche Waffen- und Munitions-Fabrik] to view machinery that might be acquired for a factory in Guatemala. When Krupp received an order for two artillery batteries in April 1914, the German minister became suspicious. He thought the French had encouraged the acquisition in order to place Germany in a bad light before the United States, which was engaged in a conflict with Mexico. World War I intervened to cancel the delivery.[42]

The prospect of a functioning canal sharpened competitive spirits and burdened U.S.-German relations, which had deteriorated steadily since the 1880s. In mid-1910, with the Panama canal nearing completion, the U.S. government amazed the German government by demanding a denial of any intention to acquire the Galápagos Islands. Later, although the United States retreated from this aggressive stance after declaring that it would never approve the sale or mortgaging of the Galápagos, U.S. distrust of German activity remained. French minister Jules Jusserand observed that "the German government shares the honor with the Japanese government" of always being under suspicion in Washington.[43]

German officials expected German firms to participate in an economic upswing on the west coast of Latin America after the canal opened. Seelinger assumed that HAPAG-Atlas, Kosmos, Roland, Nord Deutsche Lloyd, Hansa, and the German-owned Australian steamship companies wanted to share in the anticipated development. "Trade, industry, banks, and shipping should join together," he proposed, and "in goal-oriented, systematic proceedings strive to exploit the new economic situation created through the opening of the new communication route." He questioned whether German shippers should even seek a coaling site near the canal zone because the Lodge Corollary threatened any foreign acquisition there and the coaling operation could not function in a crisis. The Danish West Indies or Jamaica offered alternative coaling stations. He insisted that "the Panama canal will create . . . a great struggle to open lands still undeveloped economically and to shape new communications routes and new consumer markets." German colonists in Panama disturbed the U.S. government. However, given the widespread fear of the United States in the Hispanic countries, Seelinger expected German entrepreneurs to encounter a friendly reception.[44]

The modern communications tool—radio—loomed large in canal security. Radio's capacity to contact vessels, including submarines, in the Caribbean area rendered it a threat to ship traffic entering or leaving a canal. Despite decided U.S. opposition to "foreign" interests initiating wireless stations, German entrepreneurs ventured into radio communications on the isthmus. In 1913 a German telegraph company's plan for a wireless radio station in El Salvador was delayed because Salvadoran revenue was insufficient to maintain the project. In 1913 Telefunken's agents—Schlubach, Dauch and Company—erected a radio antenna in Guatemala City. With Empresa Eléctrica's support, Schlubach sought a concession for a nationwide radio station for Telefunken. It and Empresa were affiliated with Siemens. In light of U.S. opposition, the German government valued the Salvadoran and Guatemalan radio stations.[45]

In mid-1911 Egon Schaar, agent for a German concession in Puerto de Piñas, Panama, which included the best harbor site in the Gulf of Panama and the right to build a railroad, approached Minister Bernstorff regarding the sale of this concession to the U.S. government. Earlier, Schaar had persuaded the New York investment house Speyer and Company to supply capital for a German railroad project, until U.S. interference prompted Speyer to withdraw. U.S. intervention had earlier nullified the concession's right to extend its railroad to Panama City. Since the U.S. government assigned great strategic value to the harbor, German diplomats suspected that the concession would have to be transferred to U.S. interests because political factors kept German capital from exploiting the opportunities.[46]

When an English financial figure inquired whether the German government or German capitalists would be interested in a Colombian Atrato canal project, the government rejected participation in "a canal competitive with the Panama canal." To avoid wounding U.S. sensibility about a competitive canal, the project was revised to call for a railroad to the banana region. German interests welcomed a railroad because this region's rich agricultural land and mineral deposits lacked transportation and labor. Albingia held a concession near the proposed Atrato route. Hoping to avoid U.S. complaints, German diplomats wanted private interests to acquire the extensive land holdings. They expected German entrepreneurs to receive encouragement to develop an alternative to hated U.S. capital.[47]

Official and private German interests were manifest near the Panama canal. The French government believed that the Germans intended to use a canal concession at Atrato to compete better for markets on the west coast. The U.S. chief of staff representing the U.S. military predicted strategic problems if the Germans acquired a valid concession to a feasible route, but U.S. government officials considered the Atrato concession worthless. The French minister in Colombia recognized that "to avoid the attention of the United States, German diplomacy operated behind private businesses." Since HAPAG and Nord Deutsche Lloyd extended their west coast service to take advantage of the canal opening, the German government considered sending a vessel there periodically. The German navy's espionage activity near the canal encountered effective U.S. countermeasures. Despite disturbances in the Caribbean–Central American area in early 1914, the naval ministry recommended a minimum response until Germany possessed a base to support operations.[48]

German entrepreneurs and investors saw few reasons to refuse commercial and investment opportunities in the isthmian area. Financiers, shippers, and food wholesalers expected German resources to establish a production and distribution system to supply Europe with bananas. United Fruit resisted HAPAG experiments in the banana business. Parties on both sides of the Atlantic underlined the strategic and political aspects of such commercial activity. German financiers and geopoliticians also contemplated a jointly owned canal project and other investments that would strengthen German presence on the isthmus. A competitive canal found little support, but other communications projects won sympathy. The principal alternative transit targets were the Atrato region of Colombia, the Puerto de Piñas area in Panama, and Nicaragua. Other German investors focused on Costa Rican, Nicaraguan, or Guatemalan railroad opportunities (some of which were interoceanic routes), arguing that such projects were less likely to generate determined U.S. opposition. In some manner, Germans competed for most concessions on the isthmus.

Some German leaders sought a larger role for the German military. They considered naval stations, the establishment of military missions, and weapons sales as appropriate expressions of imperial geopolitical interests in the Caribbean and isthmian area. U.S. entrepreneurs and officials warned of the danger inherent in German penetration of a U.S. security zone. For some Americans, the Roosevelt and Lodge corollaries to the Monroe Doctrine justified the allegations. German economic, diplomatic, and maritime interests normally recognized their mutual interdependence and the relationship of their combined power to successful competition with other imperialist powers.

9

■

U.S. Displacement of German Economic Power during World War I

Before the Great War the German government had used colonization, investment, trade, and cultural institutions to compete for influence and prestige on the periphery. It expected these ingredients to generate the mix of popular, elite, and governmental influences necessary to expand German economic activity and to enrich the German migrants, the transient merchants, and homeland firms and investors. The expanding German empire challenged France, Great Britain, and the United States because its entrepreneurs achieved outstanding material success. Part of the success was due to the adoption of organized capitalism—cooperative, planned activity of the German government and private enterprise—in the pre–World War I decades. Germans lost much property in Central America (and Latin America) between 1914 and 1918, as their success was undone. In the postwar years recapturing momentum on the isthmus was considered important because the German economy would need to recover its domestic vitality and foreign ties to rebuild German well-being.[1]

The burgeoning U.S. political economy used the disruption of World War I to undermine German, French, and British activity in Central America. The war seriously burdened the ability of all European powers to supply shipping for trade or capital and technology to continue existing operations or implement uncompleted projects. Moreover, as the war endured, the need of all engaged European powers for revenue nudged taxes up and prompted entrepreneurs to liquidate foreign interests. Often these foreign holdings could not be maintained properly and their sale generated funds for the home office. Existing U.S. entrepreneurs and enterprises as well as new investors encountered opportunities in these wartime sales. Although the German government had planned to use force in the Caribbean in the event of war with the United States, in 1914 the United States did not go to war. Since U.S. policy could lead to eventual entry into the war, German officials pondered covert steps to stifle U.S. economic activity in the Caribbean–Central American area. They gathered information about U.S. military status, food and raw material movements, use of communications, and other activities. The U.S. government, even before declaring war, reduced German influence near the interoceanic routes and tried to replace German investments in Central America. Later, the United States and the allies called on wartime emotions to continue to undermine German interests even after the peace settlement, while German businesses and officials were struggling to salvage what they could.[2]

During the war, German direct trade and maritime activity with the isthmian states either dried up or were conducted clandestinely through straw men and dummy corporations. In the early postwar years, the Central American countries purchased less than 0.2 percent of the annual German exports (Table 6). During the war some German capital fled, while much of the rest was sequestered. In 1914, 2 percent of Germany's 20 billion marks of foreign investment were placed in Central America. German investment in Guatemala was estimated at 250 million marks ($60 million), in Nicaragua at 40 million marks ($10 million), and in Costa Rica at 35 million marks ($8.5 million). At war's end, in 1918, German investment in Guatemala was estimated at 867 million inflated marks and in 1920 at 1–2 billion inflated marks (Table 7). By 1918 German investment in Nicaragua had shrunk to $2.5 million, about a quarter of its prewar value.[3] In dollar terms, German capital on the isthmus shrunk appreciably during the war, but it remained a player with significant potential.

Central American leaders discovered that metropoles gave the social and economic needs and objectives of the periphery a low priority during a world crisis. The leaders from the periphery were scarcely allowed to participate in decisions about access to resources; the allocation of land, labor, and capital; or the distribution of production. One powerful but often overlooked critique of the metropoles, most of which espoused a marketplace outlook, is that their leaders, when confronted with a grave crisis, abandoned the market economy for centralized planning (for example, during World War I). They did not use socialist models for these excursions into a centralized, planned economy, because such models would have restricted private accumulation, required an equitable price-wage mechanism, and limited the use of gain for projects of social utility. Instead, they relied on organized capitalist models that permitted continued privatization of profits, manipulation of price-wage mechanisms to enhance the extraction of wealth from the workforce, and distribution of costs and burdens to the whole society. Even while building the centralized planning agencies, the elite continued to advocate a market economy. It needed to justify the continued individualization of wealth (if the wealth was produced by social effort, no one individual had a claim to a larger share of it) during the period of public, planned economic growth, and it intended to return to a private management of the economy at war's end. In the immediate postwar years, the metropole governments and businesses reinstituted limited market-controlled relations with Central America, after they reasserted their authority over the financial and distribution institutions so that they could resist the pressure to increase raw material prices.[4] Organized capitalism maintained individual and collective arguments so that one view could be called on when profits were distributed (individualism) and the other when costs, losses, or burdens had to be dealt with (collective responsibility).

The German residents drew on their material success and sociocultural reputation in Central America to conduct a successful propaganda contest with Britain and France during World War I. German diplomats and residents, especially in Guatemala and Honduras, obtained influence in the local press after war broke out and monitored allied propaganda work. Key to an effective propaganda system was raising funds for those subsidies the local papers required to print dispatches arriving from abroad. A "friendly" (subsidized) editor could supply access to the educated readership, and an "unfriendly" (unsubsidized) editor eliminated the viewpoint of one side. German minister Kurt Lehmann claimed that cables arriving over the signature of a German official received even greater credence than items from U.S. news correspondents in Berlin. Three Guatemalan newspapers, *El Eco alemán*, *La República*, and the weekly *La Esfera*, received subsidies to print items favorable to the German war effort. *El Eco alemán* was placed under the care of Dr. H. Schnitzler—a major figure in German propaganda in Latin America—after *La República* refused to print one of his articles. German businesspeople agreed to purchase enough advertising in *El Eco alemán* to pay for cables from the German-American Chamber of Commerce of New York. If this project flourished, Lehmann intended to ask the government for aid to continue.[5]

The German colony in Guatemala—cut off from its coffee and merchant income and facing declining land values and decreasing rental revenues—exhausted its resources in subsidizing the three newspapers.

When a Belgian pamphlet attacking Germany appeared in Guatemala, Lehmann used government funds to bear three-fourths of the cost of a response; *El Eco alemán* paid the remaining fourth. In March 1915 Lehmann reported that the newspaper subsidies would end in May unless the government assumed payment. If the imperial government could afford to contribute 2,000 marks per month, he could supply *El Eco alemán* with 1,000 marks per month, *La República* with 500 marks per month, and continue *La Esfera* and other propaganda activity. He considered the propaganda effective and he wanted to send *El Eco alemán* free to selected local leaders. The foreign minister agreed to supply 2,000 marks monthly, but he wanted the propaganda to reach native circles where papers like *El Eco alemán* apparently had little access.[6]

Lehmann saw potential advantage from distributing several hundred free copies of the Spanish-language edition of the *Hamburger Nachrichten* in Guatemala; however, the cost raised problems. If the paper could not be distributed free, he inquired whether merchants in Bremen, Hamburg, and Latin America could cover distribution expenses. Otherwise, a small subscription price might keep the news within reach of the intended audience.[7]

It was also necessary to subsidize propaganda work in areas without German settlers but where the empire wished to present its story. Schlubach, Thiemer, and Company and the German residents in Guatemala wanted the war reports sent to El Salvador. The Schlubach firm, which raised and spent 156,000 marks in Guatemala, noted: "This news service has been precisely a necessity for Germandom abroad because Germany's opponents in foreign areas have shaped public opinion in this manner for years." Walther Dauch of Schlubach doubted that the colony could afford the additional expense of regular cables to El Salvador. Still, Schlubach partner Dr. Karl Sapper, functioning as an intelligence agent, ordered the news cabled to El Salvador at the expense of the legation in Guatemala.[8] The foreign ministry wanted propaganda disseminated beyond Guatemala.

In Honduras, German residents raised 16,000 marks to support the war effort and several newspapers, including the official church newspaper, *Amigo del pueblo*, which published information sympathetic to Germany. Two German priests called this an example of the political side-benefits from cultural influence. The Honduran government brushed aside the protest of French merchants against German propaganda with an observation about freedom of the press. Despite the large sums raised in the early burst of enthusiasm, the propaganda campaigns endured only when the Germans or their government could cover regular subsidies. The subsidies severely taxed the wealth of Germans on the isthmus, who raised a half million marks in cash in addition to contributions of goods and services.[9]

The propaganda successes delayed the U.S. goal of replacing German investments in Central America. Entente agents counterattacked. The combined propaganda assault of the United States, Britain, and France led to the sequestration of German property and the jailing or exiling of many Germans throughout Middle America, except in El Salvador. Despite the labor of *El Eco alemán* and *La República,* the French minister in Central America judged that popular opinion increasingly sympathized with the entente cause. British agents found ample outlet for their cables in Guatemala and suppressed German cables headed toward Honduras. Lehmann conceded that the entente propaganda weakened the value of German capital in Guatemala and undermined German propaganda.[10]

Predictably, the war raised havoc with the budgets of the Central American countries because the reduced trade sliced ominously into customs revenue. Honduran revenues suffered a drastic decrease and Guatemala's political economy was in shambles due to disrupted international economic activity. Germans owned so much property in Guatemala, especially in the coffee business, that it was impossible to act against them without magnifying Guatemala's crisis. When U.S. diplomats pressured Guatemala to sever relations with Germany, yet U.S. interests were unwilling to purchase the coffee harvest, Guatemala faced unhappy Germans and a sour economy. U.S. intelligence sources detected a danger of revolution, sparked by disgruntled Germans.[11]

In late 1917 the Guatemalan government, facing mounting financial hardship, asked the U.S. government to allow it to export coffee and sugar. It assured U.S. officials that while it would have to purchase crops from some Germans, it would see that none profited from this activity. Guatemala warned that without access to this revenue, it could not pay principal or interest on its loans, which would result in grave international consequences. It did not expect the United States to "permit such misfortune to buffet a friendly and brother nation." One report projected "a heaven sent opportunity for crushing German commercial supremacy and with it, accompanying German intrigue and propaganda in the richest and strongest country of Central America" if the U.S. government vigorously aided Estrada Cabrera's government.[12] It is not clear whether the U.S. government allowed the sale.

Entente and central power officials engaged in a tug-of-war for the sympathy and support of Costa Rican society. The Costa Rican government wished to preserve its neutrality, but missteps by its citizens as well as metropole pressure pulled it toward war. The Costa Rican government was embarrassed in late 1914 when its minister in the United States, Roberto Brenés Mesén, issued a provisional patent to a British coaling vessel. Then in early 1917 a powerful radio station possessed jointly by a friend of former president Alfredo González and by his German adviser, Juan Kümpel, was destroyed in Heredia, Costa Rica. Costa Rican minister Peralta warned that the clandestine radio station and the coaling vessel affair lent credence to charges that Costa Rica was not neutral. He insisted that it must not lend further support to that charge.[13]

The activities of entente citizens in Costa Rica further endangered its neutrality. The French consul in San José persuaded the Costa Rican Chamber of Commerce to distribute some leaflets that boosted a Lyon Fair as an alternative to the prestigious Leipziger Messe (fair) and disparaged Germany and Austria. The German members resigned, endangering the existence of the chamber. Minor Keith, president of the chamber, personally requested them to withdraw their resignations. After the chamber took appropriate action, they rejoined. The Germans regretted that Keith, who had expressed opposition to Germany, had responded inadequately to the French propaganda. Some Germans questioned his suitability to continue as HAPAG agent, while others argued that given his business ability, reputation, and influence, his incorrect political views were probably not the best grounds for removing him.[14] Metropole entrepreneurs constantly faced the dilemma of choosing between actions that served their firm's, as opposed to their government's, best interests.

The outbreak of war resurrected the discussion of a German coaling station on the west side of Panama. In 1914 Gustav Krautiger offered to sell the German government a coaling station site near the Panama canal. The government considered a station superfluous because its vessels were required to take on coal during the docking in Colón. In 1915 a retired German major, working for the Balboa Pacific Estates Company, noted that the British and Japanese were keeping coaling vessels in Puerto Piñas, Panama. The German government rejected his recommendation to build a coaling and radio station there. It also received an offer of a site at Areal in Chiriquí province, but the U.S. government opposed any strengthening of Germany's position on the isthmus. In fact, by mid-1916 the U.S. government had adopted precautionary surveillance of Germans in the Canal Zone. In early 1918 a German diplomat in Stockholm wanted to know if he should delay the sale of the Balboa Pacific Estates

Company for 300,000 marks to allow the German government to tender a bid. The foreign minister rejected any acquisition of Panamanian terrain, however, because the navy could not defend it.[15]

Entente control of sea routes hampered German merchant activity in Central America. Merchants from the entente nations were creeping into areas normally dominated by German traders. British business was moderately effective in supplanting German enterprises, but French businesses experienced such financial problems that they were unable to take advantage of Germany's difficulties. German businesses fought back. Over 1,700 German individuals or firms organized an Economic Group for South and Middle America to resist decline. The government projected minimal economic losses from a short war, but it presumed that U.S. firms would profit most from a long war. German trade was expected to recover after the war, if credit was made available.[16]

All metropoles valued radio stations in the Caribbean–Central American region, but the U.S. government considered any metropole radios near the isthmus a threat to canal transit. During the war, the Germans sought to retain the use of various radio stations in Colombia, Central America, and Mexico. A German radio agent and his wife who lived in San Andrés, a Colombian island near Panama City, sent clandestine radio messages until both collapsed of nervous fatigue from constant surveillance. Such radio stations linked Germany with the Pacific Ocean region as well as the Middle American–Caribbean area. The assault on German radio traffic was widespread: on the one hand, the British, French, U.S., and Portuguese governments claimed that the German stations violated the neutrality of the host country; on the other, the U.S. government monitored German radio and telegraph cables in the Caribbean and censored German message traffic with Latin America and Asia even before it declared war on Germany. German agents schemed to acquire a radio station on the isthmus beyond U.S. censorship, while U.S. officials labored to deny them a station outside its supervision. After the war, the Japanese government joined German radio interests to protest U.S. policies of exclusion.[17]

Mexico, in conflict with the United States after 1913, supported German objectives in Central America as a means to divert U.S. attention elsewhere. Peralta was concerned that Mexican leader Venustiano Carranza planned to extend the German-Mexican alliance into Central America. He urged his government to avoid such a scheme because he expected the proposal of German foreign minister Alfred Zimmermann—which involved an alliance of Germany, Mexico, and Japan if the

United States entered the war—to collapse, and he did not want Costa Rica buried in the debris. Mexico became a spot for plotting against U.S. interests. The U.S. military attaché in Mexico suggested—though he had no evidence—that Adolph Stahl, "the leading German [actually German-American] banker of Guatemala," was acquiring weapons for Guatemala, El Salvador, and Mexico and had established a German submarine base near Puerto Barrios. He proposed that United Fruit employees should monitor wireless activity in the Caribbean.[18]

Mexican and German agents judged that Salvadoran officials might share their desire to limit U.S. penetration of Central America, in part because U.S. officials aggressively sought to control Fonseca Bay. Just after Zimmermann's note to Mexico was made public, Mexico presented the Salvadoran government with a Telefunken wireless radio station and several water-based airplanes. U.S., British, and Spanish diplomats expected the Telefunken system to serve German interests and to spread German propaganda in El Salvador. The Salvadoran and Mexican governments pursued an anti-U.S. policy. Yet Salvadoran criticism of U.S. policy in Fonseca Bay was muffled after the U.S. declaration of war on Germany. In early 1918 the Honduran government compelled the German consul to leave Fonseca Bay and seized several German lighters, which the U.S. government wanted turned over to the New York Honduras Rosario Mining Company. German consul D. Drechsel considered these actions a new sign of U.S. desire to dominate Fonseca Bay.[19]

U.S. policy was rather indifferent to which national interests were removed to make room for U.S. capital and entrepreneurs. Displacing any metropole interest increased U.S. security and well-being. The German consul in Costa Rica claimed that British, French, and Italian entrepreneurs were in no position to replace German capital, so U.S. firms were the principal threat. Until late 1915, however, U.S. merchants had little success in acquiring the German share of the import market. Nevertheless, German political economist Hermann Levy did not see U.S. competition for trade as a great danger to postwar Germany, unless the United States acquired special, unfair advantages. If this pitfall could be avoided, he expected German trade to rebound strongly once goods were available again.[20]

Guatemalans who looked on German pervasiveness with disfavor used the war to reduce German privilege. In one significant act, it terminated the bilateral trade agreement. Hamburg Syndicus Dr. Gutschow regretted the lapse of the Guatemalan-German trade treaty, which contained three clauses advantageous for Germany: (1) the most-favored-nation clause,

(2) the assurance that children born in Guatemala to German parents would remain German nationals, and (3) an arrangement placing inheritance matters under the control of the consulate. This third matter was important because it shielded German estates from suits by illegitimate children who had the same inheritance rights as legitimate children under Guatemalan law. Guatemala's elite had long opposed the clause that preserved German nationality for children born in Guatemala. Still, Gutschow speculated that if Germany had objected strongly, Guatemala would not have terminated the treaty. In his opinion, Germany could scarcely conceive of a more favorable treaty and should strive to resurrect it after the war. The U.S. minister insisted that "too much stress can scarcely be laid upon the strong position of the German colonists," who owned all the large enterprises in Guatemala except for United Fruit and the International Railways of Central America. He and the French minister considered the treaty's termination a severe blow to German prestige.[21]

In addition to confiscation of German property used in commerce, the entente powers blacklisted firms that traded with the central powers. The blacklist aimed to deprive Germany of raw materials and to destroy its financial and commercial power. German businesses avoided the entente net by using dummy firms such as the Dutch Nederlandsche Handel Maatshappy to trade in neutral Scandinavia and Holland. In 1915 the French consul protested that thinly disguised German goods arrived in Panama on Dutch or Italian ships. When the British tightened restrictions against ships carrying goods for Germans, the Dutch and Italian firms closed down. French officials were ardent about the blacklist. French chargé Chayet complained that British minister Alban Young protected German trade over Belize, avoided public condemnation of German activity, and blamed the French for blacklisting. Despite Chayet's charges, one German in Guatemala credited the British spy network with making the blacklist effective. Not all "allied" powers welcomed the blacklist. Some German agro-businesspeople of Guatemala circumvented the blacklist by selling to U.S. middlemen. Allegedly, Estrada Cabrera was unhappy with the blacklist because it affected "too many of his German friends."[22]

The hostility in Europe could adjust to New World conditions. In late 1917 the Bremen Chamber of Commerce supported retaining English citizen Hugo Fleischmann at Quetzaltenango as the German consular agent because he was protecting German interests. Moreover, the ruptured international communications would hamper any search for a suitable replacement. The fact that German property in Guatemala had remained untouched spoke strongly in favor of Fleischmann. The chamber worried that any effort to displace him might direct his appreciable influence against German interests.[23]

After the U.S. government entered the war in April 1917, the Central American republics were under pressure to sever relations with Germany. All except El Salvador complied, but only Guatemala and Costa Rica declared war. However, Estrada Cabrera insisted that the German residents need not fear any special burden, and the public received Guatemala's declaration of war on Germany without enthusiasm. Still, Max Obst—a longtime resident of Guatemala, a manager of Empresa Eléctrica prior to the war, and a former diplomat—claimed that after the break in relations, the government adopted surveillance, domestic passports, and armed guards to observe some Germans. Generally it dropped these measures after a brief period. German coffee plantations in Guatemala suffered from the depressed economy. The Nicaraguan population did not disturb Germans in the domestic trade and the Nicaraguan government resisted pressure to confiscate German property.[24] With a few exceptions, the Germans in Guatemala and Nicaragua were treated normally after relations were severed.

In Costa Rica, usurper Federico Tinoco's coup overthrew Alfredo González Flores's government, awoke the unrepenting displeasure of Woodrow Wilson, and complicated the role of German residents. Tinoco's government hoped to win recognition by conforming to U.S. wishes. Costa Rica's agent in Washington informed the secretary of state that it had dismissed five Germans serving as consuls, including its consul in Boston, as proof of the merit of Tinoco's government. Although Costa Rican officials assured German agents that the break in relations did not endanger Germans and their property, they conducted surveillance of "suspicious" Germans who might attempt reprisals. Still, the U.S. government refused recognition.[25]

According to Dr. Vincente Castro Cervantes, the Costa Rican public considered the decision to sever relations with Germany not an unfriendly act but the consequence of U.S. pressure. Costa Ricans preferred German imperialism, which was based on education, technology, culture, and military power, he insisted, to U.S. imperialism, which was based on the "Shylock principle" of extracting a pound of flesh and immorality. He expected Germany to remain a force in the world after the war.[26]

In late 1917 U.S. intelligence agents linked considerable German activity to Costa Rica. They believed that the Mexican and even the U.S. mail services carried correspondence between Costa Rica and Germany through the Swiss and Swedish legations. Supposedly, Archbishop Storck forwarded funds to Germany through the Catholic Church in Switzerland. Confidential British evaluations discounted the allegations of improper German influence in Costa Rica. The British consul in San José rejected the wild charges that German priests controlled Costa Rican public schools and taught "Germanism and anti-Americanism." First, priests were not allowed to teach in the public schools and, second, the few German priests who taught in private schools had "little if any effect on the great majority of the population." Likewise, he denied that the Germans were unmolested and prospering. All German export business was halted, and German coffee merchants were unable to buy coffee from third parties. A few German businesses avoided the hindrance. Some found third parties who fronted for sales, while others conducted internal commerce. The British consul could not understand the nervousness, because "in the entente countries, Germans of good behavior are guaranteed personal and property security."[27]

A. T. Harrison, a longtime U.S. resident in Costa Rica, emphasized that the revolt of Federico (and his brother Joaquín) Tinoco against González Flores "was in no sense a protest against German influence and was purely of local and personal interest." The brutal treatment of Juan Kümpel, a talented but conceited person, was not an expression of anti-Germanism but of his anti-Tinoco activity in Costa Rican politics. Tinoco charged Kümpel with organizing a pro-German revolt in order to justify the brutal treatment of one of the few Germans who publicly supported Germany's war effort. Many Germans could scarcely leave Costa Rica, however, because they were unable to assure their property. In early 1918 Tinoco tried to win U.S. recognition by severing relations with Germany and sequestering German property, but his government left the German community undisturbed, except for Kümpel and other supporters of González Flores.[28]

In 1918 the González Flores faction spread a rumor that Germans had aided Tinoco and that Tinoco in turn sympathized with Germany. U.S. intelligence officials discounted the charges that Tinoco's government was allowing Germans to aid Germany in any appreciable form. U.S. and French intelligence acknowledged that Bishop Storck and other Germans circulated anti-entente propaganda and that these activities were not interfered with if done quietly. Several U.S. officials criticized Storck's *La Nueva era.* One recommended suppressing it because it was "violently anti-American and strictly 'neutral,' i.e. pro-German." One U.S. intelligence official suggested that any plan for a German plot against the Panama canal would likely be found in a modern steel vault in Juan Knohr's new building in San José. He reported, however, that most Germans in Costa Rica "refrained from active participation in the war."[29]

On April 23, 1918, Estrada Cabrera's Guatemala reluctantly declared war on Germany. Later, it seized the property of those German firms that supplied a public service. It named a U.S. engineer, Daniel B. Hogdsdon, as intendant general to manage these properties. Guatemalan-German relations deteriorated after October 1918, when the Guatemalan government, responding to U.S. pressure, confiscated Empresa Eléctrica. Hogdsdon managed the enterprise with a German staff because he could not find qualified replacements. Siemens claimed that the loss of Empresa, "an essential supporting point for the continual marketing of Siemens electro-technical products in Guatemala," seriously impaired the market for electrical products.[30]

Estrada Cabrera had always conducted business with Germans in coffee and sugar. He used straw men to continue to do so during the war. While he had assured the allies that no coffee would leave German plantations, one German sold his coffee to Spanish middlemen. Estrada Cabrera delayed the confiscation and sale of enemy property because he collected $.50 per sack exported. French officials were very disappointed when Estrada Cabrera hesitated to act against German interests. They had awarded the Grand Croix de la Légion d'honneur to him and lesser honors to other Guatemalan officials. They believed that Estrada Cabrera's real estate holdings in Germany, estimated at between 40 million marks and 100 million francs ($10–20 million at prewar exchange rates), influenced Guatemalan-German relations.[31]

The confiscation and sale of Empresa Eléctrica prompted Siemens, owners of a large share of Empresa, businessman Friedrich Köper from Bremen, and local planter Erwin Paul Dieseldorff to inquire nervously at the German foreign ministry about countermeasures. Thirty-six firms initiated the Hamburg Association of Guatemalan Firms to monitor German interests. The Hamburg Association wanted an arbitrator to settle property disputes between Germans and the Guatemalan government. In late 1918 the German and U.S. governments agreed that no further liquidations of German property would take place after the armistice because neither Guatemala nor its citizens had suffered war damages. Dieseldorff feared that the loss of over 100 million marks of property would so seriously injure retail houses that any hope of exporting German manufactures would disappear. However, Germany could apply pressure to settle property confiscation claims because it purchased almost all of Guatemala's coffee. Other shadows darkened the situation. The forced liquidation of property where money was scarce produced large losses, and Guatemala's confiscation policy encouraged Germans to surrender their citizenship to avoid the penalty of being German. Köper believed that the confiscations indicated the improper intentions of the U.S. government and the need for the German government to intervene, for U.S. success in Guatemala might prove destructive to German interests in other countries. The U.S. government hinted in early 1919 that Guatemala's invitation to the Paris Peace Conference depended on a general confiscation decree. The invitation arrived six days after the confiscation decree was issued.[32] Guatemala acted against German property in response to U.S. pressure. Still, the confiscation created an opportunity for Estrada Cabrera and several North Americans to make a fortune.

Germans in coffee production often faired well, while those in commerce faced a troubled time in postwar Guatemala. German resident Adrian Rösch claimed that the Guatemalan declaration of war proved a boon to many German coffee barons, particularly the absentee landlords, because Guatemala required that all profits be invested in a Guatemalan credit institute. The administrator of the German fincas sold the coffee, distributed funds to keep the fincas operating, and deposited the rest in banks. Then in 1920 the finca owners reacquired both their coffee plantations and the undistributed income in hard currency. German merchants, who without the ability to send capital to Germany could not purchase goods there, interpreted a restriction on capital repatriation in the postwar years as an attempt to destroy them and injure German recovery.[33]

Planning for a recovery of Germany's role in the isthmian economies began shortly after the war started. Various German entrepreneurs, intellectuals, and government agents speculated about a postwar political economy and society. In 1915 an economic analyst proposed constructing new mercantilist (or "state socialism") institutions—such as importation monopolies, a state policy for stockpiling raw materials, state control of raw material prices, the use of profits from the raw material monopoly to promote trade expansion, and tariff protection—that would be useful in the postwar years. The new mercantilist world order would require state-guided social and economic policy, thus changing Germany's domestic economy. The Committee of Economic Organizations to Advance German Demands on Enemy Countries viewed the future differently. It found that the government was not taking adequate steps to protect Germans and their capital in foreign areas. The government needed a speedy commercial revival after the war. Germany's future would depend on official support for foreign trade.[34]

Near war's end, the Hamburg government and merchants circulated a highly confidential report, "Hamburg's Proposals for the New Orientation of Germany's Foreign Service," which contended that the foreign service of a world power had to eschew the passive role of protector and adopt aggressive conduct to promote its political economy. To achieve this goal, the report urged establishing a political reputation to match Germany's military and commercial position. The Hamburg Chamber of Commerce wanted commercial groups drawn into the decision-making process.[35]

The German naval staff reacted with a proposal that stressed geopolitical considerations and recommended selecting only older military men for the consular and diplomatic corps. It hoped to preserve Germany's world power status by developing a strong navy or by reaching an understanding with Great Britain or the United States. It argued that Britain had not declared war on Germany because of the naval building program but because of its rapid economic development. Since a new government would seek rapid economic recovery, England would remain an enemy even after the conflict.[36]

The Hamburg government and merchants were convinced that German policy had to pursue "only the interests of Germany and of German citizens." To this end, the foreign service bureaucracy had to be changed. The diplomatic corps must ruthlessly adopt talent rather than the traditional preference for nobility as the criteria for appointment and would have to institute adequate pay, an expanded personnel skilled in the economic areas, and other reforms that strengthened the role of commerce in the foreign office. The German government reaffirmed its confidence in the capacity of colonization, investment, trade, and culture to enrich settlers, transient merchants, and homeland firms and investors. Most German leaders assumed that domestic well-being depended on international trade and investment.[37] The Versailles peace settlement stripped Germany of its colonies in Africa and Asia, largely demilitarized it, and saddled it with large reparations payments. Rebuilding strong economic participation in Latin America assumed more importance under such conditions.

Still, with capital and other resources short, Germany struggled to reestablish its ties with the world economy. The Hamburg Association of Guatemalan Firms wanted the armistice commission to create conditions for reviving trade. It wanted all confiscations canceled and German property either returned or compensated for in U.S. currency. It observed that foreign trade was essential to Germany's existence. In May 1920 a memorandum recognized that Germany had to remain a single customs unit, to redevelop its vital shipping industry, and to preserve its property in foreign areas.[38]

French and U.S. officials assumed that the Germans would adopt strategies to recover the economic power and political influence they had lost in Central America during the war. U.S. official John Hays Hammond pointed out that "Germany, driven from her old markets under the British flag, . . . already is attempting to regain and enlarge her sphere in Latin America. We shall meet her at every turn. Her unscrupulous agents will be found in every market and their activities will bear fruit." The U.S. minister complained when a large number of Germans returned to Guatemala bearing Spanish passports, but Estrada Cabrera pointed out that a U.S. vessel had carried them from Cuba to Guatemala.[39]

At war's end, German organizations labored to mend breaches. The German Foreign Institute acted to undo the damage done by entente propaganda, so that Germans could successfully reenter Latin America. The German Economic Union of South and Middle America regretted that so many German businesspeople in Latin America had either served Germany's enemies during the war or selected foreigners as agents. The head of an entrepreneurial group hoped to strengthen the shared feelings between domestic and overseas Germans.[40] Many Germans had difficulty recognizing that in the world economic system, foreigners served German firms, just as Germans served foreign firms. Nationalism faded as transnational activity increased.

The pride and arrogance of nationalism remained influential in metropole relations with peripheral states. German diplomats and businesspeople wanted to reward El Salvador because it alone among the Central American states had not severed relations with Germany. In 1919 and 1920 many smaller Latin American states emulated the large entente powers and sent only chargés to Germany. Whereas the German government had to accept such treatment from the great powers, it did not have to from small powers. One German official insisted that the small Central American countries should name full ministers so German diplomats would bear rank equal to U.S. agents. Germany should only allow exceptions when its interests required the immediate exchange of agents. For example, after Münzenthaler died in Guatemala, Germany needed to dispatch an agent to prevent the sale of sequestered German property.[41] German officials assumed that they could dictate the parameters of the bilateral relationship, although they conceded Germany's dependence on foreign economic activity.

In the unsettled conditions of postwar Germany and Guatemala, prospects were slim that migrants to Central America could make a fortune. Still, Germans might easily recover their prewar economic and political position. The Hamburg Chamber of Commerce expected some Germans to emigrate to escape the domestic disorder. In 1920 about 1,000 German males found Guatemala an attractive place. Opportunities for young Germans had worsened, in fact, because Guatemala continued to hold confiscated property. Generally, it was assumed that a guided emigration policy would sustain the recovery of foreign markets.[42]

The longtime, tacit alliance between the German colony and Estrada Cabrera had dissolved after the president saw opportunities for gain from confiscating German property. When a domestic revolt overthrew Estrada Cabrera in early 1920, the French chargé suggested that Germans had aided the opposition in order to prevent the sale of confiscated property. Estrada Cabrera and the German colony besmirched each other's reputation before U.S. opinion. La Tribuna alleged that Estrada Cabrera decreed the confiscation and nationalization of some alien property in retaliation after some Germans had funded the Central American Union party's anti–Estrada Cabrera activity. The German community denied this allegation. Estrada Cabrera might have initiated the rumor to persuade U.S. officials that the Central American Union party was a German propaganda agency. In early 1920 German officials presumed that German property in Guatemala was not in danger because most of the new cabinet ministers were related to German property owners by marriage. Still, Obst cited the potential damage to underline the pressing need for a diplomat.[43]

Köper—whose two Guatemalan firms and a Bremen business were in jeopardy—pleaded for a diplomatic agent to monitor damage. He charged Estrada Cabrera with declaring war on Germany so that U.S. firms could acquire the German coffee plantations. He feared that Guatemalan obligations to the U.S. and French governments might hinder the release of German property. He argued that a diplomat was needed to separate the personal property of German import-export firms and private agricultural holdings from the large German corporate firms and to have the Guatemalan government quickly return the personal property and agricultural holdings. Köper suspected that the new Guatemalan government would await U.S. recognition before it returned the property because the United States only approved subservient governments.[44]

Evidence "liberated" from the presidential residence during the 1920 revolt allegedly proved that Estrada Cabrera's confiscation decree was theft planned in cahoots with U.S. swindlers. In April 1920 the new Guatemalan government discovered that Daniel Hogdsdon, Henry W. Catlin, Carlos Miron, and Estrada Cabrera had signed a contract with the object of "acquiring the major German fincas [with a prewar value of $8 million] sequestered by the Guatemalan government, forming in effect a company with a capital of $3,000,000 gold to purchase those properties, under the urging of Estrada Cabrera, for less than half of their value, with the intention of reselling them later at great advantage." Catlin had organized a company for this purpose in Delaware in 1919. The Guatemalan government wanted Catlin's conduct and his character brought to the attention of the U.S. government and of his employers—General Electric and Electric Bond and Share Company—in order to dampen his protest when it annulled this contract. German residents argued that this startling evidence could only end confiscation if a German diplomat was present because the Guatemalan government ignored public opinion. When the Guatemalan government hesitated to normalize relations after Germany had received U.S. recognition, the German foreign ministry became perturbed.[45]

In mid-1920 the firm of Schlubach, Thiemer, and Company was on the verge of an unofficial breakthrough of the logjam related to the property seized in Guatemala. It cooperated with the large Hamburg coffee plantation firms and with U.S. and French agents to arrange for the release of German property, valued at between 1 and 2 billion depreciated marks, in return for a onetime payment of about 40 million depreciated marks. The Hamburg Chamber of Commerce lamented that a large payment was necessary to release the property. The Schlubach firm asked the German government to refuse to reveal the value of German property in Guatemala, even at the Paris Peace Conference, until the matter was resolved. The German government, once satisfied that it would not be obligated to repay the bribe, agreed that the accord was a marvelous step. This agreement allowed German agent Wilhelm Erythropel to prepare to move the legation to Guatemala in late 1920.[46]

The return of confiscated property was hampered by delays in Honduras, where public opinion leaned toward Germany. Before a declaration of war, the Honduran government had seized German property in Amapala, including the lighters of Theodore Köhncke's firm, and had forced the German residents to vacate the area. It appointed a U.S. inventor to manage German property. In early 1920, it returned two seized firms: Cornelsen in Tegucigalpa and Siercke in Choluteca. The return of two Amapala firms, Rössner and Köhncke, which owned choice land at this Pacific harbor, was initially delayed, then delayed further when the U.S. minister forced the Honduran government to renounce a promise to return all sequestered property because the lighter business was vital to U.S. interest in Amapala harbor.[47] The German firms eventually removed the restrictions with difficulty.

In the immediate postwar years, German agents labored to obtain recognition. Yet, reestablishing relations with Costa Rica posed a possible embarrassment for Germany because Tinoco's government had broken relations in a fruitless attempt to win U.S. recognition. Erythropel proposed that if Costa Rican officials expressed interest in reestablishing relations, the consul or Bishop Storck could explain that the state of German-U.S. relations made such a step impossible. Erythropel rejected the charge that Germany was responsible for Tinoco's coup. Tinoco and his propaganda vehicles had been unfriendly toward Germany until the U.S. government refused to recognize him. Then, after his overthrow, he experienced a sudden urge to travel to Germany and look after the millions he had stashed in Europe. In 1920 the new Costa Rican government, appreciative that the German government extended it a friendly hand before any entente power, declared that the Costa Rican people had never approved the severing of relations with Germany.[48]

Various problems required attention before Germany and Costa Rica could reestablish normal relations. After World War I, Juan Kümpel and two other Germans filed claims against the Costa Rican government for injury to their persons and property during the Tinoco regime. Although Kümpel had aided the revolutionary plotting of the González Flores faction, Erythropel considered his treatment unjustified. However, Erythropel and the German colony disapproved of Kümpel's request to withhold recognition of Costa Rica until his claim was satisfied. Erythropel suspected that the claim settlement was difficult because Kümpel was more interested in a large indemnity than in justice.[49] The claim strained German–Costa Rican relations for years.

In 1920 Costa Rica acted to reestablish relations with Germany. It offered the German government a choice between a temporary official, Arnoldo Andre, or the permanent appointment of Peralta, who was already serving in Belgium and France. German diplomat Franz von Tattenbach recommended rejecting Andre, who had denounced his German citizenship without cause. The German government wanted Peralta to present his credentials quickly; it might have been less enthusiastic if it had realized that Peralta had argued that the Versailles settlement was too easy on Germany. Peralta hesitated because his multiple diplomatic offices might be uncomfortable for Germany. Erythropel speculated, however, that Peralta delayed a visit to Berlin out of fear that excessive friendliness toward Germany might handicap Costa Rica's admittance to the League of Nations.[50]

Initially, Erythropel encountered difficulties in Costa Rica because the German colony mistakenly assumed that he had recommended recognition of the Tinoco government. In early 1921, however, Erythropel earned himself considerable respect when he flew the German flag at half-mast from his hotel room in San José in recognition of the death of Bishop Storck. The French hotel owner claimed that U.S. officers demanded the flag's removal. To avoid a scene, Erythropel removed the flag and left the hotel. He blamed the French hotel owner and denied that the U.S. officers had anything to do with the incident. His wise conduct created a wave of anti-French feelings and sympathy for Germany without alienating powerful U.S. forces.[51]

World War I and its aftermath disrupted Europe's presence in Central America. During these years much German material success and prestige in Central America was destroyed. The war was a heavy blow to traditional German power sources—the monarchy, aristocracy, and army—yet it created few new sources of social strength. The war underscored the maturing of the U.S. political economy, which, essentially isolated from the European war, had secured formal political and strategic and informal economic power in the Caribbean–Central American area. The weakened European powers—including Germany—wished to reenter this vital area but, lacking the material or political capacity to force equal opportunity, had to settle for whatever crumbs the United States allowed to fall from its table. The German government struggled to recover its vitality and foreign ties after 1918. German entrepreneurs who had operated in Central America sought to rebuild their businesses, to find alternative economic activities or investment areas, and to reestablish prewar ties with German importers and financiers.

10

■

Reestablishing Germany's Role, 1920–1925

German reentry into Central America's political economy and culture faced obstacles. The U.S. government remained determined to dominate the Caribbean-isthmian area. The loss of political and economic power by Britain, Germany, and France during the war eased the ability of the United States to secure its own objectives. U.S. military strength expanded generally but obtained a dominant position in the Caribbean. Although in the early 1920s many Central Americans disliked the comparatively unchallenged position of the United States, it was only later, with the rise of opposition figures—Augusto César Sandino in Nicaragua and Faribundo Martí in El Salvador—and sympathy for the Apristas, that the underlying dissatisfaction grew visible. However, none of the European governments showed much interest in challenging the new U.S. authority; the human and material costs of World War I made such opposition unproductive. As long as the European powers could regenerate commercial and investment activity, there was little desire to challenge the U.S. role. Additional obstacles to German reentry included financial and exchange matters, disrupted and inadequate communications services, and the unwillingness of many emigrants from the German empire to accept the Weimar Republic as their fatherland.

Rebuilding Germany was difficult in the 1920s. There were psychological as well as ideological and material problems. In the economic sphere, historian Gerald Feldman insisted that old industry, not the new sectors and product areas, dominated the postwar German political economy. Historian Peter Krüger characterized the Weimar Republic as "a premature, unloved republic born in defeat." He excused much of its failed foreign policy because the government carried an extra burden.[1] But Weimar's failures were essentially European. Its activity in Central America encountered considerable success.

Since Germany, more than most countries, relied on trade and foreign investment to maintain a living standard suitable to a cultured great power, it had to avoid exclusion from any significant part of the world economy. German society had to develop the means to protect its interests in world trade and isthmian interoceanic transit. In the early postwar years, German officials and businesses, with little capital, scarce shipping, and a host of uncertainties about the nation's future, could not grant priority to rebuilding ties with Central America. In 1924 the Bureau of German Chambers of Commerce in Latin America was founded to promote economic relations with the region. The Central American countries, after suffering economic disruption and loss during World War I, were eager to reestablish trade relations with a good customer like Germany. Germany, with its future at stake, struggled to secure influence in this region without disturbing the U.S. government's sense of security.[2]

Some German government projects followed a rocky path. In late 1920, Erythropel complained that the newly organized postwar German foreign ministry failed to function as planned. Two months after opening his legation, the foreign trade section and the Middle American specialist still had not sent adequate information to promote German trade. Without information, he could not reply to inquiries about German market conditions. These problems were worrisome because Central Americans still placed great trust in Germany. Shoddy U.S. goods and the prewar reputation of German products foretold success, should a competent program be established to rebuild markets for German industry.[3]

The weakened European powers wished to reenter the Caribbean and Central American area, but they lacked the capacity to force equal opportunity there. The U.S. political economy had strengthened its role in this vital area during the war, and the United States continued an aggressive policy throughout the 1920s. The postwar disorder and political tension in Europe handicapped Germany's challenge to the U.S. position on the isthmus. The French occupation of the Ruhr area in 1923 and the subsequent inflation delayed the revival of the German economy. However, the setback encouraged the economic recovery of Germans abroad and induced the migration of disgruntled citizens who, after the turmoil of the war, were further disheartened by the disruption of the early 1920s. Worker organizations could not decide whether to push for reform of the Weimar government or to seek radical change. The Weimar government was burdened with war guilt, disorder, and debt. Still, German entrepreneurs overcame the various hurdles to make considerable recovery at home and abroad in the 1920s.[4]

The share of Central American products in German importation rose to 0.7 percent in 1924 before settling at about 1 percent for the rest of the

1920s. Although less than 0.2 percent of German exports went to Central America, viewed from the Central American perspective, German imports obtained a significance not surpassed since 1889–1897 (Tables 5 and 6). By 1925 German products supplied 10 percent of Guatemalan imports, 8 percent of Costa Rican imports, and 5 or 6 percent of Honduran, Salvadoran, and Nicaraguan imports. Germans consumed one-third of Guatemalan and Salvadoran exports in 1924 and 1925. German acquisition of Costa Rican and Nicaraguan products recovered to 4 percent by 1924 and 1925, but the German share of Honduran export trade remained below 1 percent. In the postwar period, German investment in Guatemala climbed back to about $40 million, or about 170 million marks (Table 7). German colonization rebounded quickly. French officials reported that during a two-month period in early 1921, 140 Germans reentered Guatemala despite financial problems and a scarcity of passenger space. They reported that 253 Germans emigrated to Central America in 1922, and 408 in 1923. German capital, colonists, and trade might restrict aggressive "Yankee imperialism."[5]

In the postwar years, the Central American societies faced persisting disruptions—social turmoil, coups, and revolutions—that were reactions to the failures of the liberal socioeconomic orders to perform as advertised. Central American societies were required to contribute more, through material and cultural sacrifices, to the preservation of metropole well-being and security. Compradors—the local partners or allies of metropole economic and political activity—escaped much of the sacrifice because they were in privileged positions. Some Guatemalans hoped to take advantage of the disrupted German domestic economy by acquiring real estate there. More commonly, however, the comprador politicians met resistance and disfavor while enforcing metropole demands at home. As the world economy recovered in the 1920s, the Central American political economies found some respite because the need to extract extra value to finance the rebuilding of the world economy declined.[6]

On the isthmus, rebuilding profitability for German entrepreneurs appeared tied to the recovery of the confiscated property. Cultural affairs and political influence were intertwined with the return of confiscated property and the revival of the German economic role on the isthmus. German officials, media, and business interests had to restore reputations damaged by wartime entente propaganda if they wished to reenter Latin American socioeconomic life successfully. They relied extensively on the print media to recapture public sentiment in Latin America. The German Foreign Institute proposed to rebuild Germany's reputation with a weekly publication, *Deutsche Auslandskorrespondenz* [German Foreign Correspondence], which would stress culture while slipping trade information into the background. "Even the appearance of propagandizing must be avoided," it warned, "otherwise opponents will immediately take counter measures, and the weekly will earn the reputation of a German economic promotion." It recommended confidentially sending the *Auslandskorrespondenz* to trustworthy people in foreign countries who would place items casually in the local press. The propaganda value of another paper, the *Münchener neueste Nachrichten*, was reduced because it was too involved with politics and technical matters. For a periodical to have success in Latin America, Tattenbach recommended that it include literary contributions, poems, sketches, and items from Latin American writers. A regular feature on beautiful German women, he observed, would boost distribution.[7]

The French diplomat Revelli was impressed with how cleverly the Germans managed their propaganda campaign in Central America in comparison with France's weak showing. The Germans sent stories meant for the Guatemalan audience to newspapers in neighboring countries, aware that the propensity to believe the printed word would bring the stories back to Guatemala. He complained that a subsidy for the newspaper *Batidor* in Honduras and a 3,000 franc annual subsidy to the French lycée in Guatemala were insufficient steps to counter German influence.[8]

The French wanted to liquidate confiscated German property in Guatemala because they assumed that the immense loss would greatly reduce German influence. French minister Jules Jusserand assured Washington that U.S. capitalists would profit more from liquidation than French financiers. However, Leo S. Rowe, director of the Panamerican Bureau, did not want a one-time gain to undermine long-term influence. The appearance of U.S. interference with the release of German property might generate a backlash in Guatemala. If the U.S. government was not responsible for the delays in releasing German property, he wanted its role publicly clarified. Jusserand hoped to diminish German influence while Rowe wanted to protect the U.S. position and its reputation for fairness.[9]

Under strong U.S. pressure, all of the Central American states except El Salvador had severed relations with Germany, sequestered German property, and detained German subjects. During Central America's centennial celebration on September 15, 1921, the German government faced an awkward situation. Erythropel proposed special congratulations for Costa Rica, El Salvador, and Honduras in recognition of their efforts to reestablish amicable relations. Since Nicaragua was unwilling to allow Erythropel to function in that country, its celebration could be ignored. He advised ignoring Guatemala's centennial festivities also unless that country moved to restore German property and to resolve other differences. Of course, nonparticipation could entail sacrifice. Some French aviation officials saw these festivities as an opportunity to showcase their capabilities. They recommended that French airplane firms participate in the celebration of Central American independence in order to undermine the German reputation in military technology.[10]

Erythropel and Obst regretted that Guatemala was delaying the return of confiscated property and the normalization of representation. Guatemala had adopted a stance, they agreed, "which earlier no Middle American state would ever have allowed itself with regard to Germany." Erythropel assigned the crude behavior to Foreign Minister Luis P. Aguirre, who was close to the French chargé. Although Guatemala was counting on German weakness, Erythropel insisted that Germany had some leverage because the new government wanted the maximum number of foreign diplomats in its capital.[11]

Germans attempted to use cultural policy to guide Guatemalan opinion about German society. In early 1922 Tattenbach protested the showing of the film "Four Horsemen of the Apocalypse" because it disparaged Germany. The friendly *El Universo* claimed that a movie house failed in its public duty when it showed a film that excited "odium and a thirst for revenge against the Germans." It claimed: "The mission of the theater is to influence everything good, true, and beautiful in the public. A theater which instead of fulfilling this sacred duty, poisons the consciences, constitutes a menace for public morals." German influence on Guatemala's elite had always had limits; the postwar years reduced this influence even more. Yet, the *Berliner Börsenzeitung* reported that the propagating of German culture in Guatemala was doing well in mid-1922. It expected good relations between German residents and the new president. Some organizations in Germany considered aiding Guatemalan students to study in Germany but were slow to act. The German government encouraged cultural relations and the minister promoted the language and culture among Guatemalans.[12]

For many years, the clerics Thiel and Storck had represented German culture as bishops in Costa Rica. In mid-1923 Erythropel attended the elevation of Augustin Hombach, a German priest, to archbishop at Tegucigalpa, Honduras. He observed that Hombach was well-liked even among Protestant Germans and had labored effectively for Germany during the war. Erythropel expected Hombach to represent German culture in Honduras. In 1925 the German foreign ministry, considering Hombach possibly the most important German in Central America, praised and welcomed him when he visited Germany.[13]

Good commercial relations, from the German perspective, combined with rebuilt diplomatic relations should encourage entrepreneurs, investors, and emigrants to consider Central American opportunities. The Hamburg Chamber of Commerce judged that the Guatemalan economy suffered less than many others on the periphery because coffee prices had fallen less than many other raw materials. The reestablishment of regular service by Hamburg-Amerika, Kosmos, and Roland, the financial stabilization of the new Guatemalan government, and modest improvement in the prices of coffee and sugar soon allowed German products to regain ground lost to U.S. and British merchandise. Guatemala's unstable currency, however, burdened importers.[14]

Currency stability, exchange rates, and other financial matters hindered the reestablishment of German–Central American trade relations in the postwar years. By 1921 commerce had recovered sufficiently to remove the difficulty in ordering from Germany. German merchants were regaining the business of Amapala, Honduras, which they had dominated before the war. One persistent dilemma for German commerce was whether to set price quotations in dollars or marks, for it was not immediately apparent which would better promote sales: non-German importers preferred dollar prices; German import firms and most import-export firms in Nicaragua and Costa Rica preferred mark prices but welcomed dollar payment; German commission agents preferred mark payment. German economists were concerned that reliance on dollar payments might weaken the mark and induce merchants to select dollar goods to the detriment of mark manufactures because they could avoid currency exchange charges, delays, and losses.[15]

The mark lacked the numerous institutional connections (banks, merchant and financial houses, and insurance companies) between homeland and isthmus that the dollar and pound sterling enjoyed. Thus, German firms suffered large exchange losses in purchasing marks to settle debts, thereby adding uncertainty and extra cost to trade and investment. Even the German bank Tafel in Costa Rica maintained an enormous spread between selling and buying marks due to the uncertain exchange rates. Tattenbach hoped that quoting orders and bills in dollars and reviving contact with large Hamburg firms and German banks would reduce exchange problems (not necessarily for the mark, however). Consul Bunge warned that Nicaraguan banks conspired to earn high exchange profits—up to 14 percent—from "inkasso" transactions (holding paper for collection), even on the British pound sterling. To avoid this exploitation, he advised German firms to use dollar prices or to convert currencies only at the end of business. The German foreign ministry announced that at least one German firm (Schlubach and Sapper) in Guatemala handled inkasso commissions at reasonable terms.[16] Doing business in marks was often inconvenient and expensive.

German officials searched for banks at home and in Central America that would tie capital, production, and commerce into an effective whole on the isthmus. Some Germans on the isthmus had capital. While Germany suffered financially from the occupation of the Ruhr, two German-Guatemalan investment houses—Schlubach-Sapper and Nottebohm—reportedly advanced the Guatemalan government $1 million to purchase AEG electrical equipment, and they were prepared to invest $8 million in the Guatemalan National Bank.[17]

In the summer of 1921 French naval Lieutenant LeCoq was surprised that German merchants, despite the drastically fallen mark, were extending long-term credit. He accepted the wisdom of the policy because the Schlubach and Rosenthal merchant bankers were extraordinarily important in Guatemala's economic life. In mid-1922 L. Cotty, an employee of the Compagnie Générale Transatlantique, informed the French foreign ministry that Germany was regaining its prewar influence on the isthmus. He reported that U.S. firms tied credit or loans to the purchase of U.S. merchandise because their goods could not compete with German products. France was not neglected. He regretted that both U.S. and German agents adopted anti-French propaganda for commercial reasons.[18]

German interests moved rapidly in the early 1920s to reenter the wireless communications sector. In 1921 the U.S., Britain, France, and Germany agreed to form a consortium to develop radio communications with Latin America, but the agreement bore little fruit. Since United Fruit circumvented the Costa Rican law prohibiting foreign control of wireless stations, the Telefunken agent sought straw men to launch a German wireless station. His offer to build a new station was rejected, however. The Germans succeeded with a circuitous route when Costa Rica and El Salvador accepted Mexican gifts of Telefunken equipment. The firm All American Cables in Costa Rica charged messages to Germany at double the rate to New York, but the Telefunken service was expected to offer German businesses a competitive fee scale.[19] German technology and determined marketing earned German communications firms access to Central America.

The prewar reputation of German products helped German industry to reenter Central American markets and enabled one chemical firm, E. Merck of Darmstadt, to establish an agent in Costa Rica. The complaint persisted, nevertheless, that German products were too expensive. Tattenbach advised German exporters to pack their products to match comparable U.S. goods. German products could not rely only on prewar reputations; they had to match U.S. competition in quality, price, and packaging.[20]

Several problems arose for German officials and businesses in late 1921 when the Central American Republic—a short-lived union of Guatemala, El Salvador, Honduras, and Nicaragua—prohibited member states from maintaining diplomatic representation outside of Tegucigalpa. Tattenbach considered it unwise to try to push Guatemala out of the union because a backlash against Germany might occur throughout the isthmus. While reluctantly concurring, Bremen businesspeople insisted that a special agent should oversee the extensive investments and trade in Guatemala. Tattenbach suggested establishing a professional consul in Guatemala and postponing the decision to move the diplomatic mission to Tegucigalpa. He advised waiting for the reaction of other European states and Washington before recognizing the Central American Republic. The German ambassador in France questioned his instructions to solicit the French attitude toward the new Central American Republic because France might use this opportunity to undermine Germany's position in Central America.[21]

Köper and other Bremen businesspeople wanted to formalize relations with the new Guatemalan government because German investments required a stable political situation. Köper worried that the Guatemalan government might look longingly at German real estate and commercial property if it faced financial problems and there was no German diplomat to compel realistic conduct. He knew that the Guatemalans and North Americans were jealous of Germany's recovery. The Guatemalan government had long objected to the German government taxing money earned in Guatemala. It argued that the profits and tax revenue earned on investments should contribute to improving Guatemala. Köper warned that if the German government did not protect Germans and their property, many might surrender their citizenship.[22]

If German officials and businesspeople hoped to restore economic and financial bonds with Central America, they had to rebuild speedy and secure postal connections. Postal service from Germany to Costa Rica was too slow. British letters took seventeen days, while German mail needed four weeks. Moreover, parcel post and fund transfers were unreliable. Business needed a reliable parcel service. The Nicaraguan postal minister suggested that Kosmos and Roland should carry postal packages and thus strengthen German-Nicaraguan ties. In early 1923 the Kosmos, Roland, and Hamburg-Amerika lines accepted packages between Germany and Nicaragua or Costa Rica under reciprocal conditions and fees.[23]

German officials monitored Central American postal fees and regulations to prevent competing nations from acquiring advantages. In October 1923 a Costa Rican–French treaty on postal fees for printed matter left only Germany and Great Britain, among the heavily participating countries, without a reduced postal fee treaty. In 1924, after England persuaded Nicaragua to reduce postal fees, Germany's consul targeted a similar reduction. Likewise, when the United States negotiated an agreement on parcel post packages with Nicaragua, Tattenbach successfully pursued a similar agreement. In accord with the Stockholm world postal agreement, Costa Rica welcomed a pact reducing fees on German books, newspapers, and journals.[24] Improved postal service remained a major concern of the Central American and metropole governments.

The demise of the German empire and rise of the Weimar Republic severely tested the patriotism of many Germans on the isthmus. Many of these residents were second, third, or perhaps even fourth generation. The inability of the empire to protect them and their property during the war prompted a few to surrender their citizenship. For many the monarchy and the empire were the pride of their citizenship. When Erythropel submitted his credentials in Nicaragua in April 1922, the German colony was indifferent. He assigned the coolness to the disdain of numerous monarchists for the Weimar Republic. In Costa Rica on Germany's national day, most foreign countries flew their flags, but the French and numerous German monarchists did not. In 1924 the Germans in Guatemala remained away from the legation on Germany's national holiday. Disorder in Nicaragua in the mid-1920s persuaded most Germans that only the agent of a recognized nation would protect their property, so they made peace with the Weimar Republic. When consular official D. O. Lutz saw the imperial flag over the German Club in Costa Rica, he argued that the colony had to accept the Weimar flag in order to preserve its strong economic position.[25] Germans in Central America either accepted the protection of the republic or changed their citizenship. Slowly the need for protection undermined the disgust the monarchists felt toward Weimar.

After Guatemalan officials rebuffed Consul E. Peper several times when he sought to reestablish relations, Peper decided that it was up to Guatemala to request the reestablishment of relations, so that Germany would not risk another rebuff. To avoid even the appearance that Germany sought contact, in 1922 he sent a private citizen to make arrangements when Foreign Minister Adrián Recinos expressed interest in reviving official contact. The brief delay was intended to be instructive rather than punitive, however, given the significance of German interests in Guatemala.[26]

In April 1923 Köper complained that a decree compelling German export-import firms to present bills of lading with commercial information to Guatemalan officials burdened trade with extra work and offered a golden opportunity for commercial espionage. He asked the Bremen Chamber of Commerce to join the protests of the Italian and British chambers. The Bremen Chamber presumed that the decree encouraged espionage because price data was unnecessary in Guatemala, which leveled its customs by weight. Tattenbach pointed out that this view was in error. Since the existing laws required price information for administrative purposes, bureaucratic indiscretion was already possible. Moreover, the Guatemalan government lost appreciable revenue due to the common underestimation of price and weight data on bills of lading. He had warned German firms not to wander too far from the truth. While the various chambers of commerce might object, he expected the Guatemalan government to reject any formal protest and point to the underevaluations.[27]

Governments of peripheral states encountered difficulties punishing metropole businesspeople, even when they were exposed in illicit activity. One strategy employed to protect the guilty was to point to equally culpable members of the comprador elite. When Guatemala issued a decree allowing the deportation of any foreigner not considered of utility to Guatemala, many foreigners became uneasy. The decree was presumably directed at the German manager of an American bank who had manipulated currency exchanges to the detriment of Guatemala. The German minister sought to have the owners of the bank, who had ordered the transactions, punished as severely as the manager.[28] Defense through finger-pointing, rather than the demonstration of innocence, is a political and diplomatic device sometimes employed by the guilty to avoid judicial resolution of an allegation.

German officials were divided over what kind of agreements would best aid commercial relations with Guatemala. In late 1923 the chancellor's office designated the promotion of German foreign commerce as one of its most important tasks because the whole economy depended on reestablishing foreign trade. German industry and export-import businesses were depending on the reestablishment of access to the world market to acquire needed raw materials and to market their finished goods. The German minister for agriculture warned that if Germany did not negotiate successfully in Guatemala, the coffee crop might go to France, which had just concluded an advantageous trade treaty. Guatemala had been Germany's second most important coffee source before World War I. To counteract French claims that Germany was no longer a good market for Guatemalan products, the minister asked Hamburg and Bremen merchants for data on German and French importation of Guatemalan products. Nevertheless, German interests, including the Hamburg Association of Guatemalan Firms, were undecided about the need for a trade treaty. David Sapper of the Schlubach firm suspected that Guatemala placed little importance on a trade treaty with Germany. Tattenbach agreed, but he considered a consular treaty or a treaty to protect trademarks appropriate. The German foreign minister intended to mollify key prewar trading partners.[29]

When the Guatemalan government indicated that it would welcome a treaty with Germany similar to the French-Guatemalan trade treaty of 1922, the German government responded quickly to minimize France's advantage. It organized a meeting of representatives from the senates of Hamburg and Bremen and the Hamburg Association of Guatemalan Firms to hammer out terms to present to Guatemala. The meeting favored a treaty based on the most-favored-nation principle, but free of clauses injurious to Guatemala's dignity, such as the clause in the 1887 treaty freeing Germans from military service in Guatemala. German officials welcomed the most-favored-nation clause, but they rejected reciprocity. Germany ordered Tattenbach, on leave, to return immediately and to assume negotiations. He praised President José María Orellana in an article in the *Hamburger Fremdenblatt* and the *Weser Zeitung*, which "strengthen[ed] my [Tattenbach's] position with [him]." In October 1924 Germany and Guatemala signed an unconditional most-favored-nation trade treaty. Guatemala wanted the agreement kept secret temporarily, but in late November 1924, its existence, but not the terms, was publicized in Guatemala.[30]

By late 1923 French officials recognized that Germany was rapidly recovering its economic position in Central America. They were impressed with the revival of shipping, propaganda, credit facilities, the numerous colonists, and the language ability of German sales personnel. The appointment of veteran diplomat Wilhelm von Kühlmann as minister in 1924 underscored the German recovery. Kühlmann found German influence surrounding the Guatemalan foreign ministry. The British minister in Guatemala was married to a German; U.S. minister Arthur H. Geissler was born in Dresden; and Robert Loewenthal, who had a German Jewish background and cherished his German roots, had succeeded Foreign Minister Adrián Recinos in 1923. Tattenbach considered Loewenthal less talented than the Francophile Recinos, but the change was advantageous for Germany. At the conclusion of the trade negotiations, Kühlmann suggested rewarding Loewenthal with a copper engraving of Mannheim, the hometown of his parents. Guatemalan subsecretary of foreign relations Sinforoso Aguilar had married a German woman. Some observers grumbled about the Germanization of Guatemala. French officials were concerned with the shift from Francophile to Germanophile influences in Guatemala's foreign office.[31]

German officials welcomed President Orellana's efforts to produce stability in Guatemala, particularly because Germans possessed large investments there. German capital continued to migrate to Guatemala. For example, Dr. Altmannsberg, associated with Schlubach and Company, searched Guatemala for new markets for German potassium firms. Tattenbach contended that the historic lack of serious difficulties for German investment explained the large flow of capital to Guatemala. In his view, Germany had closer relations with Guatemala than any country in Latin America.[32]

German entrepreneurs had comparable success rebuilding commerce and investment elsewhere on the isthmus. In 1921 Nicaragua, which had broken trade ties with Germany in 1914, found itself in grave economic straights when U.S. merchants greatly reduced purchases of coffee and sugar. A German official proposed using Nicaragua's plight to extract recognition and favorable trade terms. In 1922 Nicaraguan businessman and sometime diplomat Cristiano Medina conceded that a trade treaty with Germany might help sell sugar when world prices are falling, but he wondered whether Nicaragua would benefit in normal market conditions. Still, both nations should benefit from stabilized trade relations.[33]

The Nicaraguan consul in Chicago drafted a German-Nicaraguan trade treaty that was to be concluded in Washington, presumably because U.S. forces controlled the country and U.S. officials would have to approve any important treaty. The German government wanted a treaty but speculated that this mysterious pact might be unauthorized. In fact, the principal civil servant in the Nicaraguan foreign ministry claimed to know little about the Chicago draft. Erythropel found the Nicaraguan government reluctant to conclude any commercial treaty because it was assessing the economic consequences of the Central American treaty of 1922. He suggested a careful study of the Chicago draft, however, because it could form the basis for treaties with other Central American states.[34]

The German foreign ministry saw little prospect for a treaty. Nicaragua, conceded most-favored-nation treatment in Germany by the Versailles treaty, was willing to resurrect the 1896 treaty without the mutual most-favored-nation clause, but Germany did not want it without that clause. The Nicaraguan government took small steps to encourage trade. It awarded French and Italian nationals modest trade concessions and decreed that fees paid by German vessels would be no higher than those paid by other nations. Erythropel tried to persuade Dr. Burgheim, a personal friend of President Diego Chamorro, to undertake a mission to Germany to negotiate a trade treaty. After Chamorro died in late 1923, no responsible Nicaraguan pursued a commercial pact with Germany.[35]

In January 1924, Nicaragua renounced its option under the Versailles treaty to take action against German property and asked for a temporary trade agreement on the most-favored-nation principle, pending a permanent treaty. Erythropel conceded that a treaty offered uncertain value to Germany, yet he pursued the opportunity because normally Nicaraguans rejected the most-favored-nation clause. He and Foreign Minister Urtecho acted confidentially and quickly because they expected U.S. customs collector Clifford W. Ham to oppose a German-Nicaraguan agreement. In June 1924 an exchange of notes reactivated the treaty of 1896 and conceded German merchants the advantages of the Franco-Nicaraguan treaty. The temporary agreement shielded Nicaragua and Germany from a period of unregulated trade. Germany reached mutual most-favored-nation agreements with the Central American republics and Panama before the one-sided most-favored-nation clause of the Versailles treaty lapsed on January 10, 1925.[36]

Under the inspiration of Foreign Minister Gustavo Guerrero, who became convinced that the most-favored-nation clause was disadvantageous for El Salvador, the government abrogated all of its trade treaties.

Guerrero sought reciprocity treaties that created markets for Salvadoran coffee in return for reduced tariffs on specific imports. German officials believed that they had the leverage to receive most-favored-nation treatment because Germany purchased most of El Salvador's coffee. Moreover, the League of Nations had designated most-favored-nation clauses as the preferred basis for modern trade treaties and Germany's trading system would only accept an unconditional most-favored-nation treatment.[37]

Nicaraguan president Carlos Solarzano sought good relations with other states to avoid subservience to the United States. U.S. interference was undeniable. In early 1925, Ham held up approval of the permanent German-Nicaraguan trade treaty for a month. Solarzano was largely responsible for overcoming Ham's opposition to the tariff reduction on German goods. Despite Nicaragua's friendly attitude toward German trade, Kühlmann assumed that German merchants would be best served if U.S. interests controlled Nicaragua's Pacific coast railroad. The U.S. hold over Nicaragua was so thorough, however, that Germans often obtained business only when they agreed to use or represent U.S. products.[38]

The German interests wished to reestablish access to isthmian transit. Kosmos and Roland reinitiated regular steamer visits to Panama City in 1921 and a Panamanian legation opened in Berlin in 1922. In 1923, Lutz, the Panamanian consul in Leipzig, planned a short trip to help regenerate German trade and culture in Middle America and the Caribbean. Upon his return he noted the powerful U.S. influence in Panama but observed that President Belisario Porras had great respect for anything German. The chief Panamanian newspaper, the *Star*, Lutz conceded, received funds from the French and was anti-German. The Panamanians and the Spanish residents, however, were friendly toward Germans. Key to this pro-German attitude was, in Lutz's view, the Panamanian school system, in which Richard Newmann had been a major influence. Newmann, who had served as assistant inspector general of education and director of the National Institute, had adopted Panamanian citizenship to escape internment during the war. Lutz regretted that Germany maintained neither a diplomat nor a professional consul in Panama to exploit this advantage.[39]

German authorities assumed some responsibility to supervise emigration and to protect the citizen-colonist. In 1924 two projects to attract settlers to Panama—one linked to Panama's consul Eckelmann and his partner August Dziuk and the second linked to the sons of former president Porras—were widely promoted in Germany. The Eckelmann project languished because the two schemers were untrustworthy and the site was unsuitable for settlement. The president's sons sought German families to work on those Porras land holdings situated in a rather inhospitable location. The Hamburg *Korrespondent* warned about the difficulties of migrating to a tropical land. The German minister of the interior hoped for restraint from advocates of the colonization projects. He preferred not to alarm the public by condemning the locations as dangerously unhealthy.[40]

French observers in Guatemala were impressed with the discipline, cultural cohesion, and business acumen of the German colony. Lieutenant Lecoq described the German colony in Guatemala as "extremely hierarchical and submissive to a strict discipline." The French minister listed nine reasons why Germans were influential in Guatemala: (1) they were the most numerous foreigners; (2) two important firms, Schlubach-Sapper and the Nottebohm Brothers, supported their action; (3) over 1,500 Germans had married local women, some from the best Guatemalan families; (4) Germans owned some newspapers and influenced others through advertising; (5) German artists and intellectuals performed in Central America; (6) Germans owned over 50 percent of the most productive sugar and coffee plantations; (7) Germans owned 60 percent of the large and mid-sized retail stores; (8) Germans were closely linked to German-American bankers, industrialists, and capitalists; and (9) three of the seven important banks were German.[41] Large numbers, active social and cultural relations, the media, and entrepreneurial activity sustained the Germans.

German officials needed to recommend candidates carefully when Central American governments requested specialists because the quality of the people chosen affected the spread of German influence. Erythropel considered President Alfonso Quiñones's plans to conduct a geological survey of El Salvador as an opportunity to demonstrate German technical capabilities to the Central American elite. The German government recommended a professor to head the survey. When El Salvador's president suggested that a German military mission run the military academy, he displeased the U.S. legation and prompted the Spanish and French to propose alternative missions. Early Salvadoran interest in German educational personnel widened to include inquiries about employing Germans as gardeners, veterinarians, police trainers, and instructors of the bureaucracy.[42] Germans competed for many showpiece and skilled positions with considerable success.

German businesses perceived potential benefit from the U.S. role as a stabilizing force in Honduras because the continued disorder injured German-owned businesses such as Siercke and Rössner and non-German businesses that operated with goods obtained on credit from German firms. In 1925 Kühlmann expected a U.S. loan to Honduras to bear some relationship to the compensation Germans might receive for their claims—around 1,095,000 silver pesos (about 2 million marks)—arising from disorder on the north coast. He assumed there would be no payment without a major U.S. loan.[43]

German technology had sold well on the isthmus since the late nineteenth century. In the 1920s, German businesses new to Central America—such as Allgemeine Elektrizitäts Gesellschaft (AEG) and Wayss-Freytag in El Salvador and Costa Rica—and veterans like Siemens competed for concessions in road construction, city sanitation, engineering, urban transportation, and public utilities. Tattenbach asked AEG to exercise special care with the quality of material and the conditions of delivery for a small $20,000 order of electrical equipment for San Ramón, Costa Rica, because it would be the first postwar delivery of German machinery to Costa Rica. A satisfactory delivery could mean much for the future of the German electrical industry in Central America. Since the equipment was good quality at a fair price, Tattenbach expected Germany virtually to eliminate competition.[44]

German firms benefited when the Central Americans intended to use foreign investment to undermine U.S. hegemony. In 1924 U.S. minister Geissler intervened twice with the Guatemalan government in contract matters on behalf of Westinghouse, but AEG obtained both contracts, one of which was worth $3 million. The German bankers Schlubach, Sapper and Company and a German-American banking firm, Schwartz and Company, sustained AEG's search for concessions in Guatemala.[45]

German entrepreneurs, of course, were not always victorious in competition with U.S. firms. In 1925 El Salvador dropped its plans to employ ten German engineers for road construction because the U.S. firm Keilhauer and Hebard won several street and road contracts. German firms had little prospect of acquiring orders to deliver materials for these projects because Keilhauer, of Alsace Jewish descent, was unfriendly toward Germany.[46]

Although the Hamburg Chamber of Commerce recognized that U.S. predominance in the Caribbean region limited Germany's share of trade and investment, it welcomed steady improvement in German activity in Central America during the 1920s. Germany ranked thirteenth on the list of nations using the Panama Canal in 1921, and fourth in 1924. Germany was the sixth largest purchaser of Salvadoran coffee in 1923, and the first in 1925 and 1926. German products diligently worked their way up to third place in imports to El Salvador, behind U.S. and British goods. Germans purchased about half of the Guatemalan coffee crop and competed strongly against geographically advantaged U.S. goods for first place in imports. By 1925 Germany was again a major purchaser of native Central American products.[47]

It was evident that German products and entrepreneurs had not lost their reputation. The ties between Germany and Central America (especially Guatemala) rested on links with large German firms and thousands of travelers and colonists who had visited or settled on the isthmus between 1830 and 1914. These historic connections allowed Germans to restore their profitable and powerful position in Central America so quickly that they aroused the envy of the U.S., British, and French officials and governments. The hindrances German officials and entrepreneurs had to overcome included inadequate and costly exchange facilities, deteriorated communications, the monarchical bend of many older colonists, and the resistance of some isthmian governments to the most-favored-nation clause that was supposed to level the playing field for German businesses. By the mid-1920s German businesses had recovered most of the ground they lost during the war.

The return of German capital, colonists, and trade offered Central American leaders options to aggressive "Yankee imperialism." German officials and businesses encountered metropole firms, most commonly U.S. enterprises, that had acquired markets, investments, or contacts that Germans had held before the war. The other metropole interests were less competitive. These competitors also faced major economic burdens as a consequence of the war and often, as in the case of France, assigned Germany responsibility for their own economic and financial disorders. In the 1920s German entrepreneurs and investors produced a success story in the area of trade and investment in Central America.

11

∎

A Revived German Presence
in Central America, 1924–1929

Germany's leaders labored to continue the nation's recovery in international trade and investment. They promoted economic and political stability and the maintenance of an elevated living standard. The leaders of the German political economy dreamt of a great Soviet market early in the postwar years. That market grew slowly, so German entrepreneurs turned to old reliable economic partners. The German economy counted on extracting labor value and raw materials, reestablishing the coffee trade, gaining markets, and placing investment capital in peripheral areas like Central America. Central America was also a stepping stone to vastly greater economic opportunities in the Pacific basin. Although U.S. sensitivities to foreign activity in this area were well known, Germany's vision of future prosperity did not allow it to abandon the region. Germans in such areas commonly retained a commitment to the home country's economy and thus could play a significant role in the fatherland's economic recovery.[1]

By the late 1920s the number of German residents and firms in Central America equaled or surpassed prewar levels, even in Guatemala. The German population in Guatemala reached about 2,950 by 1930. German immigrants were either returning after the war or escaping a chaotic domestic economy. The growing number of German firms in Costa Rica and Honduras coincided with the increase in German males residing in Costa Rica (up 685) and Honduras (up 400) in the late 1920s (Tables 9 and 10).

By the mid-1920s German merchants were again major purchasers of Central American products. The Central American share of Germany's import trade rose to 1.1 percent by 1927, as German merchants acquired 35 percent of Guatemalan exports, 30 percent of Salvadoran exports, and between 5 and 10 percent of the exports of the other Central American states. German investment in Guatemala also recovered, reaching about

$40 million in 1926, despite German domestic needs (Table 7). Central America received 0.2 percent of German exports, but German products captured a significant share of Central America's import trade. They constituted 15 percent of Costa Rica's importation, 13 percent of Guatemala's, and between 5 and 10 percent of the importation of the other Central American states. In 1929 Germany ranked second among importers in Guatemala and Costa Rica and third in Honduras, El Salvador, and Nicaragua.[2]

As German recovery advanced, even critical commentary from officials could dampen progress. The Krupp Gusswerk was upset when Panamanian consul von Streitberg reported negatively on business conditions in Germany. Krupp officials conceded that German industries were having trouble, but his accurate report hampered the capacity of firms to work out their difficulties. German officials investigated the private life of Streitberg, but they found no damaging material that might have persuaded him to adjust his reports.[3] Public and private sectors in Germany had cooperated without success in an attempt to blackmail a consul into altering his reporting.

German entrepreneurs pursued new business opportunities—some of which challenged U.S. hegemony—in addition to restoring the old. The U.S. military wished to exclude foreign airlines from competing for landing rights in Central America and the Caribbean because it considered the region crucial for the defense of the canal. U.S. military officials gave special attention to the Sociedad Colombiana-Alemana de Transportes Aéreas (Scadta) [Colombian-German Air Transport Company] because it eyed privileges near the Canal Zone. Although Scadta was a Colombian firm with private German capital participation, it quickly established ties with the German national airline, the predecessor of Lufthansa. U.S. officials viewed this firm's projects in Central America as a threat to U.S. security.[4]

The U.S. military attaché in Venezuela expected Scadta to canvas the Central American republics with the same deceptive tactics used in Venezuela, where the company boldly and deceitfully claimed "the full and favorable support of U.S. authorities and a definite contract from the U.S. Post Office." Later, Scadta agents contacted the isthmian governments. Costa Rican officials considered allowing Scadta to establish air postal service at Puerto Limón to connect with Colombia and the outside world. The attaché believed that Scadta would suffer a significant defeat if it could be shown that it did not have full U.S. support. The U.S. Post Office responded with a declaration that only a U.S. company using U.S.

airplanes could obtain a mail contract. The attaché also warned that Scadta's contracts had "distinctly military features" that were "a potential menace to the Canal Defenses." The U.S. military in the Canal Zone wished to deny non-U.S. nationals access to the airfields in Colón and Panama because planes landing at these airports could attack the canal fortifications and public utilities plants before countermeasures could be taken. After surveying the German-U.S. competition to dominate aviation on the isthmus, a French report concluded that the United States "apparently has decided to monopolize the major aerial communication lines in South America." Indeed, Acting Secretary of State Joseph C. Grew expected Minister Geissler to prevent a Scadta contract in Central America.[5]

Germany's weapons industry had historically done well in Central America, so suspicions arose regarding its reappearance in the 1920s. A German merchant did supply used weapons to the *putch* forces that failed in El Salvador in 1927. The German government, however, rejected Nicaraguan Juan Bautista Sacasa's allegation that Emiliano Chamorro's revolutionary faction obtained weapons from Krupp. The German government observed that Central America possessed considerable Krupp war materials of pre-1914 manufacture.[6]

Although the Salvadoran government diversified the foreign influence on its security forces, it frequently turned to Germany. In response to a solicitation for assistance, the Prussian Secret Police [Geheimpolizei] suggested hiring a German police specialist to aid in the formation of El Salvador's secret police. Four countries contributed to the improvement of El Salvador's army. Germany supplied the bandmaster, Spain and France gave advanced officers' training, and the Rockefeller Foundation paid a Salvadoran officer to receive sanitation training in the United States. The German bandmaster ordered musical instruments from Germany in 1928.[7] Through involvement in security, there were more market opportunities than merely arms, just as there were areas of influence in public health and culture—music and education—beyond military training.

German cultural influence in Guatemala remained strong through the continued arrival of immigrants, the widely distributed Spanish-language *Gaceta de Munich*, the visits of German writers and artists, and the activity of the German Club. The Guatemalan minister of education consulted the German director of El Salvador's National Teachers Institute before engaging a dozen German teachers. José Matos, Robert Loewenthal's replacement in the Guatemalan foreign ministry, reputedly had strong links to France, but he had worked on the production of a dictionary of civil and commercial law for German users and had been friendly to German visitors. The German foreign ministry intervened with the army and justice ministries, the Academic Bureau for Foreigners, and the rector of Bonn University to facilitate the participation of Guatemalan youth in various programs.[8]

Leaders on the periphery recognized that foreign firms reserved clerical and other service jobs for foreign nationals. Citizens of the periphery could perform bureaucratic labor with minimum training, but they were seldom hired. Clerical work was cleaner, more prestigious, and better paid than the manual work assigned the local labor force. White collar jobs would train a domestic labor force to serve the local economies. In 1926, Guatemala, Panama, El Salvador, and Nicaragua established a minimum percentage of natives that each foreign firm must employ. The Guatemalan and Panamanian laws required the employment of 75 percent nationals, while the Salvadoran law called for 80 percent nationals. After considerable protest, Panama revised its law to phase in the change over five years. The German consul suggested that the exemption of technical fields where qualified Panamanians were not available would make implementation difficult. The Hamburg Chamber of Commerce became upset when Kühlmann did not protest the Guatemalan law energetically. The minister, however, after consulting local German businesspeople and European diplomats, concluded that the law might never be enforced. He advised observing the U.S. reaction first and then acting in concert with other European agents to minimize the damage from any nationalist reactions.[9]

The Hamburg Chamber observed that while retail firms might comply with new national employment laws, wholesale firms needed employees with advanced foreign language skills and experience in foreign countries. Still, Kühlmann advised waiting because the Salvadoran law might be found inconsistent with the pending U.S.-Salvadoran commerce treaty, in which case Germany could gain its objective through the most-favored-nation clause, and the odium for defeating the law would fall on the United States. The Salvadoran government, however, stopped negotiating with the United States. The Hamburg Chamber insinuated that Kühlmann was not using every opportunity to advance German interests. He considered the Hamburg Chamber's critique impolite, self-serving, and ignorant of isthmian affairs. The laws were aimed at U.S. firms and would probably have little detrimental impact on German businesses.[10]

The German government sought to improve its understanding of the isthmus in order to pursue fruitful policies. Two Germans of elevated status visited the isthmus in the mid-1920s and analyzed German activity in the region. Retired general Johannes Kretzschmar, traveling in Central America in 1925, quipped that the southern border of the United States and the northern border of Panama were identical. He found a small, well-respected German community of modest influence in El Salvador and Germans who produced sugar, corn, and cattle in addition to much coffee in Guatemala. The community in Guatemala was well organized, rich, nationalistic, and enjoyed good relations with the government, although Guatemalans occasionally found its influence irritating.[11]

As German economic activity in Central America accelerated in the mid-1920s, the Berlin government sent Gustav Noske on an extensive trip through Latin America. He was the former minister president of Hanover and a renowned Social Democratic politician who had gained infamy as minister of defense [Reichswehrminister] for his role in suppressing Berlin laborers during the Kapp-Putsch (coup) in 1920. Germans occupied a powerful economic position in Costa Rica, he reported, but were most numerous and influential in Guatemala. He valued the assessment of a German consul and large plantation owner: "We [Germans] play about the same role in Guatemala, as the anti-Semitics alleged against the Jews in Germany. As economic exploiters of the country, we are every bit as loved as the Jews are loved normally by us in the homeland." As the competition for accumulation grew sharper, the gap between the haves and have-nots expanded. Noske commented incisively on this in the mid-1920s. Most emigrés wanted to return home with a fortune. The harm was made worse because the accumulators paid almost no taxes. (The Guatemalan elite also often placed capital in foreign countries.) He recognized that Guatemalans would not tolerate this huge capital drain forever.[12]

One means of weakening the periphery and making it more susceptible to metropole exploitation was to use the ill-defined concepts of civilization, westernization, or modernization to undermine the local culture, institutions, and value system; metropoles manipulated racism, education, progress, and expertise to degrade the peripheral societies. "Ethnic" (class-race) assignment of occupations and economic roles were common in all forms of export-oriented economic enterprise. In the long run, Noske warned, white foreigners could not rule Latin America. The Guatemalan natives inevitably compared the exalted lifestyle of Germans to their own hard labor and wretched existence. Until the native population finally asserted itself, however, Noske recommended that Germans continue conducting business because the United States would continue to extract profits.[13] The metropole humanitarians often recognized the injustice of their conduct but saw no escape, because liberal rhetoric considered competition fundamental.

Many German emigrants had problems balancing their nationality and business, especially when the fatherland made their return difficult. Noske encountered conditions in Central America that hampered the preservation of German culture and nationalism. He cautioned against the use of the misleading term "German-friendly [Germanophile] state," which he understood to mean a state with a numerous, wealthy, and powerful German colony. One German merchant said: "Naturally, patriotism does not go so far that I will buy a German machine which is higher priced and also of lower quality than a comparable U.S. machine." U.S. products were marketed aggressively, but German products of high quality and moderate price competed. Noske traced the disrespect for the Weimar Republic's flag to the monarchism of the emigrated Germans and to the war-decimated investments of overseas Germans. These Germans confronted such high taxes when they wished to repatriate their wealth that many opted for homes in Holland or Switzerland.[14] The wartime and postwar experience of many overseas Germans left them uncertain about their loyalty.

German-Honduran relations were uneventful in the late 1920s. Consul Cornelsen observed happily that Germans were generally well respected in Honduras. The Honduran government arranged a small emergency loan from Tegucigalpa businessmen, including the heads of four German firms. The U.S. government delayed this loan because it did not want the Honduran government to escape its financial pressure. In March 1926 the Reichstag approved the resurrection of the 1887 Honduran-German commerce treaty with its most-favored-nation clause. German trade with Honduras developed advantageously.[15]

Efforts to settle German claims in Honduras arising from World War I and the revolts of the early 1920s met a frustrating sort of success. President Rafael López Gutiérrez recognized claims of $60,000 due to Germans, but the Honduran Congress denied their validity. Kühlmann urged not pressing unsubstantiated claims: they would be rejected and could no longer be collected by force. He advised diplomatic intervention only after political and judicial recourse failed.[16]

When Honduras postponed the implementation of a special customs fund to repay debts and claims, Germany was asked to join France, Spain, and Italy in expressions of regret at the delay. The German foreign ministry hesitated. While Cornelsen judged that a joint note might strengthen the efforts of private German creditors to obtain repayment, the Honduran government might not understand the determination behind a joint note. The U.S. government was unlikely to participate because U.S. firms regulated their disputes unilaterally. The U.S. fruit companies used their periodic financial activity with the Honduran government to assure that they suffered no losses. Cornelsen, reflecting on the overbearing U.S. role in Honduran disturbances, judged that Germany's more reserved role should prove rewarding in the long run. He and Kühlmann wished to create an atmosphere in which commerce would grow and Germans would be welcomed.[17]

German firms were trying to enter the Nicaraguan market. A German economic agency reported that German firms frequently hired agents in Managua who were isolated from the potential marketing opportunity on the Atlantic coast. Neither the German firms nor the Managuan agents understood the credit and reliability of the agency business on the Atlantic coast. Compounding the problem was the fact that Nicaragua was flooded with German traveling salesmen and commission agents who sold to anyone on credit and often did not even forward the initial payment to the principal.[18] The unreliable agents and traveling salesmen increased the risk of loss and sullied the reputation of German businesses.

Despite this drawback German consumer goods and machinery established markets in Nicaragua. German manufacturers used reliable sales agents and a reputation for quality work to build markets. A Nicaraguan merchant house, noting the predominance of U.S. cotton textiles, sought a German manufacturer who would supply textiles under an exclusive contract. German textile manufacturers refused exclusive contracts; they preferred to sell indirectly, using Hamburg export houses as middlemen. The vice consul on Nicaragua's Atlantic coast reported only modest opportunities for German products. However, after the Bluff customs house acquired a Siemens dynamo and a diesel motor from Mannheim Motoren Werke to supply electricity, he hoped more orders for electric and power machines would follow. Generally, the small machines in Nicaragua came from the United States or Germany.[19]

The metropoles competed to sell machinery for the agro-export industry and for consumer use. Costa Rica contracted with a German chemical engineer to perfect import substitution products at the state-owned liquor factory. The German minister encouraged local production because French, Dutch, and British firms exported more liquors to Costa Rica than German distilleries. British firms dominated the sale of coffee processing machinery, but Krupp-Gruson and Boehm-Wahlen sold a few machines. A commercial agent advised that any German firm could sell coffee machines if it made accurate replicas of British John Gordon machines because interchangeable parts would permit convenient repairs.[20]

Apparently, Central Americans were convinced that U.S. industry possessed superiority in several product areas. Even die-hard consumers of German products often purchased U.S. automobiles, record players, and records. German automobiles were expensive, and although German record players and records were cheaper, they were of lower quality. Consul Lutz described a simple, clever stratagem Ford Motor Company used in Panama: Ford trained local mechanics to service its automobiles. Meanwhile, German cars sold poorly because local mechanics could not repair them. In 1928 the German consul in Guatemala reported that U.S. models dominated the limited market for trucks, although the Büssing truck, considered a luxury vehicle, sold a few units annually. The United States and Britain supplied most of the agricultural tools, and German manufacturers found a few buyers.[21]

In 1927 the German Economic Service compiled lists of important foreign and native commercial firms in several Central American countries (Table 11). These lists revealed that German entrepreneurs played important roles in Nicaragua, Honduras, and Costa Rica. Unfortunately, comparable lists were not located for Guatemala and El Salvador. The German Economic Service [Deutscher Wirtschaftsdienst] distributed confidentially a blacklist of firms consular agents had verified were unreliable in business relations.[22]

In late 1927 a German committee studying commerce found no major economic or political disadvantages for German businesses in Middle America. It concluded that German exports were competitive with products of all nations but the United States. With the exception of El Salvador, it found the isthmian countries friendly to emigrants bearing capital. The Hamburg Chamber of Commerce reported that German trade with Central America remained strong, German shipping carried an appreciable portion of Guatemala's trade, and Kosmos and Roland received subsidies from the Salvadoran government. On the downside, Honduras lacked direct maritime connections and was unable to finance imports after the banana disease broke out. The Hamburg Chamber assumed that faster, regular steam vessels would improve Germany's 8 percent share of Nicaragua's trade. Although U.S. financiers supplied a loan to Nicaragua in 1929, Kühlmann expected that a share of the business the loan generated would go to Germany. German trade progressed well everywhere except in Panama, where the United States jealously guarded against competition.[23]

Germany's leaders presumed that closer ties with Central America would alleviate some internal socioeconomic ailments and bolster the nation's security and prosperity. In 1928 the German minister for the economy recognized that consumer capacity was saturated. He concluded that "in the future everything must be done for German industry to penetrate foreign markets. The German government had to assure that this expansion did not occur under the appearance of crisis signals." As one step to encourage entrance into foreign markets, the German government systematically informed business organizations of opportunities in Central America.[24]

The coffee market strongly influenced European–Central American relations. A sharp decline in world coffee prices brought coffee producers and coffee wholesalers together in the late 1920s. The League of German Food Wholesalers and Costa Rican officials shared a concern with the sharp drop in purchases of Costa Rican coffee in comparison with prewar years. They assigned the erosion to the disruption of the war, postwar inflation, the introduction of ersatz coffee (a roasted grain substitute) during the war, and the health community's campaign against caffeine. The wholesalers expected Costa Rican support for propaganda to revive coffee sales.[25]

The Costa Rican consul general blamed the decline in sales of Costa Rican coffee on the German practice of calling all coffee of high quality "coffee of Costa Rica"—which led to the selling of other high-quality coffees as Costa Rican—and on the high tariff that was levied on coffee by weight. Moreover, the coffee tax veiled the price and quality differences inherent in a quarter pound of coffee (the most common purchase) because the variation in price would only be a few pfennigs (less than U.S.$.01).[26]

Although in 1929 Germany remained the leading importer of Guatemalan and Salvadoran coffee and a significant importer of Costa Rican and Nicaraguan coffee, depressed coffee prices and unstable sugar prices left many German plantations and firms in Guatemala in a precarious position. Financial problems increased for all but the best firms. Kühlmann advised businesspeople to use banks to check German-Guatemalan firms before extending credit because the legation could not evaluate their creditworthiness reliably. In fact, German officials gathered detailed information for foreign ministry studies regarding which firms in Middle America were creditworthy and which were credit risks. Kühlmann assumed that the declining world coffee prices affected all major coffee-exporting countries.[27]

German experience with Central American diplomats and consuls was uneven. In the 1920s, Hamburg and Bremen—the coffee ports—attracted Guatemalans anxious to experience German society, frequently as honorary consuls. The Hamburg Association of Guatemalan Firms and the German foreign minister welcomed the Guatemalan consul general in Hamburg, Horacio Espinosa, a close friend of the Guatemalan president and a friend of Germany. Later, Emilio Escamilla, who had written articles favorable to Germany during the war and who had labored to release confiscated German property, arrived. Federico Mora, who had tried to bring German teachers to Guatemala while minister of education, was named Guatemalan consul general in Hamburg in 1926 and elevated to minister in 1928. He studied mental institutions and institutes of psychology in Germany because he planned to open a mental hospital on his return. Guatemala appointed Flavio Andrade, who had studied in Germany, honorary consul general in Bremen in 1928 to grant him prestige and a modest income while he furthered his medical studies.[28]

Whereas many Guatemalans served with mutual benefit to the two societies, Ricardo Chávez, named consul general to Hamburg in November 1924, left a stain on the relationship. He had been dismissed, after questionable activity, as head of a hospital in Quetzaltenango. Although the father of a large family, Chávez impregnated a young German woman and then persuaded her to have an illegal abortion. He also became involved in various civil suits that led to his recall in late 1925. In spite of the fact Chávez threatened to contact the Guatemalan press about the intrigues and antipathy he had encountered in Hamburg, he had little overt impact on future German-Guatemalan relations.[29]

Honduras also made a disastrous consular appointment to Germany. Consul General Pineda's lifestyle in Hamburg was beyond his income, so he extorted money and misused Honduran consular funds. When word got out, he accused Cornelsen and other Germans of damaging Honduras's reputation. However, he was dismissed because he had become a liability to Honduras and to Hamburg merchants.[30]

Nicaragua's internal tension complicated its relations with Germany in the mid-1920s. The continuing disturbances produced incidents involving German residents and interests and unverified stories of German involvement in the Nicaraguan civil war. An infamous (but unidentified) "General Müller" engaged in the fighting. Several Germans were casualties of the conflict and German businesses suffered from the economic slowdown related to the civil war. A former consulate employee was expelled for conspiring with the liberals against the conservatives. Wild rumors circulated that a Japanese-Mexican-German secret project aimed to overthrow all conservative governments in Latin America and that Russians were aiding Mexico to reestablish the Central American liberals. Events belied such unsubstantiated rumors. After the United States, Britain, Italy, Honduras, and El Salvador had recognized the Adolfo Díaz government, Consul Bunge hoped Germany would not hesitate to extend recognition. Although some German newspapers labeled Chancellor Gustav Stresemann's government a house servant of the United States for recognizing the Nicaraguan government, Bunge and other German diplomats argued that stability, security, and compensation for losses would depend on the U.S. government's response to Nicaraguan affairs.[31]

When Sandino operated against U.S. forces in early 1928, after the United States had announced his elimination, U.S. prestige and German interests suffered. Sandino's campaign inflicted significant property losses on Germans. Regretfully, Germans around Matagalpa, Jinotega, and Estelí had to turn to U.S. officials for protection. Even the Nicaraguan government had asked the U.S. government to protect foreigners. Kühlmann speculated that Germans might receive favorable treatment from Nicaraguan president José María Moncada because they had lent him money at crucial moments and because one of Moncada's chief advisers was German. After Moncada took a strong stand against Sandino, German chargé Dietrich von Lentz recommended that the German press should distance itself from the rebel leader.[32]

German–Costa Rican trade grew considerably after 1925 and was capable of further expansion under favorable conditions. German merchants argued that economic penetration needed a treaty. Any goodwill might evaporate if fierce metropole competition called forth the use of comprador political pressure. In 1928 the Costa Rican government seemed receptive to a commerce treaty based on most-favored-nation status.[33]

The Juan Kümpel claim clouded Costa Rican–German relations and specifically trade negotiations throughout the 1920s. Kühlmann hoped to separate this claim from the trade negotiations while using the friendly atmosphere of the trade talks to nudge the claim closer to resolution. The Costa Rican foreign minister wanted this unwarranted claim terminated. In his view, Kümpel hoped to recuperate large business losses through judicial and diplomatic activity. Kümpel had lost a suit in Costa Rican courts. The foreign minister argued that in view of the fact a German citizen had just won a suit against the Costa Rican government, Kümpel must have lost because his case lacked merit. The German colony even petitioned the German foreign ministry to distance itself from the claim because Kümpel had been involved in Costa Rican politics.[34]

Costa Rica insisted that the German government drop the Kümpel claim if it wished an advantageous trade treaty. After Kühlmann's efforts to resolve the claim through a contract awarding Kümpel money for some services plus a written apology was leaked to the public, the Costa Rican government refused any concession. Even the popular government of González Víquez would face intense public condemnation if it tried to satisfy Kümpel's claim. Kühlmann and the German business community were unable to persuade Costa Rica that the Kümpel affair and the treaty negotiations were separate matters.[35] The Kümpel claim went unresolved, remaining so for many years and possibly indefinitely.

The Central American governments welcomed the reentry of German firms. German businesses competed well against U.S. enterprises. AEG, Siemens, and the Wayss-Freytag construction firm of Frankfurt brought German technology, capital, and products to the isthmus in the 1920s. In 1925 AEG received the telephone concession in Guatemala, which U.S. military intelligence considered "an excellent piece of business from the German point of view." AEG won major projects in Guatemala, Costa Rica, El Salvador, and Honduras, while Wayss-Freytag obtained major contracts in Costa Rica. In 1926 Siemens named Schlubach, Thiemer, and Company to supervise its organization in Central America.[36] Large German firms were active and successful.

German officials and entrepreneurs expected concessions for technology and engineering in Guatemala where German economic power had revived. Kühlmann encouraged Wayss-Freytag to consider road construction opportunities and AEG to seek both the concession for an electric railroad connecting Quetzaltenango with Guatemala City and related projects for an electric power station. Guatemala's financial difficulties forced AEG to delay projects or to raise funds privately. The Guatemalan legislature, Lentz recorded, refused to approve paving and sewage projects for the capital and refused to fund an urgently needed water project contracted with AEG. Stymied by this inaction, AEG and the Banco Occidental del Salvador raised the $500,000 for the water project privately. Lentz expected this popular project to elevate AEG's image. A lack of funds also delayed AEG's project to double the 2,000 telephones in the capital.[37]

Costa Rican president Ricardo Jiménez, concerned about growing U.S. influence, asked German engineer Walter Sprung to prepare a project for an alternate harbor on the Atlantic coast (where United Fruit dominated

Puerto Limón) and to supervise the water system for Puerto Limón and the dock for Puntarenas. The Puntarenas project, worth $1,100,000, was originally intended for a U.S. firm until Sprung's cheaper plans were adopted. To finance these and other projects, the Costa Rican government sought an $8 million loan. Knowing the difficulty of attracting German firms into an area where the United States was so powerful, Sprung guided business to German firms by sending them specifications on the projects before the official request for bids.[38]

With many major projects under consideration in Costa Rica, the competition became intense. President Jiménez claimed that only "sharks"— promoters in frenzied search for concessions—came to see him. In 1927 the Costa Rican government negotiated with AEG for the electrification of the San José–to–Puntarenas railroad. Naturally, the Costa Ricans were interested in a lawsuit against AEG in Guatemala for allegedly misappropriating $400,000 from a railroad and power station project. The court of first instance found AEG guilty, but there was an appeal. The Costa Rican minister in Guatemala investigated the charges. He concluded that "the railroad as well as the electric plant are very good and well constructed. The material and the machinery are of the best available quality." He learned that Guatemalans had viewed the railroad project since its inception under Estrada Cabrera as a fountain of graft. He considered AEG, which had little control over funds, a scapegoat for the misconduct of Guatemalans. He expected the appeals court to reverse the judgment. The French minister in Guatemala, no friend of any German firm, suspected that the affair originated in intrigues by U.S. interests desirous of AEG's contracts. The Costa Rican government, quieted in its concern, still sought a guarantor of AEG's contract in Costa Rica. Once assured that the British Hambros Bank, Ltd. and the Berliner Handelsgesellschaft [Berlin Trade Society] would guarantee AEG's contracts, it awarded AEG the contract for electrification of the railroad.[39]

German firms occasionally competed bitterly with each other. After AEG was awarded the contract for an electrical railway to Puntarenas, Siemens's agent persuaded Costa Rican officials to postpone the project. AEG returned the favor by undermining a Siemens contract for a hydroelectric work at Alajuela. Kühlmann was incensed. He complained that the squabbling discredited German business, pushed concessions to other countries, and contributed toward dividing the German colony in Costa Rica. He wanted the foreign ministry to talk to the firms about joint projects and cooperation. Siemens's management assured the foreign ministry that the bitter struggle reflected personal animosity between the agents in Costa Rica and that the two firms were not engaged in mutually damaging competition.[40]

The intense competition among metropole firms fostered bribery charges and countercharges within the Costa Rican community. In 1925 Sprung had acquired both influence with Jiménez and a position administering development projects after exposing a cabinet minister who had ordered a bridge for $125 per ton even though a German firm had bid $80 per ton. In 1927, however, Sprung was forced to resign amid charges that he had used dummy firms to skim funds. This was a bitter pill for Jiménez, who had paid Sprung more than double the salary of a cabinet minister. In addition, Jiménez and Lentz were embarrassed because they had defended Sprung initially against the allegations of misconduct. They assumed these complaints arose because Sprung would not allow local politicians and firms to "profit" from the construction contracts. Jiménez presumed the flaw was personal and replaced Sprung with another German engineer.[41]

In late 1927, in one of his last acts, Sprung gave Wayss-Freytag premature notification that Costa Rica would open bidding for a $600,000 contract to pave the streets of the capital. The Frankfurt firm won the contract in spite of fierce competition from U.S. firms. Then Wayss-Freytag asserted that U.S. competitors launched political intrigues to sabotage the concession. It asked the German foreign ministry to intervene indirectly because the contract forbad diplomatic interference in matters related to the contract. At stake was not only a 2.5-million-mark project, Wayss-Freytag officials argued, but also the opportunity for German firms to acquire subsequent contracts. The foreign ministry acted to stymie the intrigue, for if Wayss-Freytag were successful, German firms would benefit in competition against U.S. businesses elsewhere in Central America.[42]

In the fall of 1928, Consul Cornelsen used AEG as a tool to extract revenge for an earlier defeat at the hands of a U.S. firm. The U.S. firm Westinghouse believed it had no competition for a contract for electric light and power in Tegucigalpa. Cornelsen wired an AEG engineer in Guatemala to prepare the necessary papers. Although Westinghouse and the U.S. minister scrambled to block the competitive bid, Honduran officials decided to purchase AEG equipment. Cornelsen rejoiced when Honduran public opinion judged his maneuvers a knockout punch to the North Americans. He expected further contracts to follow, while the U.S. minister conceded that the setback might generate a significant, rippled impact. AEG's success in Guatemala, Costa Rica, and Honduras underscored the recovery of powerful German influence on the isthmus.[43]

In the 1920s there were various projects to colonize Germans in Costa Rica. Noske recognized that the plans were not maturing because small German farmers would not do well as long as Costa Rica's economy was not strong. Even German artisans had little chance to earn a living there in the mid-1920s because prime consumers—large German firms and settlements of 100 or more Germans—were rare. Karl Lachner-Sandoval, the grandson of the composer Vinzenz Lachner, suggested that an agricultural colony of former German soldiers near the projected Nicaraguan canal route might demonstrate to U.S. officials the possibility of feeding the excavation crews from local production. The Costa Rican government was intrigued with the idea of former soldiers as colonists because the project would also protect its border.[44]

A wealthy Dresden entrepreneur, Hubert Renz, sought appointment as Costa Rican consul in order to further a scheme to colonize German farmers in Costa Rica. Lachner, though acknowledging the wealth and influence of Renz, was convinced that the culturally conservative German peasants would not be content in a climate, culture, political milieu, and community setting so alien to their lifestyle. He proposed an alternative: the Costa Rican–German Commercial Circle, which would send individuals and family groups of suitable skills to Costa Rica after preparing the site and the terms of emigration. His proposal established German settlements yet responded to Costa Rican needs for larger coffee markets, capital and technological inflows, and improved communications. He was adamant that potential migrants needed preparation before departing and support once they arrived in Costa Rica. The settlers would grow only foodstuffs the first year or two, then gradually add coffee and other commercial crops without losing the capacity to meet their own basic needs. The Commercial Circle would propagandize the products of each society in the other and facilitate the entrance of Costa Rican students into German agricultural schools. Lachner wanted the colonization project to incorporate cultural and commercial ties.[45]

Some of the tension between Germany and France manifested itself on the isthmus. Between 1927 and 1929, Germany and France engaged in a contest for reputation and influence in El Salvador. The bust of Field Marshal Helmut von Moltke was proposed for the Hall of Honor of El Salvador's Military School. The French objected to the display of Moltke alongside their World War I hero Marshal Ferdinand Foch. The central figure in this dispute was El Salvador's ambitious minister to Germany, Ismael G. Fuentes, who had studied in, and was sympathetic to, Germany. He claimed that U.S. and French intrigue blocked the placement of Moltke's bust at the military school. He suggested that the German government might prevent such inconveniences if it named highly esteemed Theodor Benecke as permanent consul to replace the honorary consul. Since El Salvador maintained a permanent mission in Berlin and Guatemala did not, he wanted Germany to move its legation to El Salvador. The German foreign ministry left the legation in Guatemala.[46]

The reputation and prestige of resident Germans helped new migrants achieve positions of influence, power, and material success. U.S., British, and French officials were jealous that these Germans could obtain profit and influence so quickly. The Germans created envy among foreign powers in Central America when they reacquired their powerful commercial positions. In late 1928 a French memorandum, conceding the successful German recovery from the setback of World War I, concluded that the United States, Britain, and Germany would compete vigorously for economic preponderance in Latin America.[47]

Unable to resolve the difficulties of the political economy, German leadership was forced to continue relying on social imperialist policies to ameliorate tensions. German–Central American relations were influenced when German special agents like Kretzschmar and Noske traveled the isthmus seeking contacts that would relieve some domestic disorder and problems. The activity of AEG, Siemens, Wayss-Freytag, Sprung, and Scadta sought to insert colonists, capital, technology, and production into Central American economies. There were efforts to send colonists to the isthmus to revitalize prewar levels of commercial and entrepreneurial activity. However, German officials had difficulty responding to the Kümpel affair, the Sandino movement, and the fate of old coffee planters in Guatemala; slow or inadequate responses in these matters slowed German reappearance on the isthmus.

The postwar years marked an era of recovery and renewal of competition and expansion, as if little had been learned from the earlier struggles and tensions of competition in the search for foreign-generated wealth to supply material success to a disordered domestic political economy. German entrepreneurs scurried to reenter isthmian public works projects as a means to introduce advanced technological products that would aid the recovery of Germany's high technology industries. German banks financed enterprises in the coffee trade and in public utilities. Despite the advantages U.S. firms had acquired during the war, by 1929 German firms had regained their prewar commercial position in Central America. Some leaders in Central America expected German capital, colonists, and trade to mitigate aggressive "Yankee imperialism." U.S. officials envisioned their hegemony in Central America as endangered by the German success. The contradictory and unstable nature of organized capitalism (an ill-defined, competitive, yet confused in its goal-orientation combination of laissez-faire ideology and bureaucratic-corporatist structures) allowed little room for self-confidence in a competitive world system.

Conclusion and Epilogue

■

The focus on British and U.S. relations with Central America in the nineteenth and early twentieth centuries has veiled German involvement in Central America. German relations with Central America changed between 1823 and 1929. From 1823 to the 1850s, several German states—the Hansa cities, Hanover, and Prussia—established relations with Central America. During these early years, Prussia manipulated Customs Union relations with Central America in the expectation of undermining Austria's Grossdeutschland aspirations with its own Kleindeutschland vision of Germany's future. Preference in the inner German struggle gravitated toward the state that could offer security, national pride, and economic opportunities to most of the major economic interests in Germany.

Prussia was an early defender of German interests in Middle America. It considered the transit area vital for its plan to attract the Hansa cities, the developing industrial areas of northern and western Germany, and ultimately even the south German states. The port cities needed access to interoceanic transit and worldwide trade, and the industrial areas needed raw materials and markets for manufactures. The right isthmian policies would help the agrarian regions to transport their displaced population to foreign areas in a manner beneficial to Prussian and kleindeutsch interests. Beginning in the 1840s, some leaders had presumed that closer, more intimate ties with Central America would alleviate some German ailments and facilitate German security and prosperity. These aspirations encountered similar perspectives among the leadership of the United States, Britain, and France.

Although societies have sought trade for millennia, national economies exploiting the technological innovation and capital accumulation of industrialism developed increased needs for raw materials, markets for their surpluses, opportunities to place surplus capital and technology, and an ideology (liberalism) that designated the fulfillment of these needs as essential for survival and progress. Great Britain, engaged in responding to such problems for several generations, was already securely settled on the isthmus. Both Germany and the United States entered rapid industrialization during the mid- and late nineteenth century. Both became particularly involved in the Central American–Caribbean area because interoceanic transit was essential in the search for more and cheaper raw materials, markets for surplus production, and investment opportunities in the world economy. Germany expected to achieve important communications objectives and significant investment and migration goals in the Caribbean area. Its activity stimulated a U.S. reaction because German penetration collided with U.S. expansionism and undermined U.S. political and economic aspirations on the isthmus.

Around 1850 the British opted to preserve transit and commercial access to the isthmus and not to challenge U.S. political and geographical aspirations in the circum-Caribbean. The British funneled most of their expansive energy to the Middle East, South and East Asia, and Africa. Their policy shift, initiated around 1850 and emphasized in the Hay-Pauncefote treaty of 1902, illuminates the decline of U.S.-British tension from the mid-nineteenth century until World War I and the rise of U.S.-German tension during the same period.

The German political economy from the mid-nineteenth through the early twentieth centuries experienced sporadic economic cycles that raised a host of problems its leaders sought to alleviate abroad. In a key area of the world system—the Central American isthmus—German interests encountered other nations's businesspeople, whose corrupted laissez-faire ideology, evident in free trade rhetoric covering government-supported multinational business ventures, generated intense competition. Strategic, political, social, and cultural language reinforced the determination of each metropole to assure minimum access to the isthmus's capacity to unlock wealth and boost security by linking the Atlantic and Pacific worlds.[1]

From 1860 to the 1880s German unification mitigated some difficulties in the German political economy and facilitated expansion abroad in a search to resolve the internal problems of the political economy. In the 1850s Prussian privy counselor Franz Hugo Hesse had encouraged levels of German activity on the isthmus that raised warning signals from U.S., British, and French diplomats in the 1860s and 1870s. By the 1880s German entrepreneurs were busily involved in coffee, wholesale and retail commerce, banking, and shipping activity throughout the isthmus.

From the 1890s to 1918, Germany and other metropole powers competed intensely over areas in the periphery viewed as prime opportunities to exploit, to expand accumulation, and to alleviate internal problems. The steady absorption of parts of the periphery and semi-periphery, either as colonies or protectorates, made latecomers like Germany and the United States—both transforming from semi-peripheral powers to metropoles—especially anxious to claim a share of the spoils and to assure that they would not be excluded from the ever-smaller undivided areas of the globe. The isthmus had something special to offer Germany and the United States. German entrepreneurs, including Krupp, Siemens, and AEG, scurried for concessions in public utilities as a means to introduce their technological products to the isthmian political economies. German banks financed enterprises engaged in commerce, the coffee trade, and public utilities. Financial institutions from other metropoles competed, but U.S. entrepreneurs were the chief competition in technologies and public utilities.

When the social imperialist policies of the metropole states proved inadequate to ameliorate the difficulties that arose from laissez-faire industrial, social, economic, and political disorder, the tension heightened until violence—strikes, riots, repression, revolutions, and wars—exposed the problems. Around the globe, major civil disorder erupted in the periphery (the Boxer uprising; and Chinese, Mexican, Brazilian, Russian, and Arabian revolts and civil wars) and in numerous armed conflicts (Sino Japanese, Spanish-American, U.S.-Philippine, Russo-Japanese, Boer, Balkan, U.S.-Nicaragua, U.S.-Mexican, and U.S.-Haitian), often between metropoles or semi-peripheral states for control or access to these peripheral areas. Central America did not escape the aggression and hostility emanating from the escalating competition. Metropole troops landed on the isthmus in 1878 (German), 1894–1895 (British), and 1903, 1907, 1911, and 1912–1933 (U.S.), while bloody revolutions and civil wars took place in 1893 (Nicaragua), 1903–1913 (Honduras), 1906 (El Salvador), 1909–1913 and 1926–1932 (Nicaragua), 1917 (Costa Rica), and 1920 (Guatemala).

Germany's outward thrust in the period from 1870 to 1914 encountered a U.S. political economy engaged in a similar expansion. Since the late nineteenth century, the Central American states were swamped with metropole agents pushing developmental schemes. Gradually they surrendered major elements of control over their internal communications, public utilities, national debt, currency, state revenue, and other economic activity to metropole interests. In fact, the heated competition of expanding industrial states intimidated the host Central American states because they were pressured to pick sides in serious metropole conflicts, such as World War I, as well as on a smaller scale in regard to concessions for canals, steamship lines, loans, and so forth. The competition, driven by metropole claims of well-being and security, restricted the sovereignty of the Central American states. For example, the Monroe Doctrine forbade Costa Rica, Nicaragua, Honduras, or El Salvador to sell islands in their possession or to grant certain concessions (for example, related to canal routes) to non–New World states. The Central American societies struggled to find a secure role in the revised world order. The goals of the states on the periphery were severely tested by the huge power imbalances between themselves and the metropoles. The Central American states considered "liberal" progress and development to be their key to a better future, yet they were denied the authority to market their resources and concessions freely. They were incorporated by bits and pieces—often as enclaves, subject to the guidance of comprador authority on behalf of metropole objectives—into the broadening world economy.[2] As early as 1914, the burgeoning U.S. political economy used the World War I era as an excuse to undermine German (and also French and British) activity in Central America.

From 1918 to 1929 German entrepreneurs recovered well, which, of course, renewed concern among U.S. officials and businesspeople. In 1928 the German minister of the economy reiterated an old theme, namely that an expansive phase of production in Germany had saturated domestic consumer capacity. He concluded that "in the future everything must be done to penetrate foreign markets for German industry. It was the German government's job to assure that this did not occur under the appearance of crisis signals." Thus, in 1928, just as with the mission of Hesse in 1850, Germany's political and economic leadership presumed that closer ties with Central America (and other places) would alleviate Germany's internal socioeconomic ailments and facilitate security and prosperity.[3]

Germany and the United States pursued social imperialism in their relations with Central America. Both states manipulated their Central American policies in response to domestic economic and political problems. The nineteenth- and twentieth-century projects to internationalize laissez-faire—British free trade, the open door, Wilson's fourteen points—represented the frustration of faltering and bastardized domestic laissez-faire systems. The metropoles believed salvation could be achieved through expanding the area of market competition onto a world scale. They pursued this objective even though the application of laissez-faire practices had failed to produce order and stability in their domestic political economies. The consequence was intensified competition in the periphery, but with fewer mechanisms to control the abuses and excesses of entrepreneurs because the states on the periphery were overmatched in wealth and power, and the institutions of international law and order were weak.[4]

German relations with Central America and with the other metropole powers need to be investigated in order to construct a more reliable picture. There is only one history of a German entrepreneur and enterprise (Erwin Paul Dieseldorff) from Central America, although at least one other businessman and his firms (Friedrich Köper of Bremen) has left extensive records. German shipping firms—HAPAG, Kosmos, Roland—were early participants in Central American trade, but little is known of this story. The role of large German firms and entrepreneurs—Siemens, Deutsche Bank, Krupp, AEG—on the isthmus needs study, as do German views and policies with regard to the various isthmian canal projects. Above all, we need studies of all areas of German expansion except colonialism, which has received considerable attention. The informal and indeed formal (in the sense of planned) commercial and investment expansion of Germany has received only modest attention. The arguments for expansion grew out of the social and economic structural changes of the industrialization process. There was an ongoing alteration of German production forms with consequent changes in the internal and external social and economic objectives of the political elite.

Despite German progress in reviving its role on the isthmus, U.S. hegemony in Central America seemed secure in the 1930s. The contradictory and unstable nature of organized capitalism, however, allowed little room for self-confidence in a competitive world system. By 1939 Germans had reacquired immense trade and investment stakes in Central America. World War II, however, destroyed the rebuilt German economic and cultural role on the isthmus. The U.S. government again pressured the isthmian governments (including Panama) to sequester property and to intern people of German descent that the U.S. considered espionage or sabotage risks. In the post–World War II decades the rebuilding of German cultural and economic presence has occurred more slowly than after World War I. Germany has, nevertheless, slowly defined commercial, investment, and cultural roles in Central America. German technology, education, financial institutions, and culture have created a modern influence yet remained able to draw on the heritage built by migrants and their descendants during a century and a half. The new role remains subordinate to metropole tensions and competition just as in other eras. This metropole rivalry—rooted in home country internal disorders and implemented on a worldwide, highly competitive economic and strategic battlefield—unquestionably has had a profound, lasting, and transforming impact on Central American societies.[5]

Appendix: Tables

■

Table 1. Guatemalan and Costa Rican Imports from Germany, 1839–1872

Year	Guatemalan Imports		Costa Rican Imports	
	($/pesos)[a]	(% of total)	($/pesos)[a]	(% of total)
1839	13,717	2.26	—	—
1840	13,767	1.43	—	—
1842	19,349	2.95	—	—
1843	5,000	1.18	—	—
1844	9,968	1.62	—	—
1846	6,108	0.92	—	—
1847	30,409	3.65	—	—
1850	8,983	0.97	—	—
1851	58,218	3.68	—	—
1852	36,928	3.78	—	—
1853	96,164	11.00	65,000	4.48
1854	18,864	2.28	—	—
1855	67,132	5.57	—	—
1856	46,851	4.40	173,830	18.30
1857	65,355	5.78	—	—
1858	26,059	2.13	100,000	10.00
1859	62,994	4.14	—	—
1860	108,548	7.26	—	—
1861	80,546	7.90	—	—
1862	69,798	6.39	—	—
1863	47,749	6.57	—	—
1864	28,543	2.02	—	—
1865	82,678	5.01	—	—
1866	118,968	7.00	—	—
1867	110,994	7.05	—	—
1868	148,035	8.89	—	—
1870	102,031	5.34	—	—
1871	209,637	8.72	—	—
1872	352,185	15.52	—	—

SOURCES: Bremen, Bureau für bremische Statistik, *Jahrbuch für die amtliche Statistik des Bremischen Staats* (Bremen: von Halem, 1862-[annual]); Hamburg, *Tabellarische Übersicht des Hamburg Handels* (Hamburg: F. H. Nestler, 1851–1874); Guatemalan and Costa Rican archival materials, *Memoria,* and newspapers; British and U.S. consular reports.

[a]Until the 1890s, the dollar and the peso were of approximately equal value.

Table 2. Guatemalan and Costa Rican Exports to Germany, 1856–1872

Year	Guatemalan Imports		Costa Rican Imports	
	($/pesos)[a]	(% of total)	($/pesos)[a]	(% of total)
1856	—	—	10,925	1.30
1857	32,161	2.46	47,240	3.67
1858	21,581	1.10	159,195	16.51
1859	—	—	10,165	0.74
1860	20,506	1.26	—	—
1865	—	—	147,445	8.35
1866	58,194	3.46	—	—
1867	105,215	5.27	144,825	6.10
1868	290,568	13.25	—	—
1869	183,084	7.33	—	—
1870	597,095	24.97	—	—
1871	561,820	20.45	—	—
1872	528,489	19.54	—	—

SOURCES: Bremen, *Jahrbuch für die amtliche Statistik des Bremischen Staats;* Hamburg, *Tabellarische Übersicht des Hamburg Handels;* Guatemalan and Costa Rican archival materials, *Memoria,* and newspapers; British and U.S. consular reports.
[a]Until the 1890s, the dollar and the peso were of approximately equal value.

Table 3. Bremen and Hamburg Imports from and Exports to Central America, 1847–1899

| | Bremen | | Hamburg | |
Year	Imports from Cent. Amer.	Exports to Cent. Amer.	Imports from Cent. Amer.	Exports to Cent. Amer.
1847	—	4,855p[a]	—	—
1850	—	5,354M	—	—
1851	—	20,204M	—	—
1852	3,668M	5,566M	—	—
1853	—	1,587M	—	79,500m[b]
1854	—	500M	—	108,580m
1855	—	3,657M	—	140,490m
1856	—	28M	—	168,820m
1857	4,554M	—	—	189,850m
1858	—	42,373M	—	560,220m
1859	7,698M	26,230M	—	484,510m
1860	89,765M	21,670M	—	768,620m
1861	117,075M	85,601M	—	311,500m
1862	45,202M	55,904M	—	527,280m
1863	190,452M	109,070M	—	849,340m
1864	199,842M	93,291M	—	285,360m
1865	228,038M	172,937M	—	304,690m
1866	664,519m	188,468m	—	427,760m
1867	551,031m	188,647m	—	456,740m
1868	1,028,623m	117,080m	—	432,410m
1869	440,455m	87,752m	—	1,221,830m
1870	716,063m	21,370m	—	138,260m
1871	1,723,685m	263,509m	—	2,090,320m
1872	2,223,027m	592,666m	—	1,566,400m
1873	1,882,364m	545,851m	—	3,300,600m
1874	3,055,944m	224,685m	—	—
1875	1,994,717m	284,430m	—	—
1876	2,638,017m	508,266m	—	—
1895	—	—	50,441,610m	16,511,210m
1896	—	—	43,118,200m	15,451,780m
1897	—	—	47,679,460m	13,002,400m
1898	—	—	38,470,190m	8,153,610m
1899	4,641,782m	164,782m	35,248,620m	6,766,240m

NOTE: p = pesos or dollars; M = gold marks; m = Kurant marks.
SOURCES: Bremen, *Jahrbuch für die amtliche Statistik des Bremischen Staats*; Hamburg, *Tabellarische Übersicht des Hamburg Handels*; Karl Sapper, *Mittelamerikanische Reisen und Studien aus den Jahren 1888 bis 1900* (Braunschweig: Friedrich Vieweg und Sohn, 1902), 426–27.
[a]Until the 1890s, the dollar and the peso were of approximately equal value.
[b]Most likely paper marks or equivalent values (in bills of credit, for example).

Table 4. Bremen Exports to and Imports from Central America, 1847–1900 (in marks)

Years	Exports to Cent. Amer. (yearly average)	Total Exports (yearly average)	Cent. Amer. % of Total	Imports from Cent. Amer. (yearly average)	Total Imports (yearly average)	Cent. Amer. % of Total
1847–51	724,064	44,874,482	1.61	165,297	50,696,138	0.33
1857–61	630,567	88,714,662	0.71	1,165,913	143,375,414	0.81
1867–71	668,056	139,584,356	0.48	1,545,419	231,057,431	0.60
1877–81	991,990	161,907,075	0.61	2,835,016	346,009,810	0.82
1887–91	588,315	274,086,050	0.22	3,337,174	442,150,395	0.76
1892–96	667,958	328,728,444	0.20	5,019,012	502,583,449	1.00
1897–1900	465,579	406,970,059	0.11	6,640,966	684,823,090	0.97

SOURCE: Bremisches Statistik Amt, *Jahrbuch für Bremische Statistik* (Bremen: Bremisches Statistisches Landesamt, 1901).

Table 5. German Imports from Central America, 1880–1928
(in thousands of current marks)

Year	Guatemala	El Salvador	Honduras	Nicaragua	Costa Rica	Central America	Total German Imports	Cent. Amer. % of Total German Imports
1880	—	—	—	—	—	2,366[a]	2,844,268	0.08
1881	—	—	—	—	—	1,365[a]	2,990,248	0.05
1882	—	—	—	—	—	1,028[a]	3,134,656	0.03
1883	—	—	—	—	—	1,409[a]	3,248,692	0.04
1884	—	—	—	—	—	2,291[a]	3,260,999	0.07
1885	—	—	—	—	—	6,548[a]	2,975,167	0.22
1886	—	—	—	—	—	7,122[a]	2,940,772	0.24
1887	—	—	—	—	—	4,977[a]	3,186,388	0.16
1888	—	—	—	—	—	4,481[a]	3,429,403	0.13
1889	—	—	—	—	—	21,943[a]	4,087,060	0.54
1890	—	—	—	—	—	14,040	4,272,910	0.33
1891	—	—	—	—	—	19,441	4,403,404	0.44
1892	—	—	—	—	—	17,200	4,227,000	0.41
1893	—	—	—	—	—	23,300	4,134,100	0.56
1894	—	—				35,800	4,285,000	0.84
1895	—	—		—	—	39,400	4,246,100	0.93
1896	—	—	—	—	—	39,700	4,558,000	0.87
1897	29,030	2,384[b]	—	—	4,410	35,824	4,864,400	0.74
1898	19,676	2,547[b]	—	—	4,029	26,252	5,439,700	0.48
1899	22,390	3,110[b]	—	—	4,070	29,570	5,983,600	0.49
1900	21,766	2,473[b]	—	—	4,589	28,828	6,043,000	0.48
1901	26,809	3,142[b]	—	—	5,403	35,354	5,710,300	0.62
1902	23,895	3,323[b]	—	—	5,838	32,956	5,805,800	0.57
1903	20,135	4,702[b]	—	—	5,449	30,286	—	—
1904	18,316	5,284[b]	—	—	4,397	27,997	—	—
1905	22,008	5,217[b]	—	—	5,084	32,309	—	—
1906	24,254	3,607	1,047	977	5,275	35,160	—	—
1907	33,817	5,829	938	3,907	7,134	51,625	7,095,000	0.73
1908	25,617	8,486	986	3,931	3,667	42,687	6,481,000	0.66
1909	35,039	6,168	893	2,536	3,316	47,952	6,859,000	0.70
1910	29,360	8,776	1,117	2,953	4,158	46,391	7,644,000	0.61
1911	35,949	9,512	1,050	2,444	4,562	53,517	8,224,000	0.65
1912	45,183	9,042	1,359	3,488	5,369	64,441	9,100,000	0.71
1913	42,903	10,010	1,452	4,478	7,838	66,681	10,199,000	0.65
1923	8,229	2,076	183	171	823	11,482	6,116,000	0.19
1924	29,894	7,734	173	1,257	6,755	45,813	6,585,000	0.70
1925	53,008	16,667	379	1,847	15,978	87,879	9,330,000	0.94
1926	62,984	22,943	352	3,083	21,836	111,198	10,451,000	1.06

| 1927 | 69,898 | 24,209 | 676 | 3,262 | 20,981 | 119,026 | 10,823,000 | 1.10 |
| 1928 | 72,821 | 34,267 | 12,452 | 4,779 | 22,594 | 146,913 | 12,087,000 | 1.22 |

SOURCES: Germany, Reichsamt des Innern, *Auswärtiger Handel des deutschen Zollgebiets nach Herkunfts- und Bestimmungsländern in den Jahren 1880–1896* (Berlin: Puttkammer und Mühlbrecht, 1897); Germany, Kaiserliches Statistisches Amt. *Statistik des Deutschen Reichs* (Berlin: Puttkammer und Mühlbrecht, 1891–1930).

[a]Central America and Mexico combined.

[b]El Salvador, Honduras, and Nicaragua combined.

Table 6. German Exports to Central America, 1880–1928
(in thousands of current marks)

Year	Guatemala	El Salvador	Honduras	Nicaragua	Costa Rica	Central America	Total German Imports	Cent. Amer. % of Total German Imports
1880	—	—	—	—	—	2,192[a]	2,976,721	0.07
1881	—	—	—	—	—	3,089[a]	3,094,308	0.10
1882	—	—	—	—	—	3,419[a]	3,279,921	0.10
1883	—	—	—	—	—	3,138[a]	3,324,351	0.09
1884	—	—	—	—	—	3,199[a]	3,255,929	0.09
1885	—	—	—	—	—	2,408[a]	2,911,458	0.08
1886	—	—	—	—	—	3,859[a]	3,041,744	0.13
1887	—	—	—	—	—	4,534[a]	3,193,023	0.14
1888	—	—	—	—	—	6,457[a]	3,356,429	0.19
1889	—	—	—	—	—	20,895	3,256,421	0.64
1890	—	—	—	—	—	8,338	3,409,584	0.24
1891	—	—	—	—	—	8,097	3,339,755	0.24
1892	—	—	—	—	—	5,700	3,151,100	0.18
1893	—	—	—	—	—	6,500	3,244,600	0.20
1894			—	—	—	6,500	3,051,500	0.21
1895	—	—	—	—	—	10,100	3,424,100	0.29
1896	—	—	—	—	—	10,700	3,753,800	0.29
1897	3,300	2,356[b]	—	—	1,903	7,559	3,786,200	0.20
1898	1,838	1,408[b]	—	—	1,307	4,553	4,010,600	0.11
1899	1,075	1,778[b]	—	—	1,201	4,054	4,368,400	0.09
1900	1,586	2,199[b]	—	—	1,798	5,583	4,752,600	0.12
1901	2,546	1,971[b]	—	—	1,360	5,877	4,512,600	0.13
1902	2,082	3,366[b]	—	—	1,024	6,472	4,812,800	0.13
1903	898	2,133[b]	—	—	1,551	4,582	—	—
1904	2,424	3,282[b]	—	—	1,547	7,253	—	—
1905	2,914	3,214[b]	—	—	1,664	7,792	—	—
1906	2,411	1,297	734	1,070	2,055	7,567	—	—
1907	3,649	1,571	755	1,483	2,760	10,218	9,001,000	0.11
1908	2,791	1,640	837	1,018	2,073	8,359	8,077,000	0.10
1909	2,812	1,600	621	941	2,166	8,140	8,860,000	0.09
1910	3,389	1,487	861	879	2,759	9,375	9,310,000	0.10
1911	4,071	1,865	1,218	2,458	4,242	13,854	10,007,000	0.14
1912	4,462	2,182	1,651	1,778	3,388	13,461	11,018,000	0.12
1913	5,299	2,860	1,737	1,921	3,169	14,986	11,206,000	0.13
1923	5,364	1,503	913	557	1,393	9,730	6,161,000	0.16
1924	7,173	2,141	1,076	1,307	2,549	14,246	9,265,000	0.15
1925	8,342	3,477	1,663	1,975	3,280	18,737	13,080,000	0.14
1926	11,343	3,657	1,809	2,102	3,896	22,807	10,617,000	0.21

| 1927 | 11,059 | 3,490 | 1,334 | 2,479 | 5,938 | 24,300 | 14,466,000 | 0.17 |
| 1928 | 11,936 | 4,532 | 1,664 | 3,430 | 6,592 | 28,154 | 15,018,000 | 0.19 |

SOURCES: Germany, *Auswärtiger Handel des deutschen Zollgebiets nach Herkunfts- und Bestimmungsländern;* Germany, *Statistik des Deutschen Reichs.*

[a]Mexico and Central America combined.

[b]El Salvador, Nicaragua, Honduras combined.

Table 7. German Investment in Central America, 1897–1926 (in millions of German marks [M], U.S. dollars [$], or French francs [F])

Year	Guatemala	Costa Rica	Nicaragua	El Salvador	Honduras	Panama
1897	155.50M[a]	39.90M	14.10M	—	2.00F	—
1898	183.50M[b]	—	14.00M[c]	—	—	—
1899	44.03$[d]	9.52$	10.47$	1.67$	1.43$	—
1900	250.00M[e]	40.00M[f]	15.00M[f]	—	—	—
1905	300.00M[g]	25.00M	24.00M	30.00M	—	0.5M
1906	250.00M[h]	35.00M[i]	250.00M[h]	—	10.00F[h]	—
1907	—	—	50.00F[i]	—	—	—
1909	190.00M[j]	—	—	—	—	—
1913	—	35.00M[k]	50.00F	—	—	—
1914	250.00M[l]	—	—	—	—	—
1918	867.00M[m]	—	2.50$[n]	—	—	0.2$[o]
1926	35–40.00$[p]	—	—	—	—	—

SOURCES: United Nations, *El Financiamiento Externo de América Latina* (New York: UNO, 1964); OAS, *Foreign Investment in Latin America* (Washington: OAS, 1955); J. Fred Rippy, "German Investment in Guatemala," *Journal of Business* 20 (Oct. 1947):212–19.
[a]Sapper, *Mittelamerikanische Reisen*, 342.
[b]von Erckert report, [1898], alte P-II-8/97, Staatsarchiv, Hamburg.
[c]Paul Metternich to Carl Burchard, June 12, 1899, Senatskommission für die Reichs und auswärtigen Angelegenheiten, neu A III, C. 22, Staatsarchiv, Hamburg.
[d]U.S. Manufacturer's Bureau, *Monthly Consular and Trade Report*, 63:460–61.
[e]Manuel María de Peralta estimate.
[f]Henri Monod to ministère des affaires étrangères, June 28, 1900, Affaires diverses commerciales, carton 280—missions commerciales (1896–1901), Archive du ministère des affaires étrangères, Paris.
[g]Paul Behneke to emperor, May 18, 1905, RM 5/vol. 5401, Behneke to emperor, May 18, 1905, RM 5/vol. 5402, Behneke to emperor, May 18, 1905, RM 5/vol. 5432, Bundesarchiv, Militärarchiv, Freiburg.
[h]von Ammon to emperor, Feb. 3, 1906, RM 5/vol. 5402, Bundesarchiv, Militärarchiv, Freiburg.
[i]Désiré Pector, *Les richesses de l'Amérique centrale* (Paris: E. Gilmoto, [1908]), 298.
[j]Total for real estate and commerce only, Bonin to Bernhard von Bülow, July 1, 1909, Rep 120, C XIII, 16[a,] Nr. 4, Band 2, Bundesarchiv, Merseburg.
[k]Désiré Pector, *Régions isthmiques de l'Amérique tropicale* (Paris: Société d'éditions géographiques, maritimes et coloniales, 1925), 84.
[l]Nachrichtenblatt des Reichsauswanderungsamts, Dec. 15, 1920, pp. 866–69, Auswanderungsamt II, Lit. C^{II}9, vol. 1, Staatsarchiv, Hamburg.
[m]French estimate, in Chayet to ministère des affaires étrangères, Jan. 20, 1919, Amér. 1918–1940, Central America, num. 39, Archive du ministère des affaires étrangères, Paris.
[n]Chayet to ministère des affaires étrangères, Jan. 21, 1919, Amér. 1918–1940, Central America, num. 68 (Nic.), Archive du ministère des affaires étrangères, Paris.
[o]Simonin to ministère des affaires étrangères, Jan. 21, 24, Feb. 2, 1919, Amér. 1918–1940, Central America, num. 96 (Pan), Archive du ministère des affaires étrangères, Paris.
[p]Karl Sapper estimate, in Kühlmann to Auswärtiges Amt, June 2, 1926, III, Guat., Wirtschaft 13, Politisches Archiv des Auswärtigen Amtes, Bonn.

Table 8. Foreign Investment in Central America, 1839–1939 (in millions of German marks [M], U.S. dollars [$], French francs [F], or British pounds [£])

Year	French	German	British	U.S.
1839	—	—	0.1£[a]	—
1880	—	—	7.5£	—
1890	—	—	11.7£	—
1896	250–300F	—	—	—
1897	—	211.5M[b]	—	11.5$
1899	—	67.1$[c]	—	—
1900	—	250.0M[d]	—	—
1902	267F[e]	—	—	—
1906	—	300.0F[f]	—	—
1908	—	—	—	31.8$
1909	—	—	—	50.0$
1912	—	—	—	47.5$
1913	88F	—	118.6$	—
1914	—	400.0F[g]	21.0£	82.0$
1919	—	—	—	96.3$
1923	—	—	—	67.3$[h]
1924	—	—	—	119.0$
1929	—	—	—	201.7$
1930	—	—	126.3$	227.1$
1938	217F	—	—	—
1939	—	—	13.0£	—

SOURCES: United Nations, *El Financiamiento Externo de América Latina;* OAS, *Foreign Investment in Latin America;* Rippy, "German Investment in Guatemala."

[a]Central American Federation external debt upon dissolving. Victor Quintana Díaz, *Inversiones extranjeras en Guatemala* (Guatemala: Instituto de investigaciones económicas y sociales, 1973), 34.

[b]Sapper, *Mittelamerikanische Reisen,* 342.

[c]U.S. Manufacturer's Bureau, *Monthly Consular and Trade Report,* 63:460–61.

[d]Monod to ministère des affaires étrangères, June 28, 1900, Affaires diverses commerciales, carton 280—missions commerciales (1896–1901), Archive du ministère des affaires étrangères, Paris.

[e]Includes 220F million invested in the Panama canal but excludes 80F million invested in the Honduran railroad.

[f]Pector, *Les richesses de l'Amérique centrale,* 298–99.

[g]Lecoq to marine minister, Sept. 2, 1921, I BB[4]6, dossier 1921, Archive de l'armée de la mer, Paris.

[h]Grosvenor M. Jones to Emmet, March 28, 1926, RG 151, 620-Lt. Amer., NA.

Table 9. German Settlers in Central America, 1844–1930

Year	Guatemala	Costa Rica	Nicaragua	El Salvador	Honduras	Panama
1844	425[a]	—	—	—	—	—
1852	—	—	—	8[b]	—	—
1864	—	164	—	—	—	—
1865	—	400[c]	—	—	—	—
1883	—	240	—	—	—	—
1884	100[d]	—	—	—	—	—
1887	—	—	—	—	43[e]	—
1888	—	298	—	—	—	—
1891	—	—	15[f]	—	—	—
1892	—	342	—	—	50[g]	—
1897	900[h]	—	—	—	—	—
1901	—	300	—	—	—	—
1904	913[i]	120	100	—	—	—
1905	—	176[j]	400	—	—	60
1906	—	350[k]	—	—	150[l]	—
1910	7,500[m]	525	250	475	450	—
1914	1,400[n]	—	—	—	—	—
1917	1,000[n]	—	—	—	—	—
1920	—	—	310[o]	—	—	—
1923	—	250[p]	—	—	—	—
1924	550[p]	—	—	—	—	—
1927	—	685	—	—	—	50[q]
1930	2,950[r]	—	200	—	400	—

NOTE: Data from this period commonly include only males. Independent, professional women (generally, teachers or nurses) were sometimes counted; children were almost never included.

[a]Estimated German participation in Belgian colonization project at Santo Tomás, Guatemala, Ferdinand Schröder. "Deutsche Kolonisationsversuche in Zentralamerika." *Der Auslandsdeutsche* 12 (1929):268–70.

[b]Franz Hugo Hesse to August von der Heydt and Otto von Manteuffel, Oct. 30, 1852, 2.4.1. Abteilung II, Nr. 5198, Bundesarchiv, Merseburg (formerly Deutsches Zentralachiv).

[c]Nikolaus Riggenbach, *Erinnerungen eines alten Mechanikers* (St. Gallien, Switzerland, 1887), 51–52.

[d]Agenor Fournier to Admiral, Feb. 22, 1884, BB[4], 1596, Archive de l'armée de la mer, Paris.

[e]Charles A. Brand, "The Background of Capitalistic Underdevelopment: Honduras to 1913" (Ph.D. diss., University of Pittsburgh, 1972), p. 57, quoting Honduras, *Censo de 1887*.

[f]Around Managua only, Gustavo Lembke to Marshall Biederstein, Nov. 19, 1901, 09.01, Nr. 52608, Bundesarchiv, Potsdam.

[g]J. Gourdoy to marine minister, March 15, 1892, BB[4] 1596, Archive de l'armée de la mer, Paris.

[h]Sapper, *Mittelamerikanische Reisen*, 342.

[i]Germany, Reichsmarineamt, *Die Entwicklung der deutschen Seeinteressen im letzten Jahrzehnt* (Berlin: Reichsdruckerei, 1905).

[j]Behneke to emperor, May 18, 1905, RM 5/vol. 5401, Behneke to emperor, May 18, 1905, RM 5/vol. 5402, Bundesarchiv, Militärarchiv, Freiburg.

[k]Pector, *Les richesses de l'Amérique centrale*, 292, including women and children.

[l]Italy, Ministero degli Affari Esteri, *Emigrazione e colonie* (Rome: Union Editrize, 1909), 321.

[m]Ernst B. Filsinger [consul in Costa Rica and Ecuador], "Immigration—A Central American Problem," *Annals of the American Academy of Political and Social Science* 37:3 (May 1911):167.

[n]Nachrichtenblatt des Reichsauswanderungsamts, Dec. 15, 1920, pp. 866–69, Auswanderungsamt II, Lit. C(II)9, vol. 1, Staatsarchiv, Hamburg.

[o]The 1920 Nicaraguan census; Paul Serre to ministère des affaires étrangères, May 17, 1921, Amér. 1918–1940, Central America, num. 69, Archive du ministère des affaires étrangères, Paris. Nicaragua had 10,375 foreign residents.

[p]Pector, *Régions isthmiques de l'Amérique tropicale*, 44.

[q]Adult males, Richard von Kühlmann to Auswärtiges Amt, Nov. 19, 1927, III, Pan., Handel 13, Politisches Archiv des Auswärtiges Amtes, Bonn.

[r]Hugo Grothe, *Die Deutschen in Übersee* (Berlin: Zentralverlag, 1932), 70, estimates the total German presence in Central America at between 4,000 and 4,500.

Table 10. German Firms in Central America, 1852–1927

Year	Guatemala	Costa Rica	Nicaragua	El Salvador	Honduras
1852	—	—	—	1	—
1861	3[a]	—	—	—	—
1879	15[b]	—	—	—	—
1884	—	—	—	60[c]	—
1889	—	13[d]	—	—	—
1891	—	—	12[e]	—	—
1897	55[f]	8	—	11	—
1897/98	68[g]	—	—	—	—
1900	50[h]	—	—	—	—
1907	68[i]	—	—	—	—
1917	150[j]	—	—	—	—
1927	—	34[k]	37[l]	—	35[m]

[a]Includes one joint German-British firm. René Louis Marie de Botmiliau to ministère des affaires étrangères, Feb. 1, 1861, correspondence commerciale et consulaire, Guat., vol. 6, Archive du ministère des affaires étrangères, Paris.

[b]Firms signing complaint against augmented Guatemalan customs duties. Correspondence commerciale et consulaire, Guat., vol. 9, Archive du ministère des affaires étrangères, Paris.

[c]Fournier to Admiral, Feb. 19, 1884, BB[4], 1596, Archive de l'armée de la mer, Paris. Possibly he meant businessmen.

[d]Eduardo Hernández Alcarón, "Comercio y dependencia en Costa Rica durante los años 1880–1890," Anuario de estudios centroamericanos 3 (1977):258.

[e]Lembke to Biederstein, Nov. 19, 1901, 09.01, Nr. 52608, Bundesarchiv, Potsdam.

[f]Sapper, Mittelamerikanische Reisen, 342.

[g]Erckert report [1898], alte P-II-8/97, Staatsarchiv, Hamburg.

[h]Grothe, Die Deutschen in Übersee, 70.

[i]Hamburg Handel und Verkehr (1905–1907) 1:449–50.

[j]"Guatemala," Nachrichtenblatt des Reichsauswanderungsamts, Dec. 15, 1920, pp. 866–69, Auswanderungsamt II, Lit. C(II)9, vol. 1, Staatsarchiv, Hamburg.

[k]Deutscher Wirtschaftsdienst, "Wichtigere Handelsfirmen in Costa Rica," in Ahrens to Auswärtiges Amt, Nov. 15, 1927, III, CR, Handel 24, Nr. 8, Politisches Archiv des Auswärtigen Amtes, Bonn. A total of 216 firms are listed for Costa Rica.

[l]Deutscher Wirtschaftsdienst, "Wichtigere Handelsfirmen in Nicaragua," Sept. 5, 1927, III, Nic., Handel 24, Nr. 4, Politisches Archiv des Auswärtigen Amtes, Bonn. A total of 124 firms are listed for Nicaragua.

[m]Deutscher Wirtschaftsdienst, "Wichtigere Handelshäuser in Honduras," [1927], III, Hond., Handel 24, Nr. 4, Politisches Archiv des Auswärtigen Amtes, Bonn. A total of 180 firms are listed for Honduras.

Table 11. Business Firms (Foreign and Native) in Nicaragua, Costa Rica, and Honduras, 1927

Type of Business	Nicaragua		Costa Rica		Honduras	
	German	Total	German	Total	German	Total
Agricultural, cattle	—	—	—	—	3	8
Autos, cycles	1	4	—	—	0	3
Bank	1	4	1	8	1	6
Books, etc.	1	4	1	5	0	1
Brewery	—	—	—	—	2	3
Candy, sugar	—	—	—	—	0	5
Cement	—	—	—	—	1	4
Coffee export	—	—	13	109	—	—
Commission house	8	13	7	10	5	6
Construction	4	12	1	8	—	—
Electrical	2	5	2	3	0	5
Export	2	14	—	—	—	—
Foods, etc.	1	7	—	—	—	—
Forwarding agency	—	—	0	3	1	4
Fruits	—	—	—	—	0	5
General merchandise	—	—	6	18	13	46
Ice company	—	—	—	—	0	3
Jewelry, clocks	2	4	2	7	—	—
Luxury, liquors	—	—	0	6	—	—
Machine store	3	4	—	—	0	6
Mineral waters	0	4	—	—	1	3
Mining	—	—	—	—	0	2
Misc. manufacturing	—	—	—	—	0	11
Pharmacy	2	9	0	8	4	29
Photography	1	3	—	—	—	—
Porcelain	—	—	0	2	—	—
Printing	1	5	—	—	0	7
Saddle-maker	—	—	—	—	1	1
Shoes, etc.	1	4	—	—	1	4
Soap, candles	0	2	—	—	0	6
Staple wholesale	—	—	0	17	—	—
Steamship	—	—	—	—	1	7
Textiles	7	26	1	12	—	—
Theater, film	—	—	—	—	1	6
Total	37	124	34	216	35	181

NOTE: German percentage of total for each country: Nicaragua, 30%; Costa Rica, 16%; Honduras, 19%.

Notes

■

Abbreviations

AA	Auswärtiges Amt
AAM	Archive de l'armée de la mer, Paris
AGCA	Archivo General de Centro América, Guatemala City
AMAE	Archive du ministère des affaires étrangères, Paris
AMEF	Archive du ministère d'économie et des finances, Paris
AN, P	Archive national, Paris
AN, CR	Archivo Nacional, Costa Rica, San José
BAF	Bundesarchiv, Frankfurt
BAK	Bundesarchiv, Koblenz
BAM	Bundesarchiv, Merseburg (formerly Deutsches Zentralarchiv)
BAMF	Bundesarchiv, Militärarchiv, Freiburg
BAP	Bundesarchiv, Potsdam
CCC	Correspondence commerciale et consulaire, AMAE
CD	Consular Despatches
Cent. Amer.	Central America
CR	Costa Rica
DD	U.S. Department of State, Diplomatic Despatches, National Archives, Washington, D.C.
FO	Foreign Office
Fr.	France/French
GPO	Government Printing Office
IHK	Industrie- und Handelskammer
LC	Library of Congress, Washington, D.C.
MAE	Ministère des affaires étrangères
MID	Military Intelligence Division
MRE	Ministerio de relaciones exteriores
NA	National Archives, Washington, D.C.
PAAA	Politisches Archiv des Auswärtigen Amtes, Bonn
Pan.	Panama
PRO	Public Records Office, London
RG	Record Group
SAB	Staatsarchiv, Bremen
SAF	Stadtarchiv, Frankfurt
SAH	Staatsarchiv, Hamburg
SAP	Geheimes Staatsarchiv Preussischer Kulturbesitz, Berlin

Siemens-Institut   Werner-von-Siemens-Institut für Geschichte des Hauses Sie-
                    mens, Munich, Germany
Ver. St.   Vereinigte Staaten
Ver. St. von Amer. Vereinigte Staaten von Amerika

Introduction

1. U.S. Department of Commerce, Bureau of the Census, *Historical Statistics of the United States: Colonial Times to 1970*, 2 vols. (Washington, DC: GPO, 1975); B. R. Mitchell, comp., *International Historical Statistics: The Americas and Australasia* (Detroit: Gale Research, 1983), 538–601.

2. Hans-Ulrich Wehler, "Industrial Growth and Early German Imperialism," in *Studies in the Theory of Imperialism*, Roger Owen and Bob Sutcliffe, eds. (London: Longman, 1972), 71–92; Michael Stürmer, *Das ruhelose Reich. Deutschland, 1866–1918* (Berlin: Siedler, 1983); Helmut Böhme, *Prologomena zu einer Sozial- und Wirtschaftsgeschichte Deutschlands im 19. und 20. Jahrhundert* (Frankfurt: Suhrkamp, 1968); Hans-Ulrich Wehler, *Bismarck und der Imperialismus* (Cologne: Kiepenheuer und Witsch, 1969), 112–55, 434–45; Thomas McCormick, *China Market: America's Quest for Informal Empire, 1893–1901* (Chicago: Quadrangle, 1967), 21–52; Bernard Semmel, *Imperialism and Social Reform, 1885–1914* (Cambridge: Cambridge University Press, 1960).

3. On the world system or world economy theories of international relations, see Fernand Braudel, *Civilisation matérielle, économie et capitalisme, xve–xviiie siècle*, 3 vols. (Paris: Armand Colin, 1979) [translated as *The Structures of Everyday Life, The Wheels of Commerce*, and *The Perspective of the World* (New York: Harper, 1984)]; Fernand Braudel, *Afterthoughts on Material Civilization and Capitalism* (Baltimore: Johns Hopkins University Press, 1977); Immanuel Wallerstein, *The Modern World System*, 3 vols. (Orlando: Academic, 1974–1988); Immanuel Wallerstein, *Historical Capitalism* (London: Verso, 1983); Terence K. Hopkins and Immanuel Wallerstein, eds., *World-Systems Analysis: Theory and Methodology* (Beverly Hills: Sage, 1982); Theda Skocpol, ed., *Vision and Method in Historical Sociology* (Cambridge: Cambridge University Press, 1984), esp. chaps. 1, 5, 9, 10, and 11. Thomas McCormick, *America's Half-Century: United States Foreign Policy in the Cold War* (Baltimore: Johns Hopkins University Press, 1989), brilliantly applies world system theory to the United States from the 1890s to 1989. Thomas Schoonover, *The United States in Central America, 1860–1911: Episodes of Social Imperialism and Imperial Rivalry in the World System* (Durham, NC: Duke University Press, 1991), uses world system theory in a more restricted geographic and chronological manner.

4. Wehler, *Bismarck und der Imperialismus*, 112–55, 434–45.

5. Rudolph Hilferding, *Finance Capitalism* (New York: Routledge, Chapman, Hall, 1985); William Appleman Williams, *The Contours of American History* (Chicago: Quadrangle, 1961); Jürgen Kocka, "Organisierter Kapitalismus oder staatsmonopolistischer Kapitalismus? Begriffliche Vorbemerkungen," in Heinrich A. Winckler, ed., *Organisierter Kapitalismus: Voraussetzungen und Aufsätze* (Göttingen: Vandenhoeck und Ruprecht, 1974), 19–35; Tony Smith, *The Pattern of Imperialism: The United States, Great Britain, and the Late-industrializing World Since 1815* (Cam-

bridge: Cambridge University Press, 1981); Thomas Schoonover, "Metropole Rivalry in Central America, 1820s to 1929: An Overview," in Ralph Lee Woodward, Jr., ed., *Central America: Historical Perspectives on the Contemporary Crisis* (Westport, CT: Greenwood, 1988), 21–46; Thomas Schoonover, "Germany in Central America, 1820s to 1929: An Overview," *Jahrbuch für Geschichte von Staat, Wirtschaft und Gesellschaft Lateinamerikas* 25 (1988):33–59.

6. Fernando H. Cardoso and Enzo Faletto, *Dependency and Development in Latin America* (Berkeley: University of California Press, 1979); André Gunder Frank, *Capitalism and Underdevelopment in Latin America* (New York: Monthly Review, 1967); Samir Amin, *Unequal Development: An Essay on the Social Formations of Peripheral Capitalism* (New York: Monthly Review, 1976). Owen and Sutcliffe, eds., *Studies in the Theory of Imperialism,* and Wolfgang Mommsen, *Imperialismustheorien: Ein Überblick über die neueren Imperialismusinterpretationen,* 2d rev. ed. (Göttingen: Vandenhoeck und Ruprecht, 1980), are readers that introduce theoretical approaches and include some case studies.

7. Immanuel Wallerstein, "The Rise and Future Demise of the World Capitalist System: Concepts for Comparative Analysis," *Comparative Studies in Society and History* 16 (Sept. 1974):387–415; Christopher Chase-Dunn, "Core-Periphery Relations: The Effects of Core Competition," in Barbara Hockey Kaplan, ed., *Social Change in the Capitalist World Economy* (Beverly Hills: Sage, 1978), 159–76; Peter B. Evans, Dietrich Rueschemeyer, and Theda Skocpol, eds., *Bringing the State Back In* (Cambridge: Cambridge University Press, 1985); Immanuel Wallerstein, *The Politics of the World-Economy* (Cambridge: Cambridge University Press, 1984); Thomas J. McCormick, "Drift or Mastery? A Corporatist Synthesis for American Diplomatic History," *Reviews in American History* 10 (Dec. 1982):318–30; Thomas J. McCormick, " 'Every System Needs a Center Sometimes': An Essay on Hegemony and Modern American Foreign Policy," in Lloyd C. Gardner, ed., *Redefining the Past: Essays in Diplomatic History in Honor of William Appleman Williams* (Corvallis: Oregon State University Press, 1986).

8. Samir Amin, Giovanni Arrighi, Andre Gunder Frank, and Immanuel Wallerstein, *Transforming the Revolution: Social Movements and the World-System* (New York: Monthly Review, 1990).

9. Schoonover, "Metropole Rivalry in Central America," 21–46; Schoonover, "Germany in Central America," 33–59.

10. Ralph Lee Woodward, Jr., *Central America: A Nation Divided,* 2d ed. (New York: Oxford University Press, 1985), 25–148; Ciro Cardoso, "Central America: The Liberal Era, ca. 1870–1930," in Leslie Bethell, ed., *The Cambridge History of Latin America,* 5 vols. (Cambridge: Cambridge University Press, 1982–1988), 5:197–227; Héctor Pérez Brignoli, *Breve historia de Centroamérica* (Madrid: Alianza, 1985), 90–102; Ciro Cardoso and Héctor Pérez Brignoli, *Centro América y la economía occidental (1520–1930)* (San José, CR: EDUCA, 1977), 149–80; Ralph Lee Woodward, Jr., "Central America from Independence to c. 1870," in Bethell, ed., *The Cambridge History of Latin America,* 3:471–506.

11. Cardoso and Pérez Brignoli, *Centro América y la economía occidental,* 15–180; Thomas Schoonover, "Prussia and the Protection of German Transit Through Middle America and Trade with the Pacific Basin, 1848–1851," *Jahrbuch für Geschichte von Staat, Wirtschaft und Gesellschaft Lateinamerikas* 22 (1985):393–422;

Thomas Schoonover, "Costa Rican Trade and Navigation Ties with the United States, Germany, and Europe, 1840–1885," *Jahrbuch für Geschichte von Staat, Wirtschaft und Gesellschaft Lateinamerikas* 14 (1977):269–309.

12. Cardoso, "Central America: The Liberal Era," 4:197–227; Pérez Brignoli, *Breve historia de Centroamérica*, 107–13; Thomas Schoonover, "Imperialism in Middle America: United States Competition with Britain, Germany, and France in Middle America, 1820s–1920s," in Rhodri Jeffreys-Jones, ed., *Eagle Against Empire: American Opposition to European Imperialism, 1914–1982* (Aix-en-Provence, France: Université de Provence, 1983), 41–58; Walter LaFeber, *Inevitable Revolutions: The United States in Central America* (New York: Norton, 1983), 31–39.

13. Wehler, "Industrial Growth and Early German Imperialism," 71–92; Wehler, *Bismarck und der Imperialismus*, 112–55; Stürmer, *Das ruhelose Reich*, 399–407.

14. Wehler, *Bismarck und der Imperialismus*, 61–111; Wehler, "Industrial Growth and Early German Imperialism," 78; Wehler, *Das deutsche Kaiserreich 1871–1918* (Göttingen: Vandenhoeck und Ruprecht, 1973), 171–81.

15. Adam Smith, *Wealth of Nations* (1776; reprint, Harmondsworth, Eng.: Penquin, 1976); John Stuart Mill, *On Liberty* (Indianapolis, IN: Bobbs-Merrill, 1956); Auguste Comte, *The Course of Positive Philosophy* (New York: Burt Franklin, 1973); Richard Rubinson, "Political Transformation in Germany and the United States," in Hockey Kaplan, ed., *Social Change in the Capitalist World Economy*, 39–73.

1. Foundations of German Interest in Central America, 1820–1848

1. Hagen Schulze, *Der Weg zum Nationalstaat: Die deutsche Nationalbewegung vom 18. Jahrhundert bis zur Reichsgründung* (Munich: dtv, 1985), 72ff.; Peter Burg, *Der Wiener Kongress: Der Deutsche Bund im europäischen Staatensystem* (Munich: dtv, 1984), 51–107; Theodor Schieder, *Vom Deutschen Bund zum Deutschen Reich, 1815–1871* (Munich: dtv, 1975), 12–13.

2. Burg, *Der Wiener Kongress*, 73ff., 125ff.; Wolfgang Hardtwig, *Vormärz: Der monarchische Staat und das Bürgertum* (Munich: dtv, 1985), 106–72; Gerhard Bondi, *Deutschlands Aussenhandel, 1815–1870* (Berlin: Akademie, 1958); Bodo von Borries, *Deutschlands Aussenhandel, 1836–1856* (Stuttgart: Gustav Fischer, 1970); Heinrich Ludwig Biersack, *Über Schutzzölle und andere, gegen das Ausland gerichtete, Schutzmassregeln zur Förderung der inländischen Industrie, sowie über Consumtionssteuern von ausländischen Waren* (Darmstadt: E. Jonghaus, 1843); Knut Borchardt, *Grundriss der deutschen Wirtschaftsgeschichte* (Göttingen: Vandenhoeck und Ruprecht, 1978), 39–56; Karl Obermann, *Deutschland, 1815–1849* (Berlin: VEB Deutscher Verlag der Wissenschaft, 1976), 36–68.

3. Hajo Holborn, *A History of Modern Germany, 1840–1945* (New York: Knopf, 1969); Knut Borchardt, "Germany, 1700–1914," in *The Fontana Economic History of Europe: The Emergence of Industrial Societies*, ed. Carolo M. Cipolla, vol. 4, pt. 1 (Glasgow, Scotland: William Collins and Sons, 1973), 76–77, 112–13; Percy Ernst Schramm, *Hamburg, Deutschland und die Welt. Leistung und Grenzen hanseatischen Bürgertums in der Zeit zwischen Napoleon I. und Bismarck. Ein Kapitel deutscher Geschichte*, 2d ed. (Hamburg: Hoffman und Campe, 1952); William O. Henderson, *The Rise of German Industrial Power, 1834–1914* (Berkeley: University of California

Press, 1975), 23–108; Hardtwig, *Vormärz*, 88–106; Imanuel Geiss, *Der lange Weg in die Katastrophe: Die Vorgeschichte des ersten Weltkriegs, 1815–1914* (Munich: Piper, 1990), 42.

4. For the early relations of German states with Latin America, see Manfred Kossok, *Im Schatten der Heiligen Allianz: Deutschland und Lateinamerika, 1815–1830. Zur Politik der deutschen Staaten gegenüber der Unabhängigkeitsbewegung Mittel- und Südamerikas* (Berlin: Akademie, 1964); Hendrik Dane, *Die wirtschaftlichen Beziehungen Deutschlands zu Mexiko und Mittelamerika im 19. Jahrhundert* (Cologne: Böhlau, 1971), 5–6, 39–56, 78–79, 148–50; Robert M. Berdahl, "Conservative Politics and Aristocratic Landholders in Bismarckian Germany," *Journal of Modern History* 44 (March 1972):14–15; decree announcing Carl Friedrich Rudolph Klee's appointment, n.d., 1845, AA II, Rep. 6, Nr. 3518, BAM; Heinrich Lutz and Helmut Rumpler, eds., *Österreich und die deutsche Frage im 19. und 20. Jahrhundert* (Munich: R. Oldenbourg, 1982); Ralph Lee Woodward, Jr., "Los comerciantes y el desarrollo económico en las Américas, 1750–1850," *Revista del Pensamiento Centroamericano* 35 (July–Dec. 1980):17–30.

5. Burg, *Der Wiener Kongress*, 125–39; Hardtwig, *Vormärz*, 50–66, 88–106; Hubert Kiesewetter, *Industrielle Revolution in Deutschland, 1815–1914* (Frankfurt: Suhrkamp, 1989), 37–63, 310; Richard H. Tilly, *Vom Zollverein zum Industriestaat: Die wirtschaftlich-soziale Entwicklung Deutschlands, 1834 bis 1914* (Munich: dtv, 1990), 39–49, 155–57.

6. Burg, *Der Wiener Kongress*, 107–25; Tilly, *Vom Zollverein zum Industriestaat*, esp. chap. 7; Schulze, *Der Weg zum Nationalstaat*, 7–8, Kiesewetter, *Industrielle Revolution in Deutschland*, 310.

7. The data on international trade and shipping for the early decades of Central American independence only allows glimpses of German economic ties with Central America. See Tables 1, 3, and 4, and Thomas Schoonover and Ebba Schoonover, "Statistics for an Understanding of Foreign Intrusions into Central America from the 1820s to 1930," pt. 3, *Anuario de estudios centroamericanos* 17:2 (1991):85–119.

8. Cardoso and Pérez Brignoli, *Centro América y la economía occidental*, 143–79; Pérez Brignoli, *Breve historia de Centroamérica*, 79–106.

9. Woodward, *Central America: A Nation Divided*, 92–148; Ralph Lee Woodward, Jr., "Economic Development and Dependency in Nineteenth-Century Guatemala," in Richard Tardanico, ed., *Crises in the Caribbean Basin* (Newbury Park, CA: Sage, 1987), 59–78; Ralph Lee Woodward, Jr., *Central America: Historical Perspectives on Revolution and Reaction* (Greenville, NC: East Carolina University Press, 1986).

10. Kossok, *Im Schatten der Heiligen Allianz*; Charles K. Webster, *Britain and the Independence of Latin America, 1812–1830*, 2 vols. (London: Oxford University Press, 1938); Dexter Perkins, *The Monroe Doctrine, 1823–1907*, vol. 1 of 3 (Gloucester, MA: Peter Smith, 1965); Walter LaFeber, *The American Age: United States Foreign Policy at Home and Abroad Since 1750* (New York: Norton, 1989), 69–88; Charles Lyon Chandler, "United States Commerce with Latin America at the Promulgation of the Monroe Doctrine," *Quarterly Journal of Economics* 38 (May 1924):466–86.

11. Dane, *Die wirtschaftlichen Beziehungen Deutschlands*, 75–77, 148–55; Manfred Kossek, "Zur Geschichte der deutsch-lateinamerikanischen Beziehungen (For-

schungs- und Periodisierungsprobleme)," *Hansische Geschichtsblätter* 84 (1966):49–97; Percy Schramm, "Deutschland, Nord- und Südamerika im 19. Jahrhundert," *Hansische Geschichtsblätter* 81 (1963):109–23.

12. Dane, *Die wirtschaftlichen Beziehungen Deutschlands*, 56, 78–79, 148–50.

13. Formation of the Rheinisch-Westindische Kompagnie in Elberfeld, March 30, 1821, Rep. 120, C VIII1, Nr. 11, BAM: von Pomern to Heinrich von Bülow (Staatsminister für Handel und Gewerbe), March 23, 1825; Nottus to Staatsminister für Handel und Gewerbe, Jan. 13, 1820. Rep. 120, C VIII 1, Nr. 3, vol. 1, BAM, Christian Günther Bernsdorff to king, Feb. 15, 1829; Auswärtiges Amt (Geheimes Civil Kabinett), 2. 2. 1., Nr. 28166, BAM; August Beckmann, "Die Rheinisch-Westindische Kompagnie; ihr Wirken und ihre Bedeutung" (Ph.D. diss., Universität Münster, 1915); Heinrich August Winkler, *Pluralismus oder Protektionismus? Verfassungspolitische Probleme des Verbandswesens im Deutschen Kaiserreich* (Wiesbaden: F. Steiner, 1972), 6–9, 31, 33.

14. Borchardt, "Germany, 1700–1914," 105; Theodore Hamerow, *Restoration, Revolution, and Reaction* (Princeton, NJ: Princeton University Press, 1958), 15; W. Henderson, *The Rise of German Industrial Power*, 28, 39; August Sartorius von Waltershausen, *Deutsche Wirtschaftsgeschichte, 1815–1914* (Jena: Gustav Fischer, 1923), 26, 111, 116; Adolph Bienengräber, *Statistik des Verkehrs und Verbrauchs im Zollverein für die Jahre 1842–1864* (Berlin: Alexander Duncker, 1868).

15. William Carr, *A History of Germany, 1815–1945* (London: Edward Arnold, 1969), 25–26, 39–41; John L. Snell, *The Democratic Movement in Germany, 1789–1914* (Chapel Hill: University of North Carolina Press, 1976), 40–43; Heinrich Bechtel, *Wirtschaftsgeschichte Deutschlands im 19. und 20. Jahrhundert*, 3 vols. (Munich: Georg D. W. Callweg, 1956), 3:330–31; Werner Conze, "Das Spannungsfeld von Staat und Gesellschaft," in Werner Conze, ed., *Staat und Gesellschaft im Deutschen Vormärz, 1815–1848*, 2d ed. (Stuttgart: Ernest Klett, 1970), 4, 16–21, 75, 208; W. Henderson, *The Rise of German Industrial Power*, 23–27, 32, 37–38, 44, 50–53; Otto Pflanze, *Bismarck and the Development of Germany*, 3 vols. (Princeton, NJ: Princeton University Press, 1963–1990), 1:33–34; Frank B. Tipton, Jr., *Regional Variations in the Economic Development of Germany during the Nineteenth Century* (Middletown, CT: Wesleyan University Press, 1976), 3, 18; Ernst Jacob, ed., *Deutsche Kolonialpolitik in Dokumenten* (Leipzig: Dieterich'sche Verlagsbuchhandlung, 1938), 13; Reinhart Kosselleck, "Staat und Gesellschaft in Preussen, 1815–1848," in Conze, ed., *Staat und Gesellschaft im Vormärz*, 109; Wehler, "Industrial Growth and Early German Imperialism," 71–92. For an unconvincing evaluation of the Customs Union as an economic failure with no political content, see Alan J. P. Taylor, *The Course of German History: A Survey of the Development of Germany Since 1815* (New York: Capricorn, 1962), 61–64.

16. Woodward, *Central America: A Nation Divided*, 92–119; Schoonover, "Metropole Rivalry in Central America," 21–25; Schoonover, "Imperialism in Middle America," 41–46.

17. Cardoso and Pérez Brignoli, *Centro América y la economía occidental*, 162–69; Alexander Lips, *Statistik von Amerika oder Versuch einer historisch-pragmatischen und raisonierenden Darstellung des politischen und bürgerlichen Zustandes der neuen Staaten-Körper Amerika* (Frankfurt: H. Wilmans, 1828), 304–5.

18. Dane, *Die wirtschaftlichen Beziehungen Deutschlands*, 56, 78–79, 148–50.

19. Klee to Albert Friedrich Eichhorn, Oct. 15, 1844; Friedrich Lang [?] to Eduard Flottwell, Nov. 14, 1844; decree announcing Klee's appointment, n.d., 1845, AA II, Rep. 6, Nr. 3518, BAM.

20. Gustav von Alvensleben to king, Aug. 29, 1838, Rep. 120, C VIII 1, Nr. 8, BAM; Lang to Flottwell, Nov. 14, 1844, Klee to Guatemalan foreign minister, Sept. 10, Nov. 10, 1846, AA II, Rep. 6, Nr. 3518, BAM.

21. Rolf Engelsing, *Sozial- und Wirtschaftsgeschichte Deutschlands* (Göttingen: Vandenhoeck und Ruprecht, 1976), 126–28; Johann Heinrich Siegfried Schultz, *Über Colonisation mit besonderer Rücksicht auf die Colonie zu Santo Thomás, im Staate Guatemala, und die Belgische Colonisations-Compagnie* (Cologne: Dumont Schauberg, 1843), 5, 29–36; Marcus L. Hansen, *German Schemes of Colonization before 1860* (Northhampton, MA: Smith College Press, 1924), 27, 47, 56, 59; Klaus J. Bade, ed., *Population, Labour and Migration in 19th and 20th Century Germany* (New York: St. Martin's, 1987).

22. Hartmut Fröschle, "Die Deutschen in Mittelamerika (Zentralamerika)," Götz von Houwald, "Die Deutschen in Costa Rica," Ekkehard Zipser and Hartmut Fröschle, "Die Deutschen in Guatemala," and Götz von Houwald, "Die Deutschen in Nikaragua," in Hartmut Fröschle, ed., *Die Deutschen in Lateinamerika: Schicksal und Leistung* (Tübingen: Horst Erdmann, 1979), 566–68, 578–81, 597–99, 632–38; Schultz, *Über Colonisation*, 5, 29–36; William J. Griffith, "Attitudes Toward Foreign Colonization: The Evolution of Nineteenth-Century Guatemalan Immigration Policy," in *Applied Enlightenment: 19th Century Liberalism* (New Orleans: Middle American Institute, 1972), 73–110; William J. Griffith, *Empires in the Wilderness: Foreign Colonization and Development in Guatemala, 1834–1844* (Chapel Hill: University of North Carolina Press, 1965); Alfred Zimmermann, *Die Kolonialreiche der Grossmächte, 1871–1916* (Berlin: Ullstein, 1916), 184–85; Robert L. Bach and Lisa A. Schraml, "Migration, Crisis and Theoretical Conflict," *International Migration Review* 16 (summer 1982):320–41; Charles Wood, "Equilibrium and Historical-Structural Perspectives on Migration," *International Migration Review* 16 (summer 1982):298–319.

23. "Auswanderung nach dem Reiche des Mosquitokönigs, 1842," Abteilung II, Bayerische Gesandtschaft London, Nr. 479, Bayerisches Hauptstaatsarchiv, Munich; "Das Gesuch des Dr. Strecher in Mainz um Anerkennung als General Agent der Belgischen Compagnie zur Colonisation des Districts Santo Thomas Guatemala," Abteilung II, Bayerische Gesandtschaft Paris, Bayerisches Hauptstaatsarchiv, Munich; Georg Niebuhr, "Pro Memoria über die Stellung Preussens zu den deutschen Auswanderern namentlichen Rand-Amerika," Feb. 17, 1845, Bernhard Ernst von Bülow to Eichhorn, March 10, 1845, Rep. 76 II, Section 1. Gen. b, Nr. 98, BAM; "Gründung einer deutschen Colonie auf der Mosquito Küste," AA, 2. 4. 1. II, Nr. 5245, BAM; "Die Auswanderungen und deren in Anregung gebrachte Leitung betreffend," Carlsruhe, June 16, 1847, DB 1/28, vol. II, BAF; A. Fellechner, Dr. Müller, and C. L. C. Hesse, *Bericht über die im höchsten Auftrage des Prinzen Karl von Preussen und des Fürsten von Schoenburg-Waldenburg bewirkte Untersuchung einiger Theile des Mosquitolands* (Berlin: Alexander Duncker, 1845); Blondeel van Cuelebrouk, *Colonie de Santo-Tomas*, 2 vols. (Brussels: Devroye, 1846); Adolph Soetbeer, "Das hamburgische Consulatswesen," *Zeitschrift des Vereins für Deutsche Statistik* 1 (1847):86–89; H. G. Pfeiffer and A. A. Reinke, "Recognoscirungs-Reise nach

der Mosquito-Küste," *Missions-Blatt aus der Brudergemeinde* 11 (Aug. 29, Oct. 26, 1847):151–52, 189–90; Galvin B. Henderson, "German Colonial Projects on the Mosquito Coast, 1844–1848," *The English Historical Review* 59 (May 1944):257–71; Nicolas Leysbeth, *Historique de la colonisation belge à Santo Tomás de Guatemala* (Bruxelles: n.p., 1938); Pedro Pérez Valenzuela, *Santo Tomás de Castilla: Apuntes para la historia de las colonizaciones en la costa atlántica* (Guatemala: Nacional, 1956).

24. Schultz, *Über Colonisation,* 5, 30–32; Winkler, *Pluralismus oder Protektionismus?* 6–9, 31, 33.

2. Prussia and Commerce with the Pacific Basin, 1848–1851

1. Holborn, *A History of Modern Germany, 1840–1945* (New York: Knopf, 1969); Hamerow, *Restoration, Revolution, and Reaction,* 197–237; Pflanze, *Bismarck and the Development of Germany,* vol. 1; Hans Hausherr, "Der Zollverein und die Industrialisierung," in Karl Erich Born, ed., *Moderne deutsche Wirtschaftsgeschichte* (Cologne: Kiepenheuer und Witsch, 1966), 55–66; Geiss, *Der lange Weg in die Katastrophe,* 79–90; Schulze, *Der Weg zum Nationalstaat,* 7–8, 119–25.

2. Alexander von Bülow, *Die Verbindungswege des Welthandels durch Central-America* (Berlin: Deckersche Geheime Ober-Hofbuch Druckerei, 1850); Hans Rosenberg, *Grosse Depression und Bismarckzeit. Wirtschaftsablauf, Gesellschaft und Politik in Mitteleuropa* (Berlin: Walter de Gruyter, 1967), 12–21; Rudolf Braun, Wolfram Fischer, Helmut Grosskreutz, and Heinrich Volkmann, eds., *Industrielle Revolution: wirtschaftliche Aspekte* (Cologne: Kiepenheuer und Witsch, 1972); W. Henderson, *The Rise of German Industrial Power,* 80–115; Engelsing, *Sozial- und Wirtschaftsgeschichte Deutschlands,* 119–76; Wolfgang Kollmann, *Bevölkerung in der industriellen Revolution: Studien zur Bevölkerungsgeschichte Deutschlands* (Göttingen: Vandenhoeck und Ruprecht, 1974); Reinhard Spree, *Die Wachstumszyklen der deutschen Wirtschaft von 1840–1880* (Berlin: Duncker und Humblot, 1977).

3. Alexander von Bülow, *Auswanderung und Colonisation im Interesse des deutschen Handels* (Berlin: E. S. Mittler und Sohn, 1849); Comité der Berliner Colonisations-Gesellschaft für Central-Amerika, *Die deutsche Ansiedlung in Mittelamerika* (Berlin: Comité der Berliner Colonisations-Gesellschaft für Central-Amerika, 1850); Dane, *Die wirtschaftlichen Beziehungen Deutschlands,* 148–55; Friedrich Eckhard, "Die preussischen Konsularberichte von Guatemala, 1842–1850," (Diplomarbeit, Universität Erlangen-Nürnberg, 1974); H. G. Pfeiffer and A. A. Reinke, "Auszug aus der Reisebeschreibung der Brüder H. G. Pfeiffer und A. A. Reinke von Fairfield auf Jamaica nach Bluefields auf der Mosquitoküste im Jahr 1847," *Missions-Blatt aus der Brudergemeinde* 12 (1847):151–52, 189–90; Percy Ernst Schramm, *Deutschland und Übersee* (Braunschweig: Georg Westermann, 1950), 62–65.

4. Engelsing, *Sozial- und Wirtschaftsgeschichte Deutschlands,* 136–38.

5. Carl Scherzer, *Central-Amerika in seiner Bedeutung für den deutschen Handel und die deutsche Industrie* (Vienna: Carl Gerold und Sohn, 1857); Karl H. Schwebel, "Bremens Handel dringt nach Lateinamerika vor. Bremische Pionierarbeit zu Beginn des vorigen Jahrhunderts," *Mitteilungen der Handelskammer Bremen* 15

(1952):225–28; Hermann Wätjen, *Der deutsche Anteil am Wirtschaftsaufbau der West-küste Amerikas* (Leipzig: F. Meiner, 1942), 195–204.

6. Heinrich Best, *Interessenpolitik und nationale Integration, 1848/1849* (Göttingen: Vandenhoeck und Ruprecht, 1980); Helmut Böhme, *Deutschlands Weg zur Grossmacht: Studien zum Verhältnis von Wirtschaft und Staat während der Reichsgründungszeit, 1848–1881,* 2d ed. (Cologne: Kiepenheuer und Witsch, 1972); Helmut Böhme, "Thesen zur Beurteilung der gesellschaftlichen, wirtschaftlichen und politischen Ursachen des deutschen Imperialismus," in Wolfgang J. Mommsen, ed., *Der moderne Imperialismus* (Stuttgart: Kohlhammer, 1971); James J. Sheehan, *German Liberalism in the Nineteenth Century: The Wilhelmine Age, 1890–1914* (Chicago: University of Chicago Press, 1978), 274–75; Conze, "Das Spannungsfeld von Staat und Gesellschaft," 16–21; Eberhard Meier, "Die aussenpolitischen Ideen der Achtundvierziger," *Historische Studien,* vol. 337 (Berlin: Emil Ebering, 1938); Wehler, *Bismarck und der Imperialismus,* 180–93; Hans-Ulrich Wehler, "Sozialdarwinismus im expandierenden Industriestaat," in Imanuel Geiss and Bernd Jürgen Wendt, eds., *Deutschland in der Weltpolitik des 19. und 20. Jahrhunderts* (Düsseldorf: Bertelsmann Universitätsverlag, 1974), 133–42.

7. E. S. Walther, *Über die Errichtung deutscher Consulate* (Jena: F. Frommann, 1848), 12–15; "Das Reichs-Consulatswesen," C. F. Wurm, "Bericht des völkerrechtlichen Ausschusses," DB 58/14 Konsulate, BAF.

8. Ibid.

9. Ibid.

10. Franz Hugo Hesse, "Andeutungen über Mittel Amerika und seine Zukunft [Considerations regarding Middle America and its future]," AA II, Rep. 6, Nr. 3518, BAM, transcribed in Eckhard, "Preussische Konsularberichte von Guatemala," 91–97; C. W. Asher, *Über die deutschen Handelsverhältnisse zu den Ländern des westlichen Amerika* (Berlin: Wilhelm Hertz, 1850).

11. Hesse, "Andeutungen über Mittel Amerika"; Karl Bermann, *Under the Big Stick: Nicaragua and the United States Since 1848* (Boston: South End, 1986), 17–35; Richard W. Van Alstyne, *The Rising American Empire* (Chicago: Quadrangle, 1965), 147–69.

12. Hesse, "Andeutungen über Mittel Amerika"; Mario Rodríguez, *A Palmerstonian Diplomat in Central America: Frederick Chatfield, Esq.* (Tuscon, AZ: University of Arizona Press, 1964).

13. Hesse, "Andeutungen über Mittel Amerika."

14. Klee to Reichsminister der Auswärtigen Angelegenheiten, April 21, 1849, AA III, Rep. 14, Nr. 532, BAM, in Eckhard, "Preussische Konsularberichte von Guatemala," 1–3a; Klee to Smidt, April 28, July 8, 1849, enclosing an extract from Fr. vice consul to [?], March 30, 1849, 2.-C. 23.c.2, SAB; Friedrich von Rönne to Reichsminister der Auswärtigen Angelegenheiten, May 22, 1849, Aug. 12, Oct. 1, 19, 1849, Jan. 6, 1850, Deutscher Reichsgesandtschafter bei den Vereinigten Staaten, Acta Nr. 2, BAF; Robert Bunsen to Alexander von Schleinitz, Nov. 7, 20, Dec. 19, 1849, Jan. 4, 1850, Nr. 832, London: Politischer Schriftwechsel, Preussisches Ministerium des Auswärtigen, SAP; *Nassauische Allgemeine,* May 11, 1850, pp. 1–2; Hesse to Otto von Manteuffel and August von der Heydt, 29 July 1852, 2.4.1., Abteilung II, Nr. 5198 (AA II, Rep. 6, Nr. 1581), Hesse to Manteuffel, Aug. 30, 1854,

2.4.1., Abteilung II, Nr. 638 (AA II, Rep. 6, Nr. 3519), BAM; Alexander von Bülow, *Der Freistaat Nicaragua in Mittelamerika und seine Wichtigkeit für den Welthandel, den Ackerbau und die Colonisation* (Berlin: Gustav Hempl, 1849); E. A. Weimann, *Mittel-Amerika als gemeinsames Auswanderungs-Ziel* (Berlin: Deckersche Geheime Ober-Hofsdruckerei, 1850).

15. Friedrich Burgdörfer, "Die Wanderungen über die deutschen Reichsgrenzen im letzten Jahrhundert," *Allgemeines Statistisches Archiv* 20 (1930):181–96, 383–419, 537–51; Ferdinand Schröder, "Deutsche Kolonisationsversuche in Zentralamerika," *Der Auslandsdeutsche* 12 (1929):268–70; Jegór von Sivers, *Über Madeira und die Antillen nach Mittelamerika* (Leipzig: Carl F. Fleischer, 1861); Moritz Wagner and Carl Scherzer, *Die Republik Costa Rica in Central America* (Leipzig: Arnoldsche Buchhandlung, 1856); Fröschle, "Die Deutschen in Mittelamerika," 566–69; Manfred Illi, "Die deutsche Auswanderung nach Lateinamerika. Eine Literaturübersicht," *Lateinamerika-Studien* 2 (1977):1–176.

16. Hesse, "Andeutung über Mittel Amerika," 98–103; Herbert Schottelius, *Mittelamerika als Schauplatz deutscher Kolonisationsversuche, 1840–1865* (Hamburg: Hans Christians, 1939); Alexander von Bülow, *Der Freistaat Costa Rica in Mittelamerika. Seine Wichtigkeit für den Welthandel, den Ackerbau und die Kolonisation* (Berlin: Gustav Hempel, 1850); Fellechner, Müller, and Hesse, *Bericht über die bewirkte Untersuchung einiger Theile des Mosquitolands;* Hansen, *German Schemes of Colonisation,* 27, 47, 56, 59.

17. Hesse, "Andeutung über Mittel Amerika," 98–103; Carlos Meléndez Chaverri, "Intereses extranjeros en Centro América durante la primera mitad del siglo XIX," in *Memoria del primer congreso de historia Centro América-Panamá* (San José, CR: Nacional, 1956).

18. Hesse, "Andeutung über Mittel Amerika," 103–7; Friedrich List, *The National System of Political Economy* (London: Longmans, Green, 1928).

19. Hesse, "Andeutung über Mittel Amerika," 103–9; Chatfield to Palmerston, Nov. 1, 1850, FO 15 (CR), vol. 66 (microcopy reel 25), PRO; Kenneth Bourne, *Britain and the Balance of Power in North America: 1815–1908* (Berkeley: University of California Press, 1967), 170–205.

20. Hesse, addenda to "Andeutungen über Mittel Amerika," in Eckhard, "Preussische Konsularberichte von Guatemala," 110–13.

21. Hesse, "Andeutung über Mittel Amerika," 103–9.

22. Comité der Berliner Colonisations-Gesellschaft für Central Amerika to Prussian king, Oct. 29, 1850, AA II, Rep. 6, Nr. 3518, BAM, in Eckhard, "Preussische Konsularberichte von Guatemala," 114–18.

23. Manteuffel to von der Heydt and Arnold von Rabe, Nov. 13, 1850, von der Heydt to Manteuffel and Rabe, Dec. 21, 1850, AA II, Rep. 6, Nr. 3518, BAM, in Eckhard, "Preussische Konsularberichte von Guatemala," 128–30; Rabe to Manteuffel and von der Heydt, March 5, 1851, 2.4.1. Abteilung II, Nr. 637 (AA II, Rep. 6, Nr. 3518), BAM.

24. Manteuffel, von der Heydt, and Rabe to Prussian king, March 9, 1851, 2.2.1. Abteilung II, Nr. 12949 (R. 89, B. XIII 5, vol. 2 [1843–1853]), BAM.

25. Rabe to Manteuffel and von der Heydt, March 5, 1851, 2.4.1. Abteilung II, Nr. 637, BAM; Manteuffel, von der Heydt, and Rabe to Prussian king, March 9, 1851, Prussian king to Manteuffel, von der Heydt, and Rabe, March 15, 1851, 2.2.1.

Abteilung II, Nr. 12949, (R. 89, B. XIII 5, vol. 2), BAM; Manteuffel to Hesse, April 8, 1851, Rep. 120, C. XIII 16, Nr. 1, BAM (also in 2.-C.23.a. SAB).

26. Friedrich Johann Pommer Esche to Manteuffel, April 16, 1851, Manteuffel to Hesse and von Criolla, April 26, 1851, Manteuffel to von der Heydt and von Westphalen, April 26, 1851, "Denkschrift," n.p., n.d., 2.4.1. Abteilung II, 637, BAM.

27. Hesse to Ober-Kirchen-Rath, April 10, May 2, 1851, Ober-Kirchen-Rath to Hesse, April 19, May 15, 1851, EO Mittelamerika 1, Evangelische Kirche der Union Archiv, Berlin; Auguste Brindeau, *Histoire de la mission morave à la côte des Mosquitos (Nicaragua) de 1849 à 1921* (Strasbourg, France: Ch. Hiller, 1922), 99–101, 136–38.

28. See the large body of correpondence in Senat, CI VI Nr. 16^d, vol. 2a, fasc. 6, Fernere Correspondence des hanseatischen General Consul bei den Staaten von Central America, Herrn Klee (Guat.), SAH; Henry Savage to Daniel Webster, July 12, 1851, RG 59, U.S. Department of State, Diplomatic Despatches, Central America: vol. 3 (Microcopy 219/reel 6), National Archives, Washington, D.C. [hereafter DD, Cent. Amer.: 3 (M 219/r 6)]; Klee and Stephen Weems to Salvadoran foreign minister, Jan. 29, Feb. 24, 1851, Consular Despatches, Guatemala: vol. 2 (Temporary microcopy 337/reel 2) [hereafter CD, Guat.: 2 (T 337/r 2)].

29. Baron Koller to Prince Felix von Schwartzenberg, April 27, July 22, 1850, Schwartzenberg to Friedrich von Bruck, May 16, June 9, 1850, Bruck to Schwartzenberg, May 28, July 5, 1850, Schwartzenberg to Maurice Esterhazy, Feb. 28, May 12, 1851, Esterhazy to Schwartzenberg, April 11, Nov. 10, 1851, Koller to Schwartzenberg, March 3, 1851, Hulseman to Schwartzenberg, March 31, April 9, 1851, Schwartzenberg to Bruck, April 21, 26, 1851, Schwartzenberg to Hulseman, May 12, 1851, Koller to Alexander Hubner, Nov. 2, 1851, F. de Lorenzana to Esterhazy, Nov. 8, 1851, XXXIII—Ver. St. von Amer., carton 125, Politisches Archiv, Österreichisches Staatsarchiv, Vienna.

3. Franz Hugo Hesse's Mission to Central America, 1851–1858

1. Hans-Ulrich Wehler, *Deutsche Gesellschaftsgeschichte,* 3 vols. (Munich: C. H. Beck, 1987–1994), 2:3–6, 580–83, 690–702, 780–84; Schieder, *Vom Deutschen Bund zum Deutschen Reich,* 113–23; Thomas Nipperdey, *Deutsche Geschichte, 1800–1866: Bürgerwelt und starker Staat* (Munich: C. H. Beck, 1983); Siegfried Richter and Rolf Sonnemann, "Zur Problematik des Übergangs vom vormonopolistischen Kapitalismus zum Imperialismus in Deutschland," *Jahrbuch für Wirtschaftsgeschichte* 4 (1963):39–78; Volker Hentschel, *Deutsche Wirtschafts- und Sozialpolitik, 1815–1945* (Düsseldorf: Droste, 1980); L. L. Farrer, Jr., *Arrogance and Anxiety: The Ambivalence of German Power, 1848–1914* (Iowa City: University of Iowa Press, 1981); Jürgen Sandweg and Michael Stürmer, *Industrialisierung und soziale Frage in Deutschland im 19. Jahrhundert* (Munich: R. Oldenbourg, 1979); Frank B. Tipton, "The National Consensus in German Economic History," *Central European History* 7:3 (Sept. 1974):195–224; Helga Grebing, *Arbeiterbewegung: Sozialer Protest und kollektive Interessenvertretung bis 1914* (Munich: dtv, 1985), 94.

2. Nipperdey, *Deutsche Geschichte,* 684–87; Rolf H. Dumke, "Der Deutsche

Zollverein als Modell ökonomischer Integration," in Helmut Berling, ed., *Wirtschaftliche und politische Integration in Europa im 19. und 20. Jahrhundert* (Göttingen: Vandenhoeck und Ruprecht, 1984), 71–101.

3. Engelsing, *Sozial- und Wirtschaftsgeschichte Deutschlands*, 131–33, 235–38; Nicole Piétri, *Évolution économique de l'Allemagne du milieu du xixe siècle à 1914* (Paris: SEDES, 1982), 64–91, 155–60; Martin Kitchen, *The Political Economy of Germany, 1815–1914* (Montreal: McGill-Queen's University Press, 1978), 174–83, 198–99, 280–82; Schulze, *Der Weg zum Nationalstaat*, 49–101.

4. Nipperdey, *Deutsche Geschichte*, 690–92; Schulze, *Der Weg zum Nationalstaat*, 124.

5. Schoonover and Schoonover, "Statistics for an Understanding of Foreign Intrusions into Central America," pt. 3, 89–119.

6. Martial Cloquet to Alfred de Valois, May 6, 1849, CP 1871, Amér. cent., vol. 8, AMAE.

7. Hesse to Manteuffel and von der Heydt, July 1, 1852, 2.4.1. Abteilung II, Nr. 5246 (AA III, Rep. 14, Nr. 534), BAM; Hans-Peter Ullman, *Der Bund der Industriellen* (Göttingen: Vandenhoeck und Ruprecht, 1976).

8. Hesse to Manteuffel and von der Heydt, July 1, 1852, 2.4.1. Abteilung II, Nr. 5246 (AA III, Rep. 14, Nr. 534), BAM; Günther Leckebusch, *Die Beziehungen der deutschen Seeschiffswerften zur Eisenindustrie an der Ruhr in der Zeit von 1850 bis 1930* (Cologne: Rheinisch-Westfälisches Wirtschaftsarchiv, 1963).

9. Hesse to Manteuffel, Nov. 7, 1851, Hesse to Manteuffel and von der Heydt, July 1, 1852, 2.4.1. Abteilung II, Nr. 5246 (AA III, Rep. 14, Nr. 534), BAM; Hubert Kiesewetter, "Economic Preconditions for Germany's Nation-Building in the Nineteenth Century," in Hagen Schulze, ed., *Nation-Building in Central Europe* (Leamington Spa, UK: Berg, 1987), 81–105; Wolfgang J. Mommsen, "Der moderne Imperialismus als innergesellschaftliches Phänomen," in Mommsen, ed., *Der moderne Imperialismus*, 14–30; Peter Marschalck, *Deutsche Überseewanderung im 19. Jahrhundert* (Stuttgart: Ernst Klett, 1973); Wilhelm Mönckmeier, *Die deutsche überseeische Auswanderung* (Jena: Gustav Fischer, 1912); Ernst Wilhelm Johann Gaebler, "Die Statistik der deutschen Auswanderung," *Jahrbuch für Volkswirtschaft und Statistik* 1 (1852):264–72.

10. Hesse to Manteuffel and von der Heydt, July 1, 1852, 2.4.1. Abteilung II, Nr. 5246 (AA III, Rep. 14, Nr. 534), BAM; Felipe Molina to MRE, Oct. 30, 1851, MRE, caja 23, expediente-E.U., Legación de Costa Rica, Archivo Nacional, San José [hereafter MRE, caja 23, exp. leg. de CR, AN].

11. Hesse to Manteuffel, March 30, 1852, 2.4.1., Abteilung II, Nr. 5246 (AA III, Rep. 14, Nr. 534), BAM.

12. Léonce Angrand to MAE, Jan. 25, Feb. 29, March 3, 1852, CP 1871, Amér. cent., vol. 10, AMAE.

13. Hesse address to Rafael Carrera, [early 1852], 2.4.1., Abteilung II, Nr. 5246 (AA III, Rep. 14, Nr. 534), BAM; Hesse to Manteuffel, July 25, 1852, Hesse to Manteuffel and von der Heydt, July 29, Oct. 30, 1852, 2.4.1., Abteilung II, Nr. 5198 (AA II, Rep. 6, Nr. 1581), BAM.

14. Hesse to Manteuffel and von der Heydt, July 29, 1852, 2.4.1. Abteilung II, Nr. 5198 (AA II, Rep. 6, Nr. 1581), BAM.

15. Hesse to Manteuffel and von der Heydt, July 29, Oct. 30, 1852, 2.4.1., Abtei-

lung II, Nr. 5198 (AA II, Rep. 6, Nr. 1581), BAM; Angrand to MAE, June 30, Nov. 26, 1852, CP 1871, Amér. cent., vol. 11, AMAE; Angrand to MAE, Feb. 28, April 30, 1853, CP 1871, Amér. cent., vol. 12, AMAE.

16. Hesse to von der Heydt and Manteuffel, Oct. 30, 1852, 2.4.1., Abteilung II, Nr. 5198 (AA II, Rep. 6, Nr. 1581), BAM; Hesse to foreign minister, Dec. 31, 1852, 2.4.1., Abteilung II, Nr. 5197 (AA II, Rep. 6, Nr. 1589), BAM; Hesse to Manteuffel, Jan. 31, 1853, 2.4.1., Abteilung I, Nr. 7943 (AA, Z. B., Nr. 924), BAM.

17. Angrand to MAE, April 30, 1853, CP 1871, Amér. cent., vol. 12, AMAE; von der Heydt and Ernst von Bodelschwing to FO, Dec. 19, 1852, Manteuffel to Louis Simons, June 7, 1853, Simons to Manteuffel, June 16, 1853, 2.4.1., Abteilung II, Nr. 5198 (AA II, Rep. 6, Nr. 1581), BAM; Jürgen Prüser, *Die Handelsverträge der Hansestädte Lübeck, Bremen und Hamburg mit überseeischen Staaten im 19. Jahrhundert* (Bremen: C. Schünemann, 1962).

18. Manteuffel to Hesse, April 8, 1851, Rep. 120, C. XIII 16, Nr. l, BAM.

19. C. L. Merck to Rudolph Schleiden, Feb. 1, 1854, instructions to Schleiden and personal to Schleiden, Feb. 8, 1854 (both letters), Schleiden, Note Verbale, March 11, 1854, 2.-C. 23. b. 2, SAB.

20. Schleiden to José de Marcoleta, July 26, 1854, 2.-C. 23. b. 2, SAB.

21. [Packulben?] to Petkhoven, Jan. 27, 1854, Never, Minister des Handels und der öffentlichen Arbeiten, to Ministerium des Königlichen Hauses und des Äussern, Feb. 5, 1854, Petkhoven to king, Feb. 11, 1854, Abteilung II, M. A. 80041, Geheimes Staatsarchiv, Bayerisches Hauptstaatsarchiv, Munich; Hesse to Manteuffel, July 1, 1852, 2.4.1., Abteilung I, Nr. 7943 (AA, Z. B., Nr. 924), BAM; correspondence from mid-1853 through 1854, in particular a circular, Jan. 24, 1854, 2.4.1., Abteilung II, Nr. 5197 (AA II, Rep. 6, Nr. 1589), BAM; Hesse to Manteuffel, Aug. 30, 1854, 2.4.1., Abteilung II, Nr. 638 (AA II, Rep. 6, Nr. 3519), BAM; Heinrich Lutz, *Zwischen Habsburg und Preussen. Deutschland, 1815–1866* (Berlin: Siedler, 1985).

22. Correspondence from mid-1853 through 1854, circular, Jan. 24, 1854, von der Heydt and Bodelschwing to Manteuffel, June 6, 1855, 2.4.1., Abteilung II, Nr. 5197 (AA II, Rep. 6, Nr. 1589), BAM; von der Heydt to Manteuffel, July 4, 1855, 2.4.1., Abteilung II, Nr. 5198 (AA II, Rep. 6, Nr. 1581), BAM.

23. Ludwig Lehmann, Promemoria, March 2, 1856, Rep. 120, CVIII 1, Nr. 8, BAM; von der Heydt to king, May 13, 1853, Geheimes Zivilkabinett, Rep. 89, 2. 2. 1., Nr. 12950, BAM.

24. Materials relative to public meetings and colonization organizations, I Hauptabteilung, Preussisches Staatsministerium (Rep. 90), Nr. 232, SAP; *Jahres-Bericht des Berliner Vereins zur Centralisation deutscher Auswanderung und Colonisation für das Jahr 1851* (Berlin: Berliner Verein zur Centralisation deutscher Auswanderung und Colonisation, 1852), 7–8; *Geschäfts-Bericht des provisorischen Comités der deutschen Colonisations-Gesellschaft für Central-Amerika, als Vorlage für die am 21. Oktober 1852 stattfindende General-Versammlung* (Berlin: Comité der deutschen Colonisations-Gesellschaft für Central-Amerika, 1852), 3–8; *Die öffentlichen Sitzungen des Central-Vereins für die deutsche Auswanderungs- und Colonisations-Angelegenheit im Jahre 1852* (Berlin: Central-Verein für die deutsche Auswanderungs- und Colonisations-Angelegenheit, 1853), 13–14; Mack Walker, *Germany and the Emigration, 1816–1885* (Cambridge: Harvard University Press,

1964), 80–83, 148–51, 194–203, 244–46; Karl Sapper, "Ansiedlung von Europäern in Mittelamerika," *Schriften des Vereins für Sozialpolitik* 117 (1912):3–67; Schröder, "Deutsche Kolonisationsversuche in Zentralamerika," 268–70; Fröschle, "Die Deutschen in Mittelamerika," 566–67.

25. J. Mariano Rodríguez to Hesse, July 27, 1852, 2.4.1., Abteilung I, Nr. 7943, BAM; Hesse to Manteuffel, March 30, 1852, 2.4.1., Abteilung II, Nr. 5246 (AA III, Rep. 14, Nr. 534), BAM.

26. Estimates here and elsewhere of the total number of colonists were extrapolated from those sources considered reliable. In this case, since it appears only males were counted but settlements consisted primarily of families, I have multiplied the number of settlers enumerated by 2.5. Jahresberichte des Hamburger Colonisationsvereins, 1851–1855, Akten des Bundestages, DB/28, vol. 1, BAF; *Protokolle der Deutschen Bundesversammlung vom Jahre 1858* (Frankfurt: n.p., [1859]), p. 1089; Hesse to Manteuffel, Dec. 30, 1852, 2.4.1., Abteilung II, Nr. 5246 (AA III, Rep. 14, Nr. 534), BAM; Julio Castellanos Cambranes, *El imperialismo alemán en Guatemala: El tratado de comercio de 1887* (Guatemala: Instituto de Investigaciones Económicas y Sociales de la Universidad de San Carlos de Guatemala, 1977), 15–25; Julio Castellanos Cambranes, "Aspectos del desarrollo socio-económico y político de Guatemala, 1868–1885, en base a materiales de archivos alemanes," *Política y sociedad* 3 (Jan.–June 1977):7–14; Dane, *Die wirtschaftlichen Beziehungen Deutschlands*, 90–91, 119, 123, 137–44; Regina Wagner, "Actividades empresariales de los alemanes en Guatemala, 1850–1920," *Mesoamérica* 13 (June 1987):87–93.

27. Carl Scherzer to Squier, May 6, 1856, container 3, Squier papers, LC; Scherzer to Squier, Aug. 2, 17, Oct. 21, Dec. 2, 1856, container 2, Squier papers, LC; Hartmut Pogge von Strandmann, "Domestic Origins of Germany's Colonial Expansion under Bismarck," *Past and Present* 42 (Feb. 1969):140–59.

28. Hesse to Manteuffel, July 1, 1852, 2.4.1., Abteilung I, Nr. 7943 (AA, Z. B., Nr. 924), BAM.

29. Hesse to Manteuffel, Oct. 30, 1852, 2.4.1., Abteilung II, Nr. 637 (AA II, Rep. 6, Nr. 3518), BAM.

30. Hesse to Manteuffel, July 1, 1852, Jan. 31, 1853, 2.4.1., Abteilung I, Nr. 7943 (AA, Z. B., Nr. 924), BAM; Hesse to Manteuffel, Feb. 22, 1853, 2.4.1., Abteilung II, Nr. 5198 (AA II, Rep. 6, Nr. 1581), BAM; Hesse to Manteuffel, Aug. 30, 1854, 2.4.1., Abteilung II, Nr. 638 (AA II, Rep. 6, Nr. 3519), BAM; Molina to Joaquín B. Calvo, Oct. 18, 1853, MRE, caja 25, exp. leg. de CR, AN, CR; J. R. Swift to William S. Thayer, Oct. 18, 1855, William Thayer papers, University of Virginia, Charlottesville.

31. Angrand to MAE, Nov. 26, 1852, CP 1871, Amér. cent., vol. 11, AMAE; Angrand to MAE, Feb. 28, 1853, CP 1871, Amér. cent., vol. 12, AMAE; Hesse to Manteuffel, July 1, 1852, Jan. 31, 1853, 2.4.1., Abteilung I, Nr. 7943 (AA, Z. B., Nr. 924), BAM; Hesse to Manteuffel, Feb. 22, 1853, 2.4.1., Abteilung II, Nr. 5198 (AA II, Rep. 6, Nr. 1581), BAM; Hesse to Manteuffel, Aug. 30, 1854, 2.4.1., Abteilung II, Nr. 638 (AA II, Rep. 6, Nr. 3519), BAM.

32. Hesse to Manteuffel, Nov. 7, 1851, 2.4.1., Abteilung II, Nr. 5246 (AA III, Rep. 14, Nr. 534), BAM.

33. Hesse to Manteuffel, July 1, 1852, 2.4.1., Abteilung I, Nr. 7943 (AA, Z. B., Nr. 924), BAM; Hesse to Manteuffel and von der Heydt, July 25, 1852, 2.4.1., Ab-

teilung II, Nr. 637 (AA II, Rep. 6, Nr. 3518), BAM; Hesse to Manteuffel and von der Heydt, Oct. 30, 1852, 2.4.1., Abteilung II, Nr. 5198 (AA II, Rep. 6, Nr. 1581), BAM; Hesse to Manteuffel, Dec. 30, 1852, 2.4.1., Abteilung II, Nr. 5246 (AA III, Rep. 14, Nr. 534), BAM.

34. Hesse to Manteuffel and von der Heydt, Oct. 30, 1852, 2.4.1., Abteilung II, Nr. 5198 (AA II, Rep. 6, Nr. 1581), BAM; Houwald, "Die Deutschen in Costa Rica"; Werner F. Leopold, "Der Deutsche in Costa Rica," *Hamburger Wirtschaftschronik* 3 (Oct. 1966):133–214.

35. Hesse to foreign minister, June 16, 1853, 2.4.1., Abteilung II, Nr. 5198 (AA II, Rep. 6, Nr. 1581), BAM.

36. Hesse to Manteuffel, March 30, April 2, 1852, 2.4.1., Abteilung II, Nr. 5246 (AA III, Rep. 14, Nr. 534), BAM.

37. Baron C. H. de Hugel to Comte Briol Schauenstein, April 27, May 11, 1852, Schauenstein to Hugel, May 5, 1852, Esterhazy to Schauenstein, Aug. 11, Dec. 13, 1852, Calvo to Aust. foreign minister, Oct. 7, 1852, Juan María Mora to Aust. emperor, Oct. 7, 1852, Lorenzana to Esterhazy, Dec. 11, 1852, Aust. foreign minister to Graf Colloredo, Nov. 29, 1852, Colloredo to Schauenstein, Jan. 8, 31, 1853, Br. FO to Colloredo, Jan. 18, 1853, R. W. Foublanque to Lord Wodehouse, Jan. 14, 1853, Aust. foreign minister to Trade Minister von Baumgartner, March 21, 1853, [illegible] to Schauenstein, April 15, 1853, Schauenstein to emperor, April 22, 1853, emperor to Mora, April 22, 1853, Schauenstein to Calvo, April 26, 1853, Schauenstein to Esterhazy, April 26, 1853, XXXIII—Ver. St. von Amer., carton 125, Politisches Archiv, Österreichisches Staatsarchiv; Julius Fröbel, *Seven Years' Travel in Central America* (London: Richard Bentley, 1856); Thomas Karnes, *The Failure of Union: Central America, 1824–1975* (Tempe: University of Arizona Press, 1976), 96–147, 248–59.

38. Hesse to Manteuffel, Nov. 7, 1851, 2.4.1., Abteilung II, Nr. 665 (AA II, Rep. 6, Nr. 3544), BAM.

39. Hesse to Manteuffel, Feb. 12, 1852, 2.4.1., Abteilung II, Nr. 665 (AA II, Rep. 6, Nr. 3544), BAM.

40. Hesse to Manteuffel, Nov. 7, 1851, 2.4.1., Abteilung II, Nr. 5246 (AA III, Rep. 14, Nr. 534), BAM; Hesse, Denkschrift, March 30, 1852, Hesse to Klee, March 30, 1852, Hesse to Manteuffel, April 30, 1852, Hesse to Manteuffel and von der Heydt, July 25, 1852, 2.4.1., Abteilung II, Nr. 637 (AA II, Rep. 6, Nr. 3518), BAM.

41. Hesse to Manteuffel, April 30, 1852, Hesse to Manteuffel and von der Heydt, July 25, Aug. 28, 1852, 2.4.1., Abteilung II, Nr. 637 (AA II, Rep. 6, Nr. 3518), BAM.

42. Hesse to Manteuffel and von der Heydt, July 25, Aug. 28, 1852, 2.4.1., Abteilung II, Nr. 637 (AA II, Rep. 6, Nr. 3518) BAM; Hesse to Manteuffel and von der Heydt, Oct. 30, 1852, 2.4.1., Abteilung II, Nr. 5198 (AA II, Rep. 6, Nr. 1581), BAM; Angrand to MAE, April 30, 1853, CP 1871, Amér. cent., vol. 12, AMAE.

43. Hesse to Manteuffel and von der Heydt, July 25, 1852, 2.4.1., Abteilung II, Nr. 637 (AA II, Rep. 6, Nr. 3518), BAM.

44. Hesse to Manteuffel and von der Heydt, Aug. 28, 1852, 2.4.1., Abteilung II, Nr. 637 (AA II, Rep. 6, Nr. 3518), BAM.

45. Hesse to Manteuffel, Nov. 9, 1853, Aug. 30, 1854, 2.4.1., Abteilung II, Nr. 638 (AA II, Rep. 6, Nr. 3519), BAM.

46. Hesse to Manteuffel, Nov. 9, 1853, Board of Directors of the Central Union

for German Emigration and Colonisation Affairs to Manteuffel, Aug. 12, 1855, 2.4.1., Abteilung II, Nr. 638 (AA II, Rep. 6, Nr. 3519), BAM.

47. Heinrich Friedrich Wilhelm Nanne to Manteuffel, Sept. 20, 1856, 2.4.1., Abteilung II, Nr. 638 (AA II, Rep. 6, Nr. 3519), BAM; Henry F. W. Nanne Memoir, Bancroft Library, University of California, Berkeley.

48. Hesse to Manteuffel, Nov. 9, 1853, Aug. 30, 1854, 2.4.1., Abteilung II, Nr. 638 (AA II, Rep. 6, Nr. 3519), BAM.

49. Hesse to foreign minister, June 23, 1853, 2.4.1., Abteilung II, Nr. 5198 (AA II, Rep. 6, Nr. 1581), BAM; Houwald, "Die Deutschen in Nikaragua"; Craig L. Dozier, *Nicaragua's Mosquito Shore: The Years of British and American Presence* (University: University of Alabama Press, 1985).

50. Hesse to Manteuffel, Aug. 30, 1854, 2.4.1., Abteilung II, Nr. 638 (AA II, Rep. 6, Nr. 3519), BAM; Hesse to Carl Bernhard, Jan. 21, 1856, 2.4.1., Abteilung II, Nr. 5246 (AA III, Rep. 14, Nr. 534), BAM.

51. Hesse to Manteuffel, Aug. 30, 1854, 2.4.1., Abteilung II, Nr. 638 (AA II, Rep. 6, Nr. 3519), BAM; Hesse to foreign minister, Feb. 4, 1856, 2.4.1., Abteilung II, Nr. 5246 (AA III, Rep. 14, Nr. 534), BAM; Juan Knohr to Syndicus Merck, Jan. 23, 1856, Konsularberichte 1856, Punta Arenas, Handelskammer, Commerzbibliothek, Hamburg; Nikolaus Riggenbach, *Costa Rica, Land und Leute* (Oldenburg: A. Michel, [1866]); Victor H. Acuña Ortega and Iván Molina Jiménez, *El desarrollo económico y social de Costa Rica: De la colonia a la crisis de 1930* (San José, CR: Alma Mater, 1986), 81–103; Dane, *Die wirtschaftlichen Beziehungen Deutschlands*, 134–37, 144–48.

52. Hesse to Manteuffel, July 1, 30, 1852, Nov. 5, 1854, 2.4.1., Abteilung I, Nr. 7943 (AA, Z. B., Nr. 924), BAM; Hesse to Manteuffel, Aug. 30, 1854, 2.4.1., Abteilung II, Nr. 638 (AA II, Rep. 6, Nr. 3519), BAM; "Suez und Panama Kanäle," *Westermann's Jahrbuch der illustrierten deutschen Monatshefte* 2 (July 1857):478–80.

53. Hesse to Manteuffel and von der Heydt, June 28, 1852, 2.4.1., Abteilung II, Nr. 5246 (AA III, Rep. 14, Nr. 534), BAM; Hesse to Manteuffel, Oct. 29, 1857, 2.4.1., Abteilung II, Nr. 5247 (AA III, Rep. 14, Nr. 535), BAM.

54. Hesse to Manteuffel, Aug. 30, 1854, 2.4.1., Abteilung II, Nr. 638 (AA II, Rep. 6, Nr. 3519), BAM; Hesse to Manteuffel, May 16, 1856, 2.4.1., Abteilung II, Nr. 5246 (AA III, Rep. 14, Nr. 534), BAM.

55. Hesse to New Granada vice president, [1855], 2.4.1., Abteilung I, Nr. 7943 (AA, Z. B., Nr. 924), BAM.

56. Landrath Merwitz to Manteuffel, June 3, 1857, Rep. 90 (Geheimes Staatsministerium), Nr. 232, SAP.

57. Alexander von Schleinitz to Prussian king, Dec. 3, 1858, 2.2.1., Abteilung II, Nr. 12954 (R. 89, B. XIII 5, vol. 4, 1857–1860), BAM; Hesse to Schleinitz, Dec. 10, 1858, 2.4.1., Abteilung II, Nr. 639 (AA II, Rep. 6, Nr. 3520), BAM; Anthony Trollope, *The West Indies and the Spanish Main* (London: Chapman, 1859), 278, 289, 296, 299.

4. Bismarck and the Foundations of the German Empire, 1858–1871

1. Wehler, *Bismarck und der Imperialismus*, 53–61; Friedrich-Wilhelm Henning, *Die Industrialisierung in Deutschland, 1800 bis 1914* (Paderborn, FRG: Ferdinand

Schöningh, 1973). On early Prussian-German expansion into Asia and Central America, see Helmuth Stoecker, "Preussisch-deutsche Chinapolitik in den 1860/70er Jahren," in Hans-Ulrich Wehler, ed., *Imperialismus* (Cologne: Kiepenheuer und Witsch, 1976), 244–58; Schoonover, *The United States in Central America*, 28–77.

2. On the relationship between economic transformation, population growth, and migration in German society, see Toni Pierenkemper, "Labour Market, Labour Force and Standard of Living from Agriculture to Industry," in Bade, ed., *Population, Labour and Migration in 19th and 20th Century Germany*, 35–58; Marschalck, *Deutsche Überseewanderung im 19. Jahrhundert;* Emil Lehmann, *Die deutsche Auswanderung* (Berlin: Georg Reimer, 1861). For a sketch of German penetration of Central America, see Castellanos Cambranes, "Aspectos del desarrollo socio-económico y político de Guatemala, 1868–1885." On the relationship of industrialization and the domestic political situation with foreign relations, see Horst Müller-Link, *Industrialisierung und Aussenpolitik: Preussen-Deutschland und das Zarenreich von 1860 bis 1890* (Göttingen: Vandenhoeck und Ruprecht, 1977); Wehler, "Industrial Growth and Early German Imperialism," 71–92; Geoff Eley, "Social Imperialism in Germany," in *Festschrift für G. W. F. Hallgarten* (Munich: C. H. Beck, 1976), 71–86.

3. Rolf H. Dumke, "Die wirtschaftlichen Folgen des Zollvereins," in Werner Abelshauser and Dietmar Petzina, eds., *Deutsche Wirtschaftsgeschichte im Industriezeitalter: Konjunktur, Krise, Wachstum* (Königstein/Ts: Athenäum/Droste, 1981), 241–73; Borchardt, *Grundriss der deutschen Wirtschaftsgeschichte*, 41–56; Schulze, *Der Weg zum Nationalstaat*, 7–8, 95–125; Pflanze, *Bismarck and the Development of Germany*, 2:3–31; Lothar Gall, *Bismarck: The White Revolutionary*, vol. 1 of 2 (London: Unwin Hyman, 1990); Hans-Ulrich Wehler, "Bismarcks Imperialismus, 1862–1890," in Wehler, ed., *Imperialismus*, 259–88.

4. Castellanos Cambranes, *El imperialismo alemán en Guatemala*, 20–38; Dane, *Die wirtschaftlichen Beziehungen Deutschlands*, 148–55; Schoonover and Schoonover, "Statistics for an Understanding of Foreign Intrusions into Central America," pt. 3, 85–119.

5. Pérez Brignoli, *Breve historia de Centroamérica*, 90–102; Héctor Lindo-Fuentes, *Weak Foundations: The Economy of El Salvador in the Nineteenth Century, 1821–1890* (Berkeley: University of California Press, 1991), 99–190.

6. Gülich to Schleinitz, Oct. 18, 1860, von der Heydt to Schleinitz, Jan. 18, 1861, Rep. 120, A. XIV, Nr. 5, vol. 1, BAM; Martin Winckler, *Bismarcks Bündnispolitik und das europäische Gleichgewicht* (Stuttgart: Kohlhammer, 1964); Wehler, *Bismarck und der Imperialismus*, 112–26.

7. Georg Theodor Beschor to [Rudolf Schleiden?], July 6, 1860, Hp II 54, Nr. 89, Handelskammerarchiv, Bremen; Mirabeau Bounaparte Lamar to Lewis Cass, June 2, 1859, DD, Cent. Amer. (Nic.): 4 (M 219/r 11).

8. "Eine Nicaraguabahn," *Westermann's Jahrbuch der illustrierten deutschen Monatshefte* 14 (April 1863):111; "Die Durchstechung des Isthmus von Panama," *Westermann's Jahrbuch der illustrierten deutschen Monatshefte* 17 (Oct. 1864):106–8; "Die Honduras-Bahn," *Westermann's Jahrbuch der illustrierten deutschen Monatshefte* 26 (Sept. 1869):446–47; "Eine Nicaragua-Bahn," *Westermann's Jahrbuch der illustrierten deutschen Monatshefte* 22 (May 1867):238; "Note pour le ministère," April 30, 1868, 6 AQ 8, AN, P.

9. Knohr to Otto von Bismarck, Knohr to Merck, both Sept. 30, 1864, 2.4.1., Abteilung II Nr. 5247 (A. A. III, Rep. 14, Nr. 535), BAM; Knohr to Merck, Sept. 30, 1864, Bd-CR, Commerzbibliothek, Handelskammer, Hamburg. On efforts to use the circum-Caribbean as a cotton-producing substitute for the South, see Ralph Lee Woodward, Jr., "Guatemalan Cotton and the American Civil War," *Interamerican Economic Affairs* 18 (1965):87–94; Thomas D. Schoonover, "Mexican Cotton and the American Civil War," *Americas* 30 (April 1974):429–47 [also in *Historia Mexicana* 91 (Jan.–March 1974):483–506].

10. Carl Bernhard to [foreign minister], Aug. 20, 1866, 2.4.1. Abteilung II, Nr. 639 (AA II, Rep. 6, Nr. 3520), BAM; Edward Delius to foreign minister, Aug. 6, 1866, Rep. 77, Tit. 226, Nr. 118, vol. 2, BAM; Wolfgang Petter, "Die überseeische Stützpunktpolitik der preussisch-deutschen Kriegsmarine, 1859–1883" (Ph.D. diss., Universität Freiburg, 1975).

11. Delius to foreign minister, Aug. 6, 1866, Rep. 77, Tit. 226, Nr. 118, vol. 2, BAM; Helmuth Polakowsky, "Estación naval alemana en Costa Rica, 1883," *Revista de los Archivos Nacionales* 7 (1943):56–65; Tulio von Bülow, "Sobre el proyecto de base naval alemana en 1868," *Revista de los Archivos Nacionales* 7 (1943):147–49; undated extract of E. E. Verebelij letter [1867?], 09.01, Nr. 52602, BAP; Joaquín Fernández Montúfar, *Historia ferrovíal de Costa Rica* (San José, CR: n.p., [1935]). On Frémont's project, see Schoonover, *The United States in Central America*, 28–45.

12. Karl Hermann Thiel to emperor, March 27, 1867, 2.2.1., Nr. 12953 (Geheimes Civil-Kabinet), BAM.

13. Arthur Morrell to William H. Seward, May 8, 1868, enclosing Friedrich Wilhelm Franz Kinderling to J. Friedrich Lahmann, April 20, 1868, Lahmann to Julio Volio, May 1, 1868, Volio to Lahmann, May 6, 1868, U.S. Department of State, *Papers Relating to the Foreign Relations of the United States, 1868* (Washington: GPO, 1869), pt. 2 [hereafter *FRUS, 1868*, pt. 2]; Kinderling to Royal Navy High Command, May 22, 1868, 2.4.1 Abteilung II, Nr. 644 (AA II, Rep. 6, Nr. 3573), BAM.

14. Polakowsky, "Estación naval alemana en Costa Rica"; Bülow, "Proyecto de base naval alemana."

15. Morrell to Seward, May 8, 25, 1868, DD, Cent. Amer. (CR): 3 (M 219/r 20); certification of Morrell, U.S. consul, June 8, 1868, Nr. 52613, Das Bundesconsulat in San José (CR), 1868–1886, BAP.

16. Lahmann to foreign minister, July 10, 1868, Rep. 77, Tit. 226, Nr. 118, vol. 2, BAM.

17. Kinderling to Royal High Command of the Navy, May 22, 1868, 2.4.1 Abteilung II, Nr. 644 (AA II, Rep. 6, Nr. 3573), BAM.

18. Kinderling to Royal High Command of the Navy, May 22, 1868, 2.4.1 Abteilung II, Nr. 644 (AA II, Rep. 6, Nr. 3573), BAM; Thiel to emperor, March 27, 1867, 2.2.1, Nr. 12953 (Geheimes Civil-Kabinet), BAM; "Franz Kinderling," MSg 1/1101, p. 185, BAMF.

19. Circular, Rudolph Delbrück to missions in London, Paris, St. Petersburg, Vienna, Florence, and Washington, July 3, 1868, Carl Schurz to Gerolt, June 20, July 9, 1868, *Die auswärtige Politik Preussens, 1858–1871*, 10:106–9.

20. Bülow, "Proyecto de base naval alemana," 147–49; "Franz Kinderling," MSg 1/1101, p. 185, BAMF; Friedrich von Gerolt to Bismarck, Oct. 20, 1868, en-

closing an extract of Charles N. Riotte to Gerolt, Oct. 4, 1868, Nr. 52613 (AA I C, Nr. 6, Central America [San José], vol. 1, Bundes Bericht), BAP.

21. Kirchenpauer, Mayor of Hamburg, to Auswärtiges Amt, April 15, 1869, Bernhard to Bismarck, April 6, 1869, 09.01, Nr. 52602, BAP; B. Squire Cotrell to John Chandler Bancroft Davis, March 16, 1870, CD, San Juan del Norte: 5 (T 348/r 5).

22. [Illegible] to Kirchenpauer, June 16, 1870, enclosing Bernhard to [?], May 16, 1870, Hamburger Bevollmächtigter beim Bundesrat in Berlin, III. 20, SAH; Delius to Delbrück, Nov. 7, 1872[?], 09.01, Nr. 52602, see also Nr. 52603 and Nr. 52615, BAP.

23. Gerolt to Bismarck, Sept. 23, 1868, Ver. St., I C 56, Schriftwechsel mit Washington, vol. 1 (1868), PAAA; Gerolt to Bismarck, Jan. 11, 1869, Ver. St., I C 59, Schriftwechsel mit Washington, vol. 1 (1869), PAAA.

24. Riotte to Hamilton Fish, May 27, Dec. 21, 1870, Jan. 7, 1871, DD, Cent. Amer. (Nic.): 11 (M 219/r 16).

25. Karl von Seebach, *Central-Amerika und der Interozeanische Canal* (Berlin: C. B. Lüderitz'sche Verlagsbuchhandlung, 1873), 30–36.

26. Julius Fröbel, "Die deutsche Auswanderung und ihre nationale und cultur-historische Bedeutung," in Julius Fröbel, ed., *Kleine politische Schriften* (Stuttgart: J. G. Cotta'sche Buchhandlung, 1866), 93–198; Karl von Scherzer, *Statistisch-commerzielle Ergebnisse einer Reise um die Erde unternommen am Bord der österreichschen Fregatte Novara in den Jahren, 1857–1858* (Leipzig: F. A. Brockhaus, 1867).

27. News item, June 14, 1870, *Allgemeine Auswanderungszeitung*, June 30, 1870, p. 103; Wehler, *Bismarck und der Imperialismus*, 155–57; Michael W. Doyle, *Empires* (Ithaca, NY: Cornell University Press, 1986), 234–56.

5. Defining Germany's Role in Central America, 1871–1885

1. Wehler, *Bismarck und der Imperialismus*, 61–111, 434–45; Wolfgang Zank, "Vom Taumel in die Krise," *Die Zeit*, May 14, 1993, 20; Wolfgang Zorn, "Wirtschafts- und sozialgeschichtliche Zusammenhänge der deutschen Reichsgründungszeit, 1850–1879," in Wehler, ed., *Moderne deutsche Sozialgeschichte*, 254–70; Michael Stürmer and Siegfried Ziegler, eds., *Das deutsche Kaiserreich und die europäischen Grossmächte im Zeitalter des Imperialismus* (Munich: R. Oldenbourg, 1977), 6–13; Wilfried Loth, *Das Kaiserreich: Obrigkeitsstaat und politische Mobilisierung* (Munich: dtv, 1996); Günter Ogger, *Die Gründerjahre: Als der Kapitalismus jung und verwegen war* (Munich: Knaur, 1995); Hans-Peter Ullmann, *Das Deutsche Kaiserreich, 1871–1918* (Frankfurt: Suhrkamp, 1995).

2. Walther L. Bernecker and Thomas Fischer, "Deutschland und Lateinamerika im Zeitalter des Imperialismus, 1871–1914," *Ibero-Amerikanisches Archiv*, n.s., 21:3–4 (1995):273–302; Richard Tilly, "Mergers, External Growth, and Finance in the Development of Large-Scale Enterprise in Germany, 1880–1913," *Journal of Economic History* 42 (Sept. 1982):629–58; Steven Webb, "Agricultural Protection in Wilhelminian Germany: Forging an Empire with Pork and Rye," *Journal of Economic History* 42 (March 1982):309–26; Steven Webb, "Tariffs, Cartels, Technology

and Growth in the German Steel Industry, 1879–1914," *Journal of Economic History* 40 (June 1980):309–29; Steven Webb, "Tariff Protection for the Iron Industry, Cotton Textiles and Agriculture in Germany, 1879–1914," *Jahrbücher für Nationalökonomie und Statistik*, n.s., 192 (1977/78):336–57; Rolf Wagenführ, *Die Bedeutung des Aussenhandels für die deutsche Industriewirtschaft. Die Exportquote der deutschen Industrie von 1870 bis 1936* (Berlin: Hanseatische Verlagsanstalt, 1936), 38–50, 71; Castellanos Cambranes, *El imperialismo alemán en Guatemala*, 26–71.

3. Kiesewetter, *Industrielle Revolution in Deutschland*, 37–63; Hardtwig, *Vormärz*, 125–28; Klaus J. Bade, *Friedrich Fabri und der Imperialismus in der Bismarckzeit: Revolution—Depression—Expansion* (Freiburg: Atlantis, 1975); Tom Kemp, *Historical Patterns of Industrialization* (London: Longman, 1971), 80–97, 360–61; David S. Landes, "The Old Bank and the New: The Financial Revolution of the Nineteenth Century," in *Essays in European Economic History, 1789–1914*, François Crouzet, W. H. Chaloner, and W. M. Stern, eds. (London: Edward Arnold, 1969), 112–27; Michael Stürmer, *Die Reichsgründung: Deutscher Nationalstaat und europäisches Gleichgewicht im Zeitalter Bismarcks* (Munich: dtv, 1984), 82–106.

4. Borchardt, *Grundriss der deutschen Wirtschaftsgeschichte*, 58; Geiss, *Der lange Weg in die Katastrophe*, 53; Sandweg and Stürmer, eds., *Industrialisierung und soziale Frage in Deutschland im 19. Jahrhundert*; Stürmer, *Die Reichsgründung*, 101; Karl W. Hardach, "Some Remarks on German Economic Historiography and its Understanding of the Industrial Revolution in Germany," *Journal of European Economic History* 1 (spring 1972):37–99.

5. Peter-Christian Witt, "Innenpolitik und Imperialismus in der Vorgeschichte des 1. Weltkrieges," in Karl Holl and Günther List, eds., *Liberalismus und imperialistischer Staat: Der Imperialismus als Problem liberaler Parteien in Deutschland, 1890–1914* (Göttingen: Vandenhoeck und Ruprecht, 1975), 17–18; Imanuel Geiss, "Sozialstruktur und imperialistische Dispositionen im zweiten deutschen Kaiserreich," in Holl and List, eds., *Liberalismus und imperialistischer Staat*, 42; Bernecker and Fischer, "Deutschland und Lateinamerika im Zeitalter des Imperialismus, 1871–1914," 298–301; Paul Bairoch, *Commerce extérieur et développement économique de l'Europe au XIXe siècle* (Paris: Mouton, 1976); Paul Bairoch, *Révolution industrielle et sous-développement*, 4th ed. (Paris: Mouton, 1974); Christoph Buchheim, *Industrielle Revolution: Langfristige Wirtschaftsentwicklung in Grossbritannien, Europa und in Übersee* (Munich: dtv, 1994), 149–54.

6. Geoff Eley, "Deutscher Sonderweg und englisches Vorbild," in David Blackbourn and Geoff Eley, *Mythen deutscher Geschichtsschreibung: Die gescheiterte bürgerliche Revolution von 1848* (Frankfurt: Ullstein, 1980), 57.

7. Mary E. Townsend, *Origins of Modern German Colonization, 1871–1885* (New York: Columbia University Press, 1921), 50–53, 82–84, 194–96; Wagner, "Actividades empresariales de los alemanes en Guatemala," 93–95; Schoonover and Schoonover, "Statistics for an Understanding of Foreign Intrusions into Central America," pt. 3, 85–119.

8. Cardoso, "Central America," 4:197–227; Woodward, *Central America: A Nation Divided*, 120–202; Cardoso and Pérez Brignoli, *Centro América y la economía occidental*, 199–320; Pérez Brignoli, *Breve historia de Centroamérica*, 95–106; Jorge Mario García Laguardia, *La Reforma liberal en Guatemala: Vida política y orden constitucional* (Guatemala: EDUCA, 1972); 37–53.

9. García Laguardia, *La Reforma liberal en Guatemala*, 171–82; Seldon Liss, *Radical Thought in Central America* (Boulder, CO: Westview, 1991), 16–17, 26–27, 98, 128–30, 161–62; David Bushnell and Neil Macaulay, *Emergence of Latin America in the Nineteenth Century* (New York: Oxford University Press, 1988), 189–90; Burns, *The Poverty of Progress*, 18–19, 46–49.

10. Woodward, *Central America: A Nation Divided*, 149–202; Alfonso Arrivillaga Cortés and Alfredo Gómez Davis, "Antecedentes históricos, movilizaciones sociales y reivindicaciones étnicas en la costa atlántica de Guatemala," *Estudios Sociales Centroamericanos* 48 (Sept.–Dec. 1988):38.

11. Wehler, *Bismarck und der Imperialismus*, 112–26, 434–45; Hans-Christoph Schroeder, *Sozialistische Imperialismusdeutung* (Göttingen: Vandenhoeck und Ruprecht, 1973), 7–25; Paul M. Kennedy, "German Colonial Expansion. Has the 'Manipulated Social Imperialism' been Ante-Dated?" *Past and Present* 54 (Feb. 1972):134–41; Geoff Eley, "Defining Social Imperialism: Use and Abuse of an Idea," *Social History* 1 (Oct. 1976):265–90; David M. Pletcher, "1861–1898: Economic Growth and Diplomatic Adjustment," in *Economics and World Power: An Assessment of American Diplomacy Since 1789*, William H. Becker and Samuel F. Well, Jr., eds. (New York: Columbia University Press, 1984), 119–71; Fritz Stern, *Gold and Iron: Bismarck, Bleichroeder, and the Building of the German Empire* (New York: Alfred A. Knopf, 1977), 176–91, 304–11; Ralph Lee Woodward, Jr., "Conservativism, Liberalism, and Marxism in Central America," *Anthenaeum Society Review* 3 (spring 1986):5–21.

12. Wallerstein, *Historical Capitalism*, 39.

13. Pierenkemper, "Labour Market, Labour Force and Standard of Living"; Ali Mazrui, "From Social Darwinism to Current Theories of Modernization," *World Politics* 21 (Oct. 1968):69–83.

14. Fritz T. Epstein, "Germany and the United States: Basic Patterns of Conflict and Understanding," in George L. Anderson, ed., *Issues and Conflict* (Lawrence: University of Kansas Press, 1959), 290; Holger H. Herwig, *Germany's Vision of Empire in Venezuela, 1871–1918* (Princeton, NJ: Princeton University Press, 1986); Ragnhild Fiebig-von Hase, *Lateinumeriku uls Konfliktherd der deutsch-amerikanischen Beziehungen 1890–1903*, 2 vols. (Göttingen: Vandenhoeck und Ruprecht, 1986), 1:13–43; Alfred Vagts, *Deutschland und die Vereinigten Staaten in der Weltpolitik*, 2 vols. (New York: Dornan, 1935), 2:513–23; Jeannette Keim, *Forty Years of German-American Relations* (Philadelphia, 1919); Heinz Wolter, *Bismarcks Aussenpolitik, 1871–1881* (Berlin: Akademie, 1983), 320.

15. Friedrich Augener to Bismarck, Aug. 21, 1872, 2.4.1. Abteilung II, Nr. 5198 (AA II, Rep. 6, Nr. 1581), BAM; Handelsvertrag mit Guatemala, Handelsvertrag mit Honduras, Oct. 1874 [?], Bestand der hanseatischen Gesandtschaft Berlin, Neuere Registratur H. II, 13c Fasz. 7, SAH; list and addenda, Aug. 6, 1872, B99-1-6/8764B, MRE, AGCA; Wagner, "Actividades empresariales de los alemanes en Guatemala," 95–97.

16. Kurt von Schlözer to Hamilton Fish, Jan. 20, 1872, RG 59, United States, Department of State, notes from the Prussian legation: vol. 3 (Microcopy 58/reel 3), NA [hereafter RG 59, notes from Prussian leg.: 3 (M 58/r 3)]; Henry Houben to George M. Williamson, Nov. 14, 1873, John Graham to William Hunter, Oct. 1874, RG 59, CD, Guat.: 3 (T 337/r 3), NA; Williamson to William Evarts, Sept.

24, 1877, RG 59, DD, Cent. Amer.: 14 (M 219/r 33), also found in *FRUS, 1877,* pp. 18–30; E. Rumsey Wing to H. Fish, Dec. 6, 1872, Bassett to H. Fish, Jan. 30, 1873, *FRUS, 1873,* pt. 1, pp. 224, 455; Wing to H. Fish, April 6, 1874, *FRUS, 1874,* p. 396.

17. Bernard Ernst von Bülow to Hamburg Senat, July 31, 1874, Spezialakten XIX. C. 23, Geographische, politische und Verwaltungsberichte aus Honduras, SAH; Ger. foreign minister to consul in Hond., Aug. 17, 1874, 09.01, Nr. 12549/3, BAP.

18. Gustave de Belot to MRE (Guat.), Aug. 22, 1872, B99-23-1/6225, MRE, AGCA; Cabarrus to MAE, July 27, 1875, Langlade to MAE, Oct. 22, 1877, CCC, Guat., vol. 9, AMAE; José Francisco Guevara-Escudero, "Nineteenth Century Honduras: A Regional Approach to the Economic History of Central America, 1839–1914," (Ph.D. diss., New York University, 1983), 411–12.

19. Bernhard to foreign minister, June 5, 1875, 09.01, Nr. 52603, BAP; Luis Felipe González Flores, *Historia de la influencia extranjera en el desenvolvimiento educacional y científico de Costa Rica* (San José, CR: Nacional, 1921).

20. Manuel María de Peralta to H. Fish, June 25, 1876, RG 59, notes from Cent. Amer. Legs.: 5 (T 34/r 7); C. N. Riotte to H. Fish, Jan. 21, 1872, RG 59, DD, Cent. Amer. (Nic.): 12 (M 219/r 17); George Bancroft to H. Fish, Jan. 5, 1872, DD, Ger.: 1 (M 44/r 19); Nicholas Fish to H. Fish, Jan. 13, 1876, DD, Ger.: 11 (M 44/r 29); John Chandler Bancroft Davis to H. Fish, Feb. 25, 1876, DD, Ger.: 12 (M 44/r 30); H. Fish to Bancroft, Feb. 9, 1876, Evarts to Bancroft, April 17, 1877, Evarts to Andrew D. White, July 22, 1879, RG 59, DI, Ger.: 16 (M 77/r 67); Michael John Cramer to H. Fish, Jan. 14, 1874, Bancroft to H. Fish, Jan. 9, 12, 1874, John Lambert Cadwalader to Caleb Cushing, Oct. 7, 1874, Cushing to H. Fish, Sept. 16, 1874, *FRUS, 1874,* pp. 368, 439–40, 912–14.

21. *Promemoria betreffend unsere Reklamation gegen Nicaragua in der Angelegenheit des Kaiserlichen Konsulats in Leon* (Berlin: Puttkammer und Mühlbrecht, 1877), included with Ger. foreign minister to Dr. Merck, Dec. 21, 1877, Senat C1 VI, Nr. 16^d, vol. 1, Fasc. 9, SAH; Sidney Locock to Marques of Salisbury, April 27, 1878, Bayerisches Hauptstaatsarchiv, Abteilung II, MA 76002, SAM; Williamson to Evarts, June 16, July 12, 25, Aug. 18, 1877, RG 59, DD, Cent. Amer.: 13 (M 219/r 32); Schlözer to Evarts, April 24, Aug. 22, 1877, Max von Thielmann to Evarts, July 19, 18, 1877, Thielmann to Frederick W. Seward, July 18, 1877, RG 59, notes from Prussian leg.: 14 (M 58/r 14); Williamson to Evarts, Sept. 24, 1877, DD, Cent. Amer.: 14 (M 219/r 33); Maudes to marine minister, Feb. 26, 1878, BB⁴ 1090, AAM; A. d'Oncien de la Batie to du Seignlay, March 7, 1878, du Seignlay to marine minister, June 8, 1878, BB⁴ 1093, AAM; Werner von Bergen to Lorenzo Montúfar, July 8, 1878, July 5, 1879, B99-5-1/4289/93194, MRE, AGCA. For more detail, see "The Eisenstück Affair: German and U.S. Rivalry in Central America, 1877–1890," in Schoonover, *The United States in Central America,* 62–76.

22. A. Tesdorpf, *Geschichte der kaiserlich deutschen Kriegsmarine in Denkwürdigkeiten von allgemeinem Interesse* (Kiel: Lipsius und Tischer, 1889), 177–202; Karl Paschen, *Aus der Werdezeit zweier Marinen* (Berlin: E. S. Mittler und Sohn, 1908), 170–97; Paul Koch, "Aus der Zeit von Admiral v. Stosch," *Marine-Rundschau* 14 (1903):694–96; B. E. von Bülow to Bergen, March 9, 1879, Rep. I, Nr. 40, vol. 1 (1878–1883), BAP; Townsend, *German Colonization,* 83–84; Solomon Huebner, "Re-

lation of the Government in Germany to the Promotion of Commerce," *Annals of the American Academy* 24 (Nov. 1904):95–109; Ekkehard Böhm, *Überseehandel und Flottenbau. Hanseatische Kaufmannschaft und deutsche Seerüstung, 1879–1902* (Düsseldorf: Bertelsmann, 1972), 23–30, 263–65; Cornelius Fischer, "Korvetten vor Corinto," *Die Zeit,* Aug. 17, 1990, p. 12; Thomas Fischer, "Craftsmen, Merchants, and Violence in Colombia: The Sucesos de [Events of] Bucaramanga of 1879," *Itinerario* 20:1 (1996):79–99.

23. Williamson to Evarts, Sept. 24, 1877, RG 59, DD, Cent. Amer.: 14 (M 219/r 33); Cornelius Logan to Evarts, April 14, 1879, May 14, 1880, DD, Cent. Amer.: 16 (M 219/r 35); Walter Herman Carl Laves, "German Government Influence on Foreign Investments, 1871–1914" (Ph.D. diss., University of Chicago, 1927), 200–207; Helmuth Polakowsky, "Die Republik Costa Rica in Central Amerika," *Westermann's Jahrbuch der illustrierten deutschen Monatshefte* 41 (March 1877):60–62; Darío A. Euraque, "La 'reforma liberal' en Honduras y la hipótesis de la 'oligarquía ausente': 1870–1930," *Revista de historia* 23 (Jan.–June 1991):26–27.

24. Evarts to White, Aug. 6, 1880, RG 59, DI, Ger.: 16 (M 77/r 67); Logan to Evarts, Oct. 14, 1880, Jan. 7, Feb. 1, 1881, RG 59, DD, Cent. Amer.: 17 (M 219/r 37); Titus to Hunter, Sept. 20, 1881, RG 59, CD, Guat.: 4 (T 337/r 4); David Strother to Hunter, Oct. 4, 1879, *FRUS, 1879,* 838–40.

25. Bülow to Bergen, Sept. 12, 1878, Bergen to Bülow, Nov. 2, 1878, AA I C, Nr. 1, Cent. Amer., vol. 1, BAP; Alfred Weber, "Zur wirtschaftlichen Lage in den tropisch-amerikanischen Staaten," *Jahrbuch für Gesetzgebung, Verwaltung und Volkswirtschaft im Deutschen Reich* 25:1 (1901):211–37.

26. Bülow to Bergen, Sept. 12, 1878, Bergen to Bülow, Nov. 2, 1878, AA I C, Nr. 1, Cent. Amer., vol. 1, BAP; David McCreery, "Coffee and Class: The Structure of the Development in Liberal Guatemala, 1871–1885," *Hispanic American Historical Review* 61 (Aug. 1976):438–60.

27. Hofmann to Chambers of Commerce and Businessmen's Associations, June 3, 1880, Rep. 120 C. XIII 16, Nr. 8, BAM.

28. Montúfar to Crisanto Medina, April 4, 1880, B99-6/4407/93361, MRE, AGCA; Montúfur to minister in Ger., May 26, 1880, Montúfar to ministers in Germany, Brazil, and Austria, June 7, 1880, Montúfar to minister in Ger., Aug. 13, 1880,B99-7-2-1/4654/93690, MRE, AGCA; Logan to Evarts, June 14, 1880, RG 59, DD, Cent. Amer.: 16 (M 219/r 35); various correspondence in 09.01, Nr. 52614, Das Kaiserliche Deutsche Konsulat in San Jose (CR), BAP; Montúfar to Medina, August 5, 13, 1880, B99-6/4358/93269, MRE, AGCA. Lehnhoff had a damaged business reputation, see John Magee to Dow, Aug. 13, 1879, box 1, folder 17, Dow papers.

29. H. H. Leavitt to Davis, Nov. 12, 1884, April 4, 1885, RG 59, CD, Managua: 1 (T 634/r 1); unsigned confidential report [Eckardt note?], Aug. 10, 1881, Spezialakten, XIX C 20, Nr. 3, SAH; Otto Mathies, *Hamburgs Reederei, 1814–1914* (Hamburg: L. Friederichsen, 1924).

30. Dow to Federico Benito, Aug. 31, 1883, Dow to Magee, Aug. 31, 1883, Dow to J. Rufino Barrios, Sept. 18, 1883, Dow to president (Pacific Mail), Feb. 27, 1884, Dow to B. Mosley, March 8, 1884, box 4, letterbook 1883–1885, Dow papers; Dow diary (1884), entries Feb. 23, 29, March 15, 1884, box 5, Dow papers.

31. Maximilian Sigismund Rudolf von Berchem to Bremen Senat, Sept. 14, 1885, 3.-A. 3.C.1. Nr. 37, SAB; Dow to Francisco Sarg, Feb. 28, 1885, box 4, letterbook 1885–1888, Dow papers.

32. Agenor Fournier to admiral, Feb. 22, 1884, BB[4] 1596, AAM; Emile Descamps to admiral, March 7, 1885, BB[4] 1398, AAM; Emile Jacques Phillippe LeBrun to MAE, Aug. 8, 1884, CP 1896, Amér. cent., vol. 26, AMAE.

33. Evarts to White, Aug. 6, 1880, RG 59, DI, Ger.: 16 (M 77/r 67); Logan to Evarts, Oct. 14, 1880, Jan. 7, Feb. 1, 1881, RG 59, DD, Cent. Amer.: 17 (M 219/r 37); Titus to Hunter, Sept. 20, 1881, RG 59, CD, Guat.: 4 (T 337/r 4); Heinrich Claussen, "Überproduktion und Krisis," *Preussische Jahrbücher* 44 (1879):490–517; Werner Sombart, "Entwickeln wir uns zum 'Exportindustriestaate'?" *Soziale Praxis: Centralblatt für Sozialpolitik* 8 (March 16, 1899):633–37; Hans-Ulrich Wehler, "Der Aufstieg des organisierten Kapitalismus und Interventionsstaates in Deutschland," in Winkler, ed., *Organisierter Kapitalismus*, 36–57.

34. Logan to James G. Blaine, June 15, 1881, RG 59, DD, Cent. Amer.: 18 (M 219/r 38).

35. Logan to Fredrick Frelinghuysen, Feb. 10, 13, 1882, RG 59, DD, Cent. Amer.: 18 (M 219/r 38).

36. Ger. minister in Mexico to Bismarck, Oct. 27, 1881, Sept. 30, 1882, Bergen to Bismarck, Feb. 28, June 10, 27, 1882, Abteilung IA, Mex. 2, vol. 1, PAAA.

37. Logan to Evarts, April 14, 1879, May 14, 1880, RG 59, DD, Cent. Amer.: 16 (M 219/r 35); Carl von Eisendecker to Bismarck, June 11, 1884, Casímir von Leyden to Bismarck, June 23, July 24, 1884, Leyden to foreign minister, July 9, 1884, Hauptabteilung III, Nr. 1111/U.S.A., 39, SAP; William L. Merry, *The Nicaragua Canal: The Gateway Between the Oceans* (San Francisco: Commercial Publishing Company, 1895).

38. Justice minister to emperor, July 7, 1879, 2.2.1., Nr. 23571, BAM; Wilton M. Nelson, *Protestantism in Central America* (Grand Rapids, MI: Erdmanns, 1984), 10–21; Akira Iriye, "Culture and Power: International Relations as Intercultural Relations," *Diplomatic History* 3 (spring 1979):115–28.

39. E. Kraft to Bergen, March 1, 1879, 09.01, Nr. 12549/3, BAP; Alison Acker, *Honduras: The Making of a Banana Republic* (Boston: South End, 1986), 16–25; Mario Argueta and Eduardo Quiños, *Historia de Honduras* (Tegucigalpa: Escuela superior del profesorado 'Francisco Morazán,' 1978).

40. Schlözer to Fish, Nov. 20, 1872, *FRUS, 1872*, pt. 1, p. 195; Klaus J. Bade, "Massenwanderung und Arbeitsmarkt im deutschen Nordosten 1880–1914: Überseeische Auswanderung, interne Abwanderung und kontinentale Zuwanderung," *Archiv für Sozialgeschichte* 20 (1980):264–323; *Informe de la sociedad de inmigración* (Guatemala: El Progreso, [1878]); Guillermo Náñez Falcón, "Contributions to the Economic Development of the Alta Verapaz of Guatemala, 1865–1900" (M.A. thesis, Tulane University, 1961), 79–85b; Guillermo Náñez Falcón, "Erwin Paul Dieseldorff, German Entrepreneur in Alta Verapaz of Guatemala, 1889–1937" (Ph.D. diss., Tulane University, 1970), 433–54; *Deutschtum in der Alta Verapaz: Erinnerungen, 1888–1938* (Stuttgart: Deutsche Verlags-Anstalt, 1938); Carlos A. E. Hegel, *Die historische Entwicklung der Plantagenwirtschaft in Guatemala bis zum Ende des 19. Jahrhunderts* (Munich: Val. Hotling, 1930); Jean-Pierre Blancpain, "Identité nationale et tradition culturelle: Le Germanisme en Amérique latine," *Recherches*

germaniques (Strasbourg) 12 (1982):188–220; David McCreery, *Development and the State in Reforma Guatemala, 1871–85,* Monographs in Latin America Series, vol. 10 (Athens: Ohio University Press, 1983), 27–47, 87–100; Sanford A. Mosk, "The Coffee Economy of Guatemala, 1850–1918: Development and Signs of Instability," *Inter-American Economic Affairs* 9 (winter 1955):6–20; Ralph Lee Woodward, Jr., "Pensamiento científico y desarrollo económico en Centroamérica, 1860–1920," *Revista del Pensamiento Centroamericano* 172–73 (July–Dec. 1981):73–86.

41. *La Sociedad de Inmigración,* 1879; *El Quetzal,* Oct. 15, 1879; Ignacio Solis, *Sobre el fomento de la inmigración y colonización extranjeras* (Guatemala: Augusto M. Chamba, 1889), and other materials in Guatemala, Sociedad de inmigración, 1877–1889, box 1, Manuscripts and Archives, New York Public Library; W. Moeller to Hofmann and Phillip zu Eulenburg, Sept. 3, 29, 1879, Rep. 77, Tit. 226, Nr. 118, vol. 3, BAM; Ralph Lee Woodward, Jr., "Population and Development in Guatemala, 1840–1879," *SECOLAS Annuals* 14 (1983):5–18.

42. Aaron Augustus Sargent to Frelinghuysen, March 12, 1883, *FRUS, 1883,* 349–55; Klaus J. Bade, "Das Kaiserreich als Kolonialmacht: Ideologische Projektionen und historische Erfahrungen," in Josef Becker and Andreas Hillgruber, eds., *Die deutsche Frage im 19. und 20. Jahrhundert* (Munich: Ernst Vögel, 1983), 91–108; Maximilian von Hagen, *Bismarcks Kolonialpolitik* (Berlin: Deutsche Verlags-Anstalt, 1923), 54–65; Henry Ashby Turner, Jr., "Bismarck's Imperialist Venture: Anti-British in Origins?" in Gifford Prosser and William Roger Lewis, eds., *Britain and Germany in Africa: Imperial Rivalry and Colonial Rule* (New Haven: Yale University Press, 1967), 47–82; Ludwig Prager, *Die deutsche Kolonialgesellschaft, 1882–1907* (Berlin: Dietrich Reimers, 1908), 4–5, 28–31.

43. "Extraits et analyses des rapports des consuls étrangères," *Kölnische Zeitung,* Dec. 1, 1884 [translation from *British Trade Journal, Consular Supplement* (March 24, 1886)], AA Abteilung II, Rep. VI, Nr. 19, Süd Amerika, vol. II., 09.01, Nr. 12487, BAP; Bernard Harms, *Die Zukunft der deutschen Handelspolitik* (Jena: Gustav Fischer, 1925), 1–15; Gustav Schmoller, "Die Wandlungen in der europäischen Handelspolitik des 19. Jahrhunderts," *Schmoller's Jahrbuch* 24 (1900):373–82; Jean Stengers, "British and German Imperial Rivalry: A Conclusion," in Prosser and Lewis, eds., *Britain and Germany in Africa,* 337–47; James C. Hunt, "Peasants, Grain Tariffs, and Meat Quotas: Imperial German Protectionism Reexamined," *Central European History* 7 (Dec. 1974):311–31.

44. Sigmund Hinrichten to Deputation für Handel und Schiffahrt, Dec. 12, 1884, Auszug aus dem Protocoll der Deputation für Handel und Schiffahrt, Dec. 16, 1884, Senat, C1 VI, Nr. 16^{a} vol. 1, fasc. 13^{b} Cent. Amer., SAH.

45. Alfred Krupp to R. P. Negrete, Aug. 14, 30, 1875, WA II 198, Krupp Archives, Essen; Krupp to C. Medina, Nov. 7, 26, 1875, WA II 178, Krupp Archives; correspondence with Negrete and C. Medina for 1878–1880, WA III 140 and WA IV 534, Krupp Archives; "Zusammenstellung der von der Kruppschen Gussstahlfabrik gelieferten Kanonen, 1847–1875," WA VIIf 862, Krupp Archives; Krupp to C. Menshausen, Aug. 20, Nov. 5, 1884, Jan. 30, 1885, WA III 194, Krupp Archives; Menshausen to Krupp, Feb. 3, 1882, WA IV 424, Krupp Archives; Bergen to Bismarck, July 1, 1881, foreign minister to Helmut von Moltke, Sept. 20, 1881, and other items in R 85/2852, BAK; William Manchester, *The Arms of Krupp, 1587–1968* (New York: Bantam, 1970), 151–52.

46. Mayer to Krupp, May 27, June 28, July 24, 1879, Krupp (Essen) to Krupp (London), Aug. 31, 1879, WA IV 771, Krupp Archives; David J. McCreery, "Developmental Aspects of the Construction of the Guatemalan Northern Railroad: The First Attempts, 1879–1885" (M.A. thesis, Tulane University, 1969).

47. Williamson to Fish, Dec. 30, 1873, RG 59, DD, Cent. Amer.: 4 (M 219/r 27); Houben to J. C. B. Davis, June 6, 1874, RG 59, CD, Guat.: 3 (T 337/r 3).

48. Gerd Hardach, *Deutschland in der Weltwirtschaft 1870–1970* (Frankfurt: Suhrkamp, 1977), 32–39; Heinrich Rittershausen, "Die deutsche Aussenhandelspolitik von 1879 bis 1948," *Zeitschrift für die gesamte Staatswissenschaft* 105 (1948):126–68; Katja Nehls, "Zur Bewegung der Kapitalexporte des deutschen Imperialismus," in *Jahrbuch für Wirtschaftsgeschichte* 4 (1963):57–91; Alfred Weber, "Deutschland und der wirtschaftliche Imperialismus," *Preussische Jahrbücher* 116 (April 1904):298–324; Ludwig Prager, *Handelsbeziehungen des Deutschen Reiches mit den Vereinigten Staaten von Amerika bis zum Ausbruch des Weltkrieges im Jahre 1914* (Weimar: H. Böhlaus Nachfolger, 1926), 112–19.

6. Aggressive Participation in the New World, 1885–1898

1. Rosenberg, *Grosse Depression und Bismarckzeit*, 258–73; Mommsen, "Der moderne Imperialismus als innergesellschaftliches Phänomen"; Hans-Ulrich Wehler, "Das Deutsche Kaiserreich, 1871–1918," in Reinhard Rürup, Hans-Ulrich Wehler, and Gerhard Schulz, *Deutsche Geschichte*, 3 vols. (Göttingen: Vandenhoeck und Ruprecht, 1985), 3:201–404; Volker Hentschel, *Wirtschaft und Wirtschaftspolitik im wilhelminischen Deutschland. Organisierter Kapitalismus und Interventionsstaat?* (Stuttgart: Klett-Cotta, 1978), 9–21, 260–61; Piétri, *Évolution économique de l'Allemagne*, 155–56, 227–59, 338–42, 393–94; Wolfgang Zorn, "Wirtschaft und Politik im deutschen Imperialismus," in Gilbert Ziebura, ed., *Grundfragen der deutschen Aussenpolitik seit 1871* (Darmstadt: Wissenschaftliche Buchgesellschaft, 1975), 163–89; Karl W. Deutsch and Alexander Eckstein, "National Industrialization and the Declining Share of the International Economic Sector, 1890–1959," *World Politics* 13 (Jan. 1961):267–99.

2. Admiral Guido Karcher to Chief of the Admiralty, March 13, 1889, RM 5/vol. 5960, BAMF; Paul M. Kennedy, *The Rise of Anglo-German Antagonism, 1860–1914* (London: Random House, 1980); Alfred Vagts, "Hopes and Fears of an American-German War, 1870–1914," *Political Science Quarterly* 54 (Dec. 1939):514–35, and 55 (March 1940):53–76; Holger H. Herwig, *Politics of Frustration: The United States in German Naval Planning, 1889–1941* (Boston: Little, Brown, 1976), 3–39; Ragnild Fiebig-von Hase, "Die deutsch-amerikanischen Wirtschaftsbeziehungen, 1890–1914, im Zeichen von Protektionismus und internationaler Integration," *Amerikastudien* 33:3 (1988):329–57; Walter LaFeber, *The New Empire: An Interpretation of American Expansion, 1860–1898* (Ithaca, NY: Cornell University Press, 1963), 35–37, 122–23, 131, 138–40, 323–25; John A. Moses and Paul M. Kennedy, eds., *Germany in the Pacific and Far East, 1870–1914* (St. Lucia, Australia: University of Queensland Press, 1977); Robert Freeman Smith, "Latin America, the United States and the European Powers, 1830–1930," in *The Cambridge History of Latin America*, 5:83–119; Klaus Stürmer, "The Nation State and the International System

1870–1914: Changing Perspectives among Germans," in *Opinion publique et politique extérieure* (Rome: École française de Rome, 1981), 15–27; Hans-Ulrich Wehler, "1889: Wendepunkt der amerikanischen Aussenpolitik. Die Anfänge des modernen Panamerikanismus—Die Samoakrise," *Historische Zeitschrift* 201 (1965):57–109.

3. Epstein, "Germany and the United States," 290; Helmuth Stoecker, "Bürgerliche Auslegungen des Imperialismusbegriffes in der Gegenwart," in Fritz Klein, ed., *Studien zum deutschen Imperialismus vor 1914* (Berlin: Akademie, 1976); Eugen von Philippovich, ed., *Auswanderung und Auswanderungspolitik in Deutschland* (Leipzig: Duncker und Humblot, 1892); Frederic Emory, "Causes of our Failure to Develop South-American Trade," *Annals* 22 (July 1903):153–56; Imanuel Geiss, "Sozialstruktur und imperialistische Dispositionen im zweiten deutschen Kaiserreich," in Holl and List, eds., *Liberalismus und imperialistischer Staat*, 40–61; Manfred Kossok, Jürgen Kübler, and Max Zeuske, "Ein Versuch zur Dialektik von Revolution und Reform in der historischen Entwicklung Lateinamerikas (1809–1917)," in Manfred Kossok, ed., *Studien zur vergleichenden Revolutionsgeschichte, 1500–1917* (Berlin: Akademie, 1974); Wolfgang J. Mommsen, "Nationalism, Imperialism and Official Press Policy in Wilhelmine Germany 1850–1914," in *Opinion publique et politique extérieure*, 367–83; Hans-Ulrich Wehler, "Handelsimperium statt Kolonialherrschaft. Die Lateinamerikapolitik der Vereinigten Staaten vor 1898," *Jahrbuch für Geschichte Lateinamerikas* 3 (1966):183–217.

4. Henri Brunschwig, *L'Expansion allemande outre-mer du XVᵉ siècle à nos jours* (Paris. Presses universitaires de France, 1957); Henri Brunschwig, *Vom Kolonialimperialismus zur Kolonialpolitik der Gegenwart* (Wiesbaden: Franz Steiner, 1957); Adolf Grabowsky, *Der Sozialimperialismus als letzte Etappe des Imperialismus* (Basel: Weltpolitisches Archiv, 1939); Walther G. Hoffmann, "Strukturwandlungen im Aussenhandel der deutschen Volkswirtschaft seit der Mitte des 19. Jahrhunderts," *Kyklos* 20 (1967):287–306; Walther G. Hoffmann, *Das Wachstum der deutschen Wirtschaft seit der Mitte des 19. Jahrhunderts* (Berlin: Springer, 1965); Eckart Kehr, *Economic Interest, Militarism, and Foreign Policy: Essays on German History*, ed. Hans-Ulrich Wehler (Berkeley: University of California Press, 1977); Karl Helfferich, *Deutschlands Volkswohlstand, 1888–1913*, 7th ed. (Berlin: Georg Stilke, 1917); Franz Schnabel, *Deutsche Geschichte im neunzehnten Jahrhundert: die moderne Technik und die deutsche Industrie* (Freiburg: Herder, 1965); Hans-Ulrich Wehler, " 'Deutscher Sonderweg' oder allgemeine Probleme des westlichen Kapitalismus?" *Merkur* 35 (1981):478–87.

5. Karl Hammer, *Weltmission und Kolonialismus: Sendungsideen des 19. Jahrhunderts im Konflikt* (Munich: dtv, 1981), 334; Wolfgang J. Mommsen, *Der autoritäre Nationalstaat: Verfassung, Gesellschaft und Kultur im deutschen Kaiserreich* (Frankfurt: Fischer, 1990), 105.

6. Lueder to Bismarck, Jan. 9, 1886, IA, Col. 1, vol. 5, PAAA; Percheck to foreign minister, March 31, 1886, 09.01, Nr. 52622, BAP; Schoonover and Schoonover, "Statistics for an Understanding of Foreign Intrusions into Central America," pt. 1, 93–118, pt. 3, 77–119.

7. Bergen to Leo von Caprivi, April 10, 1891, IA, Guat. 1, vol. 3, PAAA; Friedrich C. von Erckert report of 1897/1898, alte P-II-8/97, Paul Metternich to Carl Burchard, June 12, 1899, Senatskommission für die Reichs- und auswärtigen An-

gelegenheiten, new A III, c. 22, SAH; Friedrich Katz, "Einige Grundzüge der Politik des deutschen Imperialismus in Lateinamerika, 1898 bis 1941," in Heinz Sanke, ed., *Der deutsche Faschismus in Lateinamerika, 1933–1943* (Berlin: Humboldt Universität, 1966), 9–69; Friedrich Lenz, "Wesen und Struktur des deutschen Kapitalexports vor 1914," *Weltwirtschaftliches Archiv* 18 (1922):42–54. On the role of foreign merchants in Latin America, see Eugene W. Ridings, "Foreign Predominance among Overseas Traders in Nineteenth-Century Latin America," *Latin American Research Review* 20:2 (1985):3–27; and comments by Carlos Marichal and D. C. M. Platt, with response by E. W. Ridings, *Latin American Research Review* 21:1 (1986):145–56.

8. Bermann, *Under the Big Stick*, 103–50; Acker, *Honduras*, 55–62; Jim Handy, *The Gift of the Devil: A History of Guatemala* (Boston: South End, 1984), 57–60; Rafael L. Menjívar, *Acumulación originaria y desarrollo del capitalismo en El Salvador* (San José, CR: EDUCA, 1980), 27–57; Dozier, *"Nicaragua's Mosquito Shore."*

9. David McCreery, "Debt Servitude in Rural Guatemala, 1876–1936," *Hispanic American Historical Review* 63 (1983):735–59; McCreery, "Coffee and Class," 438–60; Carol A. Smith, *Labor and International Capital in the Making of a Peripheral Social Formation: Economic Transformations of Guatemala, 1850–1980* (Washington, DC: Smithsonian Institute, 1984).

10. Woodward, *Central America: A Nation Divided*, 149–202; Cardoso and Pérez Brignoli, *Centro América y la economía occidental*, 199–320; E. Bradford Burns, "The Modernization of Underdevelopment: El Salvador, 1858–1931," *Journal of Developing Areas* 18 (April 1984):293–316; Lindo-Fuentes, *Weak Foundations*, 81–185.

11. Waecker-Gotter to Bismarck, March 11, April 1, 1885, Bergen to Bismarck, March 13, 1885, IA, America Generalia 5, vol. 2 [hereafter Amer. Gen. 5], PAAA; Leyden to Bismarck, Sept. 11, 1885, IA, Amer. Gen. 5, vol. 2, PAAA; Bergen to Fernando Cruz, March 31, 1885, B99-5-1/4289/93194, MRE, AGCA; George M. Fisk, "German-American Diplomatic and Commercial Relations, Historically Considered," *American Monthly Review of Reviews* 25:3 (March 1982) 323–28; Wallace McClure, "German-American Commercial Relations," *American Journal of International Law* 19 (Oct. 1925):689–701.

12. Castellón to Bergen, June 24, 1885, Bergen to Castellón, April 28, 1885, IA, Amer. Gen. 5, vol. 2, PAAA; Bergen to Bismarck, Feb. 26, Nov. 6, 1886, Feb. 28, 1887, Jan. 29, 1888, IA, Amer. Gen. 5, vol. 3, PAAA.

13. Thomas Schoonover, "Los intereses europeos y estadounidenses en las relaciones México-Guatemala (1850–1930)," *Secuencia* 34 (Jan.–April 1996): 7–30.

14. Leyden to Bismarck, Sept. 11, 1885, IA, Amer. Gen. 5, vol. 2, PAAA; Bergen to Bismarck, March 5, Nov. 6, 1886, IA, Amer. Gen. 5, vol. 3, PAAA; Henry Hall to Thomas Bayard, Nov. 22, 1887, RG 59, DD, Cent. Amer.: 28 (M 219/r 48); Hans W. Gatzke, *Germany and the United States: A "Special Relationship"?* (Cambridge: Harvard University Press, 1980); John Barrett, "England, America, and Germany as Allies for the Open Door," *Engineering Magazine* 18 (Oct. 1899):1–10.

15. Joaquín Mathe to Porter, Jan. 18, Dec. 12, 1885, RG 59, CD, Sonsonate: 1 (T 440/r 1); John M. Dow to Francisco Sarg, Feb. 28, July 17, 1885, letterbook 1885–1888, also letterbooks 1881–1883 and 1883–1885, John M. Dow papers, Cornell University, Ithaca, NY; Johann von Alvensleben to Bayard, Feb. 16, 1886, RG 59, notes from Prussian leg.: 18 (M 58/r 18).

16. Wharton to Chapman Coleman, March 11, 1892, RG 59, DI, Ger.: 18 (M 77/r 69); Barrett, "England, America, and Germany as Allies for the Open Door."

17. Bergen to Friedrich August von Holstein, Aug. 23, Dec. 31, 1886, Nachlass Friedrich von Holstein, vol. 1, PAAA (copy of Aug. 23, in 09.01, Nr. 50915, BAP); Castellanos Cambranes, *El Imperialismo alemán en Guatemala*, 165–251. For Holstein's role in German international relations, see Norman Rich and M. H. Fischer, eds., *The Holstein Papers*, 3 vols. (Cambridge: Cambridge University Press, 1955–1961).

18. Wagner, "Actividades empresariales de los alemanes en Guatemala," 97, 115–21; Denkschrift zu Nr. 179, Reichstag, II Session (1887–1888), Denkschrift, [n. d.], R 2/1453, Reichsfinanzministerium, BAK; Bergen to Bismarck, Oct. 25, 1885, Bismarck to emperor, Dec. 19, 1888, IA, Nic. 1, vol. 2, PAAA; Bergen to F. Cruz, April 2, 1887, B99-5-1/4289/93194, MRE, AGCA.

19. Bergen to Holstein, Aug. 23, 1886, Nachlass Holstein, vol. 1, PAAA; memoranda on raising rank of Cent. Amer. minister resident (Georg Humbert), Oct. 31, 1887, 09.01, Nr. 50915, BAP; Bergen to Bismarck, Feb. 19, 1889, 09.01, 50916, BAP; Humbert to Bergen, Sept. 24, 1886, 14.01 Reichskanzleramt, Nr. 50919, BAP; Bergen to Holstein, Aug. 23, 1886, Nachlass Holstein, vol. 1, PAAA; Heinrich von Kusserow to Bismarck, Dec. 2, 1887, IA, Mex. 2, vol. 1, PAAA; Bergen to Bismarck, June 6, 1888, 14.01, Nr. 50920, BAP; Herman Prowe, *Deutschlands Vertretung in Central-America* (Leipzig: Naumann, [1895]).

20. Paul Louis Reynaud to MAE, March 31, 1889, CP 1896, Amér. cent., vol. 29, AMAE; Emiliano Chamorro, *El último caudillo· Autobiografía* (Managua: Union, 1983), 248.

21. James R. Hosmer to Blaine, April 10, 1889, RG 59, DD, Cent. Amer.: 30 (M 219/r 49); Victor Vifquain to William F. Wharton, Aug. 10, 1890, RG 59, CD, Colon (Aspinwall): 14 (T 193/r 14).

22. LeBrun to MAE, Oct. 25, 1885, Jan. 25, 1886, MAE to LeBrun, Nov. 25, 1885, CCC, Guat., vol. 11, AMAE; Hall to Bayard, May 11, 1886, Jan. 6, 1887, RG 59, DD, Cent. Amer.: 27 (M 219/r 47) (copy of second dispatch also in *FRUS, 1887*, pp. 92–93); Bergen to F. Cruz, March 24, 1887, B99-5-1/4289/93194, MRE, AGCA; Dow to Sarg, Jan. 19, 1886, Dow to Adrian Collado, Aug. 31, 1887, box 4, letterbook 1885–1888, Dow papers.

23. Heinz Quast and G. H. Stande to Hamburg Chamber of Commerce, June 10, 1887, Senatsakten, C1, VT, Nr. 16^{d,} vol. 1, Fasc. 10^{b,} SAH; Rob. Mestern to Committee for Trade and Navigation, June 21, 1887, Eduard von Derenthall (for Reichskanzler) to Hamburg Senat, Aug. 14, 1887, Spezialakten, XXI c. 3, Nr. 2, SAH; Kusserow to Bismarck, Dec. 2, 1887, IA, Mex. 2, vol. 1, PAAA.

24. Bergen to Bismarck, Feb. 15, 1888, Senatsakten, C1. VI, Nr. 16^{d,} vol. 2^{a,} fasc. 11^{a,} invol. 1, SAH; MAE to commerce minister, March 6, 1888, and enclosures, F^{12} 6543, AN, P; Dow to Collado, Feb. 28, 1888, box 4, letterbook 1885–1888, Dow papers.

25. LeBrun to MAE, Oct. 25, 1885, Reynaud to MAE, Dec. 14, 1887, CCC, Guat., vol. 11, AMAE; L. Debos to MAE, June 22, 1887, CCC, San José de CR, vol. 1, AMAE; MAE to commerce minister, Oct. 21, 1887, F^{12} 7053, AN, P; Maurice Lair, *L'impérialisme allemand* (Paris: Armand Colin, 1902).

26. Excerpt from consul, Oct. 3, 1891, Nr. 2, XIX, C 24, SAH; Jorge Prado to

Gotthelf Meyer, Nov. 14, 1891, B99-6/4407/93362, MRE, AGCA; Bergen to Pedro León Paez, Jan. 11, 1892, MRE, caja 106, AN, CR; D. Lynch Pringle to E. F. Uhl, Dec. 5, 1894, CD, Guat.: 10 (T 337/r 10).

27. Bergen to Bismarck, Feb. 24, 1887, Emil Floerke to foreign minister, May 31, 1887, 09.01, Nr. 12488, BAP.

28. Bergen to Bismarck, Oct. 25, 1885, Bismarck to emperor, Dec. 19, 1888, IA, Nic. 1, vol. 2, PAAA; RM 5/vol. 5397, Nachrichten über Colombia, 1880 bis 1907, BAMF; Bermann, *Under the Big Stick*, 117–22.

29. "El Ministro alemán en el banquete de ante anoche," Jan. 17, 1888, Bismarck to Bergen, April 3, 1888, AA Rep. I, Mittel Amer., Nr. 40, vol. III, BAP; Reynaud to MAE, March 8, 1888, CP 1896, Amér. cent., vol. 29, AMAE.

30. Emmerich von Arco-Valley to Bismarck, June 26, 1888, IA, Ver. St. von Amer. 20, vol. 1, PAAA; note dated Oct. 10, 1888 in III Hauptabteilung, Nr. 1111, SAP; Bergen to Bismarck, Aug. 3, Sept. 22, 1888, IA, Mex. 2, vol. 2, PAAA; Alfred H. Fried, *Pan-Amerika. Entwickelung, Umfang und Bedeutung der pan-amerikanischen Bewegung (1810–1910)* (Berlin: Maritime, 1910).

31. Bergen to Bismarck, Jan. 14, 1890, IA, Mex. 2, vol. 2, PAAA; Wagner, "Actividades empresariales de los alemanes en Guatemala," 99–102.

32. John Rice Chandler to Wharton, Jan. 31, 1890, RG 59, CD, Guat.: 7 (T 337/r 7); Reynaud to MAE, Jan. 29, 1890, CP 1896, Amér. cent., vol. 29, AMAE; J. Gaillard to marine minister, April 3, 1890, BB^4 1596, AAM; Solis, *Sobre el fomento de la inmigración y colonización extranjeras;* Mauricio Domínguez T., "The Development of the Technological and Scientific Coffee Industry in Guatemala, 1830–1930" (Ph.D. diss., Tulane University, 1970).

33. Schmaick to Leo von Caprivi, July 16, 30, 1890, Haythausen to Caprivi, July 25, 1890, IA, S. Salv. 1, vol. 2, PAAA.

34. Bergen to Caprivi, April 10, 1890, IA, Guat. 1, vol. 3, PAAA; excerpt [1891?] in Senatsakten: C1. VI, Nr. 16^{a,} vol. 2^{a,} fasc. 11^{a,} invol. 1, SAH; Cazard to MAE, May 12, 1899, MAE to Cazard, July 21, Aug. 25, 1898, MAE to Bourtiron, Sept. 26, 1899, CP 1918, Guat., Finances publiques I, N.S. 6, AMAE; Hardach, *Deutschland in der Weltwirtschaft*, 32–39, 97–104, 139–43; Andreas Hillgruber, "Die deutsche Frage im 19. und 20. Jahrhundert—zur Einführung in die nationale und internationale Problematik," in Becker and Hillgruber, eds., *Die deutsche Frage im 19. und 20. Jahrhundert*, 3–15; Carl Brinkmann, *Weltpolitik und Weltwirtschaft der neuesten Zeit* (Berlin: Juncker und Dünnhaupt, 1936), 9–29.

35. [Rieberwig?] to Bremen Senat, Dec. 23, 1891, A. 3. C. 1. Nr. 71, SAB; excerpt from consul, Oct. 3, 1891, Nr. 2, XIX, C 24, SAH; Salazar to MRE, Oct. 29, 1888, B99-6-9/8718, MRE, AGCA; Wagenführ, *Die Bedeutung des Aussenmarktes für die deutsche Industriewirtschaft*, 42–47; Hartmut Kaelble, *Industrielle Interessenpolitik in der wilhelminischen Gesellschaft* (Berlin: Walter de Gruyter, 1967), 146–47, 163–64, 201–4.

36. Craveri to MAE, Feb. 7, 1890, Ritt to MAE, Dec. 9, 1894, CCC, San José de CR, vol. 1, AMAE; Willi A. Boelcke, ed., *Krupp und die Hohenzollern in Dokumenten* (Frankfurt: Athanaion, 1970), 14–21, 112–13; "Entwicklung des Kruppschen Vertreterswesen, 1851–1910," IV 761, Krupp Archiv; Cruz to Muñoz, Dec. 11, 1896, B99-6-4/4470/93426, MRE, AGCA; Gerhard Brunn, "Deutscher Einfluss und deutsche Interessen in der Professionalisierung einiger lateinamerikanischer Ar-

meen vor dem 1. Weltkrieg (1885–1914)," *Jahrbuch für Geschichte von Staat, Wirtschaft und Gesellschaft Lateinamerikas* 6 (1969):278–336; Manchester, *The Arms of Krupp*, 151–52; Raymond Poidevin, "Fabricants d'armes et relations internationales au début du XXe siècle," *Relations Internationales* 1 (May 1974):39–56.

37. Bergen to Caprivi, March 15, 1892, IA, Guat. 1, vol. 3, PAAA; Erckert to Hohenlohe-Schillingsfürst, June 18, 1897, III Hauptabteilung, Nr. 1025, SAP; entry Dec. 3, 1892, Vereinsbuch, Deutscher Verein Cobán, Erwin Paul Dieseldorff Collection, Special Collections, Tulane University, New Orleans, Louisiana; Salazar to Antonio Lazo Arriaga, Oct. 27, 1893, April 6, 1894, B99-6-3/4444/93400, MRE, AGCA; Lazo Arriaga to Salazar, April 28, 1894, B99-6-3/4446/93402, MRE, AGCA.

38. Francisco Borchardt to MRE, April 16, 1894, MRE, caja 114, AN, CR; Ricardo Pacheco to Joaquín B. Calvo, April 16, 1895, MRE, l.c. 74, AN, CR; Otto G. A. Littmann, *Deutsche-Kostarikanische Land-Gesellschaft* (Berlin, 1894), MRE, caja 116, AN, CR.

39. Rieberwig to Hamburg Senat, July 27, 1892, and enclosures and trade report for 1892 [n.d.–1893?], C1 VI, Nr. 16^{d,} vol. 2^{b,} fasc. 2, invol. 2, Senatsakten, SAH; Max Vosberg-Rekow, *Das britische Weltreich und der deutsche Wettbewerb* (Berlin: Siemenroth und Troschel, 1898), 58–60, 71–73; Klaus Hildebrand, "Zwischen Allianz und Antagonismus. Das Problem bilateraler Normalität in den britisch-deutschen Beziehungen des 19. Jahrhunderts (1870–1914)," in Heinz Dollinger, Horst Gründer, and Alwin Hanschmidt, eds, *Weltpolitik, Europagedanke, Regionalismus* (Münster: Aschendorff, 1982), 305–31; Paul Ostwald, *Englischer und deutscher Imperialismus: Ein Gegensatz* (Berlin: Leonhard und Simion, 1917), 22–30; Ernst Daenell, *Das Ringen der Weltmächte um Mittel- und Südamerika* (Berlin: E. S. Mittler, 1919), 4–5, 11–13.

40. Report, Berlin, June 2, 1891, 09.01, Nr. 50917, BAP; Gustavo C. Lembke to Adolf Hermann Marshall von Bieberstein, Nov. 19, 1891, 09.01, Nr. 52608, BAP.

41. Hamburg Senate Committee on Trade and Navigation to Mayor Dr. Versmann, Jan. 15, 1895, neu A III, C. 17, SAH; Bergen to Caprivi, April 12, 1891, 09.01, Nr. 52612, BAP.

42. Hamburg Senate Committee on Trade and Navigation to Versmann, Jan. 15, 1895, neu A III, C. 17, SAH.

43. Challet to MAE, May 22, 1895, Emil Joré to MAE, Sept. 29, 1895, CP 1896, Amér. cent., vol. 31, AMAE; Challet to MAE, Sept. 4, 1894, CP 1918, Guat., Finances publiques. Emprunts I, N.S. 6, AMAE; Charpentier to MAE, March 24, 1894, CCC, Guat., vol. 12, AMAE; Cruz to Jorge Muñoz, Jan. 14, 1895, B99-6-4/4469/93425, MRE, AGCA; commerce minister to MAE, June 25, 1896, commerce minister to Tours Chamber of Commerce, June 25, 1896, MAE to Challet, July 3, 1896, Challet to MAE, Oct. 2, 1896, MAE to commerce minister, Nov. 17, 1896, Affaires diverses commerciales, carton 263, AMAE; F. Vié, "Les Colonies commerciales des allemands," *Revue des deux mondes* 69 (Feb. 1, 1899):696–708.

44. Bergen to MRE, May 14, 1896, B99-5-1/4292/93197, MRE, AGCA; Cruz to Muñoz, Jan. 8, 1897, B99-6-4/4470/93426, MRE, AGCA.

45. "Aus Honduras," *Hamburgische Börsenhalle*, July 10, 1895; newspaper clipping from *Abendblatt*, Dec. 13, 1895, alt S-I-K-40/95, SAH.

46. Alvey A. Adee to sec. of state, March 27, 1896, RG 59, notes from Ger. leg.: 25 (M 58/r 25).

47. Memorial of Feb. 4, 1896, Nicaragua-Germany treaty, n.d., Rep. 84a, Nr. 2468, SAP; Bergen to Hohenlohe-Schillingsfürst, Feb. 10, 1896, R2/1453, Reichsfinanzministerium, BAK; excerpt from the Hamburg minister's note, Oct. 24, 1896, H II 13[c] fasc. 9, act. 1–15, SAH; Benjamin I. Teplitz, "The Political and Economic Foundations of Modernization in Nicaragua: The Administration of José Santos Zelaya, 1893–1909" (Ph.D. diss., Howard University, 1973).

48. Challet to MAE, Feb. 4, 1896, CP 1918, Nic., Pol. intérieure, Affaires commerciales, Chemin de fers, N.S. 1, AMAE; Lewis Baker to Walter Q. Gresham, Jan. 11, 1894, DD, Cent. Amer.: 58 (M 219/r 78); Baker to Richard Olney, April 8, 1896, DD, Cent. Amer.: 61 (M 219/r 81).

49. Enclosure with Reichskanzler to Bremen Senat, Oct. 19, 1896, A. 3. C. 1, Nr. 78, SAB: M. E. Nichol to foreign minister, Aug. 6, 1897, FO 21/v. 49 (r 13), PRO; Paul Poncelet to Alvensleben, June 21, 1898, enclosed in Alvensleben to Hohenlohe-Schillingsfürst, June 23, 1898, 09.01, Nr. 12489, BAP; Jaime Biderman, "The Development of Capitalism in Nicaragua: A Political Economic History," *Latin American Perspectives* 10 (winter 1983):7–32.

50. Memorandum über die strategische Bedeutung eines Schiffahrt-Kanals durch Mittelamerika für die Vereinigten Staaten, England und Deutschland, Gustav Adolf von Götzen, March 1, 1898, enclosed with Theodor von Holleben to Hohenlohe-Schillingsfürst, March 1, 1898, IA, Amer. Gen. 12, vol. 1, PAAA; Kürchhoff, Oberst a.D., "Flottenstützpunkte," *Beiträge zur Kolonialpolitik, Kolonialrecht und Kolonialwirtschaft* 4 (1902–1903):63–66.

51. Bergen to Hohenlohe-Schillingsfürst, Sept. 6, 1897, IA, Amer. Gen. 5, vol. 3, PAAA.

52. Wolfram von Rotenhan to Bernhard von Bülow, Sept. 24, 1897, IA, Guat. 1, vol. 4, PAAA; Auszug aus dem Protokoll der Deputation für Handel und Schiffahrt to Dr. Predöhl, Oct. 19, 1897, Senatsakten: Cl. VI, Nr. 16[d,] vol. 2, fasc. 10, Hamburgischer Consulat zu Guat., SAH; J. Tible Machado, *Le Guatémala en 1896. L'exposition Centre-américaine de 1897. Quelques notes* (Bordeaux: G. Delmas, 1896).

53. G. A. Dieseldorff to directors, April 14, 1895, box 168, Dieseldorff Collection; MAE to finance minister, Nov. 22, 1895, F[30] 393[1]: Hond., Guat., CR, AMEF; Boulard Pouqueville to MAE, Oct. 13, 1897, CP 1918. Guat., Politique intérieure 1, AMAE; Konstantin Bernhard von Voights-Rhetz to Anguiano, July 4, 1899, B99-5-1/4293/93198, MRE, AGCA; Pouqueville to MAE, Dec. 16, 1897, CCC, Guat., vol. 13, AMAE; Alfred Lansburgh, "Deutsches Kapital im Auslande," *Die Bank, Monatshefte für Finanz- und Bankwesen* 9 (1909):819–33; August Sartorius von Waltershausen, *Das volkswirtschaftliche System der Kapitalanlage im Auslande* (Berlin: Georg Reimer, 1907).

54. Erckert to Hohenlohe-Schillingsfürst, March 26, 1898, IA, Guat. 1, vol. 5, PAAA; enclosure with Paul Reichardt to Bremen Senat, April 28, 1898, A. 3. C. 1., Nr. 85, SAB; Friedrich C. von Erckert, "Die wirtschaftlichen Interessen Deutschlands in Guatemala," *Beiträge zur Kolonialpolitik und Kolonialwirtschaft* 3 (1901–1902):225–38, 269–84.

55. Challet to MAE, Feb. 4, 1896, CP 1918, Nic., Pol. intérieure, Affaires com-

merciales, Chemin de fers, N.S. 1, AMAE; Pouqueville to MAE, Dec. 16, 1897, CCC, Guat., vol. 13, AMAE.

56. Voights-Rhetz to Hohenlohe-Schillingsfürst, Aug. 6, 1898, IA, Guat. 1, vol. 5, PAAA; Erckert to Hohenlohe-Schillingsfürst, March 25, 1898, Voights-Rhetz to Hohenlohe-Schillingsfürst, Sept. 20, 1898, IA, CR 1, vol. 1, PAAA.

7. Aggressive Penetration and National Honor, 1898–1906

1. Wehler, "Das Deutsche Kaiserreich," 171–84; Katz, "Einige Grundzüge der Politik des deutschen Imperialismus in Lateinamerika," 9–69; Gregor Schöllgen, *Das Zeitalter des Imperialismus* (Munich: R. Oldenbourg, 1986), 54–57, 62–67, 128–35; essays by Thomas Nipperdey and Eckart Kehr in Wehler, ed., *Moderne deutsche Sozialgeschichte,* 37–54, 369–88; Michael Geyer, *Deutsche Rüstungspolitik, 1860–1980* (Frankfurt: Suhrkamp, 1984), 45–83; Piétri, *Evolution économique de l'Allemagne,* 256–59, 424–29; Wolfram Fischer, *Die Weltwirtschaft im 20. Jahrhundert* (Göttingen: Vandenhoeck und Ruprecht, 1979), 11–13, 35–39; Fritz Klein, *Deutschland, 1897/98–1917* (Berlin: VEB Deutscher Verlag der Wissenschaften, 1977), 16–40.

2. Fiebig-von Hase, *Lateinamerika als Konfliktherd der deutsch-amerikanischen Beziehungen,* 1:320–428; Barrett, "England, America, and Germany as Allies for the Open Door," 1–10; Hans Delbrück, "Deutschlands internationale Lage und Amerika," *Preussische Jahrbücher* 112 (April 1903):184–88; Edgar Jaffe, "Volkswirtschaft. Deutschland und die amerikanische Konkurrenz," *Preussische Jahrbücher* 108 (April 1902):146–52; Daenell, *Das Ringen der Weltmächte um Mittel- und Südamerika,* 20–22; Ernst Francke, "Weltpolitik und Sozialreform," in Gustav Schmoller, Max Sering, and Adolph Wagner, eds., *Handels- und Machtpolitik* (Stuttgart: J. G. Cotta'sche Buchhandlung Nachfolger, 1900), 103–32; Thomas Baecker, "Deutschland im karibischen Raum im Spiegel amerikanischer Akten (1898–1914)," *Jahrbuch für Geschichte von Staat, Wirtschaft und Gesellschaft Lateinamerikas* 11 (1974):167–237; Volker R. Berghahn, "Zu den Zielen des deutschen Flottenbaus unter Wilhelm II," *Historische Zeitschrift* 210 (1970):34–100; Donald Castillo Rivas, *Acumulación de capital y empresas transnacionales en Centroamérica* (Mexico: Siglo XXI, 1980), 25–42; Lester D. Langley, *The United States and the Caribbean in the 20th Century* (Athens: University of Georgia Press, 1982), 22–26.

3. Böhme, *Prolegomena zu einer Sozial- und Wirtschaftsgeschichte Deutschlands,* 96–110; P. Metternich to Dr. Burchard, June 12, 1899, Senatskommission für die Reichs- und auswärtigen Angelegenheiten, new A III, c. 22, SAH; U.S. Manufacturer's Bureau, *Monthly Consular and Trade Report* (Washington: GPO, 1900), vol. 63, No. 239, pp. 460–61; Raymond Poidevin, "Weltpolitik allemande et capitaux français (1898–1914)," in Geiss and Wendt, eds., *Deutschland in der Weltpolitik des 19. und 20. Jahrhunderts,* 237–49; Erckert, "Die wirtschaftlichen Interessen Deutschlands in Guatemala," 225–38, 269–84.

4. Oetling Brothers to foreign minister [?]. Oct. 17, 1902, Senatskommission für die Reichs-und auswärtigen Angelegenheiten, neu C. I. d. 166, SAH.

5. Schoonover and Schoonover, "Statistics for an Understanding of Foreign Intrusions into Central America," pt. 3, 77–119.

6. Cardoso, "Central America," 4:197–227; Woodward, *Central America: A Nation Divided*, 149–202; Pérez Brignoli, *Breve historia de Centroamérica*, 95–106; Daniel R. Headrick, *The Tentacles of Progress: Technology Transfer in the Age of Imperialism, 1850–1940* (New York: Oxford University Press, 1988), 3–25, 379–84; Poidevin, "Fabricants d'armes et relations internationales au début du XXe siècle," 39–56; François Crouzet, "Recherches sur la production d'armements en France, 1885–1913," in *Conjoncture économique, structures sociales: hommage à Ernest Labrousse* (Paris: Mouton, 1974), 287–318; Paul Dosal, "Guatemalan Industrial Development, 1821–1986," in Jorge Luján Muñoz, ed., *Historia general de Guatemala*, vols. 4 and 5 (forthcoming).

7. Fr. chargé to MAE, April 2, 1906, F^{30} 393^1: Hond., Guat., CR, AMEF; Lester Langley, *The Struggle for the American Mediterranean: United States–European Rivalry in the Gulf-Caribbean, 1776–1904* (Athens: University of Georgia Press, 1976), 135–93; Achille Viallate, *L'Impérialisme économique et les relations internationales pendant le dernier demi-siècle (1870–1920)* (Paris: Armand Colin, 1923).

8. Enclosure with Reichards to Bremen Senat, April 28, 1898, A. 3. C. 1., Nr. 85, SAB; Emil Jung, "Deutsche Interessen in Zentralamerika," *Beiträge zur Kolonialpolitik und Kolonialwirtschaft* 3 (1901–1902):538–40; Paul Preuss, *Expedition nach Central- und Südamerika* (Berlin: Verlag des Kolonial-Wirschaftlichen Komitees, 1901); Wilhelm Wintzer, *Die Deutschen im tropischen Amerika* (Munich: C. F. Lehmann, 1900).

9. Voights-Rhetz to Hohenlohe-Schillingsfürst, Dec. 21, 1898, enclosing extract from Schaeffer, Memorandum, n.p., n.d., A 3 C. a, Nr. 85, SAB; Marcellin Pellet to MAE, Aug. 13, 20, 1898, CP 1918, Guat. pol. intérieure I, N.S. 1, AMAE; Walter Vaughn, *The Life and Work of Sir William Van Horne* (New York: Century, 1920), 317–29; Charles A. Gould, *The Last Titan, Percival Farquhar: American Entrepreneur in Latin America* (Stanford, CA: Stanford University Press, 1964), 53–58.

10. Voights-Rhetz to Hohenlohe-Schillingsfürst, Oct. 19, 1898, Hp II 61, vol. 2 (Guat.), Handelskammerarchiv, Bremen; MAE to finance minister, Oct. 21, 1899, F^{30} 393^1: Hond., Guat., CR, AMEF; Francisco Anguiano to F. Cruz, Aug. 27, 1898, B99-6-4/4467/93423, Cruz to Anguiano, Sept. 23, 1898, B99-6-4/4472/93428, MRE, AGCA; Hans von Eyb to Hohenlohe-Schillingsfürst, May 19, 1900, 1897-P-II-8, SAH.

11. E. Heinze to Bülow, March 22, 1901, R 2/1453, BAK.

12. Promemoria, April 3, 1902, RG 59, notes from Ger. leg.: 31 (M 58/31); McNally to Hill, Sept. 10, 1901, RG 59, CD, Guat.: 13 (T 337/r 13); Voights-Rhetz to Bülow, Dec. 29, 1901, IA, Amer. Gen. 13, vol. 3, PAAA; Hunter to Hay, Feb. 26, 1902, and accompanying notes, RG 59, DD, Cent. Amer.: 46 (M 219/r 66); Xabier Gorostiaga, *Los banqueros del imperio. El papel de los centros financieros internacionales en los países subdesarrollados* (San José, CR: EDUCA, 1978).

13. H. Robinow to Hamburg Senat Deputation für Handel und Schiffahrt, March 8, 1902, alt-P-II-2/02, SAH.

14. McNally to Hill, April 18, June 12, 1902, RG 59, CD, Guat.: 14 (T 337/r 14); Heinze to Bülow, April 30, 1902, IA, Nic. 1, vol. 5, PAAA.

15. Cruz to Anguiano, July 14, 1899, B99-6-4/4473/94329, MRE, AGCA; Gustav Michahelles to Hamburg Senat Deputation für Handel und Schiffahrt, Jan.

19, 29, 1904, Carlo Z. Thomsen to Hamburg IHK, Jan. 9, 1904, neu C I. d. 165, SAH; Emily and Norman L. Rosenberg, "From Colonialism to Professionalism: The Public-Private Dynamic in United States Foreign Financial Advising, 1898–1929," *Journal of American History* 74 (1987):59–82; Elisabeth Glaser-Schmidt, "Amerikanische Währungreformen in Ostasien und im karibischen Raum, 1900–1918," *Amerikastudien* 33 (1988):359–75.

16. Jacobson to emperor, June 15, 1899, IA, Frankreich 94, Nr. 2, vol. 1, PAAA; Philippe Bunau-Varilla, *Panama, the Creation, Destruction, and Resurrection* (London: Constable, 1913); Paul Lefébure, "A la conquête d'un isthme. Les États-unis et l'Europe," *Annales de sciences politiques* 16 (Sept. 1901):600–619.

17. Albert Ballin to B. Bülow, Sept. 2, 1899, enclosing Koch to Ballin, Aug. 30, 1899, IA, Amer. Gen. 12, vol. 1, PAAA; Alfred Jacobssohn, "Zur Entwicklung des Verhältnisses zwischen der deutschen Volkswirtschaft und dem Weltmarkt in den letzten Jahrzehnten," *Zeitschrift für die gesamte Staatswissenschaft* 64 (1908):292; Paul Voight, "Deutschland und der Weltmarkt," in *Handels- und Machtpolitik*; Lamar Cecil, *Albert Ballin: Business and Politics in Imperial Germany, 1888–1918* (Princeton, NJ: Princeton University Press, 1967); Wilhelm Deist, *Flottenpolitik und Flottenpropaganda: Das Nachrichtenbureau des Reichsmarineamtes, 1897–1914* (Stuttgart: Deutsche Verlags-Anstalt, 1976).

18. Ballin to Bülow, Sept. 2, 1899, enclosing Koch to Ballin, Aug. 30, 1899, Alfred von Tirpitz to foreign minister, Oct. 29, 1899, IA, Amer. Gen. 12, vol. 1, PAAA; Marquis de Noalles to MAE, March 29, 1901, CP 1918, Pan., Canal Interocéanique II, N.S. 10, AMAE; Alfred von Tirpitz, *Erinnerungen* (Leipzig: R. F. Koehler, 1920) [translated as *My Memoirs*, 2 vols. (New York: Dodd, Mead, 1919)]; Herwig, *Politics of Frustration*, 68–92; Vorbereitung zu dem Operationsplan gegen die Ver. St. von Nordamerika, 1899–1908, RM 5/vols. 5960–64, BAMF.

19. Alfons Mumm von Schwarzenstein to foreign minister, Oct. 9, 1899, Tirpitz to foreign minister, Oct. 29, 1899, IA, Amer. Gen. 12, vol. 1, PAAA; August Sartorius von Waltershausen, *Das Auslandskapital während des Weltkrieges* (Stuttgart: Ferdinand Enke, 1915), 46–47.

20. Jules Jusserand to Delcasse, Jan. 28, 1901, Delcasse to Caillaux, June 28, 1901, F[30] 394: Pan., AMEF; Holleben to Bülow, Dec. 15, 18, 1901, Jan. 9, 1902, IA, Amer. Gen. 12, vol. 4, PAAA.

21. Operationsplan gegen die Ver. St. von Nordamerika, 1899–1908, RM 5/vols. 5960–64, BAMF; Herbert von Rebeur-Paschwitz to Tirpitz, Jan. 18, 1901, IA, Amer. Gen. 13, vol. 1, PAAA; Rebeur-Paschwitz to Tirpitz, Jan. 21, 1902, RM 5/vol. 5910, BAMF; Rebeur-Paschwitz to Tirpitz, Jan. 26, 1900, excerpt, March 1903, RM 5/vol. 5960, BAMF; Herwig, *Politics of Frustration*, 85–92.

22. Hans Ernst Schlieben to Bülow, Oct. 28, 1902, Hp II 61, vol. 2, Handelskammerarchiv Bremen; Eugen von Seefried auf Buttenheim to Bülow, July 1, 1903, alt S-I-c-4/98, SAH.

23. Voights-Rhetz to Hohenlohe-Schillingsfürst, Aug. 31, 1899, Reich-Marine-Amt to foreign minister, May 23, 1900, Dr. Ernst Henrici to Bülow, June 12, 1901, IA, CR 1, vol. 2, PAAA; Alldeutscher Verband, Memorial on Samoa-Galápagos, Nov. 1899, Alldeutscher Verband, Denkschrift an die Jungfern-Inseln, Dec. 21, 1899, IA, Galápagos Inseln, vol. 1, PAAA; Voights-Rhetz to Hohenlohe-Schil-

lingsfürst, Nov. 29, 1898, Alters to Naval Chief of Staff, Dec. 15, 1899, Office of the Naval Secretary to [?], May 9, 1900, RM 5/vol. 5401, BAMF; Alfred Kruck, *Geschichte des Alldeutschen Verbandes, 1890–1939* (Wiesbaden: Franz Steiner, 1954).

24. Zembsch to Hohenlohe-Schillingsfürst, June 12, Dec. 6, 1898, Jan. 15, Feb. 16, 1900, Holleben to Hohenlohe-Schillingsfürst, Dec. 9, 1899, IA, Galápagos Inseln, vol. 1, PAAA; Robert Jannasch, "Die amerikanische Konkurrenz auf dem Weltmarkte," *Export. Organ des Centralvereins für Handelsgeographie und Förderung deutscher Interessen im Auslande* 25 (Feb. 19, 1903):97–98; Francis B. Loomis, "The Position of the United States on the American Continent—Some Phases of the Monroe Doctrine," *Annals of the American Academy* 22 (July 1903):1–19.

25. Bülow to German Embassy in the United States, June 16, 1900, Holleben to Hohenlohe-Schillingsfürst, June 30, 1900, foreign minister to Franz von Reichenau, Jan. 26, 1904, Michahelles to Bülow, June 15, 1904, IA, Galápagos Inseln, vol. 1, PAAA; Heyking to Bülow, Dec. 18, 1900, IA, Amer. Gen. 13, vol. 1, PAAA.

26. Holleben to Bülow, Jan. 29, 1902, IA, Ver. St. von Amer. 20, vol. 1, PAAA; Howard K. Beale, *Theodore Roosevelt and the Rise of America to World Power* (New York: Collier, 1956), 346–68.

27. Krupp to Bülow, May 1, June 5, 1902, IA, Nic. 1, vol. 5, PAAA; Ernst von Simson to Kemnitz, Jan. 17, 1914, Magnus to Bethmann-Hollweg, April 23, 1914, and subsequent correspondence, IA, Guat. 4, vol. 1, PAAA; Boelcke, ed., *Krupp und die Hohenzollern*, 113.

28. Fritz Blaich, *Staat und Verbände in Deutschland zwischen 1871 und 1945* (Wiesbaden: Franz Steiner, 1979), 114–19; *Denkschrift der ältesten der Kaufmannschaft von Berlin betreffend die Neugestaltung der deutschen Handelspolitik 1900* (Berlin: R. Boll, 1901), I Hauptabteilung, Rep. 108, Nr. 5104, SAP; Guillermo Kuksiek to Cruz, Feb. 27, 1901, B99-6-4/4475/93431, MRE, AGCA; Webb, "Agricultural Protection in Wilhelminian Germany," 309–26; Webb, "Tariffs, Cartels, Technology and Growth in the German Steel Industry," 309–29; Webb, "Tariff Protection for the Iron Industry, Cotton Textiles and Agriculture in Germany," 336–57.

29. *Denkschrift der ältesten der Kaufmannschaft von Berlin betreffend die Neugestaltung der deutschen Handelspolitik 1900*, I Hauptabteilung, Rep. 108, Nr. 5104, SAP.

30. Kuksiek to Cruz, Feb. 27, 1901, BB-6-4/4475/93431, MRE, AGCA; Hugo von Radolin to Bülow, Oct. 13, 1902, IA, S. Salv. 1, vol. 4, PAAA; E. Heinze to José Trigueros, Dec. 27, 1901, Gutachtliche Äusserung zu dem von Salvador vorgelegten Entwurf eines neuen Handelsvertrages, Jan. 15, 1902, 09101, Nr. 12520, BAP.

31. Report on Empresa Eléctrica de Guatemala, Oct. 1900, Tonio Bodiker to foreign minister, Oct. 29, 1900 (copy in IA, Guat. 1, vol. 4, PAAA), Bodiker to Oswald von Richthoven, Oct. 29, 1900, Bodiker to [?], July 31, 1901, 25/Lt. 201, Siemens-Institut; Gerhard Jacob-Wendler, *Deutsche Elektroindustrie in Lateinamerika: Siemens und AEG (1890–1914)* (Stuttgart: Klett-Cotta, 1982).

32. Report on Empresa Eléctrica, Oct. 1900, Bodiker to foreign minister, Oct. 29, 1900, Bodiker to Richthoven, Oct. 29, 1900, Bodiker to [?], July 31, 1901, 25/Lt. 201, Siemens-Institut.

33. Voights-Rhetz to Hohenlohe-Schillingsfürst, June 24, 1899, IA, Guat. 1, vol.

5, PAAA; James C. McNally to David J. Hill, Sept. 21, 1900, RG 59, CD, Guat.: 13 (T 337/r 13).

34. Report on Empresa Eléctrica, Oct. 1900, Bodiker to foreign minister, Oct. 29, 1900, Bodiker to Richthoven, Oct. 29, 1900, Bodiker to [?], July 31, 1901, 25/Lt. 201, Siemens-Institut.

35. Report on Empresa Eléctrica, Oct. 1900, Bodiker to foreign minister, Oct. 29, 1900, Bodiker to Richthoven, Oct. 29, 1900, Bodiker to [?], July 31, 1901, 25/Lt. 201, Siemens-Institut; McNally to Hill, Sept. 21, 1900, RG 59, CD, Guat.: 13 (T 337/r 13); Pourtalés-Gorgies to MAE, Sept. 21, 22, 29, 1900, CP 1918, Guat., Pol. extérieure, N.S. 5, AMAE.

36. Greve to Siemens und Halske, Feb. 19, 1903, 25/LI 449, Siemens-Institut.

37. Greve to Siemens und Halske, Sept. 9, 29, Dec. 16, 1903, Greve to transportation minister, Sept. 13, 1903, Siemens und Halske to Empresa Eléctrica, Nov. 7, 1903, 25/L1 449, Siemens-Institut.

38. Greve to Siemens und Halske, Sept. 29, 1903, Siemens und Halske to Empresa Eléctrica, Nov. 7, 1903, 25/L1 449, Siemens-Institut.

39. Siemens und Halske to Empresa Eléctrica, Nov. 7, 1903, Greve to Siemens und Halske, Dec. 2, 16, 1903, enclosing decree, Dec. 12, 1903, 25/L1 449, Siemens-Institut; Zentral-Verwaltung, Übersee [ca. Nov. 5, 1908], 68/Lr 488, Siemens-Institut.

40. Stockholder list and yearly report, Dec. 31, 1910, 17/Ld 929, Siemens-Institut.

41. Arghiri Emmanuel, *Unequal Exchange* (New York. Monthly Review, 1972), Amin, *Unequal Development*, 138–54, 163–71, 195–97, 358–59.

42. E. Heinze to Bülow, June 18, 1901, new C.I.d 162, SAH; Eyb to Justo A. Facio, Feb 3, 1901, Voights-Rhetz to Ricardo Pacheco, Aug. 5, Nov. 7, 1901, MRE, caja 148, AN, CR.

43. Rosenthal to Bülow, Sept. 27, 1901, A. 3. N. 1, Nr. 4, SAB; W. E. Johannsen to Pacheco, Dec. 27, 1901, MRE, caja 145, AN, CR; see also 09.01, Nr. 12485 and Nr. 12486, BAP.

44. Heinze to Bülow, June 18, 1901, new C.I.d 162, SAH; Chamorro, *El último caudillo;* memo, Aug. 31, 1901, INK 508, SAF, distributed confidentially to interested parties but not to the press.

45. Schlieben to Bülow, April 24, 1903, 90.01, Nr. 12493, BAP (copies in R2/ 1453, BAK, and A. 3. N. 1, Nr. 4, SAB); David Healy, "A Hinterland in Search of a Metropolis: The Mosquito Coast, 1894–1910," *International History Review* 3 (Jan. 1981):20–43.

46. Max Vosberg-Rekow, *Die Errichtung einer Centralstelle zur Förderung des deutschen Aussenhandels* (Berlin: Siemenroth und Troschel, 1900); Greve to Siemens und Halske, Feb. 19, 1903, 25/LI 449, Siemens-Institut; Georg von Rheinbaben to emperor, Aug. 25, 1903, Rep. 90, Nr. 1324, SAP.

47. *Mittheilung,* confidential, Sept. 4, 1903, INK 508, SAF.

48. John Hay to William Merry, July 7, 1900, RG 59, DI, Cent. Amer.: 22 (M 77/r 34), NA; Voights-Rhetz to Hohenlohe-Schillingsfürst, March 16, 1900, Nic. 1, vol. 5, PAAA; unsigned memorandum from Ger. leg. [Oct. 15, 1901], RG 59, notes from Ger. leg.: 31 (M 58/r 31); Botho von Eulenberg to Bülow, Nov. 27, 1901, IA, Amer.

Gen. 13, vol. 2, PAAA; William Roger Adams, "Strategy, Diplomacy, and Isthmian Canal Security, 1880–1917" (Ph.D. diss., Florida State University, 1974); Edward B. Parson, "The German-American Crisis of 1902–1903," *Historian* 33 (May 1971):436–52.

49. Hay to Charlemagne Tower, Jan. 12, 1903, RG 59, DI, Ger.: 21 (M 77/r 72); Radolin to Bülow, Jan. 6, 1903, Albert Quadt to Bülow, Jan. 16, 1903, Werner von Grünau to Bülow, Feb. 28, 1903, IA, Amer. Gen. 12, vol. 5, PAAA; Hilmar Bussche-Haddenhausen to Bülow, Nov. 16, 1903, IA, Pan. 1, vol. 1, PAAA; Grünau to Bülow, Nov. 19, 1903, IA, Pan. 1, vol. 3, PAAA; Bussche to Bülow, Nov. 20, 1903, IA, Amer. Gen. 12, vol. 6, PAAA.

50. Hay to Tower, Nov. 5, 20, 1903, RG 59, DI, Ger.: 21 (M 77/r 72); Grünau to foreign minister, Nov. 14, 1903, IA, Pan. 1, vol. 1, PAAA; Bussche to Bülow, Nov. 20, 1903, IA, Pan. 1, vol. 2, PAAA; Bussche to Bülow, Nov. 21, 1903, IA, Amer. Gen. 12, vol. 6, PAAA (copy also in RM 5/vol. 5428, BAMF); Rudolph Doge to Loomis, Feb. 11, 1905 [?], Francis B. Loomis Papers, vol. 1, Stanford University; Walter LaFeber, *The Panama Canal: The Crisis in Historical Perspective*, 2d ed. (New York: Oxford University Press, 1989), 3–45; David McCullough, *The Path Between the Seas: The Creation of the Panama Canal, 1870–1914* (New York: Simon and Schuster, 1977); Schoonover, *The United States in Central America*, 97–110.

51. Von Commin to emperor, Nov. 15, 1903, IA, Amer. Gen. 12, vol. 6, PAAA; Georg Wegener, *Reisen im westindischen Mittelmeer* (Berlin: Allgemeiner Verein für deutsche Literatur, 1904), 236–37; K. von Scheller-Steinwartz, "Über den Panama Kanal," [1905] 2.2.1, Nr. 13364, BAM; Michahelles to Bülow, June 17, 1905, Senatskommission für die Reichs- und auswärtigen Angelegenheiten, alt 1905, S-I-h-24, SAH.

52. The Schlubach family was in Guatemala for many generations, during which time its members entered into a variety of partnerships, family firms, and other enterprises. Paul Behneke to emperor, April 24, 1905, RM 5/vol. 5428, BAMF; German consular report on shipping and canal, circa 1904–5, IA, Pan. 1, vols. 2 and 3, PAAA; Seefried to Bülow, Aug. 16, 1904, Hp II 61, vol. 2 (Guat.), Handelskammerarchiv Bremen.

53. Hunfl to José Astua Aguillar, April 23, 1905, MRE, caja 162, AN, CR; Behneke to emperor, May 18, 1905, RM 5/vol. 5401, BAMF; *Mittheilung,* May 21, 1906, INK 508, SAF; Wegener, *Reisen im westindischen Mittelmeer,* 236–37.

54. Schlieben to Bülow, July 3, 1903, Senatskommission für die Reichs- und auswärtigen Angelegenheiten, neu C. I. d. 162, SAH; *Mittheilungen,* confidential, Feb. 23, March 26, June 1, 1904, May 9, 1905, INK 508, SAF, which carried the warning "especially to protect against its publication in the press"; Behneke to emperor, May 18, 1905, RM 5/vol. 5402, Behneke to emperor, May 18, 1905, RM 5/vol. 5412, BAMF; Merry to Hay, Feb. 20, 1904, DD, Cent. Amer.: 72 (M 219/r 92).

55. Behneke to emperor, May 18, 1905, RM 5/vol. 5402, Behneke to emperor, May 18, 1905, RM 5/vol. 5412, BAMF; Friedrich August Heye to Bülow, Jan. 23, 1906, 09.01, Nr. 12494, BAP; Schoonover, *The United States in Central America*, 130–48.

56. Behneke to emperor, May 18, 1905, RM 5/vol. 5402, Behneke to emperor, May 18, 1905, RM 5/vol. 5412, BAMF.

57. Behneke to emperor, May 18, 1905, RM 5/vol. 5402, Behneke to emperor, May 18, 1905, RM 5/vol. 5412, BAMF.

58. Behneke to emperor, April 24, 1905, RM 5/vol. 5428, Behneke to emperor, May 18, 1905, RM 5/vol. 5401, Behneke to emperor, May 18, 1905, Ammon to emperor, Feb. 3, 1906, RM 5/vol. 5402, Behneke to emperor, May 18, 1905, RM 5/vol. 5412, Behneke to emperor, May 18, 1905, RM 5/vol. 5432, BAMF; Laves, "German Government Influence on Foreign Investments."

59. Behneke to emperor, April 24, 1905, RM 5/vol. 5428, Behneke to emperor, May 18, 1905, RM 5/vol. 5401, Behneke to emperor, May 18, 1905, Ammon to emperor, Feb. 3, 1906, RM 5/vol. 5402, Behneke to emperor, May 18, 1905, RM 5/vol. 5412, Behneke to emperor, May 18, 1905, RM 5/vol. 5432, BAMF; Arthur Dix, "Zentral-Amerika," in Ernst von Halle, ed., *Amerika* (Hamburg: Hamburger Börsenhalle, 1905), 431–65; "Mittelamerika," *Handbuch des Deutschtums im Auslande* (Berlin: Dietrich Reimer, 1906), 309–14.

60. Behneke to emperor, April 24, 1905, RM 5/vol. 5428, Behneke to emperor, May 18, 1905, RM 5/vol. 5401, Behneke to emperor, May 18, 1905, Ammon to emperor, Feb. 3, 1906, RM 5/vol. 5402, Behneke to emperor, May 18, 1905, RM 5/vol. 5412, Behneke to emperor, May 18, 1905, RM 5/vol. 5432, BAMF.

61. Abteilung II, Bayerische Gesandtschaft in Paris, MA 1921 A. V. IV, Nr. 61732, Bayerisches Hauptstaatsarchiv, Munich; Heyer to Bülow, Dec. 22, 1905, A. 3. C. 1, Nr. 104, SSB (copy in Rep. 49, vers. 3, VIII, Fasz. 71, Hauptstaatsarchiv, Baden-Württemberg, Stuttgart); Fritz Blaich, *Der Trustkampf (1901–1915)* (Berlin: Duncker und Humblot, 1975), 38 45, 142 44; Heinze, "Die United Fruit Company," *Berichte über Handel und Industrie* 4 (1906):145–51.

62. Abteilung II, Ministerium des Äussern, MA 1921 A. V. II, Nr. 53269, and Bayerische Gesandtschaft in Paris, Nr. 10402, Bayerisches Hauptstaatsarchiv, Munich; Eyb to MRE, Sept. 29, 1900, B99-5-1/4294/93199, MRE, AGCA; Heinze to Bülow, June 18, 1901, new C. I.d 162, SAH; McNally to Hill, Nov. 2, 1900, RG 59, CD, Guat.: 13 (T 337/r 13); *Mittheilung*, confidential, Sept. 30, 1902, IHK 508, SAF; Felix Hänsch-Leipzig, "Weltpolitik, Kolonialpolitik und Schule," *Zeitschrift für Kolonialpolitik, Kolonialrecht und Kolonialwirtschaft* 11 (Oct. 1907):767–75; Gerhard Weidenfeller, *VDA-Verein für das Deutschtum im Ausland. Allgemeiner Deutscher Schulverein (1881–1918)* (Bern: Lang, 1976).

63. Joré to MAE, S. José, Oct. 27, 1901, CCC, San José de C.R., vol. 2, AMAE; Houwald, "Die Deutschen in Costa Rica"; Leopold, "Der Deutsche in Costa Rica."

8. Apogee of German Power in Central America, 1906–1914

1. Mommsen, *Der autoritäre Nationalstaat*, 198–99, 318; Wehler, "Das Deutsche Kaiserreich," 192–239; Eckart Kehr, "Englandhass und Weltpolitik," in Ziebura, ed., *Grundfragen der deutschen Aussenpolitik seit 1871*, 132–62; Fritz Fischer, *Germany's Aims in the First World War* (New York: Norton, 1967).

2. Katz, "Einige Grundzüge der Politik des deutschen Imperialismus in Lateinamerika," 9–17; Clara E. Schieber, *The Transformation of American Sentiment Toward Germany 1870–1914* (1923; reprint, New York: Russell and Russell, 1973); Imanuel Geiss, *German Foreign Policy, 1871–1914* (Boston: Routledge and Kegan

Paul, 1976); Arnold Steinmann-Bucher, *350 Milliarden deutsche Volksvermögen* (Berlin: Otto Elsner, 1909), 46–51.

3. Poidevin, *Les Relations économiques et financières entre la France et l'Allemagne,* 76, 154–56, 241, 333–43; André M. Jacques d'Arlot de Saint-Saud to Rouvier, Feb. 20, 1906, Commerce, F^{12} 7054: Amér. cent., AN; E. Gómez Carrillo to MRE, Jan. 19, 1909, B99-6-9/8718, MRE, AGCA; Karl Sapper, *Die Ansiedlung von Europäern in den Tropen,* 2 vols. (Munich: Duncker und Humblot, 1912) 1:1–74; Jean Bouvier, *Le Mouvement de profit en France au XIXe siècle* (Paris: Mouton, 1965), 274–77; Célestin-Pierre Cambiaire, *Le Rôle de la France dans l'expansion des États-Unis* (Paris: Albert Messein, 1935), 222–26; Jean-Sylvian Weiller, "Long-run Tendencies in Foreign Trade: With a Statistical Study of French Trade Structure, 1871–1939," *Journal of Economic History* 31 (Dec. 1971):804–21. Students of French expansion often focus on colonialism, ignoring informal methods of expanding a political economy. See, for example, Christopher Andrew and A. S. Kanya-Forstner, *France Overseas: The Great War and the Climax of French Imperial Expansion* (London: Thames and Hudson, 1981), 10–17.

4. Poidevin, *Les relations économiques et financières entre la France et l'Allemagne,* 76, 154–56, 241, 333–43; Hans W. Gatzke, "The United States and Germany on the Eve of World War I," in Geiss and Wendt, eds., *Deutschland in der Weltpolitik des 19. und 20. Jahrhunderts,* 271–86; "Das Gespenst der 'deutschen Gefahr' in Südamerika, sein Entstehen und Vergehen," *Zeitschrift für Kolonialpolitik, Kolonialrecht und Kolonialwirtschaft* 10 (1908):155–62; Alan S. Milward and S. B. Saul, *The Development of the Economies of Continental Europe, 1850–1914* (London: Allen and Unwin, 1977), 127–39.

5. Peter-Christian Witt, "Innenpolitik und Imperialismus in der Vorgeschichte des 1. Weltkrieges," in Holl and List, eds., *Liberalismus und imperialistischer Staat,* 11.

6. Schoonover and Schoonover, "Statistics for an Understanding of Foreign Intrusions into Central America"; Rodrigo Quesada Monge, "Diplomacía y deuda externa: El caso de Honduras (1897–1912)," *Anuario de estudios centroamericanos* 10 (1984):69–80.

7. Seefried to Bülow, April 4, 1906, IA, CR 1, vol. 3, PAAA; Seelinger to foreign minister, Sept. 11, 1912, IA, Amer. Gen. 12, vol. 10, PAAA; Bussche to Theobald von Bethmann-Hollweg, July 18, 1910, Bussche to foreign minister, July 15, 1910, IA, Amer. Gen. 13, vol. 8, PAAA; Sternburg to foreign minister, Oct. 18, 1907, IA, Ver. St. von Amer., 16, Geheim, vol. 1, PAAA; Lester Langley, *America and the Americas: The United States in the Western Hemisphere* (Athens: University of Georgia Press, 1989), 104–32; Bill Albert, *South America and the World Economy from Independence to 1930* (London: Macmillan, 1983); Frank Ninkovich, "Ideology, the Open Door, and Foreign Affairs," *Diplomatic History* 6 (spring 1982):185–208.

8. Wilhelm von Schoen to Bülow, Feb 24, 1906, IA, Amer. Gen. 13, vol. 5, PAAA; Hildebrand, "Zwischen Allianz und Antagonismus," 305–31; Fritz Fischer, *War of Illusions: German Policies from 1911 to 1914* (New York: Norton, 1975).

9. Ger. minister in Rome to foreign minister, June 1907, IA, Amer. Gen. 16, Geheim, vol. 2, PAAA; Heinrich Leonhard von Tschirschky and Bögendorff to marine minister, Aug. 15, 1907, RM 5/vol. 6026, BAMF; Tirpitz to [?], Oct. 2, 1908 [?], to Baudissin, Oct. 15, 1908, RM 5/vol. 6024, BAMF; Bernhard Dernburg, "Ger-

many and American Policies," *Annals of the American Academy* 60 (July 1915):195–96; Holger H. Herwig and David Trask, "Naval Operations Plans between Germany and the United States of America, 1898–1913: A Study of Strategic Planning in the Age of Imperialism," *Militärgeschichtliche Mitteilungen* 70:2 (1970):5–32.

10. Johann Heinrich von Bernstorff to Bülow, March 1, 1909, III Hauptabteilung (A. A.), Nr. 1114, SAP.

11. Heye to Bülow, April 7, 1906, A. 3. C. 1, Nr. 105, SAB; Seefried to Bülow, April 4, 1906, IA, CR 1, vol. 3, PAAA.

12. Heye to Bülow, May 23, 26, 1906, 09.01, Nr. 12494, BAP; Seefried to Bülow, April 4, 1906, Albert C. Schwerin to Bülow, April 30, 1908, IA, CR 1, vol. 3, PAAA; d'Arlot to Léon Bourgeois, Sept. 5, 1906, AMEF, F^{30} 393^1: Hond., Guat., CR; Leslie Combs to Elihu Root, April 28, 1906, DD, Cent. Amer.: 53 (M 219/r 72); Robert Hoeniger, *Das Deutschtum im Ausland vor dem Weltkrieg*, 2d ed. (Leipzig: B. S. Teubner, 1918), 86–91, 112.

13. *Mittheilung*, Aug. 3, 1906, INK 508, SAF; Heye to Bülow, Aug. 4, 1906, enclosing Hättasch to [foreign minister], Aug. 4, 1906, 09.01, Nr. 12494, BAP; excerpt in [illegible] to Hamburg Senat, Oct. 3, 1906, Senatskommission für die Reichs- und auswärtigen Angelegenheiten, neu C. I. d. 162, SAH.

14. Critique enclosed with Michahelles to Hamburg Senat Deputation für Handel und Schiffahrt, Nov. 1, 1906, Senatskommission für die Reichs- und auswärtigen Angelegenheiten, neu/C. I. d. 162, SAH; Heye to Bülow, Aug. 6, 1906, R 2/1454, BAK.

15. Augusto C. Coeller to Ger. foreign minister, Nov. 20, 1906, R 85/687, BAK; Max Schinckel to Hamburg Senat Deputation für Handel und Schiffahrt, Feb. 15, 1907, Senatskommission für die Reichs- und auswärtigen Angelegenheiten, neu A III c. 20, SAH.

16. Bernstorff to Bethmann-Hollweg, May 28, 1910, Jan. 9, 1911, Deutsche Übersee Bank to foreign minister, June 16, 1910, Buch to Bethmann-Hollweg, July 15, 1910, IA, Hond. 1, vol. 3, PAAA; Buch to Bethmann-Hollweg, Feb. 15, 1911, IA, Hond. 1, vol. 4, PAAA; Augustin Julien Rigoreau to MAE, July 30, 1910, CP 1918, Hond., Finances, AMAE (copy in F^{12} 7222, Cent. Amer. et Chile, AN, P); Guillermo Molina Chocano, *Estado liberal y desarrollo capitalista en Honduras* (Tegucigalpa: Banco de Honduras, 1976).

17. Riderlin to Chief of Naval Staff, Nov. 3, 1910 [?], to emperor, Nov. 15, 1910, RM 5/vol. 6015, BAMF; E. A. Anderson to sec. of the navy, Nov. 24, 1910, enclosing "Commercial Project of J. E. Foster, " [n.d.], RG80, entry 19, file 8480 (14:24), NA.

18. N. Kaumanns to Bülow, Aug. 29, 1908, Senatskommission für die Reichs- und auswärtigen Angelegenheiten, neu C. I. d. 164, SAH; Wilhelm Bitter, *Die wirtschaftliche Eroberung Mittelamerikas durch den Bananentrust* (1921; reprint, Darmstadt: Wissenschaftliche Buchgesellschaft, 1971).

19. Woodward, *Central America: A Nation Divided*, 149–203; Manuel Roja Bolaños, "El Desarrollo del movimiento obrero en Costa Rica; un intento de periodización," in *Desarrollo del movimiento sindical en Costa Rica* (San José: Editorial universitaria de Costa Rica, 1981), 13–21; Víctor Meza, *Historia del movimiento obrero hondureño* (Tegucigalpa, Hond.: Guaymuras, 1980); Mario Posas, *Luchas del movimiento obrero hondureño* (San José, CR: EDUCA, 1981); Vladimir de la Cruz,

Las luchas sociales en Costa Rica, 1870–1930 (San José: Editorial universitaria de Costa Rica, 1980); Thomas F. O'Brien, *The Revolutionary Mission: American Enterprise in Latin America, 1900–1945* (Cambridge: Cambridge University Press, 1996), 47–55, 80–106.

20. Schwerin to Bülow, June 18, 1907, RM 5/vol. 6026, BAMF.

21. Hans von Wangenheim to Bülow, March 22, April 22, May 8, 30, Aug. 30, 1907, IA, Mex. 2, vol. 3, PAAA.

22. Bonin to Bülow, June 12, 1909, A. 3. C. 1, Nr. 85, SAB.

23. Hermann Johannes to Bethmann Hollweg, Sept. 3, 1913, A. 3. G. 2., Nr. 763, SAB.

24. Bonin to Bülow, July 1, 1909, Rep. 120, C XIII, 16[a,] Nr. 4, vol. 2, BAM; Seelinger to foreign minister, Aug. 1, 1912, R 85/134, BAK; Gnet to Chancellor, Sept. 12, 1912, Senatskommission für die Reichs- und auswärtigen Angelegenheiten, neu C. I. d. 164, SAH; Phillip Darby, *Three Faces of Imperialism: British and American Approaches to Asia and Africa, 1870–1970* (New Haven, CT: Yale University Press, 1987), 142–46, 169–73, 213–14.

25. Seelinger to foreign minister, Aug. 1, 1912, Kracker to Bethmann-Hollweg, July 12, 1912, R 85/134 BAK; Kracker to Bethmann-Hollweg, Dec. 28, 1911, H. Edm. Bohlen to Hamburg Senat Deputation für Handel, Schiffahrt und Gewerbe, Oct. 14, 1912, Gnet to Chancellor, Sept. 12, 1912, Senatskommission für die Reichs- und auswärtigen Angelegenheiten, neu C. I. d. 164, SAH.

26. Lester Langley and Thomas Schoonover, *The Banana Men: American Mercenaries and Entrepreneurs in Central America, 1880–1930* (Lexington: University Press of Kentucky, 1995); Charles D. Kepner and Jay H. Soothill, *The Banana Empire: A Case Study in Economic Imperialism* (New York: Vanguard, 1935); Watt Stewart, *Keith and Costa Rica: A Biographical Study of Minor Cooper Keith* (Albuquerque: University of New Mexico Press, 1964), chaps. 3–12, 15.

27. Metternich to Bethmann-Hollweg, March 12, 1910, von der Goltz to Bethmann-Hollweg, May 9, 1910, IA, Col. 1, vol. 24, PAAA; von der Goltz to Bethmann-Hollweg, March 22, April 6, 15, May 19, 1910, IA, Col. 5, vol. 2, PAAA; Kracker to Bethmann-Hollweg, July 4, 1912, enclosing article from *Nuevo tiempo,* July 4, 1912, R 85/134, BAK.

28. Ger. minister in Bogotá to foreign minister, July 10, 1912, Oscar Egersdorfer to foreign minister, July 19, 1912, R 85/134, BAK.

29. Seelinger to foreign minister, Aug. 1, 1912, R 85/134, BAK; Gnet to Chancellor, Sept. 12, 1912, Senatskommission für die Reichs- und auswärtigen Angelegenheiten, neu C. I. d. 164, SAH; Seelinger to foreign minister, Sept. 11, 1912, IA, Amer. Gen. 12, vol. 10, PAAA.

30. Richard Krauel to Hamburg Senat Deputation für Handel, Schiffahrt und Gewerbe, Oct. 4, 1909, Senatsakten, C1 V1, Nr. 16[a,] Vol. 1, Fasc. 15, SAH; Victor to Bremen Senatskommission für Reichs- und auswärtige Angelegenheiten, Oct. 16, 1909, A. 3. C. 1, Nr. 113, SAB.

31. D'Arlot to MAE, March 2, 1908, AMEF, F[30] 393[1]: Hond., Guat., C. R.; Jacques to patrons, July 19, 1909, Amérique Centrale folder, additional Jacques correspondence on Central America in New York folder, Banque de Neuflir, 44 AQ19, AN; for background, see David Joslin, *A Century of Banking in Latin America* (London: Oxford University Press, 1963).

32. Jusserand to MAE, Oct. 26, 1910, MAE to Jusserand, Nov. 17, 1910, unsigned draft, Nov. 1910, A. Gervais, "Le Rôle de la France dans le monde," *Matin,* Dec. 1, 1910, CP 1918, Amér. Latin, Questions Générale, AMAE; Rigoreau to MAE, Oct. 5, 1910, CP 1918, S. Salv., Affaires commerciales, AMAE; Rigoreau to MAE, Dec. 3, 1910, CP 1918, Guat., Pol. extérieure, AMAE; [illegible] to [illegible], INK 200, SAF; *Die Republik Guatemala und ihr Präsident, Herr Lizentiat Don Manuel Estrada Cabrera, 1911* (n.p.: n.p., 1912).

33. Bonin to Bülow, July 1, 1909, Rep. 120, C XIII, 16[a,] Nr. 4, vol. 2, BAM; Sapper, *Die Ansiedlung von Europäern in den Tropen,* 1:64–66.

34. Fritz Legnitz to Bremen Senat Kommission für Reichs- und auswärtige Angelegenheiten, Sept. 30, 1912, Hp II 57 (CR), SAB; J. Cambon to MAE, May 1, 1914, CP 1918, Amér. Latine, Questions Générales, AMAE; O. Preusse-Sperber, *Süd- und Mittel-Amerika. Seine Bedeutung für Wirtschaft und Handel* (Berlin: Otto Salle, 1913), 178–81; Weidenfeller, *VDA-Verein für das Deutschtum im Ausland,* 376–86.

35. Wilhelm Münzenthaler to Bülow, July 1909, Ger. consulate to Bethmann-Hollweg, Sept. 6, 1909, IA, CR 1, vol. 3, PAAA.

36. Ernst Goette to emperor, Dec. 19, 1910, RM 5/vol. 5432, BAMF; Ger. consulate to Bethmann-Hollweg, Aug. 17, 1911, IA, CR 1, vol. 4, PAAA.

37. Schwerin to Bülow, April 30, 1908, IA, CR 1, vol. 3, PAAA; Buch to Bethmann-Hollweg, July 15, 1910, IA, CR 1, vol. 4, PAAA.

38. Wilhelm Erythropel to Chancellor, Jan. 5, 1914, R 85/122, BAK.

39. Erythropel to Bethmann-Hollweg, Dec. 17, 1913, May 11, 1914, IA, CR 1, vol. 4, PAAA.

40. Bülow to Hamburg Mayor Dr. Predoehl, Jan. 7, 1913, Heye to Deputation für Handel, Schiffahrt und Gewerbe, Jan. 20, 1913, Senatskommission für die Reichs- und auswärtigen Angelegenheiten, neu A III c. 22, SAH; memorandum, March 27, 1913, IA, Amer. Gen. 13, vol. 8, PAAA; Falke to Bethmann-Hollweg, July 20, 1913, IA, Amer. Gen. 12, vol. 11, PAAA; Roh to Bethmann-Hollweg, March 11, 1910, A. 3. N. 3., Nr. 202, SAB; Bernstorff to Bethmann-Hollweg, Nov. 27, 1911, IA, Amer. Gen. 12, vol. 10, PAAA; Robert Freeman Smith, "A Note on the Bryan-Chamorro Treaty and German Interest in a Nicaraguan Canal, 1914," *Caribbean Studies* 9:1 (April 1969):63–66.

41. Münzenthaler to Bülow, July 4, 1907, IA, CR 1, vol. 3, PAAA.

42. Desiré Pector to MAE, May 6, 1911, finance minister to MAE, July 5, 1911, CP 1918, Hond., Pol. intérieure. Chemins de fer. Armée, AMAE; Ernst von Simson to Kemnitz, Jan. 17, 1914, Magnus to Bethmann-Hollweg, April 23, 1914, and subsequent correspondence, IA, Guat. 4, vol. 1, PAAA; Toledo Herrarte to Ernesto Mencos, Oct. 31, 1912, B99-6-3/4459/93415, MRE, AGCA.

43. Riderlin to Bethmann-Hollweg, Aug. 22, 1910, foreign minister, memorandum, Aug. 23, 1910, IA, Galápagos Islands, vol. 2, PAAA; Jusserand to MAE, April 8, 1912, CP 1918, Pan., Canal de Panama VI, AMAE.

44. Seelinger to foreign minister, Sept. 11, 1912, IA, Amer. Gen. 12, vol. 10, PAAA; Goette to emperor, Jan. 1911, RM 5/vol. 5428, BAMF; Ponsignon to MAE, Aug. 1, 1911, CP 1918, Pan., Pol. étrangère II, AMAE; Siegfried Mielke, *Der Hansa-Bund für Gewerbe, Handel und Industrie, 1909–1914* (Göttingen: Vandenhoeck und Ruprecht, 1976), 11–33, 181–86; Jantzen, *Hamburgs Ausfuhrhandel,* 17–41, 69–71; Al-

mond R. Wright, "German Interest in Panama's Piñas Bay, 1910–38," *Journal of Modern History* 27 (March 1955):61–66.

45. Company for Wireless Telegraph to foreign minister, Oct. 11, 1913, Frantzius to Bethmann-Hollweg, Dec. 13, 1913, R 85/788, BAK; David McCreery, "Wireless Empire: The United States and Radio Communications in Central America and the Caribbean, 1904–1926," *South Eastern Latin Americanist* 37 (summer 1993):23–41.

46. Bernstorff to Bethmann-Hollweg, July 12, 1911, A. Oberndorff to Bethmann-Hollweg, Sept. 19, 1911, IA, Pan. 1, vol. 7, PAAA.

47. Paul Metternich to Bülow, Oct. 12, 1908, foreign minister to Metternich, Oct. 17, 1908, IA, Col. 1, vol. 22, PAAA; Bonin to Bülow, July 1, 1909, Rep. 120, C XIII, 16^{a,} Nr. 4, vol. 2, BAM; von der Goltz to Bethmann-Hollweg, Nov. 12, Dec. 22, 1909, Albert D. Roters to J. O. Petersen, Dec. 13, 1909, enclosed in Petersen to foreign minister, Jan. 30, 1910, IA, Col. 1, vol. 24, PAAA.

48. Minister in Bogotá to MAE, Jan. 16, 1914, F^{30} 396: Pan., AMEF; MAE to commerce and industry minister, June 16, 1913, F^{12} 7226, AN; chief of staff to sec. of war, Oct. 11, 1913, box 74-Isthmian Canal Route, Frank Ross McCoy Papers, LC; Seebohm to emperor, Feb. 16, 1914, RM 5/vol. 6017, BAMF; Fr. vice consul at Southhampton to MAE, March 25, 1913, CP 1918, Pan., Canal de Panama, VII, N.S. 15, AMAE; Bizet to MAE, Jan. 23, 1914, CP 1918, Pan., Canal de Panama, VIII, N.S. 16, AMAE; Larroque to MAE, July 30, 1914, CP 1918, Amér. Latine, Questions Générales, AMAE; Kracker to Bethmann-Hollweg, Feb. 28, March 22 1914, IA, Pan. 1, vol. 8, PAAA; Tapken to Schonberg, Feb. 2, 1914, RM 5/vol. 3657, BAMF; Max Hochschiller, "L'Allemagne à la conquête du Panama et l'inertie française," *L'Information*, May 1, 1914, Panama Canal, F^{12} 8779, AN; Henri Hauser, *Les Méthodes allemandes d'expansion économique* (Paris: Armand Colin, 1916), 199–203, 235, 255–59; Lamar Cecil, "Diplomaten und Soldaten: Die Rolle des Militärs im Deutschen Auswärtigen Amt 1871–1914," in Konrad Jarausch, ed., *Quantifizierung in der Geschichtswissenschaft: Probleme und Möglichkeiten* (Düsseldorf: Droste, 1976), 218–31.

9. U.S. Displacement of German Economic Power during World War I

1. Friedrich Katz, "Die deutschen Kriegsziele in Lateinamerika im ersten Weltkrieg," *Wissenschaftliche Zeitschrift der Humboldt-Universität zu Berlin* 13 (1964):875–79; Manfred Jonas, *The United States and Germany: A Diplomatic History* (Ithaca, NY: Cornell University Press, 1984); James R. Mock, "The Creel Committee in Latin America," *Hispanic American Historical Review* 22:2 (May 1942):262–79; James A. Farrell, "Central and South American Trade as Affected by the European War," *Annals* 60 (July 1915):60–68; John Hay Hammond, "Trade Relations with Central and South America as Affected by the War," *Annals* 60 (July 1915):69–71; Philippe Bunau-Varilla, *The Great Adventure of Panama: The German Conspiracies Against France and the United States* (New York: Doubleday, 1920); Hermann Schumacher, "Deutschlands Stellung in der Weltwirtschaft," in Otto Hintze, Friedrich Meinecke, Hermann Oncken, and Hermann Schumacher, eds., *Deutschland und*

der Weltkrieg (Leipzig: B. G. Teubner, 1915); Gerald D. Feldman, "Der deutsche organisierte Kapitalismus während der Kriegs- und Inflationsjahre, 1914–1923," in Abelshauser and Petzina, eds., *Deutsche Wirtschaftsgeschichte*, 299–323. Bill Albert's *South America and the First World War* (London: Macmillan, 1983) does not discuss the Central American region, but his analysis contributes to understanding the international history of the isthmus during World War I.

2. Herwig, *Politics of Frustration*, 85–92; Small, "The United States and the German 'Threat' to the Hemisphere," 252–70; Katz, "Einige Grundzüge der Politik des deutschen Imperialismus in Lateinamerika," 9–69; Bernhard Harms, *Deutschlands Anteil an Welthandel und Weltschiffahrt* (Stuttgart: Union Deutsche Verlagsgesellschaft, 1916); Otto Hintze, "Deutschland und das Weltstaatensystem," in Hintze, Meinecke, Oncken, and Schumacher, eds., *Deutschland und der Weltkrieg*, 1–371; Ernst zu Reventlow, *Die Politik der Vereinigten Staaten* (Berlin: E. Bruckmann, 1917).

3. Claude Chayet to MAE, Jan. 20, April 26, 30, 1919, Amér. 1918–1940, Cent. Amer., num. 39, AMAE; J. Fred Rippy, "German Investments in Latin America," *Journal of Business* 21 (April 1948):63–73; Schoonover and Schoonover, "Statistics for an Understanding of Foreign Intrusions into Central America," 15(1):93–117, 16(1):135–56, and 17(2):77–119.

4. Wiebe, *The Search for Order*, 224–302; Kolko, *The Triumph of Conservatism*, 255–305; Cardoso and Pérez Brignoli, *Centro América y la economía occidental*, 199–321; LaFeber, *Inevitable Revolutions*, 49–59.

5. Kurt Lehmann to Bethmann-Hollweg, Sept. 8, Oct. 5, Nov. 2, 1914, Walther Dauch to Dr. Weber, Jan. 29, 1915, Dauch to L. Asch, March 15, 1915, IA, Guat. 5, vol. 1, PAAA; Nicolaus Cornelsen to Bethmann-Hollweg, Dec. 28, 1914, IA, Hond. 2, PAAA.

6. Lehmann to Bethmann-Hollweg, Sept. 8, Oct. 5, Nov. 2, 1914, March 28, 1915, AA to Ger. minister in Stockholm, May 8, 1915, IA, Guat. 5, vol. 1, PAAA.

7. Lehmann to Bethmann-Hollweg, Nov. 2, 1914, IA, Guat. 5, vol. 1, PAAA.

8. Dauch to Weber, Jan. 29, 1915, Dauch to L. Asch, March 15, 1915, IA, Guat. 5, vol. 1, PAAA.

9. Cornelsen to Bethmann-Hollweg, Dec. 28, 1914, IA, Hond. 2, PAAA; Lehmann to Bethmann-Hollweg, Sept. 8, Oct. 5, Nov. 2, 1914, March 28, 1915, IA, Guat. 5, vol. 1, PAAA; on the collected funds, see R 85 (AA), vols. 2327, 2328, 2329, 2331, 2337, 2523, 2524, 2526, 2528, 2529, 2535, 2569, 2570, and 2571, BAK; Adrian Rösch, *Allerlei aus der Alta Verapaz* (Stuttgart: Ausland und Heimat, 1934), 101.

10. Fr. minister to MAE, Nov. 22, 1914, CP 1918, Guat., Négociations et affaires commerciales, AMAE (copy in F^{30} 393^1: Hond., Guat., CR, AMEF).

11. Cornelsen to Bethmann-Hollweg, Dec. 28, 1914, IA, Hond. 2, PAAA; "Wirtschaftliche Lage und Handel in Honduras während des Krieges," March 13, 1915, IHK 200, SAF.

12. Toledo Herrarte to Méndez, Dec. 24, 1917, B99-6-3/4461/93417, MRE, AGCA; Office of Naval Intel. to St. Dept., Feb. 5, 1918, RG 165, MID, 87-6, NA; Chayet to MAE, Oct. 1, 1918, Amér. 1918–1940, Cent. Amer., num. 21, AMAE.

13. Manuel Castro Quesada to Roberto Brenés Mesén, Dec. 31, 1914, MRE, l.c. 166, AN, CR; Peralta to Carlos Lara, March 10, 12, 1917, MRE, caja 236, leg.-Francia III (1917), AN, CR.

14. Erythropel to Lehmann, Feb. 15, 1916, Senats-Kommission für die Reichs- und auswärtigen Angelegenheiten, C I d 162, SAH.

15. Franous to Bethmann-Hollweg, April 29, May 16, 1914, Gustav Krautinger to AA, May 16, 19, 1914, Deutsches Kohlen Depot, G.m.b.H. to Krautinger, May 18, 1914, Krautinger to Fritz Roechling, Jan. 27, 1915, AA to Ger. ambassador to Rome, Feb. 1, 1915, J. Heinrich Munz to Kolonialamt, Feb. 19, 1915, AA to Munz, March 21, 1915, IA, Pan. 1, vol. 8, PAAA; Ferdinand Rothe to AA, Nov. 29, 1915, AA to Rothe, Dec. 20, 1915, IA, CR 1, vol. 4, PAAA; Schmidt-Reder to Naval Staff, Jan. 19, 1915, RM 5/vol. 5428, BAMF; clipping, *New York Times*, Feb. 15, 1916, RM 5/vol. 5425, BAMF; Bizet to MAE, Pan., May 6, 1916, CP 1918, Pan., Canal de Panama X, AMAE; Bethmann-Hollweg to Chief of Naval Staff, Jan. 25, 1918, naval minister to Ger. leg. in Stockholm, Jan. 31, 1918, RM 5/vol. 2738, BAMF; Wright, "German Interest in Panama's Piñas Bay," 61–66.

16. "Handelsbestrebungen Englands und der Vereinigten Staaten von Amerika in Guatemala," Oct. 10, 1914, "Handelsbestrebungen Englands und der Vereinigten Staaten von Amerika in Salvador," Oct. 24, 1914, "Handelsbestrebungen Englands und der Vereinigten Staaten von Amerika in Costa Rica," Nov. 1914, "Wirtschaftliche Lage und Handel in Honduras während des Krieges," March 13, 1915, IHK 200, SAF; Mitglieder-Liste, 1916 and 1918, IHK 201, SAF; Daenell, *Das Ringen der Weltmächte um Mittel- und Südamerika*, 27–35.

17. Correspondence in R 85/789, 810, and 811, BAK; Amann to confidential person at Cartago, Feb. 17, 1915, RM 5/vol. 5404, BAMF; Ger. minister in Haiti to Bethmann-Hollweg, Aug. 22, 1916, RM 5/vol. 5411, BAMF; minister in Sweden to AA, May 13, 1916, Chief of Naval Staff to AA, July 9, 1916, Mullendorff to AA, March 10, 1917, Reichs-Postamt to AA, July 3, 1916, R 85/788, BAK; McCreery, "Wireless Empire."

18. Peralta to Lara, March 10, 12, 1917, MRE, caja 236, leg.-Francia III (1917), AN, CR; Ibero-Amerikanischer Nachrichten- und Archivdienst to AA (A. Schmidt), July 9, 1917, R 85/789, BAK; U.S. military attaché to van Deeman, March 21, 1917, RG 165, MID, file 6370–450, NA.

19. Peralta to Lara, March 10, 12, 1917, MRE, caja 236, leg.-Francia III (1917), AN, CR; Conde de San Esteban de Cañonyo to MAE, April 15, 1917, legajo 1729 (El Salv.), Archivo del Ministerio de asuntos estranjeros, Madrid; Cornelsen to Hertling, Feb. 17, 1918 [Cornelsen?], to Hertling, May 6, 1918 [?], to Reichswirtschaftsamt, July 26, 1918, R85/5413, BAK.

20. "Handelsbstrebungen der Vereinigten Staaten von Amerika in Costa Rica," Oct. 28, 1915, IHK 1231, SAF; Eckert to Reichskanzler, July 19, 1916, IA, Amer. Gen. 13, vol. 8, PAAA; Max von Ratibor to AA, June 12, 1918, R 85/6714, BAK; Erythropel to Georg Friedrich von Hertling, May 24, 1918, Ratibor to AA, June 12, 1918, "Pro Memoria," June 3, 1918, IA, CR 1, vol. 5, PAAA; Peralta to Dr. Ferriere (Red Cross), Aug. 29, 1918, R 85/3614, BAK; Hermann Levy, *Deutschland und die amerikanische Konkurrenz* (Berlin: Admiralstab der Marine, 1917); Hans-Jürgen Schroeder, "Die politische Bedeutung der deutschen Handelspolitik nach dem I. Weltkrieg," in Gerald Feldman, ed., *Die deutsche Inflation: Eine Zwischenbilanz* (Berlin: de Gruyter, 1982), 235–51; Werner Pade, "Die Expansionspolitik des deutschen Imperialismus gegenüber Lateinamerika 1918–1933," *Zeitschrift für Geschichtswissenschaft* 22 (1974):578–90.

21. Gutschow and Rud. Crasemann to Hamburg Senats-Kommission für Handel und Industrie, July 6, 1915, Senatsakten, Cl. VI, Nr. 16^{d,} vol. 1, Fasc. 16, SAH; Gutschow to Dr. Schröder, July 6, 1915, HP II 61, vol. 2, Bremen IHK; William Hayne Leavell to sec. of state, April 1, 1915, dec. files, 714.622/1, Political relations, Guat. with other states, 1910–1929 (M657/r 27), NA.

22. Bizet to MAE, Feb. 5, Nov. 4, 1915, CP 1918, Pan., Relations et conventions commerciales II, N.S. 8, AMAE; Bizet to MAE, July 22, 1915, CP 1918, Pan., Canal de Panama X, N.S. 18, AMAE; Armando Cahens and Co. to [?], Nov. 13, 1915, F^{23} 157, Services extraordinaires des Temps de Guerre, AN, P; Kracker to Bethmann-Hollweg, Oct. 1, 1915, RM 3/vol. 3901, BAMF; lists from the *London Gazette*, RM 3/vol. 4621, BAMF; Stephen Pichon to Guat. minister, Sept. 7, 1918, Chayet to MAE, Sept. 19, 1918, Amér. 1918–40, Cent. Amer. (Guat.), num. 20, AMAE; correspondence, Nov. 1918–Jan. 1919, Amér. 1918–1940, Cent. Amer., num. 6, AMAE; Chayet to MAE, Nov. 30, 1918, CP 1918, Amér. cent., II, N.S. 2, AMAE; Office of Naval Intelligence to Chief of Naval Operations, Jan. 23, 1918, RG 165, MID, 87, NA; Erwin Paul Dieseldorff to William Owen, Oct. 9, Dec. 29, 1917, letterpress copybook 32, E. P. Dieseldorff Collection; Thomas Bailey, "The United States and the Black-list during the Great War," *Journal of Modern History* 6 (March 1934):14–35.

23. Ed Acbelis to Senat Handelskommission, Oct. 24, 1917, HP II 61, vol. 2 (Guat.), Bremen IHK.

24. Fr. minister to MAE, April 30, 1918, CP 1918, Guat., Pol. extérieure, AMAE; Bussche to Ger. embassy in Madrid, May 17, 1918, R 85/5410, BAK; Ratibor to AA, June 12, 1918, IA, CR 1, vol. 5, PAAA, (also in R 85/6714, BAK); Span. ambassador to AA, Feb. 19, 1919, R 85/3614, BAK; Max Obst to AA, Oct. 19, 1919, R 85/5642, BAK; Chayet to MAE, Feb. 18, 1919, Amér. 1918–1940, Cent. Amer., num. 39, AMAE; Span. foreign minister to Ger. minister in Spain, Nota Verbal, March 13, 1919, Botschaft Madrid (Guat.), Pol. Nr. 1^{h,} PAAA (copy in R 85/6695, BAK); annex with Erythropel to AA, Sept. 16, 1920, III, Nic., Handel 11, PAAA; Bruno Simmersbach, "Die wirtschaftlichen Zustände der Föderativrepublik Guatemala," *Schmollers Jahrbuch* 41 (1917):291–373.

25. Ibero-Amerikanischer Nachrichten- und Archivdienst to AA, May 4, 1917, declaration of the CR foreign minister, Sept. 22, 1917, Ratibor and Corvey to AA, Oct. 10, 1917, Peralta to [illegible], Nov. 2, 1917, IA, CR 1, vol. 4, PAAA; Ratibor to AA, Oct. 10, 1917, R 85/6695, BAK; Lara to Ricardo Fernández Guardia, April 27, 1917, MRE, l.c. 166, AN, CR; Luis Esquivel to MRE, Oct. 13, 1917, MRE, caja 240, leg.-Pan. V (1917), AN, CR; Hugo Murillo Jiménez, *Tinoco y los Estados Unidos: Génesis y caída de un régimen* (San José, CR: Editorial universitaria estatal a distancia, 1981).

26. Memoranda, "Wie man in Costa Rica über den Abbruch der Beziehungen denkt," IA, CR 1, vol. 4, PAAA.

27. Office of Naval Intel. to St. Dept., Dec. 11, 29, 1917, C. H. Calhoun to MID, Dec. 13, 1917, RG 165, MID, 6370, NA; Hiram B. Crosby to Director of Military Intelligence (hereaftr Dir. Mil. Intel.), Oct. 31, 1918 (2 letters), RG 165, MID, 10674-22, NA.

28. A. T. Harrison to Col. Van Deman, July 30, 1918, RG 165, MID, 10674-45, NA; Erythropel to Hertling, May 24, 1918, Ratibor to AA, June 12, 1918, "Pro

Memoria," June 3, 1918, IA, CR 1, vol. 5, PAAA; Peralta to Ferriere (Red Cross), Aug. 29, 1918, R 85/3614, BAK; "Reliable" to St. Dept., Feb. 18, 1918, New York and Honduras Rosario Mining Company to Lincoln Valentine, March 1, 1918, RG 165, MID, 10674–3, Roger to Claudio de Peralta, March 30, 1918, RG 165, MID, 10674–36, NA; "Pro-Memoria," June 3, 1918, Respuesta provisional a la Pro-Memoria, July 3, 1918, MRE, caja 241, leg.-Francia III (1918), AN, CR; Serre to MAE, Dec. 17, 1920, Amér. 1918–1940, Cent. Amer., num. 7, AMAE; Juan Kümpel, *La Bancarrota del liberalismo* (San José, CR: La Prensa Libre, 1911); Suzanne M. O'Connor, "Costa Rica in the World Community of Nations 1919–1939: A Case Study in Latin American Internationalism" (Ph.D. diss., Loyola University of Chicago, 1976).

29. E. McCauley, Jr., to Dir. of Mil. Intel., Oct. 31, 1918, Crosby to Dir. of Mil. Intel., Oct. 31, 1918, RG 165, MID, 10674–22, NA; Peralta to Lara, Oct. 10, 1917, MRE, caja 236, leg.-Francia III (1917), AN, CR; Juan Kümpel, *La Guerra: Su origen histórico, su verdadera causa, y los pretextos con que los enemigos de Alemania excusan su agresión* (Valparaiso, Chile: Victoria, 1915).

30. Dirección general de Empresa Eléctrica, Nov. 25, 1912, B126.2/8394, Obras públicas . . . Gaz y Electricidad, 1880–1927, MRE, AGCA; Chayet to MAE, Feb. 18, 1919, Amér. 1918–1940, Cent. Amer., num. 39, AMAE; Span. foreign minister to Ger. minister in Spain, Nota Verbal, March 13, 1919, Botschaft Madrid (Guat.), Pol. Nr. 1^{h}, PAAA (copy in R 85/6695, BAK); Siemens und Halske to AA, March 24, 1919, AA to Vereinigung der Guatemala-Firmen, July 18, 1919, Obst to AA, Oct. 19, 1919, R 85/5642, BAK; Alfonso Bauer Paiz, "La Eléctrica Bond and Share Company," *Revista Alero* 2 (1970):20–34.

31. Chayet to MAE, Jan. 20, Feb. 6, March 4, April 26, 30, 1919, Amér. 1918–1940, Cent. Amer., num. 39, AMAE; Chayet to MAE, Jan. 21, 1919, Amér. 1918–1940, Cent. Amer., num. 68, AMAE.

32. Toledo Herrarte to Méndez, May 2, July 22, Nov. 4, 1918, B99-6-3/4461/93417, MRE, AGCA; Siemens und Halske to AA, Aug. 23, 1918, memoranda to Armistice Committee [1919?], Dieseldorff to Brockdorff-Rantzau, Feb. 20, 1919, Friedrich Köper to AA, Feb. 24, 27, 1919 [illegible], to Rudolf Hesse, March 27, 1919, Köper to AA, April 2, 1919, eight firms to AA, April 3, 1919, Dieseldorff to Bernhard Dernburg, April 22, 1919, Obst to AA, Oct. 19, 1919, R 85/5642, BAK.

33. Seven firms to Brockdorff-Rantzau, March 3, 1919, eight firms to AA, April 3, 1919, R 85/5642, BAK; Rösch, *Aus der Alta Verapaz,* 103.

34. Wolffram, "Denkschrift," Dec. 1, 1915, Rep. 109, Seehandlung—Preussische Staatsbank, Nr. 5374, SAP; Deputation für Handel, Schiffahrt und Gewerbe, II, Spezialakten XXXIV, Nr. 209, SAH; Heinrich Class, *Zum deutschen Kriegsziel* (Munich: J. F. Lehmanns, 1917); Gerhard Schulz, *Deutschland seit dem Ersten Weltkrieg, 1918–1945* (Göttingen: Vandenhoeck und Ruprecht, 1982).

35. "Hamburger Vorschläge zur Neugestaltung des deutschen Auslandsdienstes," April 1918, "Stellungnahme von A I to A IV (Hamburger Vorschläge zur Neugestaltung des deutschen Auslandsdienstes)," May 8, 1918, RM 3/vol. 4382, BAMF; annual report, Hamburg Handelskammer, 1918, S 6, Nr. 991, Dortmund IHK.

36. "Gedanken über die zukünftige Entwickelung der Marine" (Ganz Geheim), April 23, 1916, RM 3/vol. 10, BAMF; "Stellungnahme von A I to A IV

(Hamburger Vorschläge zur Neugestaltung des deutschen Auslandsdienstes),"
May 8, 1918, RM 3/vol. 4382, BAMF.

37. "Hamburger Vorschläge zur Neugestaltung des deutschen Auslandsdienstes," April 1918, "Stellungnahme von A I to A IV (Hamburger Vorschläge zur
Neugestaltung des deutschen Auslandsdienstes)," May 8, 1918, RM 3/vol.
4382, BAMF, copy in Handelskammer Bochum, K2, Nr. 963, Dortmund IHK; Kurt Doss,
"Vom Kaiserreich zur Weimarer Republik. Das deutsche diplomatische Korps
in einer Epoche des Umbruchs," in Klaus Schwabe, ed., *Das diplomatische Korps,
1871–1945* (Boppard am Rhein: Harald Boldt, 1985), 81–100; Kurt Doss, *Das deutsche Auswärtige Amt im Übergang vom Kaiserreich zur Weimarer Republik. Die Schülerische Reform* (Düsseldorf: Droste, 1977), 92ff., 142–46.

38. Vereinigung der Guatemala-Firmen to Peace Commission, April 23, 1919,
Vereinigung der Guatemala-Firmen to Bremen Handelskammer, April 23, 1919, R
85/5642, BAK; HP II 61, vol. 2 (Guat.), Bremen IHK; Rosenbaum and Hassel-
mann, *Deutschlands wirtschaftliche Leistungsfähigkeit* (Berlin: n.p., 1920), Deputation für Handel, Schiffahrt und Gewerbe, XXXIV, Nr. 253, SAH; Chayet to MAE,
Aug. 26, 1919, Amér. 1918–1940, Cent. Amer., num. 35, AMAE; Hans David, "Das
deutsche Auslandskapital und seine Wiederherstellung nach dem Kriege," *Weltwirtschaftliches Archiv* 14 (1919):31–70, 275–300.

39. John Hays Hammond [1919], RG 151, 430-Latin America-General, 1918–
1920, NA.

40. "Ausnutzung des schwimmenden Materials der Marine im Interesse der
deutschen Volkswirtschaft nach Abschluss eines ungünstigen Friedensver-
trages," May 20, 1919, RM 23/1804, BAMF; materials in Deutsches Auslandsin-
stitut, R57/DAI 413, BAK; Conrad von Borsig to Deutscher Wirtschaftsverband
Süd- und Mittelamerika E. V., Jan. 26, 1920, RM 20/485, BAMF; August Sartorius
von Waltershausen, *Die Weltwirtschaft und die staatlich geordneten Verkehrswirtschaf-
ten* (Leipzig: G. A. Gloeckner, 1926), 157–59, 381–85; Kruck, *Geschichte des Alldeutschen Verbandes,* 218–22; Herbert Dorn, "Germany in Latin America," *Current History* 28 (March 1955):168–176.

41. Max Cohen to AA, Nov. 17, 1919, Alfred Stettiner and Co. to AA, Dec. 13,
1919, AA to Alfred Stettiner and Company, Dec. 23, 1919, IA, S. Salv. 1, vol. 7,
PAAA; L. R. von Stohrer, Memoranda, May 21, 1920, III, Guat., Pol. 10, PAAA.

42. Chayet to MAE, Dec. 16, 1919, April 25, 1921, Lucien Lévy-Bruhl, "L'Allemagne prévoit une émigration considérable après la paix," March 10, 1919, Paul
Tirand to Raymond Poincaré, May 21, 1924, Z-Europe 1918–1929, Allemagne,
num. 598 (Emigration), AMAE; Stohler, Wedel and [illegible] to AA [?], June 1920,
III Guat., Pol. 5, PAAA; *Nachrichtenblatt des Reichsauswanderungsamts,* Dec. 15,
1920, pp. 866–69, Auswanderungsamt II, Lit. C^{II}9, vol. 1, SAH; Kurt Hassert and
Otto Lutz, *Mittelamerika (Mexiko) als Ziel deutscher Auswanderung* (Berlin: Suferott,
1920); Karl Sapper, *Auswanderung und Tropenakklimatisation* (Würzburg: Kabitzsch
und Mönnich, 1921); Karl Sapper, *Mittel-Amerika* (Hamburg: L. Friedericksen,
1921), 101–10; Henri Hauser, *Frankreichs Handel und Industrie und die Konkurrenz
des Auslandes* (Jena: Gustav Fischer, 1919).

43. Perrot to MAE, May 17, June 6, 1920, Amér. 1918–1940, Cent. Amer., num.,
21, AMAE; Obst to AA, April 21, 1920, III, Guat., Pol. 5, PAAA; Annual report,
Hamburg Handelskammer, 1920, S6, 991, Dortmund IHK; Obst to AA, Jan. 30,

1920 [illegible] to Karl von Wedel, July 20, 1920, III, Guat., Pol. 2 (Guat.-Deutschl.), PAAA.

44. Köper to Bremen Senat, June 24, 1920, 4.49, 115/31 Guat., SAB (same in III, Guat., Rechtswesen 19, PAAA).

45. Leopold von Hoesch to AA, July 26, 1920, III, Guat., Pol. 10, PAAA; Span. foreign minister to Hoesch, July 19, 1920, Aide-Mémoire, Oct. 15, 1920, Botschaft Madrid (Guat.), Pol. Nr. 1[h,] PAAA; MRE to Lazo Arriaga, April 27, 1920, B99-6-3/4461/93417, Lazo to Luis P. Aguirre, Aug. 9, 1920, B99-23-6/6260, MRE, AGCA.

46. Rudolph Schlubach to AA (Simmons), Aug. 27, 1920, AA to Schlubach, Thiemer, and Company, Sept. 7, 1920, III, Guat., Rechtswesen 19, PAAA, (copies in R 2/759, BAK); AA to Reichsminister für Wiederaufbau, July 11, 1921, Reichsminister für Wiederaufbau to Reichsminister der Finanzen, July 24, 1921 (endorsed to AA, n.d.), Reichsfinanzministerium, R2/759, Kriegsschaden Deutscher in Guat., 1921, BAK; chargé to MAE, March 30, 1921, Amér. 1918–1940, Cent. Amer., num. 39, AMAE; Erythropel to Stohrer, Dec. 15, 1920, III, CR, Pol. 10, PAAA.

47. Cornelsen to AA, April 17, 1920, III, Hond., Pol. 2, PAAA; Perrot to MAE, May 17, June 6, 1920, Amér. 1918–1940, Cent. Amer., num. 21, AMAE; Theodoro Köhncke to Diedrich Drechsel, Dec. 15, 1920, III, Hond., Pol. 9, PAAA; Erythropel to AA, March 18, 1921, III, Hond., Rechtswesen 19, Nr. 1, PAAA.

48. Erythropel to H. Welczeck, Aug. 5, 1919, Erythropel to AA, Nov. 15, 1919, IA, CR 1, vol. 5, PAAA; Pinchon to Chayet, Sept. 7, 1919, Chayet to MAE, Sept. 19, Oct. 1, 1919, Amér. 1918–1940, Cent. Amer. (Guat.), num. 21, AMAE; Erythropel to AA, Aug. 13, 1920, III, CR, Pol. 2, PAAA; Span. foreign minister to Ger. minister in Spain, Nota Verbal, March 13, 1919, Botschaft Madrid (Guat.), Pol. Nr. 1[h,] PAAA, (copy in R 85/6695, BAK); AA to Vereinigung der Guatemala-Firmen, July 18, 1919, R 85/5642, BAK; Chayet to MAE, Jan. 21, 1919, Amér. 1918–1940, Cent. Amer., num. 68, AMAE.

49. Erythropel to Kraske, Sept. 29, 1920, Kümpel (brother of claimant) to AA, Nov. 4, 1920, Erythropel to AA, Nov. 5, 1920, III, CR, Rechtswesen 28, PAAA.

50. Erythropel to AA, Nov. 26, 1920, III, CR, Pol. 2, PAAA; Ger. ambassador in France to AA, Jan. 4, 1921, III, CR, Pol. 11, Nr. 3, PAAA; Franz von Tattenbach to AA, March 23, 1921, Erythropel to AA, June 2, 1921, III, CR, Pol. 9, PAAA; Peralta to Tobías Zuñiga Montúfar, May 21, 1919, MRE, caja 247, leg.-Francia III, AN, CR; Peralta to Alejandro Alvarado Quiros, Aug. 17, 1920, MRE, caja 251, leg.-Francia III, AN, CR.

51. Erythropel to [?], Sept. 17, 1920, Erythropel to AA, Jan. 26, 1921, III, CR, Pol. 10, PAAA; Serre to MAE, Jan. 26, 1921, Amér. 1918–1940, Cent. Amer., num. 7, AMAE.

10. Reestablishing Germany's Role, 1920–1925

1. Feldman, "Der deutsche organisierte Kapitalismus während der Kriegs- und Inflationsjahre, 1914–1923," 299–323; Peter Krüger, *Versailles: Deutsche Aussenpolitik zwischen Revisionismus und Friedenssicherung* (Munich: dtv, 1986), 7ff.

2. Katz, "Einige Grundzüge der Politik des deutschen Imperialismus in Latein-amerika," 14–18; Horst Möller, *Weimar: Die unvollendete Demokratie* (Munich: dtv, 1985), 11–57; Karl Buchheim, *Die Weimarer Republik: Das Deutsche Reich ohne Kaiser* (Munich: Wilhelm Heine, 1970), 24–54; Detlev J. K. Peukert, *Die Weimarer Republik* (Frankfurt: Suhrkamp, 1987), 32–86; George W. F. Hallgarten and Joachim Rad-kau, *Deutsche Industrie und Politik von Bismarck bis in die Gegenwart* (Reinbek, FRG: Rowohlt, 1981), 140–89.

3. Erythropel to AA, Oct. 7, 1920, III, CR, Handel 11, PAAA; Erythropel to Stohrer, Dec. 15, 1920, 1920, III, CR, Pol. 10, PAAA; annex with Erythropel to AA, Sept. 16, 1920, III, Nic., Handel 11, PAAA; Gregorio Rosales R. to sec. of Frankfurt IHK, Jan. 23, 1920, IHK 200, SAF.

4. Langley, *America and the Americas*, 104–32; McCormick, *America's Half-Century*, 170–204; Joseph S. Tulchin, *The Aftermath of War: World War I and U.S. Policy Toward Latin America* (New York: New York University Press, 1971); Schulz, *Deutschland seit dem Ersten Weltkrieg*, 54–91; Hartmut Bickelmann, *Deutsche Über-seeauswanderung in der Weimarer Zeit* (Wiesbaden: Franz Steiner, 1980); Peter Mar-schalck, *Bevölkerungsgeschichte Deutschlands im 19. und 20. Jahrhundert* (Frankfurt: Suhrkamp, 1984), 53–71; Klaus Schönhoven, *Reformismus und Radikalismus: Gespal-tene Arbeitsbewegung im Weimarer Sozialstaat* (Munich: dtv, 1989), 7–8; Peukert, *Die Weimarer Republik*, 13–31.

5. Handelskammer Hamburg, *Bericht über das Jahr 1926* (Hamburg: Handels-kammer Hamburg, 1926); *Hamburger Nachrichten*, Nov. 21, 1925, Senatskommis-sion für die Reichs- und auswärtigen Angelegenheiten, N.R., III, B 94, SAH; Wil-helm von Kühlmann to AA, May 25, 1926, March 11, Dec. 31, 1927, Nov. 12, 1929, III, S. Salv., Wirtschaft 1, PAAA; José María Orellana to E. P. Dieseldorff, Nov. 22, 1922, Dieseldorff Collection, box 4, folder 19; Chayet to MRE, Apr. 25, 1921, Paul Tirand to Raymond Poincaré, May 21, 1924, Z-Europe 1918–1929, Allemagne, num. 598 (Emigration), AMAE; Karl Sapper, *Mittel-Amerika* (Halle [Saale]: Max Niemeyer, 1927), 108–16; Schoonover and Schoonover, "Statistics for an Under-standing of Foreign Intrusions into Central America."

6. Victor Bulmer-Thomas, *The Political Economy of Central America Since 1920* (Cambridge: Cambridge University Press, 1987), 25–47; Woodward, *Central Amer-ica: A Nation Divided*, 182–223; Pérez Brignoli, *Breve historia de Centroamérica*, 107–33; LaFeber, *Inevitable Revolutions*, 54–67.

7. Various correspondence, memoranda, drafts in Deutsches Auslandsinsti-tut, R57/DAI 413, BAK; Tattenbach to AA Presseabteilung, Sept. 8, 1921, III, CR, Pol. 12, PAAA; Pade, "Die Expansionspolitik des deutschen Imperialismus gegenüber Lateinamerika," 578–84.

8. Revelli to Poincaré, Jan. 20, 1922, Revelli to MAE, March 6, 1922, Amér. 1918–1940, Cent. Amer., num. 30, AMAE; Fr. minister to MAE, April 26, 1922, F^{30} 1956, AMEF.

9. Général Charles Mangin, "Autour du continent latin avec le 'Jules Michelet.' II, Le Guatémala—Panama," *Revue des deux mondes* 92 (Oct. 1922):559–79; Fr. chargé to MAE, March 20, 1921, MAE to Jusserand, May 7, 1921, Amér. 1918–1940, Cent. Amer., num. 39, AMAE; Leo S. Rowe to A. G. Bates, June 29, 1921 and enclosures, Pacific Mail Steamship Company records, box 50, folder Central American Republics, Huntington Library, San Marino, California.

10. Erythropel to AA, July 8, 1921, III, Guat., Pol. 2 (Guat.-Deutschl.), PAAA; AA to Reichspräsident, Sept. 9, 1921, III, M.-Amer., Pol. 2, PAAA.

11. Erythropel to AA, July 27, 1921, III, Guat., Pol. 10, PAAA; Revelli to MAE, Aug. 22, 1922, Amér. 1918–1940, Cent. Amer., num. 26, AMAE.

12. "Teatro Abril," *El Universo,* March 23, 1922, in Heinrich Johannes Kroeger to José Andrés Alvarado, April 26, 1922, MRE, caja 261, AN, CR; Revelli to MAE, Sept. 22, 1922, Amér. 1918–1940, Cent. Amer., num. 30, AMAE; "Deutschtum in Mittelamerika," *Berliner Börsenzeitung,* May 1, 1922, Guat., Pol. 3 (Guat.-Ver. St.), PAAA; Friedrich Heilbron to Ger. minister in Guat., Feb. 12, 1925, III, Guat., Handel 13, PAAA; Kühlmann to AA, Nov. 13, 1924, III, Guat., Handel 13, PAAA.

13. Erythropel to AA, Sept. 22, 1921, III, M.-Amer., Pol. 15, PAAA; Erythropel to AA, March 19, June 21, 1923, III, Hond., Pol. 2, PAAA; Augustin Hombach to Reichskanzler, May 20, 1923, III, Hond., Pol. 16; AA, Aufzeichnung, Nov. 16, 1925, III, Hond., Pol. 11, Nr. 6, PAAA.

14. Mayer to AA, April 15, 1921, III, S. Salv., Pol. 9, PAAA; Handelskammer Hamburg, *Bericht über das Jahr 1921* (Hamburg: Handelskammer Hamburg, 1921), S6–991, Dortmund IHK; Sapper, *Mittel-Amerika* (1921), 101–10.

15. Unsigned telegram to MID, April 26, 1921, RG 165, MID, 2515-p-3, NA; Erythropel to AA, March 18, 1921, II, Hond., Rechtswesen 19, Nr. 1, PAAA; Tattenbach to AA, Sept. 20, Oct. 23, 1921, III, CR, Handel 11, PAAA; Reichskommissar for import and export licences to all foreign trade bureaus, III, M.-Amer., Zollwesen 15, PAAA (also in IHK/200, SAF).

16. Tattenbach to AA, Aug. 16, 1922, III, Nic., Handel 11, PAAA; Bunge to Ger. minister in CR, April 29, 1925, III, Nic., Finanzwesen 20, PAAA; Rudolf Bobrik, Memorandum, Nov. 16, 1925, III, Guat., Rechtswesen 28, PAAA.

17. Tattenbach to AA, July 22, 1922, III, CR, Finanz 20, PAAA; Fr. minister to MAE, June 15, 1923, F^{30} 1956: Guat., AMEF.

18. LeCoq to marine minister, Sept. 2, 1921, I, BB^4 6, dossier 1921, AAM; L. Cotty to Dejean de la Batie, June 23, 1922, Amér. 1918–1940, Cent. Amer., num. 26, AMAE.

19. Tattenbach to AA, July 28, 1921, Sept. 22, 1921, III, CR, Postwesen 28, PAAA; Kroeger to AA, July 4, 1922, III, CR, Postwesen 29, PAAA; U.S. intelligence reports, July 6, 31, 1923, RG 165, MID, file 2280-P-15/16, NA; Hugh G. J. Aitken, *The Continuous Wave: Technology and American Radio, 1900–1932* (Princeton, NJ: Princeton University Press, 1985), 464.

20. Tattenbach to AA, Jan. 30, 1922, III, CR, Handel 11, Nr. 1, PAAA; Tattenbach to AA, Sept. 26, 1921, Jan. 30, 1922, III, CR, Handel 24, Nr. 8, PAAA; Handelskammer Hamburg, *Bericht über das Jahr 1922* (Hamburg: Handelskammer Hamburg, 1922), 27, S6–991, Dortmund IHK.

21. Erythropel to AA, Sept. 10, 1921, III, Hond., Pol. 10, PAAA; Erythropel to AA, Sept. 21, Dec. 16, 1921, III, M.-Amer., Pol. 4, PAAA; Fritz Arnoldi to Bremen IHK, Feb. 3, 1922, Joh. Gottfr. Schutte and Co. to Bremen IHK, Feb. 15, 1922, HP II 61, vol. 2 (Guat.), Bremen IHK; Köper to AA, Feb. 13, 1922, III, Guat., Pol. 2 (Guat.-Deutschl.), PAAA; Ger. ambassador to Fr. to AA, Jan. 30, 1922, III, S. Salv., Pol. 5, PAAA.

22. Köper to AA, Jan. 19, March 30, 1922, III, Guat., Pol. 2 (Guat.-Deutschl.),

PAAA; Arnoldi to Bremen IHK, Feb. 3, 1922, Joh. Gottfr. Schutte and Co. to Bremen IHK, Feb. 15, 1922, HP II 61, vol. 2 (Guat.), Bremen IHK.

23. Stenger to AA, April 7, 1921, III, CR, Postwesen 18, PAAA; Deutscher Transport-Versicherungs-Verband to AA, Nov. 4, 1920, Kroeger to AA, May 19, 1922, Feb. 19, 1923, III, CR, Postwesen 3, PAAA; F. Bunge to Ger. minister in CR, Feb. 11, 1923, Klaus to AA, April 9, 1923, III, Nic., Postwesen 3, PAAA.

24. Kroeger to AA, Oct. 15, 1923, III, CR, Postwesen 4, PAAA; Tattenbach to AA, July 31, Aug. 25, 1924, III, Nic., Postwesen 8, PAAA; Tattenbach to AA, Guat., Aug. 21, 25, 1924, Hübner to AA, Jan. 3, 1925, H. R. Wettstein to AA, June 10, 1927, III, Nic., Postwesen 3, PAAA; Fritz Sauter to Ger. minister in Cent. Amer., Sept. 16, 1927, Ziegler to AA, Aug. 10, 1928, III, CR, Postwesen 3, PAAA; A. Aguila Machado to A. Peña Chavarría, May 31, 1929, MRE, l.c. #128, p. 308, AN, CR.

25. Erythropel to AA, May 23, 1922, and enclosures, III, Nic., Pol. 10, PAAA; Tattenbach to AA, Aug. 15, 1922, III, CR, Pol. 10, PAAA; D. O. Lutz to AA, Jan. 26, 1924, III, Pan., Pol. 2, PAAA; Revelli to MAE, Oct. 2, 1924, Amér. 1918–1940, Cent. Amer., num. 22, AMAE; Bunge to Kühlmann, Sept. 5, 1926, III, Nic., Pol. 5, vol. 1, PAAA.

26. E. Peper to Erythropel, June 16, 1922, enclosed in Erythropel to AA, June 24, 1922, III, Guat., Pol. 10, PAAA.

27. Köper to Bremen IHK, April 20, 1923, Hp II 61, vol. 2 (Guat.), Bremen IHK; Bremen IHK to Senat Kommerzkommission, May 16, 1923, Tattenbach to AA, July 5, 1923, 3.-A.3.c.1, Nr. 132, SAB.

28. Tattenbach to AA, Sept. 29, 1923, III, Guat., Verkehrswesen 11, PAAA.

29. "Der Ausbau des Auswärtigen Dienstes zur Förderung des deutschen Aussenhandels," [1923–1924], Reichskanzlei, R43/1198, BAK; Reichsminister für Ernährung und Landwirtschaft to Reichskanzlei, July 31, 1923, R431/1174, BAK; AA to Reichswirtschaftsministerium, Sept. 27, 1923, Reichsfinanzministerium, R2/24596, BAK; Tattenbach to AA, Sept. 1, 1923, III, Guat., Handel 13, PAAA.

30. Bobrik to various German ministries, Sept. 27, 1923 (very urgent), and enclosures, AA to Ger. minister in Guat., Dec. 6, 1923, Tattenbach to AA, June 6, 1924, Kühlmann to AA, Nov. 27, 1924, III, Guat., Handel 13, PAAA; W. de Haas to AA, Sept. 27, 1923, Bremen Gesandtschaft in Berlin to Bremen Senatskommission für die Reichs- und auswärtigen Angelegenheiten, Oct. 10, 1923, 3.-S.18. Nr. 241, SAB; memo, Oct. 10, 1923, Reichsfinanzministerium, R2/24596, BAK; Hamburg Gesandtschaft to Hamb. Senatskommission für die Reichs- und auswärtigen Angelegenheiten, N.R. I.C. 2.b.21, SAH; Revelli to MAE, April 28, 1923, March 15, 1924, Amér. 1918–1940, Cent. Amer., num. 38, AMAE; Aldorf Georg Otto von Maltzan to Tattenbach, Dec. 6, 1923, III, Guat., Pol. 10, PAAA; Tattenbach to AA, Dec. 25, 1923, III, Guat., Pol. 11, Nr. 1, PAAA; Reichstag, Entwurf eines Gesetzes über das Handelsabkommen zwischen dem Deutschen Reiche und Guatemala, Nr. 41, March 9, 1925, IHK/198, SAF, (also in Reichskanzlei, R43/116, BAK); Bobrik to Hamburg Senat, Nov. 25, 1924, Senatsakten: C1 VI, Nr. 16^d vol. 1, Fasc. 20, SAH.

31. Louis Stirnemann to Abbé E. Wetterlé, June 27, 1923, MAE to minister in Cent. Amer., Aug. 2, 1923, MAE to Wetterlé, Aug. 2, 1923, Amér. 1918–1940, Cent. Amer., num. 76, AMAE; "Amérique du Sud. Développement du commerce alle-

mand," Sept. 8, 1923, 7N3374, dossier 2, AAM; Revelli to MAE, Oct. 22, 1924, Amér. 1918–1940, Cent. Amer., num. 7, AMAE; Tattenbach to AA, March 24, 1923, III, Guat., Pol. 5, PAAA; AA to Ger. foreign minister, May 29, 1926, III, Guat., Pol. 11, Nr. 3, PAAA; Revelli to MAE, Feb. 20, 1925, Amér. 1918–1940, Cent. Amer., num. 22, AMAE.

32. Revelli to MAE, March 7, 1925, clipping, *Diario de Guatemala,* March 6, 1925, Amér. 1918–1940, Cent. Amer., num. 30, AMAE; "Guatemala," *Weserzeitung,* Feb. 25, 1924, III, Guat., Pol. 11, Nr. 1, PAAA; Revelli to MAE, March 9, 1924, Amér. 1918–1940, Cent. Amer., num. 29, AMAE; Tattenbach, "Guatemala und Deutschland," enclosed in Tattenbach to AA, June 7, 1924, III, Guat., Handel 13, PAAA.

33. Ger. ambassador in Fr. to AA, Nov. 18, 1921, Mayer to AA, June 2, 1922, III, Nic., Handel 13, PAAA; [n.n.] to Tattenbach, Dec. 19, 1921, III, Nic., Wirtschaft 1, PAAA.

34. Ger. ambassador to AA, July 10, 1922, AA to Ger. minister in S. Salv., Sept. 23, 1922, Erythropel to AA, Oct. 2, 1922, III, Nic., Handel 13, PAAA.

35. AA to Erythropel, Dec. 31, 1922, Erythropel to AA, April 27, Dec. 27, 1923, III, Nic., Handel 13, PAAA; Erythropel to AA, Oct. 18, 1923, Bunge to Kühlmann, Oct. 7, 1924, III, Nic., Pol. 11, Nr. 1, PAAA; Tattenbach to AA, Sept. 1, 1924, III, Nic., Pol. 5, vol. 1, PAAA.

36. J. A. Urtecho to Ger. minister in El Salv., Jan. 9, 1924, III, Nic., Rechtswesen 19, Nr. 19, PAAA; Erythropel to AA, Jan. 25, 1924, March 7, 1924, Tattenbach to AA, June 11, 1924, Bobrik to Ger. minister in Guat., July 23, 1924, III, Nic., Handel 13, PAAA; Entwurf eines Gesetzes über die Wiederinkraftsetzung des Freundschafts-Vertrages zwischen Deutschland und Nicaragua vom Februar 25, 1896, Nr. 421, Reichsfinanzministerium, R2/24614, BAK; "Deutsche Verordnung über den Zollverkehr," Jan. 10, 1925, IHK 200, SAF; Stolten to AA, Feb. 17, 1925, Bobrik to Hamburg Senatskommission für die Reichs- und auswärtigen Angelegenheiten, Senatsakten: C1 VI, Nr. 16^{d}, vol. 1, fasc. 19, SAH.

37. Extract of Kühlmann letter, May 28, 1929, Haas, Aufzeichnung, June 19, 1929, AA to Ger. minister in Guat., July 7, 1929, III, S. Salv., Handel 13, PAAA.

38. Continental Caoutchouc and Gutta-Percha Compagnie to AA, March 21, 1923, Kühlmann to AA, Feb. 26, 1925, III, Nic., Handel 13, PAAA; Kühlmann to AA, March 12, 1925, III, Nic., Pol. 5, vol. 1, PAAA; Bunge to Kühlmann, Oct. 7, 1924, III, Nic., Pol. 11, Nr. 1, PAAA.

39. Tomás Arias to AA, Nov. 30, 1922, N. N. to Eugen Will, Feb. 7, 1923, III, Pan., Wirtschaft 6, PAAA; Lutz to Will, July 27, 1923, III, Pan., Pol. 9, PAAA; Lutz to AA, Jan. 26, 1924, III, Pan., Pol. 2, PAAA; Arthur Dix, *Schluss mit 'Europa': Ein Wegweiser durch Weltgeschichte zu Weltpolitik* (Berlin: E. S. Mittler, 1928), 54–65, 87–90.

40. AA to Ger. minister in S. Salv., Oct. 26, 1923, III, Pan., Handel 13, PAAA; Lutz to Will, July 27, 1923, III, Pan., Pol. 9, PAAA; Hering to Hamburg Senat, May 8, 1924, Hamburg *Korrespondent,* Jan. 21, 1925, Auswanderungswesen, II, Lit. AV, 24, vol. 1, SAH; Stotten to interior minister, Oct. 24, 1924, Damann to interior minister, Oct. 13, 1924, enclosing Soehring to Pan. cons. gen., Aug. 26, 1924, Pan. cons. gen. to AA, July 26, 1924, Senatskommission für die Reichs- und auswärtigen Angelegenheiten, III, D.2.Fasc. 35, SAH.

41. LeCoq to marine minister, Sept. 2, 1921, I, BB⁴ 6, dossier 1921, AAM; Revelli to MAE, Jan. 27, 1924, F³⁰ 1956: Guat., AMEF.

42. Erythropel to AA, July 26, 1923, Bobrik, memo, Aug. 31, 1923, AA to Ger. minister in S. Salv., Nov. 27, 1923, Erythropel to AA, Jan. 11, April 22, 1924, Will, Memo, Feb. 15, 1924, L. Späth to AA, Sept. 10, 1924, Victoriano Luis Quiros to Weidner, May 15, 1923, AA to Erythropel, Sept. 10, 1924, III, S. Salv., Industrie 30, PAAA; correspondence, Jan. 14, 1924, legajo H1730 (El Salv.), Archivo del Ministerio de asuntos estranjeros, Madrid; "Visite du ministre du Salvador, A. M. Deperetti," July 5, 1924, memo, July 8, 1924, Amér. 1918–1940, Cent. Amer., num. 10, AMAE; Kühlmann to AA, March 2, 1925, III, S. Salv., Pol. 5, PAAA; Kühlmann to AA, Nov. 19, 1925, III, S. Salv., Wege- und Strassenwesen 1, PAAA.

43. Cornelsen to Kühlmann, Nov. 19, 1924, Kühlmann to AA, May 14, 1925, III, Hond., Pol. 5, PAAA; Kühlmann to AA, June 10, 1925, III, Hond., Rechtswesen 28, PAAA.

44. Tattenbach to AA, Oct. 10, 1921, III, CR, Handel 30, PAAA; Tattenbach to AA, Oct. 10, 1921, AEG to AA, Nov. 14, 1921, III, CR, Handel 24, Nr. 8, PAAA; Tattenbach to AA, March 6, 1922, III, Nic., Handel 30, Nr. 1, PAAA; Nehls, "Zur Bewegung der Kapitalexporte des deutschen Imperialismus," 68–72; Wagenführ, *Die Bedeutung des Aussenmarktes für die deutsche Industriewirtschaft,* 47–50.

45. Revelli to MAE, Jan. 27, 1924, F³⁰ 1956: Guat., AMEF; Revelli to MAE, Oct. 6, 1924, Amér. 1918–1940, Cent. Amer., num. 22, AMAE; Hardach, *Deutschland in der Weltwirtschaft,* 146–49.

46. Kühlmann to AA, June 23, 1925, III, Nic., Wirtschaft 6, PAAA; Salv. leg. to AA, July 22, 1925, Kühlmann to AA, Sept. 9, Nov. 19, 1925, III, S. Salv., Wege- und Strassenwesen 1, PAAA.

47. Handelskammer Hamburg, *Bericht über das Jahr 1925* (Hamburg: Handelskammer Hamburg, 1925), 118–19, S6–991, Dortmund IHK; Tattenbach, "Guatemala und Deutschland," enclosed in Tattenbach to AA, June 7, 1924, III, Guat., Handel 13, PAAA; Handelskammer Hamburg, *Bericht über das Jahr 1926; Hamburger Nachrichten* Nov. 21, 1925, Senatskommission für die Reichs- und auswärtigen Angelegenheiten, N.R., III, B 94, SAH; Kühlmann to AA, May 25, 1926, March 11, Dec. 31, 1927, Nov. 12, 1929, III, S. Salv., Wirtschaft 1, PAAA.

11. A Revived German Presence in Central America, 1924–1929

1. Möller, *Weimar,* 163–205; Hallgarten and Radkau, *Deutsche Industrie und Politik,* 180–219; Katz, "Einige Grundzüge der Politik des deutschen Imperialismus in Lateinamerika," 14–18; H.-J. Schroeder, "Die politische Bedeutung der deutschen Handelspolitik"; Hardach, *Deutschland in der Weltwirtschaft,* 105–10.

2. Kühlmann to AA, June 2, 1926, III, Guat., Wirtschaft 13, PAAA; Kühlmann to AA, Jan. 26, 1929, III, M.-Amer., Allgemeines 3, PAAA; Pade, "Die Expansionspolitik des deutschen Imperialismus gegenüber Lateinamerika," 584–89; Schoonover and Schoonover, "Statistics for an Understanding of Foreign Intrusions into Central America."

3. Reichsverband der Deutschen Industrie to AA, Oct. 6, 1925, Wiesbaden IHK to AA, Feb. 27, 1926, III, Pan., Pol. 9, PAAA. On the state of the German

economy, see Engelsing, *Sozial-und Wirtschaftsgeschichte Deutschlands*, 180–82; Hentschel, *Deutsche Wirtschafts-und Sozialpolitik;* Friedrich-Wilhelm Henning, *Das industrialisierte Deutschland, 1914 bis 1972* (Paderborn, FDR: Ferdinand Schöningh, 1974), 114–16.

4. Chief of Air Service Mason M. Patrick to Adjutant General [1925], RG 165, MID, 183–76, N. E. Margetts to U.S. attaché Caracas, April 2, 1925, W. G. Peace to U.S. attaché Guat., May 22, 1925, RG 165, MID, 2538–21, NA; Anthony Sampson, *Empires of the Sky: The Politics, Contests and Cartels of World Airlines* (New York: Random House, 1984), 33–35.

5. C. A. Willoughby to G-2, July 7, 1925, William Lassiter to Adj. Gen., Aug. 21, 1925, Joseph C. Grew to sec. of war, Aug. 28, 1925, Grew to Geissler, Aug. 21, 1925, RG 165, MID, 2538–21, NA; Fritz Sauter to Ger. minister Cent. Amer., Sept. 16, 1927, Ziegler to AA, Aug. 10, 1928, III, CR, Postwesen 3, PAAA; "Les germes de conflit en Amérique du Sud et la situation respective des puissances intéressées," Oct. 3, 1928, 7N3375, dossier 5, AAM.

6. AA to Reichsministerium des Innern, Oct. 26, 1926, Preussischer Minister des Innern to Reichsminister des Innern, Jan. 24, 1927, III, Nic., Pol. 13, PAAA; Kühlmann to AA, Dec. 23, 1927, III, S. Salv., Pol. 5, PAAA.

7. Rosenblum brothers to criminal division (Berlin), Oct. 28, 1925, AA to Tattenbach, April 27, 1926, and enclosures, III, S. Salv., Innere 6, PAAA; Kühlmann to AA, March 22, 1927, March 20, 1928, Ger. leg. to AA, April 6, 1929, III, S. Salv., Pol. 13, PAAA; Kühlmann to AA, April 25, 1929, III, S. Salv., Pol. 11, Nr. 1, PAAA.

8. "Influence allemande au Guatemala," enclosed with C. Chartier to war minister, Dec. 31, 1925, 7N3376, dossier 2, Archive de l'armée de la terre, Paris; Dietrich von Lentz to AA, Jan. 29, 1927, enclosing F. Mora to Peter Bock, Jan. 28, 1927, III, Guat., Pol. 26, PAAA; AA to Ger. minister in Guat., Aug. 23, 1928, III, Guat., Pol. 13, PAAA; Kühlmann to AA, Nov. 5, 1926, III, Guat., Pol. 11, Nr. 3, PAAA; Kühlmann to Bobrik, April 28, 1927, Bobrik to Kühlmann, May 18, 1927, III, Guat., Handel 13, PAAA; AA to Preussisches Justizministerium, March 1, 1929, III, Nic., Verkehrswesen 10, PAAA; AA to Ger. minister in Guat., Nov. 14, 1929, III, Guat., Pol. 11, Nr. 1, PAAA.

9. Hamburg Handelskammer to Hamburg Deputation für Handel, Schiffahrt und Gewerbe, June 7, July 24, 1926, Georg Ahrens to Ger. minister in Guat., Dec. 14, 1927, Kühlmann to AA, Dec. 30, 1927, III, Guat., Sozialpolitik 1, PAAA; Kühlmann to AA, June 8, 25, Sept. 23, Nov. 9, 1926, Neumann to Ger. minister in Guat., Dec. 20, 1926, Jan. 28, 1927, III, Pan., Sozialpolitik 2, PAAA.

10. Kühlmann to AA, June 8, 25, Sept. 23, Nov. 9, 1926, Neumann to Ger. minister in Guat., Dec. 20, 1926, Jan. 28, 1927, III, Pan., Sozialpolitik 2, PAAA.

11. Johannes Kretzschmar, "Bemerkungen über die Verhältnisse in Guatemala, San Salvador und Mexiko auf Grund einer Ende 1925 ausgeführten Reise," July 14, 1926, III, N.-Amer., Pol. 5, PAAA.

12. "Reisebericht," Gustav Noske to Preussischer Minister des Innern, June 28, 1927, III, M.-Amer., Pol. 15, PAAA; AA to Noske [Dec. 15, 1926], III, M.-Amer., Verkehrswesen 12, PAAA; Wallerstein, *Historical Capitalism*, 72, 82; Gustav Noske, *Erlebtes aus Aufstieg und Wiedergang einer Demokratie* (Offenbach, FRG: Karl Drott, 1947), only treats domestic events.

13. "Reisebericht," Noske to Preussischer Minister des Innern, June 28, 1927, III, M.-Amer., Pol. 15, PAAA.

14. "Reisebericht," Noske to Preussischer Minister des Innern, June 28, 1927, III, M.-Amer., Pol. 15, PAAA; AA to Noske [Dec. 15, 1926], III, M.-Amer., Verkehrswesen 12, PAAA.

15. Walter de Haas, Denkschrift (circular to German ministries and state governments), Aug. 31, 1925, Reichsfinanzministerium, R2/24601, BAK; Kühlmann to AA, Nov. 9, 1925, III, Hond., Pol. 5, PAAA; Entwurf eines Gesetzes über das Handelsabkommen zwischen dem Deutschen Reiche und Honduras [March 4, 1926], Reichskanzlei, R431/1096, BAK; Cornelsen to Ger. minister in Guat., Dec. 9, 1927, III, Hond., Sozialpolitik 1, PAAA; Hamburg Handelskammer, *Bericht über das Jahr 1927* (Hamburg: Handelskammer Hamburg [1927]), 174–75, S6-991, Dortmund IHK; Zweigstelle des AA für Aussenhandel to AA, Jan. 10, 1927, AA to Zweigstelle des AA für Aussenhandel, Jan. 10, 1927, III, Hond., Handel 30, PAAA; extract of commercial report, Dec. 15, 1927, 4.49.58/14, Hond., SAB.

16. Kühlmann to AA, Feb. 10, Sept. 8, 1926, III, Hond., Rechtswesen 28, PAAA; Cornelsen to Kühlmann, April 1, 1927, III, Hond., Pol. 5, PAAA.

17. Kühlmann to AA, Aug. 31, 1927, AA to Ger. minister in Guat., Oct. 20, 1927, Deutsche Botschaft Rom, M.-Amer., Pol. 3, PAAA; Kühlmann to AA, Sept. 24, 1927, III, Hond., Rechtswesen 28, PAAA.

18. Francisco José Calderón to AA, May 1, 1927, Deutscher Wirtschaftsdienst to AA, June 28, 1927, III, Nic., Handel 11, Nr. 5, PAAA; Bunge to AA, Dec. 17, 1927, III, Nic., Handel 24, Nr. 8, PAAA; Wellstein to [?], Jan. 16, 1928, III, Nic., Wirtschaft 1, PAAA.

19. Extract of a letter, June 10, 1929, enclosed with Zentralstelle für wirtschaftlichen Auslandsnachrichtendienst to AA, July 8, 1929, III, Nic., Handel 11, PAAA; extract from German consulate to [?], Aug. 19, 1929, 4.49 73/18 (Nic.), SAB.

20. Kühlmann to AA, Sept. 12, 1925, III, CR, Industrie 30, PAAA; extract from a commercial report, Dec. 14, 1927, 4.49.56/14, Guat., SAB.

21. Extract of consular dispatch, Dec. 7, 1927, 4.49.56/16, Guat., SAB; "Beantwortung des Fragebogens des Enquete-Ausschusses für die Republik Panama," [1927], III, Pan., Handel 11, PAAA; "Beantwortung des Fragebogens des Enquete-Ausschusses für die Republik Costa Rica," [1927], III, CR, Handel 11, PAAA; "Beantwortung des Fragebogens des Enquete-Ausschusses für den Freistaat El Salvador," [1927], III, S. Salv., Handel 11, PAAA; Lentz to Kühlmann, Sept. 25, 1927, III, Pan., Handel 11, PAAA; extract of consular report, April 25, 1928, 4.49.56/14, SAB; Sauter to AA, Sept. 16, 1927, III, CR, Handel 24, Nr. 8, PAAA; Karl Sapper, *Reise nach Süd- und Mittelamerika, 1927/28* (Würzburg: E. Mönnich, 1929), 144–45.

22. Deutscher Wirtschaftsdienst, "Wichtigere Handelsfirmen in Nicaragua," Sept. 5, 1927, III, Nic., Handel 24, Nr. 4, PAAA; Deutscher Wirtschaftsdienst, "Wichtigere Handelsfirmen in Costa Rica," enclosed with Ahrens to AA, Nov. 15, 1927, III, CR, Handel 24, Nr. 8, PAAA; Deutscher Wirtschaftsdienst, "Wichtigere Handelshäuser und Unternehmen in Honduras," [1927], III, Hond., Handel 24, Nr. 4, PAAA; Meyeren to all Regierungspräsidenten, Feb. 25, 1928, III, CR, Handel

22, PAAA; Zentralstelle für den wirtschaftlichen Auslandsnachrichtendienst to various service stations, April 2, 1928, and annexes, Ahrens to AA, May 13, 1928, III, CR, Handel 39, Nr. 1, PAAA.

23. Kühlmann to AA, April 6, 1927, III, S. Salv., Handel 20, PAAA; "Beantwortung des Fragebogens des Enquete-Ausschusses für die Republik Panama" [1927], III, Pan., Handel 11, PAAA; "Beantwortung des Fragebogens des Enquete-Ausschusses für Costa Rica" [1927], circular, Zentralstelle für den wirtschaftlichen Auslandsnachrichtendienst, Feb. 6, 1928, III, CR, Handel 11, PAAA; "Beantwortung des Fragebogens des Enquete-Ausschusses für El Salvador," [1927], III, S. Salv., Handel 11, PAAA; Kühlmann to AA, Dec. 21, 1927, April 3, 1928, Jan. 22, 1929, III, Nic., Pol. 5, vol. 2, PAAA; Hamburg Handelskammer, *Bericht über das Jahr 1927*, 174–75, Hamburg Handelskammer, *Bericht über das Jahr 1928* (Hamburg: Handelskammer Hamburg, 1928), S6–991, Dortmund IHK; Jantzen, *Hamburgs Ausfuhrhandel*, 67–71.

24. Reichswirtschaftsminister to Reichskanzlei, Feb. 16, 1928, R431/1175, BAK.

25. Dr. Goetz to CR con. gen., Aug. 2, 1927, MRE, caja 294, leg.-Alemania, AN, CR; Kühlmann to AA, Jan. 26, 1929, III, M.-Amer., Allgemeines 3, PAAA.

26. Ronaldo Fálconer Davenport [Sept. 1927], MRE, caja 294, leg.-Alemania, AN, CR; Louis Delius and Co. to Bremen IHK, Sept. 9, 1929, HP II 57 (CR), Bremen IHK.

27. Ger. leg. [?] to AA, Oct. 21, 1929, 4.49, 56/14, SAB; Kühlmann to AA, Oct. 30, 1929, III, M.-Amer., Handel 11, PAAA; corres. 1928–1929, III, M.-Amer., Handel 24, Nr. 6, PAAA.

28. Leon Guttmann to AA, July 15, 1922, Mora, Ansprache des Gesandten, May 1928, III, Guat., Pol. 9, PAAA; Vorsitzender des Vereins guatemalischer Firmen to Bobrik, Sept. 19, 1922, Bobrik to Polizeipräsidium in Wiesbaden, Sept. 21, 1922, Kühlmann to AA, March 20, 1928, III, Guat., Pol. 11, Nr. 3, PAAA; "Aufzeichnung über die Persönlichkeit des Gesandten von Guatemala Federico Mora," with AA to Reichskanzlei, May 5, 1928, Reichskanzlei, R431/102b, Süd-America, 1928–1933, BAK.

29. Hamburg Senatskommission für die Reichs- und auswärtigen Angelegenheiten to AA, Dec., 24, 1925, and other corres., III, Guat., Pol. 9, PAAA.

30. Cornelsen to Kühlmann, Feb. 13, 1929, Staatsamt für auswärtige Angelegenheiten, Feb. 22, 1929, III, Hond., Pol. 9, PAAA.

31. Bunge to Kühlmann, Nov. 4, 1925, Sept. 26, Nov. 7, Dec. 4, 1926, March 27, 1927, Kühlmann to AA, Dec. 4, 1925, April 15, 1926, Nov. 25, 1926, April 7, 1927, III, Nic., Pol. 5, vol. 1, PAAA; "Deutschland als Hausdiener der Vereinigten Staaten," *Die Welt am Abend*, Jan. 15, 1927, III, Nic., Pol. 2, PAAA; Bunge to Ger. minister in Guat., Jan. 16, 1927, III, Nic., Rechtswesen 28, PAAA; Lentz to AA, Jan. 21, 1927, III, Nic., Pol. 3 (Nic.-Ver. St.), vol. 1, PAAA.

32. Kühlmann to AA, Dec. 21, 1927, April 3, 1928, Jan. 22, 1929, III, Nic., Pol. 5, vol. 2, PAAA; Wilhelm Hüper to Ger. cons. in Nic., May 31, 1928, Hüper to Lentz, Sept. 29, 1928, III, Nic., Pol. 10, PAAA; Lentz to AA, Feb. 5, 1929, III, Nic., Pol. 2, PAAA; Ute Hasse, "Probleme des antiimperialistischen Kampfes in Lateinamerika in den Jahren 1927–1932 in der Darstellung der zeitgenössischen deutschen Presse," *Wissenschaftliche Zeitschrift der Universität Rostock* 14 (1965):131–52.

33. [Illegible] to Bremen IHK, Sept. 26, 1929, HP II 57 (CR), Bremen IHK; III, Ahrens to Ger. leg. in Guat., July 5, 1928, endorsed by Lentz, July 16, 1928, Haas, memo, Dec. 9, 1928, Kühlmann to AA, July 17, 1929, III, CR, Handel 13, PAAA.

34. MRE to CR inspector general of consuls, Sept. 7, 1928, MRE, caja 309, leg.-Consules de CR en el extranjero, AN, CR; Kümpel, *La bancarotta del liberalismo*.

35. Extract of a Kühlmann letter, May 28, 1929, Kühlmann to AA, July 17, 1929, Aug. 20, 1929, Reichswirtschaftsminister to AA, Sept. 12, 1929, Hamburgische Gesandtschaft to AA, Nov. 1, 1929, III, CR, Handel 13, PAAA; Deutscher Industrie- und Handelstag to Bremen IHK, Sept. 5, 1929, Teodoro Gathmann and Co. to Bremen IHK, Sept. 18, 1929, Frankfurt IHK to Deutscher Industrie- und Handelstag, Sept. 25, 1929 [illegible], to Bremen IHK, Sept. 26, 1929, HP II 57 (CR), Bremen IHK.

36. "Guatemala—Installation of Modern Telephone System," June 22, 1925, RG 165, MID, 2280-P-28, NA; "Mitteilung Nr. 17, Nachtrag 9, Übersee-Abteilung," Nov. 10, 1926, Organisation der Vertretungen in Mittelamerika, 1894–, 68/Li 260, Siemens Institut; Kühlmann to AA, Jan. 26, 1929, III, M.-Amer., Allgemeines 3, PAAA.

37. Henri Eugène Aymé-Martin to MAE, Aug. 25, 1927, F^{30} 1956: Guat., AMEF; Kühlmann to AA, Sept. 2, 1927, III, Guat., Pol. 5, PAAA; Lentz to AA, Oct. 15, 1928, III, Guat., Wege- und Strassenwesen 1, PAAA.

38. Kühlmann to AA, Sept. 16, 25, Nov. 24, 1925, Aug. 31, 1926, Aug. 10, Dec. 21, 1927, Walter Sprung to Kühlmann, Nov. 6, 1925, May 5, Sept. 27, 1926, Feb. 28, April 1, June 6, July 28, 1927, Lentz to Kühlmann, Aug. 26, 1927, AA to Ger. minister in Guat., April 27, 1927, Haas to Ger. leg. in Guat., Jan. 17, 1929, Kühlmann to AA, Aug. 29, 1929, Wayss-Freytag, Oct. 14, 1929, III, CR, Industrie 30, PAAA; Kühlmann to AA, Jan. 11, 1928, Lentz to AA, July 23, 1928, III, CR, Handel 30, Nr. 1, PAAA; Hamburg Handelskammer, *Bericht über das Jahr 1928*.

39. CR minister to Ricardo Castro Beeche, June 1, 1927, MRE, caja 300, leg.-Guat., Rafael Oreamuno to Castro Beeche, Sept. 27, Oct. 12, Nov. 7, 1927, MRE, caja 297, leg.-EU, AN, CR; MRE to CR cons. gen. in Hamburg, Oct. 20, 1927, MRE, l.c. 215, AN, CR; Aymé-Martin to MAE, Aug. 25, 1927, F^{30} 1956: Guat., AMEF; Ahrens to AA, Sept. 30, 1928, III, CR, Eisenbahnwesen 18, PAAA.

40. Kühlmann to AA, Sept. 16, 25, Nov. 24, 1925, Aug. 31, 1926, Aug. 10, Dec. 21, 1927, Sprung to Kühlmann, Nov. 6, 1925, May 5, Sept. 27, 1926, Feb. 28, April 1, June 6, July 28, 1927, Lentz to Kühlmann, Aug. 26, 1927, AA to Ger. minister in Guat., April 27, 1927, III, CR, Industrie 30, PAAA.

41. Kühlmann to AA, Sept. 16, 25, Nov. 24, 1925, Aug. 31, 1926, Aug. 10, Dec. 21, 1927, Sprung to Kühlmann, Nov. 6, 1925, May 5, Sept. 27, 1926, Feb. 28, April 1, June 6, July 28, 1927, Lentz to Kühlmann, Aug. 26, 1927, III, CR, Industrie 30, PAAA.

42. Kühlmann to AA, Jan. 11, 1928, Lentz to AA, July 23, 1928, III, CR, Handel 30, Nr. 1, PAAA; Haas to Ger. leg. in Guat., Jan. 17, 1929, Kühlmann to AA, Aug. 29 1929, Wayss-Freytag, Oct. 14, 1929, III, CR, Industrie 3, PAAA.

43. Cornelsen to Kühlmann, Dec. 4, 1928, III, Hond., Industrie 10, PAAA.

44. "Reisebericht," Noske to Preussischer Minister des Innern, June 28, 1927, III, M.-Amer., Pol. 15, PAAA; Lutz to AA, Jan. 26, 1924, III, Pan., Pol. 2, PAAA;

Karl Lachner to MRE, May 22, Aug. 1, 1928, MRE, caja 303, leg.-Alemania, AN, CR; MRE to Lachner, Sept. 5, 1928, MRE, caja 309, leg.-Consules de CR en el extranjero, AN, CR; Sapper, *Mittel-Amerika* (1927), 108–16.

45. Lachner to MRE, March 11, Nov. 22, Dec. 17, 1929, and enclosures, Guido von Schröter to Lachner, April 22, 1929, MRE, caja 315, leg.-Alemania I, AN, CR.

46. "Aufzeichnung über die Persönlichkeit des Gesandten von El Salvador, Ismael G. Fuentes," AA Protokoll, Oct. 24, 1927, Reichskanzlei, R431/102a, Süd-Amerika, 1919–1927, BAK; Aymé-Martin to MAE, April 26, 1929, E. Gissot to MAE, Aug. 2, 1929, Amér. 1918–1940, Cent. Amer., num. 8, AMAE; Kühlmann to AA, Sept. 9, 1929, AA draft memo of conversation, Nov. 29, 1929, III, S. Salv., Pol. 2, PAAA.

47. "Les Germes de conflit en Amérique du Sud et la situation respective des puissances intéressées," Oct. 3, 1928, 7N3375, dossier 5, AAM; Pade, "Die Expansionspolitik des deutschen Imperialismus gegenüber Lateinamerika," 584–89.

Conclusion and Epilogue

1. Lothar Gall, ed., *Liberalismus* (Königstein/Ts.: Verlagsgruppe Athenäum, Hain, Scriptor, Hanstein, 1980); Herbert Goldhammer, *The Foreign Powers in Latin America* (Princeton, NJ: Princeton University Press, 1972); Bernard Lietaer, *Europe and Latin America and the Multinationals* (Westmead, Eng.: Saxon House, 1979); Fritz Stern, *The Failure of Illiberalism: Essays on the Political Culture of Modern Germany* (New York: Alfred A. Knopf, 1972).

2. Fischer, *Die Weltwirtschaft im 20. Jahrhundert*; Hallgarten and Radkau, *Deutsche Industrie und Politik von Bismarck bis in die Gegenwart*, 229–538; Edelberto Torres-Rivas, "Poder nacional y sociedad dependiente," in Edelberto Torres-Rivas, ed., *Financiamiento extranjero en América Central* (San José, CR: EDUCA, 1974), 15–42.

3. Reichswirtschaftsminister to Reichskanzlei, Feb. 16, 1928, R431/1175, BAK.

4. Evans, Rueschemeyer, and Skocpol, eds., *Bringing the State Back In*; William Appleman Williams, *The Tragedy of American Diplomacy* (New York: Dell, 1972).

5. Edward B. Glick, *Germany and Latin America* (Santa Monica, CA: Rand Corporation, 1968); Stanley E. Hilton, "Latin America and Western Europe, 1880–1945: The Political Dimension," in Wolf Grabendorff and Riordan Roett, eds., *Latin America, Western Europe, and the United States* (New York: Praeger, 1985); Hans-Jürgen Puhle, "Die Politik der USA in Mittelamerika: Eine self-fulfilling prophecy," *Vorgänge. Zeitschrift für Gesellschaftpolitik* 54 (1981):29–41; Manfred Scharbius, "Zur Politik des deutschen Faschismus in Mittelamerika und Westindien," in Heinz Sanke, ed., *Der deutsche Faschismus in Lateinamerika, 1933–1943* (Berlin: Humboldt, 1966), 145–57.

Research Resources on Germany in Central America

■

Much of the material for this study came from obvious, traditional sources. In addition to the Politisches Archiv des Auswärtigen Amtes (Bonn), the Bundesarchive in Freiburg, Merseburg, Potsdam, and Koblenz and the Staatsarchive in Hamburg and Bremen supplied valuable materials. Documents in the Krupp and Siemens archives offered special perspectives. Additional documentation came from archives in Munich, Frankfurt, Berlin, and Stuttgart.

The records of other nations present different views of German activity on the isthmus. The U.S. National Archives, Record Group 59 (and to a lesser extent RGs 40, 80, 151, and 165), and the French foreign ministry archives contain numerous reports on German activity. The Spanish foreign ministry archives also offered insights into German activity. The Costa Rican Archivo Nacional and the Guatemalan Archivo General de Centro América supplied material on the German presence in Costa Rican and Guatemalan societies. Germans engaged in the coffee industry, numerous colonies, and a variety of enterprises and investments. The extensive Erwin Paul Dieseldorff collection at Tulane University contains interesting material on German coffee planter activity in Guatemala. Branches of the Friedrich Köper family resided in Germany and Guatemala; its business and family papers at the Bremen Staatsarchiv should prove extremely valuable when organized and ready for examination.

No broad studies focus on German–Central American relations. Hendrik Dane, *Die wirtschaftlichen Beziehungen Deutschlands zu Mexiko und Mittelamerika im 19. Jahrhundert* (Cologne: Böhlau, 1971), offers a fact-oriented study of the 1820 to 1870 period. Julio Castellanos Cambranes, *El imperialismo alemán en Guatemala: El tratado de comercio de 1887* (Guatemala: Instituto de Investigaciones Económicas y Sociales de la Universidad de San Carlos de Guatemala, 1977), and "Aspectos del desarrollo socio-económico y político de Guatemala, 1868–1885, en base a materiales de archivos alemanes," *Política y sociedad* 3 (Jan.–June 1977):7–14, interprets German-Guatemalan relations in the late nineteenth century. Several of my publications describe German relations with Central America in an international perspective: "Imperialism in Middle America: United States Competition with Britain, Germany, and France in Middle America, 1820s–1920s," in Rhodri Jefferys-Jones, ed., *Eagle Against Empire: American Opposition to European Imperialism, 1914–1982* (Aix-en-Provence, France: Université de Provence, 1983):41–58;

"Metropole Rivalry in Central America, 1820s to 1929: An Overview," in Ralph Lee Woodward, Jr., ed., *Central America: Historical Perspectives on the Contemporary Crisis* (Westport, CT: Greenwood, 1988), 21–46; *The United States in Central America: Episodes of Social Imperialism and Imperial Rivalry in the World System* (Durham, NC: Duke University Press, 1991).

My understanding of German society from the 1820s to the 1930s benefited from the works of Lothar Gall, *Bismarck: The White Revolutionary,* trans. J. A. Underwood, 2 vols. (London: Urwin Hyman, 1990); Gerd Hardach, *Deutschland in der Weltwirtschaft, 1870–1970: Eine Einführung in die Sozial- und Wirtschaftsgeschichte* (Frankfurt: Campus, 1977); William O. Henderson, *The Rise of German Industrial Power, 1834–1914* (Berkeley: University of California Press, 1975); Hajo Holborn, *A History of Modern Germany, 1840–1945* (New York: Knopf, 1969); Otto Pflanze, *Bismarck and the Development of Germany,* 3 vols. (Princeton: Princeton University Press, 1963–1990); Nicole P`iètri, *Evolution économique de l'Allemagne du milieu du XIXe siècle à 1914* (Paris: SEDES, 1982); Reinhard Rürup, "Deutschland im 19. Jahrhundert, 1815–1871," in Reinhard Rürup, Hans-Ulrich Wehler, and Gerhard Schulz, *Deutsche Geschichte,* 3 vols. (Göttingen: Vandenhoeck und Ruprecht, 1985), 3:3–200; James J. Sheehan, *German Liberalism in the Nineteenth Century: The Wilhelmine Age, 1890–1914* (Chicago: University of Chicago Press, 1978); Michael Stürmer, *Das ruhelose Reich. Deutschland, 1866–1918* (Berlin: Siedler, 1983); and Hans-Ulrich Wehler, *Das deutsche Kaiserreich, 1871–1918* (Göttingen: Vandenhoeck und Ruprecht, 1973). Hubert Kiesewetter, "Economic Preconditions for Germany's Nation-Building in the Nineteenth Century," in Hagen Schulze, ed., *Nation-Building in Central Europe* (Leamington Spa, UK: Berg, 1987), 81–105; and Michael Stürmer, *Die Reichsgründung: Deutscher Nationalstaat und europäisches Gleichgewicht im Zeitalter Bismarcks* (Munich: dtv, 1984), facilitate understanding of the formation of a unified German state.

Various German scholars have illuminated specific periods in German history: Hagen Schulze, *Der Weg zum Nationalstaat: Die deutsche Nationalbewegung vom 18. Jahrhundert bis zur Reichsgründung* (Munich: dtv, 1985); Peter Burg, *Der Wiener Kongress: Der Deutsche Bund im europäischen Staatensystem* (Munich: dtv, 1984); Theodor Schieder, *Vom Deutschen Bund zum Deutschen Reich, 1815–1871* (Munich: dtv, 1975); Wolfgang Hardtwig, *Vormärz: Der monarchische Staat und das Bürgertum* (Munich: dtv, 1985); Helmut Böhme, *Deutschlands Weg zur Grossmacht: Studien zum Verhältnis von Wirtschaft und Staat während der Reichsgründungszeit, 1848–1881,* 2d ed. (Cologne: Kiepenheuer und Witsch, 1972); Hans-Peter Ullmann, *Das Deutsche Kaiserreich, 1871–1918* (Frankfurt: Suhrkamp, 1995); Richard H. Tilly, *Vom Zollverein zum Industriestaat: Die wirtschaftlich-soziale Entwicklung Deutschlands, 1834 bis 1914* (Munich: dtv, 1990); Wilfried Loth, *Das Kaiserreich: Obrigkeitsstaat und politische Mobilisierung* (Munich: dtv, 1996); Günter Ogger, *Die Gründerjahre: Als der Kapitalismus jung und verwegen war* (Munich: Knaur, 1995); Fritz Klein, *Deutschland, 1897/98–1917* (Berlin, GDR: VEB Deutscher Verlag der Wissenschaften, 1977); Peter Krüger, *Versailles: Deutsche Aussenpolitik zwischen Revisionismus und Friedensicherung* (Munich: dtv, 1986); Wolfgang Ruge, *Deutschland, 1917–1933* (Berlin, GDR: VEB Deutscher Verlag der Wissenschaften, 1978); Horst Möller, *Weimar: Die unvollendete Demokratie* (Munich: dtv, 1985); Karl Buchheim, *Die Wei-*

marer Republik. Das Deutsche Reich ohne Kaiser (Munich: Wilhelm Heine, 1970); Detlev J. K. Peukert, *Die Weimarer Republik* (Frankfurt: Suhrkamp, 1987).

The Zollverein spurred on German industrialization and, indirectly, German expansion; see Rolf H. Dumke, "Der deutsche Zollverein als Modell ökonomischer Integration," in Helmut Berding, ed., *Wirtschaftliche und politische Integration in Europa im 19. und 20. Jahrhundert* (Göttingen: Vandenhoeck und Ruprecht, 1984):71–101. German industrial growth can be followed in Werner Abelshauser and Dietmar Petzina, eds., *Deutsche Wirtschaftsgeschichte im Industriezeitalter. Konjunktur, Krise, Wachstum* (Düsseldorf: Athenäum/Droste, 1981); Rudolf Braun, Wolfram Fischer, Helmut Grosskreutz, and Heinrich Volkmann, eds., *Industrielle Revolution: Wirtschaftliche Aspekte* (Cologne: Kiepenheuer und Witsch, 1972); Hubert Kiesewetter, *Industrielle Revolution in Deutschland, 1815–1914* (Frankfurt: Suhrkamp, 1989); Reinhard Spree, *Die Wachstumszyklen der deutschen Wirtschaft von 1840 bis 1880* (Berlin: Duncker und Humblot, 1977); Hans Rosenberg, *Grosse Depression und Bismarckzeit*, 2d ed. (Berlin: Walter de Gruyter, 1976); Wolfram Fischer, *Wirtschaft und Gesellschaft im Zeitalter der Industrialisierung* (Göttingen: Vandenhoeck und Ruprecht, 1972); George W. F. Hallgarten and Joachim Radkau, *Deutsche Industrie und Politik von Bismarck bis in die Gegenwart* (Reinbek: Rowohlt, 1981); Jürgen Sandweg and Michael Stürmer, *Industrialisierung und soziale Frage in Deutschland im 19. Jahrhundert* (Munich: R. Oldenbourg, 1979). Christoph Buchheim, *Industrielle Revolution: Langfristige Wirtschaftsentwicklung in Grossbritannien, Europa und in Übersee* (Munich: dtv, 1994), links industrialization to expansion.

My comprehension of German foreign policy profited from Imanuel Geiss, *Der lange Weg in die Katastrophe: Die Vorgeschichte des Ersten Weltkriegs, 1815–1914* (Munich: Piper, 1990); Imanuel Geiss, "Sozialstruktur und imperialistische Dispositionen im zweiten deutschen Kaiserreich," in Karl Holl and Günther List, eds., *Liberalismus und imperialistischer Staat: Der Imperialismus als Problem liberaler Parteien in Deutschland, 1890–1914* (Göttingen: Vandenhoeck und Ruprecht, 1975):40–61; Wolfgang Mommsen, *Der autoritäre Nationalstaat: Verfassung, Gesellschaft und Kultur im deutschen Kaiserreich* (Frankfurt: Fischer, 1990); Wolfgang Mommsen, "Der moderne Imperialismus als innergesellschaftliches Phänomen," in Wolfgang J. Mommsen, ed., *Der moderne Imperialismus* (Stuttgart: Kohlhammer, 1971):14–30; Hans-Ulrich Wehler, "Der Aufstieg des organisierten Kapitalismus und Interventionsstaates in Deutschland," in Heinrich August Winkler, ed., *Organisierter Kapitalismus: Voraussetzungen und Aufsätze* (Göttingen: Vandenhoeck und Ruprecht, 1974):36–57; Wehler, "Industrial Growth and Early German Imperialism," 71–92. Kurt Doss, *Das deutsche Auswärtige Amt in Übergang vom Kaiserreich zur Weimarer Republik. Die Schülerische Reform* (Düsseldorf: Droste, 1977), describes reform of the early-twentieth-century German foreign ministry.

German expansion is often linked to the Bismarck era. The following scholarship outlines German expansion in the Bismarck years: Fritz Stern, *Gold and Iron: Bismarck, Bleichroeder, and the Building of the German Empire* (New York: Alfred A. Knopf, 1977); Klaus J. Bade, *Friedrich Fabri und der Imperialismus in der Bismarckzeit: Revolution—Depression—Expansion* (Freiburg: Atlantis, 1975); Hartmut Pogge von Strandmann, "Domestic Origins of Germany's Colonial Expansion under Bismarck," *Past and Present* 42 (1969):140–59; Hans-Ulrich Wehler, *Bismarck und der*

Imperialismus (Cologne: Kiepenheuer und Witsch, 1969); Wolfgang Zorn, "Wirtschaft und Politik im deutschen Imperialismus," in Gilbert Ziebura, ed., *Grundfragen der deutschen Aussenpolitik seit, 1871* (Darmstadt: Wissenschaftliche Buchgesellschaft, 1975):163–89; Holl and List, eds., *Liberalismus und imperialistischer Staat.* In the 1870s, Heinrich Claussen, "Überproduktion und Krisis," *Preussische Jahrbücher* 44 (1879):490–517, tied overproduction to expansion. Cornelius Fischer's "Korvetten vor Corinto," *Die Zeit,* Aug. 17, 1990, p. 12, is a graphic narrative of the German military landing at Corinto, Nicaragua, in 1878.

Some theories that seem relevant to German expansion are free trade expansion, world system, social imperialism, and organized capitalism. Fernand Braudel, *Civilisation matérielle, économie et capitalisme, xvᵉ-xviiiᵉ siècle,* 3 vols. (Paris: Armand Colin, 1979) [translated as *The Structures of Everyday Life, The Wheels of Commerce,* and *The Perspective of the World* (New York: Harper, 1984)]; Fernand Braudel, *Afterthoughts on Material Civilization and Capitalism* (Baltimore: Johns Hopkins University Press, 1977); and Immanuel Wallerstein, *The Modern World System,* 3 vols. (Orlando: Academic Press, 1974–1988), are closely associated with world system theory. Christopher Chase-Dunn, "Core-Periphery Relations: The Effects of Core Competition," in Barbara Hockey Kaplan, ed., *Social Change in the Capitalist World Economy* (Beverley Hills: Sage, 1978), 159–76, examines the relationship of core country competition on the periphery (for instance, areas like Central America). Theda Skocpol, "Wallerstein's World Capitalist System: A Theoretic and Historical Critique," *American Journal of Sociology* 82 (March 1977):1075–102, and Theda Skocpol, ed., *Vision and Method in Historical Sociology* (Cambridge: Cambridge University Press, 1984), critique and evaluate world system theory. Andre Gunder Frank, *Capitalism and Underdevelopment in Latin America* (New York: Monthly Review, 1967), and Fernando H. Cardosos and Enzo Faletto, *Dependency and Development in Latin America* (Berkeley: University of California Press, 1979), are the standard works on dependency theory. John Gallagher and Ronald Robinson, "The Imperialism of Free Trade," *Economic History Review,* 2d ser., 6 (1953):1–15, is the basic work on free trade imperialism. Perhaps the first study of social imperialism was Adolf Grabowsky, *Der Sozialimperialismus als letzte Etappe des Imperialismus* (Basel: Weltpolitisches Archiv, 1939). Owen and Sutcliffe, eds., *Studies in the Theory of Imperialism;* Wolfgang Mommsen, *Imperialismustheorien: Ein Überblick über die neueren Imperialismusinterpretationen,* 2d rev. ed. (Göttingen: Vandenhoeck und Ruprecht, 1980); Peter F. Klaren and Thomas J. Bossert, eds., *Promises of Development: Theories of Change in Latin America* (Boulder, CO: Westview, 1986); Jonathan Hartlyn and Samuel A. Morley, eds., *Latin American Political Economy: Financial Crisis and Political Change* (Boulder, CO: Westview, 1986); Edward Weisband, ed., *Poverty Amidst Plenty: World Political Economy and Distributive Justice* (Boulder, CO: Westview, 1989); George T. Crane and Abla Amawi, eds., *The Theoretical Evolution of International Political Economy* (New York: Oxford University Press, 1991), introduce readers to theoretical approaches and some case studies.

The debate over continuity and discontinuity and over organized capitalism, social imperialism, and the critiques of these theories are found in the works of Geoff Eley, "Defining Social Imperialism: Use and Abuse of an Idea," *Social History* 1 (1976):265–90; Geoff Eley, "Social Imperialism in Germany," in *Festschrift für George W. F. Hallgarten* (Munich: C. H. Beck, 1976):71–86; Volker Hentschel, *Deutsche Wirtschafts- und Sozialpolitik, 1815–1945* (Düsseldorf: Droste, 1980); Volker Hentschel, *Wirtschaft und Wirtschaftspolitik im wilhelminischen Deutschland. Organisierter Kapitalismus und Interventionsstaat?* (Stuttgart: Klett-Cotta, 1978); Kocka, "Organisierter Kapitalismus oder staatsmonopolistischer Kapitalismus? Begriffliche Vorbemerkungen," in Winckler, ed., *Organisierter Kapitalismus,* 19–35; Hans-Ulrich Wehler, "Sozialdarwinismus im expandierenden Industriestaat," in Imanuel Geiss and Bernd Jürgen Wendt, eds., *Deutschland in der Weltpolitik des 19. und 20. Jahrhunderts* (Düsseldorf: Bertelsmann Universitätsverlag, 1974):133–42.

Germans migrated in large numbers, quite a few to Latin America. Klaus J. Bade, ed., *Population, Labour and Migration in 19th and 20th Century Germany* (New York: St. Martin's, 1987); Jean-Pierre Blancpain, "Identité nationale et tradition culturelle: Le Germanisme en Amérique latine," *Recherches germaniques* (Strasbourg) 12 (1982):188–220; Peter Marschalck, *Deutsche Überseewanderung im 19. Jahrhundert* (Stuttgart: Ernst Klett, 1973); and Wilhelm Mönckmeier, *Die deutsche überseeische Auswanderung* (Jena: Gustav Fischer, 1912), treat German colonization more generally. A useful bibliography is Manfred Illi, "Die deutsche Auswanderung nach Lateinamerika. Eine Literaturübersicht," *Lateinamerika-Studien* 2 (1977):1–176.

The German colonization in Central America was extensive already in the 1830s and 1840s. The Belgian settlement project at Santo Tomás in Guatemala is described in William J. Griffith, *Empires in the Wilderness: Foreign Colonization and Development in Guatemala, 1834–1844* (Chapel Hill: University of North Carolina Press, 1965), and Nicolas Leysbeth, *Historique de la colonisation belge à Santo Tomás de Guatemala* (Bruxelles: n.p., 1938). Useful for the study of German migration to the Central American isthmus are the relevant essays in Harmut Froeschle, ed., *Die Deutschen in Lateinamerika: Schicksal und Leistung* (Tübingen: Horst Erdmann, 1979):565–76, 577–96, 597–606, 631–49; Götz von Houwald, *Los alemanes en Nicaragua* (Managua: Banco de América, 1975); Werner F. Leopold, "Der Deutsche in Costa Rica," *Hamburger Wirtschaftschronik* 3 (Oct. 1966):133–214; Karl Sapper, "Ansiedlung von Europäern in Mittelamerika," *Schriften des Vereins für Sozialpolitik* 117 (1912):3–67; Herbert Schottelius, *Mittelamerika als Schauplatz deutscher Kolonisationsversuche, 1840–1865* (Hamburg: Hans Christians, 1939); Galvin B. Henderson, "German Colonial Projects on the Mosquito Coast, 1844–1848," *English Historical Review* 59 (May 1944):257–71.

The roles of Germans and German influences in Latin American and Central American societies are described in various studies: Walther L. Bernecker and Thomas Fischer, "Deutschland und Lateinamerika im Zeitalter des Imperialismus, 1871–1914," *Ibero-Amerikanisches Archiv,* n.s., 21:3–4 (1995):273–302; Gerhard Brunn, "Deutscher Einfluss und deutsche Interessen in der Professionalisierung einiger lateinamerikanischer Armeen vor dem 1. Weltkrieg (1885–1914)," *Jahrbuch für Geschichte von Staat, Wirtschaft und Gesellschaft Lateinamerikas* 6 (1969):278–336; Gerhart Jacob-Wendler, *Deutsche Elektroindustrie in Lateinamerika: Siemens und AEG (1890–1914)* (Stuttgart: Klett-Cotta, 1982); Friedrich Katz, "Einige Grundzüge der Politik des deutschen Imperialismus in Lateinamerika, 1898 bis 1941," in Heinz Sanke, ed., *Der deutsche Faschismus in Lateinamerika, 1933–1943* (Berlin: Humboldt-Universität, 1966):9–69; Manfred Kossok, *Im Schatten der Heiligen Allianz. Deutsch-*

land und Lateinamerika, 1815–1830. . . . (Berlin: Akademie, 1964); Werner Pade, "Die Expansionspolitik des deutschen Imperialismus gegenüber Lateinamerika, 1918–1933," *Zeitschrift für Geschichtswissenschaft* 22 (1974):578–90.

Central American scholars have studied the impact of Germans or foreigners generally on their society: Luis Felipe González Flores, *Historia de la influencia extranjera en el desenvolvimiento educacional y científico de Costa Rica* (San José, CR: Nacional, 1921); Carlos Meléndez Chaverri, "Intereses extranjeros en Centro América durante la primera mitad del siglo XIX," in *Memoria del primer congreso de historia Centro América-Panamá* (San José, CR: Nacional, 1956); Regina Wagner, "Actividades empresariales de los alemanes en Guatemala, 1850–1920," *Mesoamérica* 13 (June 1987):87–123; Donald Castillo Rivas, *Acumulación de capital y empresas transnacionales en Centroamérica* (Mexico: Siglo XXI, 1980).

Several scholars have examined the nature of German investment in Central America: J. Fred Rippy, "German Investments in Guatemala," *Journal of Business* 20 (Oct. 1947):212–19; J. Fred Rippy, "German Investments in Latin America," *Journal of Business* 21 (April 1948):63–73; Rodrigo Quesada Monge, "Diplomacía y deuda externa: El caso de Honduras (1897–1912)," *Anuario de estudios centroamericanos* 10 (1984):69–80; Victor Quintana Díaz, *Inversiones extranjeras en Guatemala* (Guatemala: Instituto de investigaciones económicas y sociales, 1973); Gert Rosenthal K., "La inversión extranjera en Centroamérica," *Nueva Sociedad* 11/12 (March–June 1974):24–58. Xabier Gorostiaga, *Los banqueros del imperio. El papel de los centros financieros internacionales en los países subdesarrollados* (San José, CR: EDUCA, 1978), has examined the impact of financial power on underdeveloped countries, with some reference to the Central American experience.

Aspects of the Central American political economy are investigated in Jaime Biderman, "The Development of Capitalism in Nicaragua: A Political Economic History," *Latin American Perspectives* 10 (winter 1983):7–32; Sanford A. Mosk, "The Coffee Economy of Guatemala, 1850–1918: Development and Signs of Instability," *Inter-American Economic Affairs* 9 (winter 1955):6–20; Antonio Murga Frassinetti, "Economía primaria exportadora y formación del proletariado. El caso centroamericano (1850–1920)," *Economía política* (UNAH, Tegucigalpa) 18 (1979–1980):40–78; José Luis Velázquez, "La incidencia de la formación de la economía agroexportadora en el intento de formación del estado nacional en Nicaragua: 1860–1930," *Revista conservadora del pensamiento centroamericano* 157 (Oct.–Dec. 1977):11–31. Carlos A. E. Hegel, *Die historische Entwicklung der Plantagenwirtschaft in Guatemala bis zum Ende des 19. Jahrhunderts* (Munich: Val. Hotling, 1930), discusses the growth of plantations, including German projects.

U.S. relations with Germany and Central America were intertwined. On U.S.-German relations, see Manfred Jonas, *The United States and Germany: A Diplomatic History* (Ithaca, NY: Cornell University Press, 1984), and Alfred Vagts, *Deutschland und die Vereinigten Staaten in der Weltpolitik*, 2 vols. (New York: Dornan, 1935). On U.S. interests in Central America, see Walter LaFeber, *Inevitable Revolutions: The United States in Central America* (New York: Norton, 1983); Lester D. Langley, *The Struggle for the American Mediterranean: United States–European Rivalry in the Gulf-Caribbean, 1776–1904* (Athens: University of Georgia Press, 1976); Lester D. Langley, *The United States and the Caribbean in the 20th Century* (Athens: University of Georgia Press, 1982); Schoonover, *The United States in Central America*; Lester D.

Langley and Thomas Schoonover, *The Banana Men: American Mercenaries and Entrepreneurs in Central America, 1880–1930* (Lexington: University Press of Kentucky, 1995). The numerous books of travelers, settlers, and businesspeople collectively add details and anecdotes.

U.S. and German competition in the Caribbean basin is examined in Thomas Baecker, "Deutschland im karibischen Raum im Spiegel amerikanischer Akten (1898–1914)," *Jahrbuch für Geschichte von Staat, Wirtschaft und Gesellschaft Lateinamerikas* 11 (1974):167–237; Ragnhild Fiebig-von Hase, "Die deutsch-amerikanischen Wirtschaftsbeziehungen, 1890–1914, im Zeichen von Protektionismus und internationaler Integration," *Amerikastudien* 33:3 (1988):329–57; Ragnhild Fiebig-von Hase, *Lateinamerika als Konfliktherd der deutsch-amerikanischen Beziehungen, 1890–1903*, 2 vols. (Göttingen: Vandenhoeck und Ruprecht, 1986); Robert Freeman Smith, "Latin America, the United States and the European Powers, 1830–1930," in Leslie Bethell, ed., *The Cambridge History of Latin America*, 8 vols. (Cambridge: Cambridge University Press, 1982–1993), 5:83–119.

The best studies of Central America are Ralph Lee Woodward, Jr., *Central America: A Nation Divided*, 2d ed. (New York: Oxford University Press, 1985); Ralph Lee Woodward, Jr., "Central America from Independence to c. 1870," in Bethell, ed., *The Cambridge History of Latin America*, 3:471–506; Ciro Cardoso and Héctor Pérez Brignoli, *Centro América y la economía occidental (1520–1930)* (San José, CR: EDUCA, 1977); Ciro Cardoso, "Central America: The Liberal Era, ca. 1870–1930," in Leslie Bethell, ed., *The Cambridge History of Latin America*, 5 vols. (Cambridge: Cambridge University Press, 1982–1988), 5:197–227; Héctor Pérez Brignoli, *Breve historia de Centroamérica* (Madrid: Alianza, 1985); James Dunkerley, *Power in the Isthmus: A Political History of Modern Central America* (London: Verso, 1988); and Victor Bulmer-Thomas, *The Political Economy of Central America Since 1920* (Cambridge: Cambridge University Press, 1987). Edelberto Torres-Rivas, *Interpretación del desarrollo social centroamericano*, 7th ed. (San José, CR: EDUCA, 1977), is a standard work on development and change in Central American society.

Among the most rewarding studies of individual isthmian countries are Ralph Lee Woodward, Jr., *Rafael Carrera and the Emergence of the Republic of Guatemala, 1821–1871* (Athens: University of Georgia Press, 1993); Jim Handy, *The Gift of the Devil: A History of Guatemala* (Boston: South End, 1984); David McCreery, *Development and the State in Reforma Guatemala, 1871–85*, Monographs in Latin America Series, vol. 10 (Athens: Ohio University Press, 1983); Alison Acker, *Honduras: The Making of a Banana Republic* (Boston: South End, 1986); Darío A. Euraque, "La 'reforma liberal' en Honduras y la hipótesis de la 'oligarquía ausente': 1870–1930," *Revista de Historia* 23 (Jan.–June 1991):17–27; Guillermo Molina Chocano, *Estado liberal y desarrollo capitalista en Honduras* (Tegucigalpa: Banco de Honduras, 1976); E. Bradford Burns, "The Modernization of Underdevelopment: El Salvador, 1858–1931," *Journal of Developing Areas* 18 (April 1984):293–316; Rafael L. Menjívar, *Acumulación originaria y desarrollo del capitalismo en El Salvador* (San José, CR: EDUCA, 1980); Mario Flores Macal, *Origen, desarrollo y crisis de las formas de dominación en El Salvador* (San José: Universidad de Costa Rica, 1978); Héctor Lindo-Fuentes, *Weak Foundations: The Economy of El Salvador in the Nineteenth Century, 1821–1890* (Berkeley: University of California Press, 1991); Alberto Lanuza, Juan Luis Vázquez, Amaru Barahona, and Amalia Chamorro, *Economía y sociedad en la con-*

strucción del estado en Nicaragua (San José, CR: Instituto centroamericano de administración pública [ICAP], 1983); José Luis Vega Carballo, *Orden y progreso: La formación del estado nacional en Costa Rica* (San José, CR: ICAP, 1981); and Victor H. Acuña Ortega and Iván Molina Jiménez, *El desarrollo económico y social de Costa Rica: De la colonia a la crisis de 1930* (San José, CR: Alma Mater, 1986).

Primary Materials and Published Sources

■

Primary Materials

Austria
    Österreichisches Staatsarchiv, Vienna
    Politisches Archiv
Costa Rica
    Archivos Nacionales, San José
    Relaciones Exteriores
      cajas, 1–233
      libros copiadores
Federal Republic of Germany
    Bayerisches Hauptstaatsarchiv, Abteilung II, Munich
      Bayerische Gesandtschaft, London
      Bayerische Gesandtschaft, Paris
      Ministerium des Äussern
    Bundesarchiv, Frankfurt
      Akten des Bundestages
      Deutsche Reichsgesandtschaft, Vereinigte Staaten
    Bundesarchiv, Koblenz
      Auswärtiges Amt (R 85)
      Deutsches Auslandsinstitut (R 57)
      Reichsfinanzministerium (R 2)
      Reichskanzlei (R 43)
    Bundesarchiv, Merseburg (formerly Deutsches Zentralarchiv)
      Abteilung I, Auswärtiges Amt
      Abteilung II, Auswärtiges Amt
      Rep. 76, Ministerium für Wissenschaft, Kunst und Volksbildung
      Rep. 77, Ministerium des Innern
      Rep. 81, Zentral-Amerika
      Rep. 89, Geheimes Civilkabinett
      Rep. 120, Ministerium für Handel und Gewerbe
    Bundesarchiv, Militärarchiv, Freiburg
      Reichsmarine: RM 3, RM 5, RM 6, RM 20, MSg
      Reichsheer: RH 2
    Bundesarchiv, Potsdam (formerly Zentrales Staatsarchiv)
      Auswärtiges Amt (09.01)
      Reichskanzleramt (14.01)

Commerzbibliothek, Handelskammer, Hamburg
  Consulatsberichte: Guatemala
Evangelische Kirche der Union (EKU) Archiv, Berlin
  E. O.—Mittelamerika
Geheimes Staatsarchiv Preussischer Kulturbesitz, Berlin
  I Hauptabteilung
    Preussisches Justizministerium (Rep. 84a)
    Preussisches Staatsministerium (Rep. 90)
  III Hauptabteilung
    Auswärtiges Amt
    Preussische Gesandtschaft, Dresden
    Seehandlung (Rep. 109)
Handelskammerarchiv, Bremen
  Hp II: Costa Rica; Guatemala; Honduras; Nicaragua; Panama; San Salvador
Hauptstaatsarchiv, Stuttgart: E 14; E 46; E 150
Historisches Archiv, Friedrich Krupp GmbH., Essen
Historisches Archiv der Stadt Köln, Cologne
Industrie- und Handelskammer, Dortmund
  Handelskammer, Bochum (K 2, Nr. 132)
    Jahresberichte, Handelskammer: Berlin (S6-910); Bremen (S6-988); Crefeld (S6-966); Hamburg (S6-991); Hanover (S6-876); Leipzig (S6-971)
Niedersächsisches Staatsarchiv, Aurich
  Rep 21 a: Consulate in Costa Rica, Guatemala, Honduras, Nicaragua, and Panama
Politisches Archiv des Auswärtigen Amts, Bonn
  Abteilung I A: Amerika Generalia; Columbien; Costarica; Frankreich; Galápagos Inseln; Guatemala; Handel; Honduras; Mexiko; Nicaragua; Panama; San Salvador; Spanien
  Abteilung I C: Vereinigte Staaten
  Abteilung II: Wirtschaft—Frankreich/Costa Rica
  Botschaft, Heiliger Stuhl
  Botschaft, Madrid
  Nachlass Friedrich von Holstein
  Politische Abteilung II: Vatikan
  Politische Abteilung III: Costa Rica; Guatemala; Honduras; Mittel-Amerika; Nicaragua; Panama; San Salvador
Rheinisch-Westfälisches Wirtschafts-Archiv, Cologne
  Handelskammer zu Köln
Staatsarchiv Bremen
  Gesandtschaften
  Handelskommission des Senats
  Senatsakten
  Senatskommission für Reichs- und auswärtige Angelegenheiten
Staatsarchiv Hamburg
  Auswanderungswesen
  Deputation für Handel, Schiffahrt und Gewerbe

Hanseatische Gesandtschaften: Berlin; Washington
Senatsakten
Senatskommission für die Reichs- und auswärtigen Angelegenheiten
Spezialakten
Staatsarchiv Lübeck
Stadtarchiv Arnsberg: Bestand 4/1
Stadtarchiv Frankfurt: Industrie- und Handelskammer
Werner-von-Siemens-Institut für Geschichte des Hauses Siemens, Munich
    Organisation der Vertretung in Mittelamerika
    Schriftwechsel mit Empresa Eléctrica de Guatemala
France
  Archive de l'armée de la mer, Paris
    Series: BB^4, BB^7
  Archive de l'armée de la terre, Paris
    2eme Bureau, Attachés militaires
  Archive du Ministère de l'économie et des finances, Paris
    Series: F^{30}
  Archives Nationales, Paris
    Archives d'entreprises: 6 AQ, 44 AQ
    Fonds du Ministère de commerce: F^{12}, F^{23}
  Archive du Ministère des affaires étrangères, Paris
    Affaires diverses, commerciales
    Correspondence commerciale et consulaire (CCC), 1793 1901: Guatemala;
    San José de Costa Rica
    Correspondence politique (CP) à 1871: Amérique Centrale
    Correspondence politique (CP), 1871 à 1896: Amérique Centrale; Costa
    Rica; Guatemala; Honduras; Nicaragua; San Salvador
    Correspondence politique et commerciale (CP), 1897–1918 (Nouvelle série):
    Amérique Centrale; Costa Rica; Guatemala; Honduras; Nicaragua; Pan-
    ama; El Salvador
    Série B. Amérique, 1918–1940: Centre Amérique
    Série Z. Europe, 1918 1929
Great Britain
  Public Record Office (PRO)
    Foreign Office (FO): FO 15 (Costa Rica); FO 21 (Central America/Guate-
    mala); FO 39 (Honduras); FO 53 (Mosquito Coast); FO 56 (Nicaragua); FO
    66 (San Salvador)
Guatemala
  Archivo General de Centro América. Guatemala City.
    legajo 1395 (Santo Tomás)
    Ministerio de Relaciones Exteriores
      Legación y consulados de Guatemala en Alemania
      Legación y consulados de Alemania en Guatemala
      Legación y consulados de Guatemala en los EEUU
      Legación y consulados de los EEUU en Guatemala
      Legación y consulados de Guatemala en otros estados
      Legación y consulados de otros estados en Guatemala

Spain
  Ministerio de Asuntos Exteriores, Madrid
United States
  Huntington Library, San Marino, California
    Pacific Mail Steamship Company
  Library of Congress, Washington, D.C.
    Frank R. McCoy
    Ephraim George Squier
  National Archives, Washington, D.C.
    RG 59, Department of State
      Country Series, 1776–1906
        Consular Instructions, 1801–1834 (M-78)
        Despatches from the U.S. Commission to Central and South America, 1884–1885 (T-908)
        Despatches from U.S. Consuls: Colón (T-193); Guatemala (T-337); San José (Costa Rica) (T-35); San Juan del Norte (T-348); Sonsonate (T-440)
        Diplomatic Despatches, Central America (M-219)
        Diplomatic Despatches, Germany (M-44)
        Diplomatic Instructions (M-77): Central America; Germany
        Notes from Foreign Legations: Central America (T-34); Germany (Prussia) (M-58)
        Notes to Foreign Legations (M-99): Germany (Prussia); Hanseatic States
      Decimal File Series, 1910–1929
        Guatemala and other states (M-657)
    RG 80, Department of the Navy
    RG 151, Bureau of Foreign and Domestic Commerce
    RG 165, War Department, General and Special Staffs
  New York Public Library, New York City
    Sociedad de inmigración
  Stanford University, Special Collections
    Francis Butler Loomis
  Tulane University, New Orleans
    Erwin Paul Dieseldorff
  University of Virginia, Alderman Library, Charlottesville
    William Sydney Thayer

Published Sources

Bienengräber, Adolph. *Statistik des Verkehrs und Verbrauchs im Zollverein für die Jahre 1842–1864*. Berlin: Alexander Duncker, 1868.

Bigelow, Poultney. *Prussian Memories, 1864–1914*. New York: G. P. Putnam's Sons, 1915.

Bremen. Bremer Staatsarchiv. *Statistisches Jahrbuch der Freien Hansestadt Bremen [1866–1873]*. Bremen: Bremisches Statistisches Landesamt, 1867–1874.

————. Bureau für Bremische Statistik. *Jahrbuch für die amtliche Statistik des bremischen Staats.* Bremen: von Halem, 1862–.

Bülow, Alexander von. *Auswanderung und Colonisation im Interesse des deutschen Handels.* Berlin: E. S. Mittler und Sohn, 1849.

————. *Der Freistaat Costa Rica in Mittelamerika. Seine Wichtigkeit für den Welthandel, den Ackerbau und die Colonisation.* Berlin: Gustav Hempel, 1850.

————. *Der Freistaat Nicaragua in Mittelamerika und seine Wichtigkeit für den Welthandel, den Ackerbau und die Colonisation.* Berlin: Gustav Hempel, 1849.

————. *Die Verbindungswege des Welthandels durch Central-America.* Berlin: Deckersche Geheime Ober-Hofbuchdruckerei, 1850.

Bunau-Varilla, Phillippe. *The Great Adventure of Panama: The German Conspiracies Against France and the United States.* New York: Doubleday, 1920.

Chamorro, Emiliano. *El último caudillo: Autobiografía.* Managua: Unión, 1983.

Comité der Berliner Colonisations-Gesellschaft für Central-Amerika. *Die deutsche Ansiedlung in Mittelamerika.* Berlin: Comité der Berliner Colonisations-Gesellschaft für Central-Amerika, 1850.

Cuelebrouk, Blondeel van. *Colonie de Santo-Tomas.* 2 vols. Brussels: Devroye, 1846.

Dernburg, Bernhard. "Germany and American Policies." *Annals of the American Academy* 60 (July 1915):195–96.

Deutsches Reich. Reichstag. *Stenographische Berichte über die Verhandlungen des Deutschen Reiches.* 3. Legislaturperiode, 2. Session (1877–1878), 9. Sitzung.

Deutschtum in der Alta Verapaz: Erinnerungen, 1888–1938. Stuttgart: Deutsche Verlags-Anstalt, 1938.

Erckert, Friedrich C. von. "Die wirtschaftlichen Interessen Deutschlands in Guatemala." *Beiträge zur Kolonialpolitik und Kolonialwirtschaft* 3 (1901–902):225–38, 269–84.

Fellechner, A., Dr. Müller, and C. L. C. Hesse. *Bericht über die im höchsten Auftrage des Prinzen Karl von Preussen und des Fürsten von Schoenburg-Waldenburg bewirkte Untersuchung einiger Theile des Mosquitolands.* Berlin: Alexander Duncker, 1845.

Fröbel, Julius. "Die deutsche Auswanderung und ihre nationale und culturhistorische Bedeutung." In *Kleine politische Schriften,* ed. Julius Fröbel, 93–198. Stuttgart: J. G. Cotta'sche Buchhandlung, 1866.

————. *Seven Years' Travel in Central America.* London: Richard Bentley, 1856.

Germany. Kaiserliches Statistisches Amt. *Statistik des Deutschen Reiches.* Berlin: Puttkammer und Mühlbrecht, 1891–1930.

————. Reichsamt des Innern. *Auswärtiger Handel des deutschen Zollgebiets nach Herkunfts- und Bestimmungsländern in den Jahren 1880–1896.* Berlin: Puttkammer und Mühlbrecht, 1897.

————. Reichsarchiv historischer Kommission. *Die auswärtige Politik Preussens, 1858–1871.* 10 vols. Oldenburg: G. Stalling, 1932–1945.

————. Reichsmarineamt. *Die Entwicklung der deutschen Seeinteressen in den letzten Jahrzehnten.* Berlin: Reichsdruckerei, 1905.

————. *Statistisches Jahrbuch für das Deutsche Reich . . . 1907.* Berlin: Puttkammer und Mühlbrecht, 1907.

Geschäfts-Bericht des provisorischen Comités der deutschen Colonisations-Gesellschaft für Central-Amerika, als Vorlage für die am 21. Oktober 1852 stattfindende General-Versammlung. Berlin: Comité der deutschen Colonisations-Gesellschaft für Central-Amerika, 1852.

Guzmán, Enrique. *Editoriales de la prensa 1878.* Managua: Banco de América, 1977.

————. *Las gacetillas, 1878–1894.* Managua: Banco de América, 1975.

Handels-Archiv. Wochenschrift für Handel, Gewerbe und Verkehrsanstalten, 1847–1859.

Hänsch-Leipzig, Felix. "Weltpolitik, Kolonialpolitik und Schule." *Zeitschrift für Kolonialpolitik, Kolonialrecht und Kolonialwirtschaft* 11 (Oct. 1907):767–75.

Harms, Bernhard. *Deutschlands Anteil an Welthandel und Weltschiffahrt.* Stuttgart: Union Deutsche Verlagsgesellschaft, 1916.

————. *Gegenwartsaufgaben der deutschen Handelspolitik.* Jena: Gustav Fischer, 1925.

————. *Die Zukunft der deutschen Handelspolitik.* Jena: Gustav Fischer, 1925.

Holstein, Friedrich. *The Holstein Papers.* Eds. Norman Rich and M. H. Fischer. 3 vols. Cambridge: Cambridge University Press, 1955–1961.

Informe de la sociedad de inmigración. Guatemala: El Progreso, [1878].

Jacob, Ernst Gerhard, ed. *Deutsche Kolonialpolitik in Dokumenten.* Leipzig: Dieterich'sche Verlagsbuchhandlung, 1938.

Jahres-Bericht des Berliner Vereins zur Centralisation deutscher Auswanderung und Colonisation für das Jahr 1851. Berlin: Berliner Verein zur Centralisation deutscher Auswanderung und Colonisation, 1852.

Jung, Emil. "Deutsche Interessen in Zentralamerika." *Beiträge zur Kolonialpolitik und Kolonialwirtschaft* 3 (1901–1902):538–40.

Krupp, Alfred. *Krupp und die Hohenzollern in Dokumenten.* Ed. Willi A. Boelcke. Frankfurt: Athenaion, 1970.

Kümpel, Juan. *La bancarrota del liberalismo.* San José, CR: La Prensa Libre, 1911.

————. *La guerra: Su origen histórico, su verdadera causa, y los pretextos con que los enemigos de Alemania excusan su agresión.* Valparaiso, Chile: Victoria, 1915.

Kürchhoff, Oberst a.D. "Flottenstützpunkte." *Beiträge zur Kolonialpolitik, Kolonialrecht und Kolonialwirtschaft* 4 (1902–1903):63–66.

Lehmann, Emil. *Die deutsche Auswanderung.* Berlin: Georg Reimer, 1861.

Littman, Otto G. A. *Deutsche-Kostarikanische Land-Gesellschaft.* Berlin: n.p., 1894.

Öffentliche Sitzungen des Central-Vereins für die deutsche Auswanderungs- und Colonisations-Angelegenheit im Jahre 1852. Berlin: Central-Verein für die deutsche Auswanderungs- und Colonisations-Angelegenheit, 1853.

Organization of American States. Interamerican Economic and Social Council. *Foreign Investments in Latin America.* Washington: Pan American Union, 1955.

Ostwald, Paul. *Englischer und deutscher Imperialismus: Ein Gegensatz.* Berlin: Leonhard, Simion, 1917.

Pan American Union. *Foreign Trade of Latin America, 1910–1929.* Washington, DC: Pan American Union, 1930.

————. *Foreign Trade Series* for Costa Rica, El Salvador, Guatemala, Honduras, and Nicaragua, [Nos. 1–214]. Washington, DC: Pan American Union, 1918–1950.

Paschen, Karl. *Aus der Werdezeit zweier Marinen.* Berlin: E. S. Mittler und Sohn, 1908.

Pfeiffer, H. G., and A. A. Reinke. "Auszug aus der Reisebeschreibung der Brüder H. G. Pfeiffer und A. A. Reinke von Fairfield auf Jamaica nach Bluefields auf der Moskitoküste im Jahr 1847." *Missions-Blatt aus der Brüdergemeinde* 12 (1847):18–26.

———. "Recognoscirungs-Reise nach der Mosquito-Küste." *Missions-Blatt aus der Brüdergemeinde* 11 (Aug. 29, Oct. 26, 1847):151–52, 189–90.

Preuss, Paul. *Expedition nach Central- und Südamerika.* Berlin: Verlag des Kolonial-Wirtschaftlichen Komitees, 1901.

Preussiches Handelsarchiv (also *Deutsches Handelsarchiv*), 1860–1933.

Promemoria betreffend unsere Reklamation gegen Nicaragua in der Angelegenheit des Kaiserlichen Konsulats in Leon. Berlin: Puttkammer und Mühlbrecht, 1877.

Riggenbach, Nikolaus. *Costa Rica, Land und Leute.* Oldenburg: A. Michel, [1866].

———. *Erinnerungen eines alten Mechanikers.* St. Gallen, Switz.: C. Detloff, 1887.

Rösch, Adrian. *Allerlei aus der Alta Verapaz.* Stuttgart: Ausland und Heimat, 1934.

Sapper, Karl. *Mittelamerikanische Reisen und Studien aus den Jahren 1888 bis 1900.* Braunschweig: Friedrich Vieweg und Sohn, 1902.

———. *Reise nach Süd- und Mittelamerika, 1927/28.* Würzburg: E. Mönnich, 1929.

Scherzer, Carl. *Central-Amerika in seiner Bedeutung für den deutschen Handel und die deutsche Industrie.* Vienna: Carl Gerold und Sohn, 1857.

———. *Travels in the Free States of Central America: Nicaragua, Honduras, and San Salvador.* 2 vols. London: Longman, Brown, Green, and Roberts, 1857.

Schoonover, Thomas, and Ebba Schoonover. "Statistics for an Understanding of Foreign Intrusions into Central America from the 1820s to 1930." *Anuario de estudios centroamericanos* 15:1 (1989):93–118, 16:1 (1990):135–56, 17:2 (1991):77–119.

Schultz, Johann Heinrich S. *Über Colonisation mit besonderer Rücksicht auf die Colonie zu Santo Thomás im Staate Guatemala und die Belgische Colonisations-Compagnie.* Cologne: Dumont Schauberg, 1843.

Seebach, Karl von. *Central-Amerika und der Interozeanische Canal.* Berlin: C. B. Lüderitz'sche Verlagsbuchhandlung, 1873.

Sivers, Jegor von. *Über Madeira und die Antillen nach Mittelamerika.* Leipzig: Carl F. Fleischer, 1861.

Soetbeer, Adolph. *Statistik des Hamburgischen Handels, 1842, 1843, 1844.* Hamburg: Hoffman und Campe, 1846.

———. *Über Hamburgs Handel. Statistik des Hamburgischen Handels, 1839, 1840, 1841.* Hamburg: Hoffman und Campe, 1842.

Solis, Ignacio. *Sobre el fomento de la inmigración y colonización extranjeras.* Guatemala: Augusto M. Chamba, 1889.

Streber, Friedrich L. *Zweiter Bericht aus Central-Amerika.* Schneeberg: Carl Moritz Gartner, 1851.

Tabellarische Übersichten des Hamburgischen Handels, [1850–1872]. Ed. Ernst Baasch. Hamburg: F. H. Nestler, 1851–1875.

Tirpitz, Alfred Peter Friedrich von. *Erinnerungen.* Leipzig: R. F. Koehler, 1920. [Translated as *My Memoirs.* 2 vols. New York: Dodd, Mead, 1919.]

United States. Congress. *Commercial Relations of the United States.* Washington, DC: GPO, 1852–.

———. *Serial Set.* Washington, DC: GPO, 1788–.

United States. Department of State. *Papers Relating to the Foreign Relations of the United States.* Multiple vols. Washington: GPO, 1861–1934.

———. Manufacturer's Bureau, *Monthly Consular and Trade Report.* Vol. 63: no. 239, pp. 460–61. Washington: GPO, 1900.

Vié, F. "Les Colonies commerciales des allemands." *Revue des deux mondes* 69 (Feb. 1, 1899):696–708.

Voight, Paul. "Deutschland und der Weltmarkt." In *Handels- und Machtpolitik.* Eds. Gustav Schmoller, Max Sering, and Adolph Wagner. Stuttgart: J. G. Cotta'sche Buchhandlung Nachfolger, 1900.

Wagner, Moritz, and Carl Scherzer. *Die Republik Costa Rica in Central-Amerika.* Leipzig: Arnoldsche Buchhandlung, 1856.

Wegener, Georg. *Reisen im westindischen Mittelmeer. Fahrten und Studien in den Antillen, Colombia, Panama und Costarica im Jahre 1903.* 2d ed. Berlin: Allgemeiner Verein für deutsche Literatur, 1904.

Weimann, E. A. *Mittel-Amerika als gemeinsames Auswanderungs-Ziel.* Berlin: Deckersche Geheime Ober-Hofsbuchdruckerei, 1850.

Index

About the Author

■

Thomas Schoonover received his master's degree from Louisiana State University and his doctorate from the University of Minnesota. He is the author of three other scholarly studies in the area of Latin American studies and foreign relations: *Dollars over Dominion: The Triumph of Liberalism in Mexican-United States Relations, 1861–1867; The United States in Central America, 1860–1911;* and (with Lester D. Langley) *The Banana Men: American Mercenaries and Entrepreneurs in Central America, 1880–1930.*